Real Stories
of the Rails

First-hand

accounts of

railroaders

from the 1920s

to the 1990s

On the cover: We don't know much about the conductor in this photo from the *Trains* magazine archives. We know the image was captured around 1940, but we don't know this railroader's identity or what railroad he worked for. It's just a beautiful photo of a railroader going about his job. This unknown conductor represents tens of thousands of fellow railroad employees of his generation. All had stories to tell—some frightening, some exasperating, some funny, but all fascinating—and the stories in this book likewise represent all railroaders of their eras. *Photo by H. Armstrong Roberts*

Back cover: Top left: A Norfolk & Western passenger conductor smiles as he takes tickets in a coach in a publicity photo. Top right: The engineer of Western Pacific F7 No. 913, hand on the throttle, maintains a steady 49 mph near Tracy, Calif., in 1978 (*photo by Ted Benson*). Bottom: A night hostler tosses a scoop of coal into the firebox of Rio Grande narrow gauge 2-8-2 No. 476 in 1966 (*photo by Glenn Beier*).

Kalmbach Media
21027 Crossroads Circle
Waukesha, Wisconsin 53186
www.KalmbachHobbyStore.com

Published in 2019
23 22 21 20 19   1 2 3 4 5

Manufactured in China

ISBN: 978-1-62700-587-6
EISBN: 978-1-62700-588-3

Editor: Jeff Wilson
Book Design: Lisa Bergman

Library of Congress Control Number: 2018967287

Contents

Foreword

We who are fascinated by railroads tend to be drawn to them as children by their sheer mechanical majesty. Whether the trains we first came to know were steam, diesel, or electric, the sight and sound of hundreds of tons of steel in motion on flanged wheels hooked us.

As we got older, we learned there were different kinds of trains, and we delighted in distinguishing between them. Then we developed favorites, and might try to see or photograph every locomotive owned by a particular railroad, or every member of a certain engine class. We'd note that one railroad used one type of lineside signals, while its neighbor favored another. We'd marvel at how welded rail was laid, in seeming defiance of the laws of physics.

Of course, all those trains and tracks and signals did not spontaneously spring into existence for our enjoyment. They were designed, produced, and used by people. The late William L. Withuhn, longtime curator of transportation at the Smithsonian, stressed that the locomotives on which we lavish so much attention were merely tools that humans used to do a job: move 3,000 tons of freight from Point A to Point B, deliver 200 passengers to their destination, or group freight cars from various tracks into a single train. Indeed, the whole railroad network is simply a massive assemblage of tools, brought to life by millions of hands over the industry's nearly two centuries of history.

In this collection of 40 stories from the pages of *Trains* and *Classic Trains*, we hear from the people who used those tools, and their tales make for fascinating reading. Among the trades represented are engineers, conductors, operators and towermen, dispatchers, even a ticket agent. All take the reader inside a world with a rich culture that's largely inaccessible to outsiders.

Significantly, there are more stories in this collection—seven—from locomotive firemen than any other craft. Firemen were uniquely positioned to offer compelling tales. Their job put them right where the action was, the locomotive cab. But as the junior member of the two-member engine crew, the fireman was part participant, part observer. Hoping one day to be promoted to engineer, he absorbed all he could. For young men like Lloyd Arkinstall, Chuck LeFever, and John Crosby, trips with veteran engineers were formative experiences that remained fresh in their minds decades after they occurred.

It's also worth noting that, with one exception, the stories here are from 1980 or before. The next-to-last decade of the 20th century saw wrenching changes in the railroad industry, including major reductions in the number of employees. Freight train crews, for example, were cut from five members to two. Cabooses vanished. The ranks of operators and towermen continued to thin. With fewer railroaders on the job, it's inevitable that fewer stories come out of their shared experiences.

Today, as railroading strives for ever more efficiency, there's a push to run some trains with just a single person aboard, and technology offers the possibility of trains with no crew members at all. That's a sobering prospect for those of us who enjoy reading firsthand accounts of life inside our favorite industry.

If the great era of railroad stories has indeed passed, we can still rejoice in the many voices from years gone by represented in this volume.

Robert S. McGonigal
Editor, Classic Trains

Comparing watches before leaving Los Angeles Union Station on Union Pacific's *City of Los Angeles* in March 1951 are conductor H.C. Brown, engineer Van Santongue, and fireman Walter Thrall. FRANK J. PETERSON.

My first night as a roundhouse foreman

By E. L. O'Connell
Roundhouse Foreman

1920s

From *Trains* magazine,
February 1970

On May 20, 1920, I was at my evening meal when the night round-house foreman, Wiley Innis, called and asked me to substitute for him for a few nights because he had suddenly become ill. He suggested that I also be prepared to substitute for a longer time in case his illness persisted.

I had worked a shift that day, but since I would be paid overtime for doubling over and on the succeeding nights after the eighth hour, I consented.

On May 10 I had been a machinist for the Missouri Pacific at Nevada, Mo., for 15 years. I was the local president of the machinists, and this post entailed duties such as shop committee chairman and delegate to the district meetings. I performed duties for the other craft unions, and at times the company put me in charge as extra foreman. I was 29 years old.

The shop was 21 blocks from my house, and I arrived at the office at 6:30 p.m., just as the day foreman departed. The engine dispatcher also was an extra man, but a good one. He was still in high school, but like myself he had been practically reared on a railroad. He was the son of W. C. Bevington, the division superintendent. His name was Earl but we usually called him Bevy. While he marked the bulletin board and got his lineup from the train dispatcher, I scanned the situation. Fourteen engines were lined up from the edge of the turntable pit on south over the cinder pit and down into the yard. There would be six more arrivals, in addition to the through passenger trains that might have to change engines. Two fire cleaners and one engine watchman were working.

The inside men did not go on duty until 7 p.m., but some of them had already checked in. I walked through the shop to see if there were any empty pits. The drop pit and the one next to it were vacant. Both of these pits and the transfer pit connecting them were level with water. I turned on the siphon but it did not remove any of the water so I turned off the steam. A drop pit is constructed so that drive wheels can be lowered into it and transferred out or to another pit for repairs to the journals or boxes.

I had started back to the office when the boiler washer caught up with me and reported that there was no water coming from the roundhouse hydrants. At the office I learned that the water service men had been working on the mains and had left without turning on the water. I was unable to find someone who knew where the shutoff valves were located, so we called in the water service man.

The engine watchman reported that he had more engines than he could handle and that the 162 was hot with no water visible in the glass or showing from gauge cocks. There were three engines in front of 162 that we had to run onto the turntable and back onto the sandhouse track before we could get her in the house. We ran her in next to the drop pit and shook the fire out into the water. This left a fine ash on top of the water and over the transfer pit which looked exactly like solid ground.

Three other engines were low on water when I got to the cinder pit, so I helped the engine watchman until Earl could get a day man to double over. It was nearly 7:30 and the train dispatcher wanted to talk to me. He wanted a start on the 169 and some other information, and I gave him a 9:30 on the engine. The machinists found some trainline leaks and I called out a pipe fitter. The hostler reported that the coal-chute engine had broken down and no coal could be lifted into the tipple until it was repaired, so I called in a day machinist. When I returned to the house the 169 was hot. When the crew turned on her old-style Pyle dynamo for a headlight test, the ball-bearing retainer promptly screwed itself forward until the turbine jammed against the housing and stopped. Since a machinist could not be spared and calling in a day man would cause a delay, I crawled up on the side of the boiler, and crouching with my feet on the handrail, removed the brush holder and armature, screwed the retainer back flush, tightened the set screw, and replaced the parts. From my perch 3 feet from a blasting pop I still had to run a roundhouse, screaming at those who tried to talk to me in spite of the noise.

We backed the 169 across the table to the coal chute and discovered that the pipe from the sand bin at the top of the chute was stopped. We had started the night without water, coal, or sand. The engine had a short supply but we sent her on her way. A fire cleaner was finally persuaded to go aloft and inspect the chute. He found a pair of overalls covering the opening. He said nobody was in them.

The train dispatcher wanted to send the 817 to Butler for the Interstate local the next morning, but she was nine deep on the pit. We took a start on the 1251, then found a broken brake rod and called a blacksmith to make the weld and a machinist to assist. We moved 162 from the flooded drop pit to the one vacated by the 169 for pit work. At midnight we had a blacksmith, pipe fitter, two machinists, two fire cleaners, and an engine watchman from the day force working with the night men and yet we had barely scratched the work reports. We sent a machinist from the day force to Butler to cobble the local engine there for another trip while we worked on the 817.

A transformer blew at that time and the men were forced to scurry about with only the light from their coal oil torches. Unwarned of the ashes over the flooded transfer pit, day machinist Jimmy McConnell stepped onto what he believed to be solid ground and disappeared from

Roundhouses were filled with life, from steam locomotives to the workers who maintained them. This is a 2-8-2 in the Galesburg, Ill., roundhouse of the Chicago, Burlington & Quincy in the 1950s. JIM SHAUGHNESSY.

sight. When the ashes had closed over him and he did not emerge, his helper came to the office yelling that we had lost a machinist. Everybody got a tool from the cinder pit and work ceased while we sounded the depths with flue augers and slash bars and dragged the pit with pan hoes and clinker hooks. As Bevy ran to the office to notify the coroner and police, he found Jimmy in the nearby boiler room. Jimmy's clothes were soaking in a 2-gallon bucket, and he was taking a shower with the cold water squirt hose, shivering and

using outrageous language. I tried to talk some reason into him, telling him that this was no way to speak to his foreman and brother in the machinists' lodge, that only switchmen talked like this, and finally, that if he didn't stay out of the pit, the boiler washers would raise hell. He threw the bucket and several chunks of coal at me as I ducked out the door. We went back to the work routine.

The 1251 was now ready for service, but when we backed her out the rear

tender truck wheel dropped onto the turntable and the brake beam came down, tearing up a section of the track and blocking the table so we could get nothing into the house or out of it. We called tank men, and the roadmaster sent a section crew to repair the track. The tank men got an assist from the sectionmen and we got the locomotive on the table, but we could not turn her because the turntable tractor had become uncoupled. We were running out of time, so with a tank man's help and risking the wrath of the shop committee I coupled it. The 1251 took the Red Ball out on schedule.

The 162 was ready for the extra and we stored her on a spur. At 5 a.m., when the 2361 for the Minden local was on the turntable, a hostler helper told me that he could not get steam pressure to turn her. I rushed to the boiler room and found Slim the boiler fireman in a kitchen chair, leaning fast asleep against the coal bin beneath the flue blower air cock. A torch was over the steam gauge and a lantern hung on a gauge cock lighting the water glass. He had a dying fire and 40 pounds of steam.

I ran to the office and got a ball of shipping twine. Bevy and I went to the boiler room, pushed the cold water hose up Slim's pants leg to his waist, and tied the leg to the chair. I raised the water pressure, turned it on, and walked outside. Bevy yanked the air cock open, the torch blew out, and the air was filled with soot and dust. We could see a little by the dim light of the lantern. Slim thought the water glass had blown. Dragging the hose and chair, with water squirting out of his pants, he dived at the valve and shut off the bottom cock, and ran out through the doorway as far as the hose permitted. Fearing that the glass would blow with only steam in it, I ran inside, reopened the valve, and collided with Slim in the darkness and got soaked. I went back to the office and soon heard the 2361 move off the table onto the coal-chute track.

A storm had been threatening all night and torrents of rain broke over us. There were still six engines on the track and over the cinder pit. The 71 was the last one in. There was no report on her except leaky flues. Boilermaker Ingalls got the fire cleaners to cover the fire with wet slack and to throw some wet planks into the firebox. Then, with the blower on, fire a few inches below his feet, and surrounded by 80 pounds of steam and plenty of coal gas, he caulked the flues. Such a dangerous practice was strictly forbidden, but that is what was done and we sent No. 71 out on a Pleasant Hill turnaround. We had finished what was necessary, which is all that is expected of a night force. Engines had been worked inside and outside of the roundhouse and fires had been cleaned—when necessary—on the ground.

As I sat down at the desk for the first time that night, the hostler, Gainey, brought some of the storm in and said, "Mr. Boss, there is another small chore demanding attention before we call it a night. My helper is standing in the rain with his hands high above his head on top of the coal pile in the tender of the 2361. He is not praying; he is holding the coal chute apron up because the balance or whatever keeps it up when it is not dumping coal has ceased to function. I could have him jump off as I move her forward, but that side of the chute would empty all the coal onto the east track and on top of him. Or I could get laborers to relieve him in relays until we think of something better."

I got 50 yards of bell rope out of the storeroom, gave it to a laborer, and told him to help McGuire tie the apron up until the maintenance men could make proper repairs. I told Gainey to shuffle the engines on the cinder pit and to take coal from the west side of the chute. Then after taking a good look at poor McGuire holding the apron up as sheets of rain smothered him, I picked up my lunchbox and started my 21-block walk home in the rain.

Two beautiful ladies were waiting to have breakfast with me when I arrived home at West Arch Street. One of them was almost 5 feet tall and the other was about 28 inches. One of them hugged my knees and the other kissed me, then touched the grime on my face. "Did you have a hard night?"

"Not really."

She opened my lunchbox. "Why, you never even touched this lovely lunch I fixed for you."

On the way to work that evening at the depot I met the engineer who made the Pleasant Hill turnaround. He was just off the 71, and he was dirty and extremely tired. I tried to avoid him but he stopped me.

"Hello, Taylor, did you just get in?" I asked.

"Hell, no, I just got out of bed," he replied. "I always sleep this dirty. What did you do to that damned cap and ball you hung on me last night?"

"Just caulked the flues. There was nothing else reported."

"There is now. Don't you have inspectors anymore?"

When I got to the shop the machinist committee was waiting for me. It was a matter of not calling one of them to repair the dynamo on the 169 and to couple the turntable tractor. It took at least 30 minutes of diplomatic give and take to compose them.

Then I looked in on Slim. The boiler was popping and he was much cleaner than usual. I checked inside and outside the house and went back to the office where Bevy was marking the board. After checking the dispatcher's lineup, Bevy and I decided to write a letter to Slim. We wrote it on official stationery and forger Bevy signed it.

Office of Master Mechanic
Joplin Division
Nevada, Mo.
May 21, 1920

Stationary Fireman Smith
Nevada, Mo.

Dear Mr. Smith:
There is a report on my desk covering the 18-minute deferred departure of train 795 this a.m., which was caused by the tardy arrival of engine 2361 at point-of-exit track No. 4 in the yard. Her delay has been explained as owing to insufficient steam pressure to operate the tractor which moves the turntable. This in turn was caused by you being asleep on the job. If the report is released as it is now recorded, it will pass over President Baldwin's desk and you will be dismissed from service. We would rather that this did not happen to such a valuable employee because of innocent dozing. In order to vacate this dilemma you will reimburse the company by handing the sum of $7.18 to the night roundhouse foreman. This is the amount of terminal time credited to the crew. On receipt of the money we will adjust our information in the interest of terminating correspondence.

T. M. Douglas
Master Mechanic

Bevy went to the boiler room and told Slim that the Boss wanted to see him. Slim entered, came over to the desk, and from his towering height looked down on me with a sorrowful expression. Trying to look like an official, I handed over the letter. He opened it, stared at it for a few minutes, then wadded our beautiful letter into a ball and stuffed it in his overalls. He walked over to the door, and just before he slammed it said, "Nuts." It was like General McAuliffe at Bastogne. Bevy heaved a deep sigh, "He sure was onto us." I thought so too but I later learned that he was not. He couldn't read.

Hell Gate + hurricane = locomotive test

By Forman H. Craton
Mechanical Engineer

1938

From *Trains* magazine,
March 1971

May 18, 1938 was the first day of revenue operation for the New Haven's spanking-new GE-built 11,000-volt A.C. passenger locomotives 0361 to 0366.

That evening swank all-Pullman extra-fare Boston-to-New York train *Merchants Limited,* hauled by old 0313, left New Haven on her fast nonstop electrified run to Grand Central Terminal. Two minutes later, nondescript No. 59 behind sleek new 0362 departed from New Haven also New York-bound. Four miles later at the crest of West Haven hill, No. 59 overhauled the *Merchants,* and the extra-fare patrons in the observation-lounge got a fleeting glimpse of the proletariat streaking by in a string of coaches on the adjacent track.

Jim Bracken, mechanical engineer of the New Haven's Van Nest Shops, who was riding 0362, remonstrated with Dick Shaft, the engineer, about this flagrant disrespect for the sacrosanctity of the *Merchants.* Bracken expostulated, "I caught hell once for passing the *Merchants* with just a test train!"

Dick Shaft, more familiarly known as Sir Richard, twitched his bushy eyebrows, turned his 250-pound bulk toward Bracken, and replied, "Aw, hell, Jim, I had to pass him. He was late and I'd be late too if I hadn't done it." But the word quickly got around that the new engines were "a ball of fire." The railroad soon decided to make some test runs to establish loading limitations for its new power and also to collect data in freight service for future use. This is the story of those test runs, which culminated under circumstances never to be forgotten by the New Haven Railroad.

Number 0362's ability to overtake the *Merchants* was predictable. The new locomotives had nearly double the power of the 0300 class, which were built between 1919 and 1928. Under favorable adhesion conditions an 0361 could deliver 7,600 hp at the rims of her 12 driving wheels. This would be useful on the heavy frequent-stop commuter trains and the still-extensive high-class passenger business between New York and Boston, including the Hell Gate bridge runs from Penn Station.

First some brief comments on the 0361 design: Weight on drivers was 136 tons; continuous rated horsepower, 3,600; and maximum speed, 93 mph (although the overspeed relays were set at 76 mph). The electrical apparatus, ventilating equipment, train-heating boiler, and miscellaneous auxiliaries were housed in the symmetrical double-ended streamlined cab. The 2-C+C-2 running gear with six twin motors and quill drive provided a smooth ride. The control was complicated by the 600-volt D.C. operation into Grand Central. Otherwise things were straightforward enough.

I was the GE commercial engineer from Erie handling liaison between the railroad and our locomotive designers. My job was to keep everybody happy in both the customer's and GE's organizations, an idealistic objective at best.

The first test, on September 14, 1938, had 0364 hauling 18 Pullmans, 1,580 tons, from New Haven to Penn Station nonstop and return, about 150 miles. We took readings each minute of controller notch, miles per hour, motor current, and temperatures of major equipment. The test was largely uneventful, with Charlie Hess, road foreman of engines, running the locomotive. Charlie, a bullet-headed veteran in his 60s, performed flawlessly with one exception. Returning, he delayed his release approaching New Rochelle Junction, where the Grand Central and Penn Station lines converge, and stalled on the crossovers; but he hauled out masterfully, commenting, "She done a nice job pullin' eighteen wagons out of there."

In New Haven, the force in the electrical engineer's office complained that while we were accelerating the train, we'd drawn a fantastic 12,500 kilowatts. We assured them that without the 0364's being geared to the track, we could not possibly draw more than 7,000. However, they were unhappy, with visions of a rapidly disintegrating distribution system.

The following day we ran a 20-Pullman test from New Haven to Penn Station and return. To avoid blocking Penn Station, we made a quick turnaround and left in 35 minutes, permitting little cooling. Although it was evident we were nearing the heating limitations of the traction motors, transformer, and other apparatus, all went impressively well. This concluded the passenger testing.

It had been duck soup.

The three freight tests, which were somewhat of an afterthought, remained to be carried out: (1) New Haven to Bay Ridge (Brooklyn) with 2,000 tons; (2) Bay Ridge to New Haven with 2,500 tons; and (3) New Haven to Bay Ridge and return with 3,000 tons. All three tests would negotiate Hell Gate bridge with its relatively long, heavy grade approaches, and test No. 3 particularly had the potential of causing severe electrical equipment heating in a high-speed passenger locomotive.

Before undertaking the freight tests, we had had to sell them to Stanley MacKay, general superintendent of transportation. Stanley was a stocky, vigorous man of about 45, full of pep and ideas. Talking about train resistance, he admitted there were factors that couldn't be calculated and cited an example. At a place called Wickford Hill on the New Haven was a cut where the wind would strike boxcars quartering and sometimes actually would stall a train even though calculations would indicate this was impossible. We were to recall this comment a few days hence.

Freight tests 1 and 2 were conducted on September 20. The rain that morning

9

threatened a flood as we left Cedar Hill yard at New Haven with 16 battleships of coal and 43 empty boxcars, 2,050 tons. Tracks in New Haven station were submerged as we splashed through. However, we had no trouble until we reached the east approach to Hell Gate bridge. Down to 29 mph because of a speed restriction, we suddenly slipped, tripping the main breaker. By the time the engineer shut off, reset the breaker, and notched out again, we'd lost several miles an hour, only to slip again, and then again. We soon stalled ignominiously. Finally two Westinghouse freight-motors boosted us over the summit—a bitter pill. At Bay Ridge we were cheered slightly to find our A-side sanders plugged, explaining our trouble.

The return trip to Cedar Hill with 2,500 tons went without a hitch. Everything ran comparatively cool despite the 3,000 amps that were held for what seemed an eternity until we got her swinging. With the sanders fixed and a good rail the next day, there should be no problem with 3,000 tons. We were unimpressed with the near-flood conditions from the all-day rain—or the fact that the morrow would be September 21, bordering the autumn equinox, when anything is possible.

But before proceeding, meet several people participating in the 3,000-ton test: Charlie Hess again was running the engine, with the engineer and fireman standing by. There was Clark Scovill, an engineering assistant from Van Nest Shops. Besides me, the following from GE were aboard: Jim Smith, a wiry, witty, stable old-timer from our New York office who'd followed the New Haven for years; Felix Konn, a young high-caliber but excitable engineer who'd designed the traction motors; Alf Bredenberg, quiet and completely reliable, who'd devised the locomotive circuitry; and Bob Walsh, a young Englishman who had supervised the apparatus layout. Collectively this bunch had railroaded plenty, but I doubt if even the veteran Charlie Hess had experienced a day like the one before us.

September 21 dawned heavily overcast and pouring. We coupled to our 3,000 tons at Cedar Hill and pumped up the train. Then we waited. The downpour would moderate briefly, only to rain harder than ever. Finally we eased out of the yard with a helper. He soon dropped off, and we were on our own until we reached Oak Point at the foot of the east approach to Hell Gate some 70 storm-swept miles away.

As we passed New Haven station, poor visibility forced Charlie to slow down to a fast walk. Once past the station area he notched up rapidly, trying to hold her just below the slipping point to get a swing for West Haven hill which was soon upon us. But despite his skill, he kept slipping and losing speed. The assignment was a brutal one for a high-speed passenger engine. Equipment heating soared.

Felix was reading traction motor temperatures, the signals being transmitted from thermocouples embedded in the motor windings to meters in the rear cab. As we faltered toward the summit, Felix tore to the front end to inquire excitedly why Charlie persisted in exceeding 2,200 amperes only to slip. Charlie ignored him. I explained to Felix that Charlie was trying to avoid stalling and was doing okay. As Felix retired, Charlie snarled, "I suppose they want me to go up here in notch seven or eight and stall! To hell with that stuff!" About this time we reached the summit and that crisis was over.

From the West Haven crest, we bowled along without incident to Oak Point, where we got our helper, a dubious-looking 85-ton switcher. Then we started up Hell Gate. It was raining and blowing hard. The pickup was agonizingly slow. I thought of Stanley MacKay and Wickford Hill. We labored up to 12 mph, and with the whole train now on the 1.2 percent grade, just hung there. Things were heating up fast. Suddenly we slipped and the breaker opened like a cannon, showering sparks into the apparatus-cab aisle. When Charlie had picked it up again, we'd lost 3 to 4 mph. Then we buckled down to an unyielding 3,000 amps as we struggled on 8 mph.

Bob Walsh burst in, yelling, "My God, the motor-control units are hot!" Charlie Hess glanced down the B-aisle and saw smoke emerging from the pigs (bridging reactors in the main-transformer circuit). The intercab phone rang and Felix, affecting an unconvincing calm, inquired, "How long are we going to keep this up?" I said, "How hot are you?" He said, "The motors are 150 degrees [C] and rising." We kept on a minute longer. The summit was still 4 minutes away and the pigs would probably blow up before that. I told Charlie to shut off. Again we called for help.

Soon two freight-motors were reported on our rear. The start was tough but we had to get out; tying up the main line was regarded with disfavor. Once we got her swinging, we lay back and let the pushers do most of the work while we cooled.

Beyond the summit, it was easy going into Bay Ridge. However, the weather was deteriorating rapidly—the rain coming harder and harder, and the wind rising alarmingly.

We ran around our train at Bay Ridge and waited for a helper to boost us up the outgoing 0.7 percent grade. The storm's fury was accelerating. In the cut where we stood, the water was rising fast. The ground men wore boots and all the rubber coats and hats they could find. The wind was driving the rain horizontally. We tried to start, but after a half dozen unsuccessful attempts found we had no helper. When we finally got one, we dragged out at a singeing 3,400 amps. But we got over the hump, the pusher dropped off, and we were alone again.

Ahead the tracks disappeared into a pond—the cut was flooded. We shut off and drifted through it, the locomotive nose lifting water almost to the trolley wire. Then it settled in sheets over the windshield and washed through the side grilles, drenching Jim Smith, who was back in "the cave of the winds" taking blower-intake temperatures. Rain drove onto the equipment. Jim closed all grille covers except the one that would have fouled the thermocouple leads. Then he stood in front of this opening desperately holding the engineer's raincoat up to protect the apparatus. Finally, soaked and chilled, he cut the wires, stopping Felix's readings, and closed the slide. But Jim's sense of humor was inexhaustible. He declared that the engines were well named "battleships"—he'd ridden the "hurricane deck" all day, and when we hit the flood in the cut, he thought the "bow plates" would buckle.

Charlie Hess passed the foot of Hell Gate at 50 mph and topped the grade nicely, although the rain was so blinding that with the wipers running top speed, the engineer, his face glued against the glass, had difficulty seeing the signals. On the main span of the bridge, the wind rocked the boxcars alarmingly behind us. We eased down the east side and stopped near Oak Point—where we stayed 3 hours.

It was late afternoon. We first thought we were being held for the commuter traffic. The wind and rain were rampant. People could scarcely fight their way along the streets below the viaduct on which we stood. Umbrellas were snapping inside out wherever we looked. The air was turning much colder now as the berserk wind drove the heavy sheets of rain before it. Then we learned we were through. Neither

The first of New Haven's new 3,600-hp General Electric passenger-service electric locomotives, No. 0361, poses for its builder's photo in 1938 in a scene much more serene than sister 0364 would encounter during testing a few months later. GENERAL ELECTRIC.

0364 nor any other freight would be on the main line that night. The wires were down at Stamford. The last train to leave New Haven was No. 11 around 1 p.m. Everything was completely demoralized. We would remain where we were until room could be found for us in Oak Point yard.

Some of us went to a nearby lunch wagon for food and coffee. While we were there, a gang of washout-fighting gandy dancers were marched in by their boss. Charlie said they were recruited from the bowery, anywhere; frequently well-educated men were among them, men completely down on their luck. He said there was a civil engineer in that crowd. They'd work a few days and quit. Some quit before they drew their pay.

Back on the locomotive, we started the train-heating boiler to dry ourselves out. An open motor car shot by going up the bridge. It carried a section man dispatched to investigate reported washouts in the cut near Bay Ridge. The man was trying it alone, although he could be blown off the track on Hell Gate. Soon after he'd passed, we got orders to pull into the yard, cut off, and take 0364 to Van Nest. The test was called off because of the storm and havoc.

We drifted into Oak Point yard and dropped our train. En route to Van Nest the regular crew let us off at abandoned Hunt's Point station. It was dark. We poked around with flashlights. Finding the exit boarded up, we fought along the cut in the howling wind and stinging rain looking for a place to climb the steep bank. Finally we scrambled up through mud and dripping bushes to come out on 149th Street. Soon we were on the subway en route downtown, where we parted company with Charlie, Jim Smith, and Clark Scovill.

At Grand Central, Felix, Alf, Bob, and I inquired how the New Haven was running. The reply: "Where you going?"

"New Haven."

"Train at 8:55."

"How about the eight o'clock?"

"Canceled. The only train to New Haven tonight is the 8:55, and that's subject to delay."

Alf and I went down to see Clem Bellairs, the engine dispatcher. Clem was using two or three phones simultaneously. He had no engines and didn't know when he'd get any. West River had inundated the tracks at New Haven, stopping trains in or out. There was no power for switches or signals. Bay Ridge was isolated by washouts; we'd left just in time. We were

fast realizing that this was one of the greatest storms ever to strike the Northeast. The dead were multiplying into the hundreds and damage was mounting into hundreds of millions.

We sought shelter at the Commodore. We were a motley crew. My costume consisted of a battered hat soaked black; old brown sport jacket wrinkled and soggy; dirty, baggy tweed pants turned up at the cuffs; a greasy sweat shirt under my jacket; and wet, mud-caked loafers. The others were in similar condition. We had no luggage; it was in New Haven. But the Commodore took us in, loaned us toilet kits, and we soon hit the sack, exhausted.

The next day we returned to New Haven, which was a shambles. The storm was over, but the two-day rainfall had been 10.15 inches, the most in 64 years. The railroad was crippled, with no service east of New Haven or north of Hartford. Boston was isolated, with all railroads and highways blocked. Long Island was racked and torn. And the never-to-be-completed 3,000-ton freight test was never to be forgotten.

Riding K4s 5399 —to 94.7 mph!

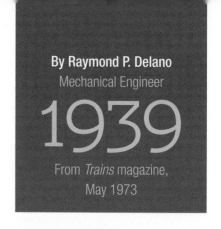

By Raymond P. Delano
Mechanical Engineer

1939

From *Trains* magazine,
May 1973

A chill fog lay in the hollows and there was a nip in the October morning air as I climbed into the cab. Harry Allen, road foreman of engines, eased back the throttle and we rolled through the Pennsylvania's Fort Wayne (Ind.) yards.

I was so absorbed in studying the firebox slope sheet with its piping and gauges that I nearly hit the deck when we lurched through a switch. After that I held onto something. The fireman and the regular engineer shared my feeling of tension. This was the day we were to find out if the changes that had been made to K4s engine 5399 would be effective enough to challenge diesel power.

We had worked for more than two years developing 5399's new poppet valve gear. Her new cylinders had separate dual intake and exhaust valves at each end. The valves were opened and closed by cams driven from a timing control box. The valve openings and the timing of the valve events were arranged for the most efficient use of steam.

Number 5399 had been modified at the Lima Locomotive Works. I had spent a week squatting under her, operating the big air motor which rolled her drivers to check valve events. When a valve opened or closed, a string was pulled and I stopped the motor while the crosshead position was measured and recorded. Each evening after I walked back to the Argonne Hotel, my ears rang for an hour until the noise of that motor wore off.

Next we had spent a couple of weeks at Fort Wayne running preliminary road tests with 5399, a dynamometer car, and light trains. I had been cooped up for too many hours with piles of test data and a slide rule. But today the big test was to occur. We were going to rerun—just a year later—the 1938 AAR Passenger Locomotive Road Test over the same track, the Fort Wayne Division between Fort Wayne and Valparaiso. The only change was to be the application of the Franklin System of Steam Distribution. We were to see what a good valve gear could do for a fine locomotive, and I was riding a cab for the first time.

We left the yards fast as Harry shortened the cutoff and worked the throttle wide open. He kept it there for 100 miles on some of the best straight and level track in the country. The staccato bark of the exhaust from poppet valves had a unique sound. The exhaust, pumping the flue gas up the stack, became sharper as the cutoff was shortened. The valve gear worked beautifully, and I began to sense the power of our 3,000 horses.

I found that a locomotive rocks and pitches. She waddled along, swinging with every revolution of the 80-inch driving wheels. Heat flowed back from the firebox. The tender tried to tear off the drawbar. A full gale blew around the cab. The experience was like racing down a rough road while standing in a coal truck that rode on solid rubber tires. Fly ash, coal dust, and cinders piled up on the back of my neck. I was glad I had tucked a bandanna under my collar to keep out the dirt. I was surprised to discover that my closest comparable experience was when I rode my heavy old Harley 74 motorcycle. I had the same feeling of tremendous life and power.

We accelerated. I timed us with my watch by the passing mileposts: 80 mph, 90, and finally 94.7—that was all Harry could nurse out of her. But 5399 went 5 mph faster than any others of her class, and she showed a good increase in horsepower with less steam.

The fireman gave me his seat, and I watched the rails being sucked beneath us. About a mile ahead, an ancient automobile slowly rattled up a section road to a grade crossing. The driver glanced our way and saw our train far off. Slowly he bumped across the tracks. I held my breath. We would hit that crossing in 40 seconds. He made it. I looked at the fireman, who shook his head. We both knew that our engine and tender weighed 250 tons. The dynamometer car and 15 heavy coaches weighed another 1,000 tons. If that auto had stalled, Harry would have thrown the brakes into emergency but we would have slid for 3 miles past the crossing on locked and flattened wheels.

Halfway toward Chicago, the water gauge showed that the level in the tender was too low for us to finish the run, so we slowed to take water from a trough

between the rails. Harry was in a hurry and slowed to only 40 mph instead of the regulation 20. At the mark he dropped the scoop. There was a terrifying crash, and the air was filled with flying water. (We learned later that a stone from the track ballast had been thrown by the water against the eastbound track and had bounced through a window two cars back in our train.) Harry lifted the scoop as fast as he could, but it tore up a few ties beyond the trough and nearly was ripped from the tender. The gauge showed the tender was full. The top of the tank had a new slight bulge.

We accelerated, and 5399 settled down at 90 mph for the rest of the run. As we ticked off the miles I speculated about the condition of the boiler. Two hundred pounds of steam pressure was tearing at every stay in the back sheet and trying every pipe joint. And I was standing with no place to go 2 feet from the possibility of getting a scalding or worse.

I glanced back at the tender and noticed that the stoker had stopped taking coal. The screw was running empty. The fireman saw it too and got busy pulling down coal. The fuel had stopped feeding for not more than a minute, but the steam pressure was dropping; it did not return to 200 pounds for 10 minutes. I began to understand what a sensitive monster this machine was and how responsive it was to the whims of its masters. The iron horse had been well named. When we turned on the wye west of Valparaiso to run back to Fort Wayne, I was sorry to give up my place in the cab.

We set a record that day, and we had the satisfaction of a task well done. But our efforts and those of many other loyal advocates of steam power were in vain— diesel power won the contest. Before steam died, though, the Pennsy's T1 class steam locomotives with our valve gear made many fast runs with heavy trains on that same Fort Wayne Division.

Pennsylvania K4s 4-6-2 No. 5399, built at the railroad's Juniata shops in 1923, was rebuilt by Lima in 1939 with a front-end throttle and poppet valves to improve performance and efficiency. LIMA LOCOMOTIVE WORKS.

"It's gonna be one of those trips, Captain"

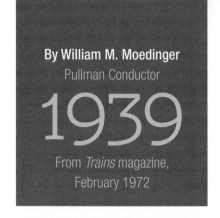

By William M. Moedinger
Pullman Conductor

1939

From *Trains* magazine,
February 1972

A Pullman conductor began his career by spending two weeks in a classroom. Now, two weeks in a classroom was by no means the complete answer to training a conductor, and no one knew this better than The Pullman Company.

Months of in-service experience were required before a man was adequately qualified. Consequently, the company regarded a conductor's first six months on the payroll as probationary. During this period, which was an indispensable part of the training program, the company reserved the right to dismiss a conductor for any cause without the formality of a hearing.

Actually, dismissals were relatively rare. The company throughout its long history had observed that virtually every conductor hired had threatened at least once during the training period to turn in his punch and keys. Therefore, it was relatively easy for a superintendent simply to accept the resignation of any trainee whose progress in the direction of a full-fledged conductor left something to be desired. By the same token, superintendents needed considerable diplomacy and skill in the not-so-simple art of persuading promising young conductors who were bent on resigning that they should reconsider. If the Kansas City District superintendent of nearly 30 years ago hadn't possessed those qualities, my career as a Pullman conductor (see page 44) would have ended before I had been on the road for two weeks.

From the beginning—even in the classroom—I found the work extremely attractive. I had some bad moments, of course, but they only served as challenges which tended to make the work even more interesting. Then came the inevitable bad trip. I was westbound on a military move between Fort Mitchell, Ala., and Fort Ord, Calif., when my tour of duty was suddenly terminated at Kansas City. There I was issued a trip pass on the Burlington and ordered to Denver for duty the following day, where I was signed out on the Santa Fe's *Centennial State,* which departed in mid-afternoon for Kansas City. The *Centennial,* normally a one-car Pullman operation manned by a porter-in-charge, that afternoon had in its consist three tourist sleepers in addition to the regular line car *Red Pheasant*. Although the brakeman who was assigned to work with me was fresh out of freight service and would have accepted a Chinese wash check as a ticket, our initial lift moved along smoothly, albeit slowly. My diagram for the regular car and my orders for the three tourist sleepers (which were to be boarded at Colorado Springs by military personnel from Camp Carson) indicated a comfortable load, with enough space left over to take care of a duplicate sale or two and to provide me with office space. The tourist cars were manned by relatively inexperienced porters, but my porter on the *Red Pheasant* was a good-natured, knowledgeable veteran whose long years of service and ample qualifications were manifested by gold service bars extending halfway to the elbow of his blue uniform sleeve. I was thoroughly confident that if I ran into any serious problem, my veteran porter's vast experience and co-operative attitude would stand me in good stead. Santa Fe train No. 101 arrived in Colorado Springs precisely on the advertised that early spring afternoon with its Pullman conductor right on top of his job.

After Colorado Springs the story was altogether different. The trip became a grim tale of a steadily deteriorating situation that finally reached its climax four hours later as the *Centennial's* marker lights disappeared into the chilly night just east of the little plains town of Lamar, Colo. My tourist sleepers, with a combined maximum capacity of 120 soldiers (based on the military wartime standards of two men to each lower berth, one man to each upper, and occupancy of the three drawing room sofas), were boarded by 130 men with their duffel bags, nearly 30 more men than my orders indicated. I rationalized by consoling myself that the problem was the responsibility of the train commander. But I learned that he was in charge of only 69 of the men; the other 60 were traveling on individual orders. This would have presented no problem for an experienced conductor; he simply would have honored the individual TR's (Government Transportation Requests) first. In this way every TR would have been honored for at least some space. A TR was nothing more than a blue piece of paper about the size of a dollar bill which entitled the bearer to berth space, if available, between two stipulated points. Most GI's, however, believed that a TR was the equivalent of a ticket; if no space was available, the GI's thought they were being deprived of a berth for which the government had already paid. In my ignorance, I first honored the blanket TR covering the train commander and the 69 men under him; the result was that I could honor only 34 of the individual TR's. By doubling up in lowers, as Army regulations dictated at that time, only 10 men were left without sleeping space. Nevertheless, all 26 men believed that The Pullman Company had shortchanged them by not providing the individual berths their TR's authorized.

Any wishful thoughts I entertained about accommodating the 10 men in the *Red Pheasant* were promptly dispelled when I commenced my lift there. Somewhere the Pullman reservation system had blown a fuse. To a plaintive glance in the direction of my veteran porter came the disquieting response, "It's gonna be one of those trips, sure as you were born, Captain." There were a couple of duplicate sales, which was just about par

Pullman conductor William Moedinger strikes a pose for a staged photo after his career had concluded. He learned quickly that some situations weren't covered in the classroom or training, and that some trips were certainly better than others. JON W. SIMPSON.

for the course in those busy days. At Colorado Springs, a ticket had been issued each for a lower in space normally held for Pueblo sale and for a lower marked "on Rocky Ford" on my diagram.

Also there had been the problem of two misdated tickets which I had honored leaving Denver, the solution to which entailed issuing refunds for the difference in price between a lower and an upper. At Pueblo someone boarded with a ticket for the space that had been released to Colorado Springs. Between Pueblo and Rocky Ford I discovered that I was short one porter on the tourist cars; the porter on another car said the missing man had gone into the Pueblo station for a snack, and the train had left without him. Somewhere along the line one of the tourist cars had lost its generator belt, so its lights, along with those in the car train-lined to it, were failing rapidly.

"On Rocky Ford" was a sample-case-laden drummer holding a ticket for the lower that had been boarded at Colorado Springs. At the very mention of a duplicate sale he waxed belligerent,

refused either an upper or a refund, and threatened to roust the other passenger who had already retired. Fortunately, the salesman's bark was worse than his bite, and he ultimately but reluctantly accepted an upper. He refused the refund and let it be known that he had powerful and influential friends in high places within The Pullman Company who, at his merest nod, would cheerfully accommodate him by having me fired on the spot. At this point the porter from the one remaining tourist car with lights informed me that the ladies' room of his car was flooded and that his car at the moment was out of water. The GI's in his car had piled their duffel bags on the washstands, and one of the supports had snapped under the weight, causing the whole fixture to collapse, breaking the cold-water pipe in the process.

The Pullman way of life had lost much of its glamour in those past three hours. One more encounter with an irate passenger or with a malfunctioning sleeper could very well have left me completely disenchanted with the business

of conducting. That encounter was just minutes away, waiting impatiently on the Lamar station platform for the *Centennial's* headlight to appear over the western horizon.

After we left La Junta I settled down in the *Red Pheasant's* smoking room, by then deserted, to catch up with the paperwork which had accumulated since Colorado Springs. One upper was due on at Lamar, but my porter offered to cover the stop for me. Except for two brief interruptions by the 10 berthless GI's, who had stepped into the smoking room to glare menacingly at me as though they were contemplating mayhem on my person in retribution for the shabby treatment they had received from The Pullman Company, no one entered. This was just as well, for I had discovered that the 34 individual TR's were for points east of Kansas City, which meant a transfer for each one had to be cut.

I heard the muffled clasp of brake shoes as the train slowed for Lamar, but I kept working. To properly endorse 35 TR's with all information the government required before it would pay the company

Conductors had a tremendous amount of paperwork to complete, not to mention dealing with unhappy passengers, equipment problems, train schedules, and seating issues. NORFOLK & WESTERN.

was a long, tedious task. My mountain of paperwork had melted considerably, but more of it still was ahead of me than was behind me, and the prospect of having to issue 34 transfers had not improved my disposition one iota. A Pullman transfer, incidentally, was more than a foot long and rather difficult for an inexperienced conductor to fill out and punch. If the transfer was not executed properly, it could be worthless to the bearer and a headache later to the issuing conductor.

Suddenly the curtains parted. A tall man stepped into the room and asked for the Pullman conductor. Even though I was surrounded by a vast assortment of tickets, TR's, Pullman forms, and sundry other tools of my calling and was wearing a cap with the words PULLMAN CONDUC-TOR emblazoned across the front, he was certain that I was not the Pullman conduc-tor of the *Centennial State*. The Pullman conductor was to be on the platform at all station stops without fail to render assistance to his passengers. Also, the Pullman conductor wore the regulation uniform, not a blue-patterned sports suit which happened to satisfy his sartorial whim at the moment. Before I had an opportunity to vent the venom which was

building up within me, he proffered a Pullman annual pass which identified him as one of the company's roving inspectors.

I admitted to being improperly attired because I did not yet own a uniform — wartime shortages, you know. I also admitted to not hitting the platform at Lamar, but I assured him it would not happen again. Yes, he had my solemn word that I would hit the platform at Syracuse, Kan., the next stop, because that was where I was getting off. Anyone as stupid as I had no business masquerading as a Pullman conductor. To make sure that he hadn't missed the point, I removed my cap and tossed it, along with my keys and punch, on the leather sofa beside him. From there on in he was to be the conductor.

When he finally regained his speech, he argued and pleaded for me to reconsider. I suggested that he save his breath, for after he endorsed those 35 TR's, completed his earnings diagrams, posted his call cards, restored the lights in the two dark tourist sleepers, and repaired the plumbing in the ladies' room of the third, he still had 34 transfers to issue for the GI's destined for points east of Kansas City. He threw his arms up in despair. He hadn't

worked as a conductor for years; what was he to do? I informed him just what he could do. While my precise words do not bear repetition here, the essence of my suggestion was that he ram four 80-ton sleepers up a particular area of his anatomy. Meanwhile, I proceeded to assemble my personal belongings in preparation for detraining at the next stop, which was just minutes away.

The curtain parted again, and my porter on the *Red Pheasant* beckoned me to follow him. We retired to the ladies' room at the far end of the car, out of hearing distance. He had overheard the whole exchange, and he didn't blame me one bit. But would I, as a favor to him, stay on to Kansas City? If I didn't, he would have to write out those transfers, because he knew the inspector wouldn't. I went forward and told the inspector that the porter had talked me out of getting off at Syracuse. A trace of humanity had crept into the inspector's personality, and he suggested that I retire—he would cover the next three stops for me. I asked the porter to call me at 4 a.m.; I wanted those GI's to get their transfers.

My entrance into the Kansas City District office on the following morning was accompanied by an unusual attitude of friendliness and efforts to be of help by everyone I met. As I sat down at a table in the cashier's office, another inspector introduced himself and offered to help me finish my work. He insisted on taking me out for breakfast and wanted to hear all about my trip from Denver. When I finally returned to the office in midmorning, there was word that the superintendent wanted to see me. He was all apologies, and he commended me on my handling of the situations on the *Centennial State*. Both the porter and the traveling inspector had stopped by that morning, and from what both had told him, he was proud to have me as a member of the Pullman family. All thoughts of quitting vanished from my mind. I could see I was a very important person. Fifteen minutes later when I emerged from his office with his promise of a very interesting assignment later that day, I realized I had done the right thing by not resigning. I was not merely a VIP; I was virtually indispensable. Pullman district superintendents earned their salaries.

The assignment *was* interesting, too, introducing me to three railroads new to my travel diary: Union Pacific, Alton, and Illinois Central. The IC portion included a segment of the Yazoo & Mississippi Valley between Memphis and New Orleans via Vicksburg and Baton Rouge, a quaint part of the world along the levees that seemed completely removed from the feverish wartime activity of the rest of the nation. At Baton Rouge my sleepers were coupled to the rear of an accommodation local with a 3 hour, 15 minute schedule for the 89 miles to New Orleans. This was not a fast carding overall but was one that required some pretty fancy throttle and brake artistry in order to arrive on the advertised after 15 intermediate stops. The trip was 89 miles of fast starts, lively sprints, and quick stops by a man on the righthand cushions who was an engineer in every sense of the word. No. 33, trailing seven heavy tourist sleepers in addition to its regular consist, arrived in New Orleans right on time.

That arrival at 5 p.m. in New Orleans marked the completion of my fifteenth day on the road. That night I drenched myself in the hospitality of the French Quarter and was able to sleep in a bed that wasn't on the move. The next afternoon I was signed out as second conductor on Louisville & Nashville's *Piedmont Limited*. Instead of going through to Philadelphia as second man, I was pulled off the train at Atlanta, deadheaded to Sand Hill, Ga., and assigned to a military move bound from there to Camp Miles Standish, Mass.— Pullman conductors, like tires and gasoline, were in short supply. Deadheading back from Boston, I was nailed at Penn Station for duty as second conductor on the *Havana Special*. I finally arrived back in Philadelphia after having been on the road 24 days and traveling 10,599 miles. The Pullman way of life had much to recommend it.

When I walked into my home district office I was advised that I had been assigned to a regular parlor car run between Philadelphia and Pittsburgh. The conductor who had been on the run had resigned, and no one had submitted a bid for it, a circumstance which automatically awarded it to the youngest man on the district's conductor roster. I was that man. Before my first month on the road ended, I made one round trip on my new assignment. In that month I had logged 11,479 miles, every one an experience if not a joy.

The itinerary of my new assignment was westbound on the Pennsylvania's Philadelphia section of the *Metropolitan*. It carried two straight parlor cars, one of which was a Buffalo-bound car I swapped at Harrisburg for a Washington-Pittsburgh parlor. Eastbound my run was on the *Duquesne,* which carried one straight parlor and one 16-seat parlor-buffet-lounge. It operated on a 7-hour, 5-minute carding that was just 3 minutes longer than the *Broadway's* time between the cities. Despite the critical motive power shortage of that time, the *Duquesne* usually was doubleheaded as far as Altoona, for No. 74 was a fast stepper which made six more stops in its 349 miles than the *Broadway*. I had been very disappointed at being pulled off the extra board with its long and varied troop runs, but I soon learned to like my new run. Parlor car operations kept a conductor busy every minute, and the time passed only too quickly.

The run was lucrative too, particularly on the *Duquesne*, which left Pittsburgh at 2 p.m. and carried a heavy-tipping clientele—a $10 tip for a seat was not unusual. Plenty of $10 tips were waiting, but the problem for me was finding enough seats. However, few potential tippers were not accommodated after I learned how to read my diagrams and how to maneuver my cash customers accordingly. Coaches were so crowded that the first-class trade would sit anywhere just to ensure that they had space in a parlor car. By exacting a promise from passengers that they would be willing to move around from time to time if I sold them a seat, I often could accommodate up to half a dozen more passengers than the two cars actually seated. This was possible by utilizing the space held by intermediate stations, such as Johnstown, Altoona, and Harrisburg, and by observing who had gone to the diner and when. The typical trip was like a giant game of checkers in which the seats were the squares and people were the checkers.

The timing of my new run ultimately led to a confrontation with my district superintendent. The company paid its employees twice a month, 15 days after the end of each pay period. Consequently, when I returned from my first 24 days on the road, I received the pay for my two weeks in the classroom. My regular assignment arrived in and departed from the old Broad Street Station, while the cashier's office was in 30th Street Station. This office was closed each day when I arrived back in Philadelphia, and my only opportunity to pick up my checks was before departure time in the morning. As a result, I simply neglected to attend to this little detail. I didn't need the checks; gratuities kept me living in fine style.

After nearly three months on the road, I was met by the Pullman platform man (the Pullman version of the railroad stationmaster), who handed me a small brown envelope containing a terse note signed by Superintendent W. A. Hartley. The note ordered me to report to Hartley's office on the following morning without fail. The platform man seemed reluctant to discuss the matter, but he hinted that it was likely not a socially oriented invitation to a meeting at which Mr. Hartley traditionally served tea and crumpets. W. A. Hartley was something of a legend in the world of Pullman, and I was one of the few conductors who had not been hired personally by him; I had been hired by his assistant. However, it was gospel around the district that an invitation to his office was never inspired by something of a picayune nature.

On the following morning, I was met by Hartley's assistant, who informed me that his boss was not in a good humor and that I should conduct myself accordingly. He proceeded to Mr. Hartley's door and announced me, and I heard the boss instruct him to send me in at once. We shook hands, and I took the proffered chair while he settled back in his chair to

Heavyweight Pullman cars trail Pennylvania Railroad train 72, the eastbound *Juniata*, at Marysville, Pa., in 1952. The train is en route from Detroit to New York City. PHILIP R. HASTINGS.

stare at me for what seemed an eternity. Finally, when I couldn't stand the silence any longer, I asked him whether I had done anything wrong. He didn't answer the question, but he revealed that he had had excellent reports on the caliber of my work from every source: Superintendent Scudder's office in Pittsburgh; inspectors who had observed me on the road; and his own cashier. He even had received letters from several passengers who had ridden my trains. His guess was that I certainly must like the work. Yes, I had to admit that I enjoyed every minute of it; to me, it was the greatest vacation I had ever had. He said that it gave him a lot of pleasure to see someone who really enjoyed what he was doing, but there was one thing he would like me to clarify for him. His records showed that I had been on the road for nearly three months, but his cashier reported that I never came in to pick up my paychecks. There were at that moment five checks of mine waiting to be picked up. Would I be good enough to explain?

For some now-forgotten reason, the question struck me as facetious. "You mean I get paid, too?" I blurted out. The unlit corona he had been dry smoking began to droop like a lower quadrant semaphore and finally dropped completely out of his mouth. He was staring at me

again, this time with an expression of utter disbelief. He concluded the interview with a violent wave of his arm that I knew was intended to inform me that I should get out of his office without further delay. I departed and stopped by the cashier's office to pick up my five checks.

The Philadelphia District was not large as far as porters and conductors were concerned, but it was important to the overall Pullman operation because it was the car distribution center for the entire eastern part of the United States. Mr. Hartley was reputed to be familiar with the floor plans and other pertinent data of at least half of the cars in the Pullman pool, which at that time numbered nearly 8,000. I was to witness his incredible knowledge of the subject several months later when I ran into him in the Pullman platform office in Broad Street Station one evening. He glanced at my OK slip (the equivalent of a railroad conductor's wheel report, listing all Pullman cars in a consist) and noticed that I had the car *Caleb Strong*. He wanted to know what I was doing with that car, as though I had any choice in the matter. He said that car had no business on my line, and he told me where it did belong. The next morning the car was missing from my consist, which

pleased me; it had a temperamental air-conditioning system.

My line, No. 2430 (every regular Pullman run had an identifying number, and that number was always carried by one car operating on the line), was unpopular with conductors because of the 21-hour layover in Pittsburgh. It would have been a fine run for Pittsburgh-based conductors, because the layover in Philadelphia was only 12 hours, 35 minutes. However, for a Philadelphia conductor who didn't mind working, the run was not bad. The Pittsburgh district was always in need of conductors. For example, if I had an extra troop sleeper destined for Cleveland in my consist, I knew for a certainty that I would be asked when I arrived in Pittsburgh to continue through to Cleveland. Occasionally, when one of the older conductors had reported in "sick," I would be asked to man B&O's train No. 35. It departed from the road's downtown station with two sleepers, one for Cincinnati and one for Hinton, W.Va., via C&O. The run was a gravy job that appealed to the older conductors. A conductor went as far as Parkersburg, and after a 50-minute layover, he returned on the northbound train. Usually the conductor had his earnings diagrams completed before he left the receiving tables. If his conscience permitted, he was free to retire.

If no road job out of Pittsburgh needed filling, a tour of station duty usually needed to be filled, either at the Pennsylvania station or across the Monongahela River at the Pittsburgh & Lake Erie station. A tour of station duty involved lifting tickets at receiving tables for sleepers which would be picked up by a through train or for through sleepers with space regularly assigned for Pittsburgh use. Two sleepers with Pittsburgh space were the New York-Memphis car and the New York-Nashville car on Pennsylvania's *Cincinnati Limited*. These cars were turned over to L&N's *Pan-American* at Cincinnati. Examples of sleepers picked up by passing trains were cars at the P&LE station, where a Chicago-bound sleeper was picked up by B&O's *Capitol Limited* and a Washington-bound sleeper from Parkersburg, W.Va., was picked up by B&O's *Chicago-Pittsburgh-Washington Express*. A station duty conductor was also a "protect" man, which meant that he was expected to report for duty prepared to fill any emergency assignment that might arise during his tour of duty. This never happened to me in Pittsburgh, but more than once a 4- or 5-hour tour of station duty developed into 10 days or two weeks on the road.

Although I facetiously referred to the Pittsburgh run as my 349-mile rut, it was far from that. Some of my most poignant memories involve those Sunday afternoon departures from Pittsburgh when the *Duquesne* ran in two sections. The Washington section, which departed a few minutes before the hour, ran nonstop to Harrisburg except for a crew change at Altoona. The regular section, which left at 2 p.m., carried the parlor cars and made all scheduled stops. The two sections always loaded across the platform from each other. Because the Washington section usually had two or three cars less than the regular section, its K4—with safety valves popping and blowers on—stood right across the platform from where my porters and I loaded our parlor cars. To many of my first class patrons, accustomed to the red-carpet serenity of prewar times, this certainly must have been a scene out of Dante's *Inferno*. Conversation at levels below a shout was impossible above the clamor of three K4's impatiently champing at the bit. To a railfan conductor who loved the sound, smell, and sight of the steam locomotive, particularly a Pennsylvania K4, this was the ultimate in railroading.

The Washington section usually would remain well ahead of us all the way to Harrisburg. Occasionally, though, primarily because our section was doubleheaded, we would catch up with it on the Pittsburgh Division. Two steam trains running side by side in the same direction always intrigued me.

One Thursday afternoon I reported for duty and noticed only one K4 was on the point. Number 74 never kept its schedule over the Pittsburgh Division without a helper, and that day was no exception. We didn't even make the 4.6 miles to East Liberty on time. A combination of insufficient motive power, poor fuel, and a green fireman relegated us to the menial status of a way freight. Our progress was so slow in places that the air-conditioning in the parlor cars remained inactivated. Our 7 p.m. arrival in Altoona meant that the *Duquesne* had maintained an average of 23 miles per hour. Everyone aboard No. 74 was pinning his hopes on Altoona, where we would get another engine. And that we did. But just as the brake test was being completed, word came that a wreck had occurred on the Middle Division, and No. 74 would be routed via the Bald Eagle branch through Lock Haven and Williamsport. The *Duquesne* arrived in old Broad Street Station at 2:20 a.m., 5 hours and 15 minutes late. No one complained, not even the Pullman conductor; he was on overtime.

In those days, every section of the 349-mile main line between the state's two largest cities could be bypassed using the PRR's own rails. Consequently, as the result of tie-ups on various parts of the system, I was able to ride over many of these alternate routes, many of which were freight-only. One of these routes was the Atglen & Susquehanna, commonly known as the low-grade freight line, between Parkesburg and Columbia. A tie-up on famous Horseshoe Curve would result in all passenger trains being routed over a freight-only line to the south that achieved the crest of the Allegheny Mountains at Gallitzin via the Muleshoe Curve. Any blockage of the four-track main line between Thorndale and Parkesburg meant a 29-mile detour westbound via the Washington main line as far as Perryville, thence north along the Susquehanna River 62 miles to where this picturesque stretch of railroad joins the Harrisburg main line at Royalton. These winding miles along the river had been freight-only since I was a boy, and this electrified route now is being used by Amtrak's trains between Washington and Harrisburg.

Conductors were required "to be on the platform at all station stops without fail to render assistance to his passengers," even if an avalanche of paperwork awaited.
TRAINS MAGAZINE COLLECTION.

As far as conductors were concerned, featherbedding was never a part of the Pullman lexicon. A conductor's basic work month consisted of 240 hours (8 hours x 30 days). The total in-service hours for my assignment for a 30-day month came to approximately 216 hours, which meant I had to accumulate 24 hours of late arrival time before I received any additional pay. Between 240 and 270 hours, a conductor received additional pay at the regular rate; anything in excess of 270 hours called for time-and-one-half pay. Only on rare occasions did my assignment's late arrivals for the month push in-service time above 240 hours. However, I frequently got into the time-and-a-half bracket because of extra assignments at the Pittsburgh end.

On July 15, 1945, all sleeping cars operating on runs of less than 450 miles were removed from service so they could be used by the military. This in effect removed the Philadelphia District from the sleeping car business. The older conductors, who feared troop movements even more than they feared parlor car operations, immediately bumped us younger conductors off our runs. I was bumped just in time to re-enter the peripatetic world of the extra board on my 32nd birthday; this was a birthday present to my way of thinking, one which I shall remember long after others have been forgotten.

Making time on the Midlander

By Chuck LeFever
Fireman

1942

From *Classic Trains* magazine,
Winter 2004

At age 18 and having been on the Erie Railroad's Kent Division extra board at Marion, Ohio, for only a short time, I was surprised by the phone call, which came just before noon.

Train 16, the Chicago-New York *Midlander*, needed a fireman between Marion and Kent, and I was next out. Pletcher, the crew caller, told me, "Report at 2 p.m. sharp; the engine is 2960. And eat a good meal." Then he added, "With Hummer, you'll need it."

The year was 1942. World War II had changed so many things. In my first few weeks as fireman, I had been called for about every job the Division had to offer except a work train. I dressed, took my metal suitcase, and set off for the railroad at the west end of Marion. On the way I stopped at Richter's Diner for lima bean soup, a Swiss steak platter, and apple pie—just what I needed on a cold December day with real work ahead.

At the caller's office I signed in and checked the Order Book for any problems east to Kent. I saw Will Shaw, our conductor, talking with Mr. O.D. Hummer, my engineer, who was enjoying a cigar. No one knew what the O.D. stood for; only company records or his family were privy to that information. Most called him Mr. Hummer, some O.D.; others, who were more his age or who were nervy enough, called him "Jim."

An Erie employee since December 14, 1909, this imposing man stood straight, fairly bulky even at 6-feet-plus, clean-shaven, and dressed from cap down in blue-striped denim. The steel frame of his glasses sparkled in the light of the bare bulb hanging from the ceiling. Standing there in conversation, he displayed a sense of quiet confidence. I knew his reputation to be one of the best engineers on the Kent Division. I decided I could not disappoint this man.

I walked alone to the out-track, where the 2960 stood waiting, nearly ready to take over from the engine that was bringing the *Midlander* in from Chicago.

The 31 class K-5 and K-5a 2900-series Pacifics were the top passenger engines on the Erie, and 2960 was the newest. Baldwin built her in 1926 as the lone member of the road's K-5b class. By 1942 she had been rebuilt to a standard K-5a, with shielded air pumps on the pilot deck, one-piece frame, Boxpok drivers, trailing-truck booster, and a big 12-wheel tender. And with 79-inch drivers, she could really fly. Climbing into the cab, I placed my case in the left-side tender cubby, then set about getting things in order.

Being anxious to have everything ready, I worked over the fire to the point that the boiler pressure reached its limit, and the safety valve let go with a tremendous gush of steam high into the cold, gray sky. By now Mr. Hummer stood on the ground at the bottom of the gangway ladder and, in a voice that chilled me but had no effect on the too-hot fire, shouted a choice selection of railroad-tested expletives and lunged for the handrails. Bounding into the cab, he glanced at the steam gauge, water-level glass, and blower setting and swiftly brought the pressure down to reasonable limits. In seconds, he had opened the feedwater injector and cut the blower draft with a dexterity that I envied. Without a word to me or a look at my anxious face, he turned and descended to the ground to resume his oiling and checking. I had heard from other firemen that conversation was not one of O.D.'s strong points.

In short order I set the lubricator, cleaned and adjusted the stoker blast jets, found the water tank full, spoke with the hostler about full sand boxes, and swept out the cab floor. When O.D. returned, he placed his case in the right-side cubby, wiped off the engineer's seat with a gob of cotton waste, then carefully cleaned the window glass on his side of the cab. He did not sit on his seat box, feel the throttle, or do any of the things most engineers did at this point. It seemed he looked upon the engine as a tool that would have to serve, and that any situation which might arise held no fears for him.

Bending to adjust a hard-to-reach valve on my side, I was startled by a command to fill the drinking-water can. It was not a loud, harsh command, but carried such impact that I stood straight so quickly that I knocked my cap off and came close to caving in my head on a protruding gauge. In this somewhat awkward condition, I looked over to see O.D. calmly relighting his cigar. I picked up my cap and dashed off with the water can.

When I returned, Mr. Hummer took out his large gold pocket watch and looked at it carefully. In this particular, he differed not at all from other engineers. He held the watch in his left hand and rubbed its face with his thumb. This is a ritual I never understood, but duly adopted as my own after observing it many times.

Replacing the watch, he signaled several short whistle blasts to indicate to all in the area that we were going to blow down the boiler. This is done to clean out scale and dead water so top efficiency may be obtained from the heating surfaces. During the blowdown, O.D. looked critically at the water-level gauge and tested each level-cock, then patiently waited for the water to reach the correct level in the glass. After we closed the blow-off valves, he tested the forward and backup sanders, booster engine, straight and automatic air-brake valves, bell, headlight, and other appliances. Again he took out his watch and calmly scrutinized its face, thumbed the crystal, and replaced it in its pocket.

Far up the track, a switchman gave the come-ahead signal. Leaving the cylinder cocks open, O.D. sounded two short blasts and started the bell. Moving slowly up the

During a Lake Erie snow squall at Stony Point, Pa., about 12 miles west of Meadville, K-5 Pacific 2924 stands in the siding as an unidentified K-5a dashes past with an eastbound. ERIE RAILROAD.

out-track past the caller's office, he opened and closed the throttle several times, worked the reverse gear, then flipped away his cigar stub. The purposeful 2960 eased away from the yard area and onto the eastward main. O.D. brought the engine over the interlocking, crossing first the Chesapeake & Ohio and then the Pennsylvania, between which was a cold crowd waiting for No. 16 on the Marion Union Station platform.

A car inspector swung up into the cab and, after a perfunctory nod to Mr. Hummer, stood behind my seatbox. He asked if this was my first run with this engineer and, to my affirmative reply,

smiled and advised, "Keep a heel in her. Heard he's a real stack-rapper and will pull every cinder off the grates if you aren't careful."

The engine came to a stop on the main, just clear of the crossover, and we waited for No. 16 to come in from Chicago. As 16's scheduled 3:11 p.m. arrival time approached, I noticed a restlessness in O.D.'s movements. He checked the fire, went out on the running board to check one thing or another, then returned to his seat to contemplate his watch. At the stroke of 3:11 he slammed his fist down on the armrest and muttered some short, brittle words. Sixteen was late!

Seventeen minutes later, the express drew into the station and its engine, 2910, was cut off as we were signaled to back onto the head car. During this maneuver, Hummer's manner changed completely. No longer casual, he was now deliberate in his movements. He handled each control crisply and surely. The coupling was made so smoothly the passengers probably never knew an engine change had been made.

The car knock signaled all was well, and O.D. checked the air line and the steam-heat lines, holding his watch in his right hand. In order to have a clear view of the baggage-handling and other activity back along the train, he thrust his broad shoulders far out the window. Soon, our conductor appeared under the window and told O.D. we would have nine cars: two baggage, three coaches, a diner, and three Pullmans, one of which was loaded with most of an Army divisional staff. The two men compared watches, and the conductor called up something about being late. O.D. only grunted.

The scheduled time for No. 16 to run the 113.7 miles from Marion to Kent was 2 hours, 24 minutes. This included four stops—Galion, Mansfield, Ashland, and Akron—which took up at least 20 minutes combined. A good average speed had to be maintained if the schedule was to be kept. Of course, with time to be made up, the average would have to be considerably higher.

Reflecting on stories I'd heard about Hummer, I realized this was just the kind of situation in which he liked to display his skill. The schedule must be maintained. The arrival time in Kent must be met. O.D. was ready to pit his experience and guile against this problem. On his side were his talents, a good engine, and an earnest but green fireman. Opposing him were a heavy train and time. In addition. it was wartime. Unforeseen delays were common. Equipment was not as well maintained as it normally was. Traffic was very heavy, with extra sections and specials. Rules were to be observed to the letter, but on occasion were relaxed. It all made for exciting railroading. I would not have traded my job for anything.

With his gloved left hand on the throttle, his watch still in his right hand, his eye on the green signal ahead, and his ear cocked for the conductor's air whistle, O.D. sat poised. I checked the fire for the hundredth time, noted that the pressure gauge was topping the maximum reading, injected a little water, and eased one more scoop of coal into the firebox as insurance against the firebox heel's being drawn out the stack.

I mulled over the carknocker's comment about Hummer's being a stack-rapper. The term comes from the use an engineer makes of the throttle and cut-off valve combination. For power, the throttle is used generously, with the cut-off valve in the full-forward position. This is used in starting a train. As speed increases, the two are eased into a more compatible and efficient setting to make the best use of the steam. However, when both speed and power are demanded, as in a situation when time must be made up on a passenger run, the valves and throttle are kept more open, causing a violent exhaust through the stack even at speed. Hence, the engineer becomes a "stack-rapper." Heaven help the fireman who allows his fire bed to become too light so the uprush of the exhaust literally cleans it off the grates.

The engine change was accomplished in the scheduled 5 minutes. At 3:33, 17 minutes behind schedule, the communication whistle sounded two peeps and O.D. quickly yanked the 2960's whistle cord twice in acknowledgement. In smooth moves, he performed like an organist. Watch into pocket. Forward sander on. Cut-off all the way down in the corner. Train airbrake valve off. Straight-air off. Cylinder cocks open. Bell set ringing. Booster cut in. Throttle heaved back.

The first exhaust to issue from the stack was a soft chuff. The next sounded angry, followed by a series of barks. The tall drivers slipped a turn. Closing the cylinder cocks, easing the throttle a bit, then out again all the way, O.D. began to pick up the load.

Eastbound out of Union Station was a slight upgrade to the Main Street crossing. My job now was to watch the stack, adjust the stoker in order to avoid too much smoke, listen to the sound as the engine picked up speed and Hummer adjusted the cut-off, and keep the pressure gauge on the peg and boiler water at the half mark. The whistle wailed as we swept past the Main Street crossing guard, who gave us an enthusiastic highball.

As we passed the Huber farm-equipment factory and the last street crossing in Marion, I stole a glance to the north toward the house where I rented a room. No supper in Marion tonight; I would eat at the Roundhouse Cafe in Kent if all went well.

How lucky I was. The blue overalls and jacket. My striped cap starched and pressed so cinders would not cling to the fabric. The red bandanna kerchief around my neck to keep out cinders and coal dust. My used Hamilton watch in its pocket. The outfit included goggles, since often one's head was stuck out the window to get a good look at the stack or to see signals on a curve. Gauntlet gloves that came up over jacket cuffs. Black, steel-toed, quarter-high shoes. Elastic pant cuff bands that snapped tight at the ankle. I was proud of this uniform and liked to keep it neat. One of the great benefits for me was to look down from the engine cab and wave to anyone in sight, especially kids, as we roared by.

From Marion to Galion, our first stop, the country was essentially flat. This was the longest stretch for fast running. As each green signal appeared, we each held up a gloved hand and shouted "Clear!" On curves, whoever saw the signal first called out what indication it showed. As we neared Caledonia, confident the way ahead was clear, O.D. jumped down on the deck and yelled in my ear, "I'll be aiming for 80 after the curve ahead. Keep her hot and the water low. Steams better on low water." He aimed a hefty punch at my shoulder and climbed back on his seat.

Low water? Being fairly new, I had never heard of low water. Most engineers wanted at least a half glass. I had just learned one of O.D.'s secrets that made his reputation for fast runs, but low water presented a problem to a fireman once we got into the hills east of Galion. I would

Number 2960, a K-5b Pacific built by Baldwin in 1926 (later rebuilt to K-5a), provided a good run for fireman LeFever and engineer O.D. Hummer as they made up time on their 1942 trip heading Erie's *Midlander*. ROBERT A. LEMASSENA.

just have to be as good as I could be.

Sure enough, by timing mileposts with my Hamilton's second hand, I saw that 2960 had reached her stride, even exceeding O.D.'s promised pace. We blew through the tiny town of Martel like a hurricane, slammed over the Toledo & Ohio Central crossing, and then past a freight train in a siding. The engine swayed from side to side. The tall drivers pounded against the rails in a furious, rollicking dance. Folks waiting at crossings waved, and I waved back. It was a glorious feeling, with sounds impossible to describe. The exhaust a sharp staccato, like hail driven against metal. The whistle crying out at every country crossing. The engine bounding, almost at a gallop, as we romped down the track.

Approaching the station, O.D. eased in the throttle and began to apply the air brakes with a velvet touch. We stormed over the first Galion crossing and slowed for the station. Ahead I could see only a wall of red lights. These signals marked the crossing of the main line of New York Central's Big Four between Cleveland and Cincinnati. If the tower allowed a freight to cross in front of us, we would lose time.

Bringing the train to a smooth stop at the station, O.D. kept staring at the red signals. There was plenty to keep me busy. I checked the tender to be sure coal would continue feeding into the stoker drive . . . opened the firedoor and placed more coal into the back corners . . . cleaned one stoker jet . . . examined the lubricator and found it OK. Then, back on my seat, I used the stoker valve to shoot coal into the firebox.

The conductor's air whistle sounded and we were off again. In the distance I could now see green signals—we would not be delayed by the Big Four. O.D. held up four fingers and patted his watch pocket, indicating how many minutes we'd gained since Marion.

From Galion all the way to Kent, the main line snaked its way around curves, crossed many bridges, and began to climb the westernmost hills of the Appalachians. No more flat, straight track. No more high-speed running. But a skilled hogger like Hummer could still make time.

Leaving Mansfield, the grade out of town past the State Reformatory was tough. Here O.D. revealed just what kind of demands he could make. He wanted power. He left the cut-off wide open, and the engine responded by digging in with all its might. He left the booster on longer than I had hoped, and the steam gauge showed a troubling decline. I had put an extra-large heel in the firebox while stopped at the station, and now all I could do was hope my fire bed would not be gutted by the hard-working engine.

We topped the hill at about 50. On past the Ohio Match Factory, the track curved to the right in a long sweep before beginning the ascent of Willow Ridge. The headlight pierced through a snow squall as dusk descended. Having made this run on freight trains, I looked forward to a slugging match between the 2960 and the grade. But to my surprise our engine was flying along. O.D. kept the throttle open and only grudgingly eased the cut-off.

The next several miles to Ashland were filled with curves left and right, and grades interspersed with straight track. If ever the carnival ride Shoot the Chutes were put on rails, this would be it. The engine would leap side to side, and bound up and down, but as far as I could see, O.D. considered the track flat and true. As we neared Ashland, he came over and called into my ear, "I hope not too many are in the dining car!" Westbound freights were frequent. At our speed, opposing traffic loomed quickly around the many curves. It was wise to move over behind the boiler to avoid being struck by some piece of loose freight.

The stop at Ashland gave me a chance to rebuild the fire. With the air pumps rhythmically pulsing as if to regain breath, I had to shake the grates since special, high-quality passenger-engine coal was no longer available, thanks to the war. We had the same coal any switcher burned, and it was full of slate. I knew Polk Hill and Creston were ahead, and we might be delayed at the Baltimore & Ohio crossing at Sterling.

With whistle blowing and stack erupting like a volcano, we thrashed out of town to the east, now only seven minutes off schedule. Feeling somewhat more confident, I stole quick glances at Hummer. I had made runs with Pangborn, Charley Bonecutter, Brillheart, and Eddy Schoor—all top engineers—but Hummer had a degree entire of intensity un-matched. He took "being on time" as a personal challenge. The use of sand was not new—every engineer used sand—but Hummer used it when running at speed so as not to risk one slip of the drivers. On curves, he used the rail washers, a spray of water behind the drivers that washed the crushed sand off the rail so as to reduce

friction for the car wheels of the train. He was a master of detail. Details made seconds. Seconds made minutes.

Through Polk, our bid to be on time seemed possible. As we approached Sterling, a little town with a dozen homes and one wonderful restaurant, we both spotted the green signal in the gloom before we raced over the B&O crossing. No delay this time.

On freight trains, Sterling was a water stop both east- and westbound. If there was a delay due to troop trains or some other problem, the conductor would announce a meal break, and the head-end crew would walk a short distance along a country road to the Rittenaurer Family Restaurant. There was served perhaps the best meals anyone could imagine: homebaked biscuits and bread, coleslaw and oven-roasted potatoes, garden salad with bacon and hot dressing, and meat loaf and gravy that, rumor had it, could be found nowhere else but inside the Pearly Gates. But this day, Sterling was passed in seconds, in a roar of flying ash and cinders.

Rushing onward, we passed another freight in a siding, and a westbound drag rumbled by. Down through Wadsworth, then Barberton, where one of my future Navy buddies lived. Past the rubber works where, it was told, they made special condoms for American servicemen. The tracks of the Erie ran alongside those of the B&O through South Akron, and we soon came to the Akron station.

O.D. brought the panting 2960 to a stop opposite the ticket office. A messenger came running out with an envelope and gave it to Will Shaw, our conductor. From the station platform he called up, "Don't look good. There's a stalled freight towards Kent."

O.D. climbed down the gangway steps to talk with Shaw. All I heard was Shaw saying, as he headed for the station office, "I'll try, but I think you're crazy."

My engineer stood on the deck and lighted another cigar. I was busy with the fire and injector. We had only 11 miles to go. O.D. checked the fire, looked at the water glass, and climbed back onto his seatbox. Soon our conductor came out of the station and shouted, "Take the westbound!" In moments, we were moving again, and miracle of miracles, we were to run east on the westbound main track all the way to Kent! Unheard of, but this was wartime railroading.

Just beyond the station, a dwarf signal showed that the crossover to the west-

bound track was clear. O.D. shouted over the noise as we picked up speed, "We have a clear track into Kent, and by grab we'll be on the money!"

We thundered along the somewhat strange track. Seeing it from a reverse direction was an odd experience. Hummer, however, seemed to know every crosstie as he opened up for speed. He made maximum use of the whistle, keeping it howling seemingly most of the distance to Kent. We passed the disabled freight and roared on. Up the final long grade, I could tell by the sound of the exhaust that O.D. was running as never before. I mentally crossed my fingers.

A lighted Christmas wreath in the west window of the station welcomed us. We glided through a crossover back onto the eastbound track and stopped at Kent station. The noble 2960 seemed fresh as ever. O.D. and I waited for the crew who was to take her and the *Midlander* on to Meadville, Pa. As I retrieved our cases, O.D. with a gob of waste cleaned the side glass and a couple of gauge glasses. Into the cab came Fred Lambert and his fireman Carl Pedersen. As they began their checks, O.D. and I descended to the snowy station platform.

As soon as No. 16 headed east, Will Shaw came over pulling out his watch, and Hummer did the same. "By my watch, I made the station stop at 5:39," said Shaw. "We were due at 5:40."

O.D. thumbed his watch, then said, "Yep, that was a good ride; that there 2960 is a strong engine. Will, can you see your way clear to join my fireman and me for supper at the cafe, say in an hour?"

Will Shaw nodded and gave me a grin. "You, young man, have got yourself a story to tell your kids and grandchildren, if you're lucky enough to have any. It's not often over a quarter of an hour is made up on Number 16."

Later, in the bunkhouse, O.D. was making out his trip report and had to ask me how I spelled my name—that's how new I was.

I am lucky to have a fine grandson. I hope he finds a job he enjoys as much as I did railroading. Not long after that fast trip to Kent, I joined the Navy and enjoyed that as well, but firing on the Erie Railroad has always held a special place in my memory. I guess it was the sense of accomplishment, of doing real work that was measurable and worthwhile. Being a fireman was my first job away from the farm, and I had measured up.

The Lady and the Pennsy

By Margot Fogg
Ticket Agent

1942

From *Trains* magazine,
December 1982

In the summer of 1942, I had just graduated from college and was staying with my parents at our cottage in Maine when I received a notice from the College Placement Bureau that the Pennsylvania Railroad was recruiting women graduates for a training course to become ticket sellers in city offices.

I wrote to inquire and was told that the first class had started, but the railroad was planning another session soon and that I should make an appointment with the Assistant General Passenger Agent in New York. I reluctantly left the cool Maine coast, returned to the city, and phoned for an interview.

I pictured an Assistant G.P.A. as an elderly man who had spent years with the railroad, so it was a shock to be introduced to a young, dark, curly-haired Adonis! I had no job experience, which I knew was a disadvantage, but I was surprised to discover that I was considered to be too young. Apparently the job description had a 25-35 age limit. I was told that a Miss Brink had been hired to oversee the program and might wish to interview me, but I left convinced I had wasted my time. I went to visit a college friend for the weekend, and on my return found a telegram asking me to meet with Miss Brink on Monday morning. I kept the appointment, and after chatting for a few minutes, she told me that I was too young and had no experience and in the next breath asked if I could be ready to start school in Philadelphia on Wednesday morning! I called the friend with whom I had spent the weekend in a Philadelphia suburb to ask if I could return for a few days until I found a place to live. Her mother insisted that I stay with them while I was in Philadelphia, and after persuading her to accept a small weekly contribution for my bed and board, I moved in and prepared to go back to school.

Arriving at the classroom, I found three other girls, all my age. Our instructor, B. J. Howard, informed us that we were an experiment. There were 10 women in the class that was already underway, all within the prescribed age limits, but it had been decided to gamble on the four of us. For six weeks we were to attend class from 9 to 5, five days a week, with homework every night and on weekends. We learned to use the *Official Guide* backward and forward, read rate books, work out itineraries, know the names of Pennsy trains and those of principal connections, and draw the Pennsy map from memory. We worked hard, but being fresh out of college we were used to studying and progressed much faster than the first class. We were paid a small amount while attending school, and when our first checks were delivered at the end of the second week, we insisted that Mr. Howard take our picture while we gleefully held up our checks—the first real pay any of us had earned.

The four of us quickly became good friends, and shared a somewhat irreverent attitude toward the whole proceedings, giving Mr. Howard a rather bad time; he was baffled by our foolishness, but proud of our accomplishments. We were asked to sign a statement agreeing to go to any city on the line, but we were assured that if it was a strange city we would be met and shown around, with a hotel room provided for two weeks to give us time to find a place to live. We were also told that we might be wined and dined by agents of connecting lines, and that if customers offered us a tip it was perfectly correct to accept. We were being handled with kid gloves, and we loved it.

During our training, Miss Brink took us on two trips. We had already been told that when we started work we were to dress like "ladies": no tight sweaters or clinging dresses or low necklines. Now that we were about to appear in public, Miss Brink was concerned that two of us had come to Philadelphia without hats. We were instructed to remedy that situation before the trips. We both hated hats but did as ordered, and I'm afraid our choice didn't please our boss; although in a nice dark grey material, they really resembled baseball caps. Miss Brink let it be known that she considered us somewhat infantile, but any hat was better than none.

Our first trip was a day in New York where we toured Pennsylvania Station, spending some time in the reservation center as well as looking over many of the name trains. Our second trip took two days and nights and was designed to acquaint us with different types of accommodations. We were each given money with which to buy our meals, and with Miss Brink as chaperone, off we went. We boarded the *General,* luxuriating in connecting double bedrooms, which we promptly opened up into one room, talking half the night. In Chicago Union Station we were met by a passenger agent who showed us the Parmelee Transfer System, the city ticket office, and the other stations. Then we were off to Cincinnati in a day coach.

Again we were met, shown the handsome Union Terminal, and taken to a hotel for a few hours of rest. None of us had ever seen such an elegant suite, being told it was normally reserved for John L. Lewis, the legendary chief of the United Mine Workers. We ordered food and drink, took welcome baths, and enjoyed the chance to stretch our legs. About midnight we took off again, this time in upper and lower berths en route to Pittsburgh. There we had very little time before boarding another train, this time in parlor chairs, to Washington. Again we were met and taken on a whirlwind tour of the sights before collapsing in a drawing room for the return to Philadelphia.

Passenger schedules changed continually during World War II. Record-breaking numbers of passengers and increased wartime traffic made issuing tickets both a difficult challenge and an art. TRAINS MAGAZINE COLLECTION.

Shortly before our final exam, we were taken to the downtown city ticket office to observe ticket sellers in action. While there I received word that my mother, who had been seriously ill for some time, was in critical condition and that I should go to my New York home immediately. The Pennsy sprang into action; a taxi was quickly provided to take me to the station, and when I got there I was met by an agent who handed me a round-trip ticket and told me to stay as long as necessary. I was not to worry about the exam, he said; if I wasn't back in time, I would graduate anyway and have a job. My mother rallied and I returned the next day, but I felt that if I could not work in New York I would have to resign. I was immediately assured that I would be assigned to New York and was offered any help the railroad could provide.

I started out in a small ticket office

on 33rd Street. I began on the phones, making reservations and giving information. One day I was handed a very long itinerary of a Mr. X who was traveling coast to coast, going west through the northern tier of states and returning on a southern route, with many stopovers along the way. It was my job to find the trains that would fit his schedule and make all the reservations; once this was done, Vic, the ticket agent, would make up the ticket. It took days and innumerable telephone calls to get all the space confirmed, but finally everything was in order and Mr. X came to pick up his tickets. When he arrived, Vic called me to the counter and introduced me as "the girl who did all the work." Mr. X thanked me and asked, "What size slip do you wear?" My jaw must have dropped, and I know I turned scarlet. Vic laughed and explained that Mr. X was a lingerie salesman and just wanted to give me a gift for a job well done. I was given a choice of pink or white, tailored or with lace, and a few days later my new slip was delivered. I had been told to expect an occasional tip, but I hadn't been warned about that kind of question!

I was at the 33rd Street office a very short time before being transferred to the Consolidated Ticket Office at 17 John Street in the heart of the business and financial district. This was a large office shared with the Baltimore & Ohio, Lackawanna, New York Central, and Reading, but the Pennsy was the biggest occupant by a wide margin. A large proportion of the customers were from big firms in the area, many of whom bought tickets on a daily basis, and the ticket sellers had regular customers. The atmosphere at times was almost that of a club or neighborhood bar, with bantering and insults flying back and forth. After a few days on the phones and a couple of weeks on the "make-up" desk learning the many varieties of tickets, I was given a dater and a spot on the counter. I was now "D for Danny 17," the first female ticket seller in the city.

The men seemed to appreciate my appearance on the scene; the regulars were so startled to see a young woman behind the counter that the noise level and crude language subsided drastically. There were 10 of us on the counter, and the customers were lined up at least 10 deep from the time the doors opened in the morning until they closed at night. The pressure was tremendous. The regulars knew what to expect and came prepared; my favorite arrived daily from Western Electric, armed with a book and an apple, ready to stand in line for 2 hours or more. But tempers often ran short among others who found themselves standing in line behind five or six office boys, each buying 8 or 10 tickets to different places.

One day was particularly hectic, and my half-hour lunch time had long since passed. I announced that I would take five more customers and then be gone for 30 minutes, and the others could wait for me or shift to another line. As I finished with the fifth customer and started to lock up, the next man asked what I thought I was doing. When I replied that I was going to lunch, as I had been announcing continuously, he exploded. His voice got louder and louder as he complained that he had been standing in line for well over an hour and that I wasn't going to walk out on him! By this time it was almost 3 p.m., and I had had enough pressure for one day. I told him that I had been standing since 9 a.m., that I was very tired and hungry, and that I was going to lunch. I thought he was going to hit me, and the men working beside me edged closer to protect me. The man yelled that he was going to report me to the ticket agent. By that time I didn't care if I was fired, and I left. When I returned from lunch, the agent stopped me and said that he had told that customer just where to go! Dear Mr. Ryan—I should have known that he wasn't going to let anyone pick on his girl.

The ones who never seemed to lose their patience or sense of humor were the girls at the reservation desk in Penn Station. I never met any of them, but I soon came to recognize their cheery voices when they'd answer "G.C. for Grand Central" or "T.F. for Tutti Fruitti." I would have to call several times a day about trains I knew were sold out, but they seemed to understand that the customers demanded it, and they usually came back with a humorous remark. They knew me only as "D for Danny 17," and I never discovered how they found my name, but when my engagement was announced I received a lovely card signed by about 15 of them.

I was not at all surprised that the two sleeper trains to Washington were sold out weeks in advance, and many times military and Government personnel with official priorities were upset when we couldn't provide space. What did surprise me was that apparently half the population of New York City wanted to vacation in Florida that winter. The *Silver Meteor* and *Tamiami Champion* were sold out at least two months in advance. Many people wouldn't believe me and offered bribes for space I was supposedly holding back. Perhaps some of the men who'd been there for years had a way of holding space up their sleeves for favored customers, though if they did I didn't know about it, and certainly as a newcomer I had no pull anywhere. The biggest problem, however,

was getting people back from Florida who'd had the foresight to make their southbound reservations very early. These reservations had to be made through the originating lines in Florida, and they were sold out for months too. We had our phone crew calling every day to confirm space, but it frequently took weeks to achieve.

Meanwhile, customers were coming in every day, hoping to pick up their tickets. I saw no reason why they should stand in line for up to two hours, only to be told that nothing had happened, so I tried to keep track of their status and signal them as soon as they came in. I assumed that other sellers did the same, but apparently many customers were not used to this consideration, for I was the recipient of profuse thanks when tickets were finally ready. Many returned a few days later with gifts—boxes of candy, perfume, even silk stockings, which were worth their weight in gold in those days!

Some problems seemed almost insoluble. A young man wanted to change a party ticket, which didn't alarm me until I discovered it was issued for six by a Western road. Four of the party wanted to return on the date for which the return ticket had been issued, but two others wanted the date changed. I had no idea of how to cope, so went to my favorite old-timer for help. He'd never faced the problem either, and after reading regulations and discussing alternatives he decided we couldn't touch the ticket and that the young man would have to go to an office of the issuing road. Then there was a Frenchman who spoke no English and wanted a sleeper to Pittsburgh. He was sent to me because I spoke some French, but my limited vocabulary couldn't translate "duplex" or "roomette," and there was the added problem that the train left at 12:01 a.m.—did he really want to leave on the date he stated or the previous day? Between my garbled French, sign language, and much laughter, we finally got everything straight—I hope!

Since selling tickets was my first job, I was eager to prove myself and was soon outselling everyone else, one day breaking the $3,000 mark to set an office record. Shortly after I had arrived at John Street, the local union representative asked if I wanted to join. When I inquired what membership would do for me, he proudly announced that the union was responsible for the seniority system. He lost me right there! I could be the best ticket seller in the city but never get a raise until someone hired ahead

of me moved up. What incentive was there to do a good job? On the other hand, I could be a useless employee and still move up. If I had stayed on the job long, I probably would have become lazy and sloppy like some of the others.

Although the railroad treated me with great consideration, the pay was terrible. I received $142.20 a month for a 48-hour-a-week job (and when the big day came when I did move up a notch on the roster, my pay increased by the sum of 20 cents a month!). And if I made the wrong change or charged the wrong amount, the difference would be deducted from my check. Fortunately, that never happened to me, although I did make one careless mistake. A minister bought tickets for himself and his wife. Clergy were given a discount, but when totaling the cost I doubled the price of his ticket and found myself $10 short at the end of the day. I realized my mistake right away, but I didn't know his name, so there was nothing I could do. The next morning there was a call for me—the minister saying he had realized that I'd made an error and was sending the money over. That $10 represented almost two full days of hard work, and it was difficult for me to express how grateful I was for his honesty. This also showed how valuable it was to be the only girl in the office—there was no question about to whom the money belonged!

One morning I awoke with a terrible case of laryngitis. I felt fine and went to work, but I couldn't be understood on the phone, so was put to work on accounts. I was horrified to discover that so many errors were made each day and that many of the men were short several days a week. I don't know how far up the roster these old-timers had moved, or how much they were paid, but those two weeks were a depressing time for me. The men had been very kind and helpful to me, and I hated to see them docked for their mistakes.

I don't know how long the Pennsy continued to train women as ticket sellers, for I left in the spring to get married. During that time I knew of only one other woman doing that job in New York; she had been in the first class and came to our office shortly before I left. As far as I know, the program was a success and Pennsy should be given credit for being the first (and only?) railroad to try it. For me, it was an invaluable experience in dealing with the public under great pressure, and despite the aching feet and miserable pay, I'm glad I was part of the experiment.

Time to unload

By John A. Terhune
Fireman
1942
From *Trains* magazine,
November 1986

I was a fireman on the Pennsylvania Railroad, hired December 2, 1941, working the extra freight list out of Jersey City, N.J. In early February 1942, I was ordered to deadhead on train 25 to Harrisburg, Pa., to work a round trip from Enola Yard to Jersey City, N.J., and return on Pool Crew No. 602.

This was my first long road trip. In fact, I didn't even know where Enola was, but other deadheads filled me in, and I paid close attention to the experienced firemen as they spoke of their trips. When No. 25 stopped at North Philadelphia, an elderly man carrying a railroader's bag walked into the head car. He looked us firemen over and said, "Who's covering the No. 602 crew with me?" I raised my hand and said, "I am, sir."

Everyone laughed as he snapped, "Don't call me sir, young man, you're not in the service yet. My name is M.P. Rogers." I felt my face redden and thought, *boy, am I off to a good start*. What a grouch! But I was wrong, because he turned out to be one of the best runners that I ever fired for. In fact, by the time I went into the service in June 1942, I was his regular fireman on the No. 602 crew.

After No. 25 left Paoli, Pa., we ran at normal speed (75 mph) and then slowed to a crawl. One of the deadheads exclaimed, "Wow! Look over on No. 1 Track." The tracks were covered with brass hats. Then I saw the reason for the officials being there. A set of wheels, cylinders, rods, and tender of a 2-10-0 stood at the front of a freight train minus the boiler. One engineer exclaimed, "Look over to the right!" There lay the boiler and cab on its side with two blanket-covered figures alongside. Rogers said, to no one in particular, "That was an I1 that blew up." He looked at my face, which was drained of color, and said in a hushed tone, "It happens sometimes, son." No. 25 resumed speed, and the card games also got going again. Once or twice I heard strained laughter and I thought, *how can they be so callous and indifferent?* But during my 38

years of service, I learned that a railroader knows that he has a hazardous job. Death is no stranger to us, so when someone is hurt or killed, we thank God that it was not us and we don't talk about it.

When No. 25 arrived at Harrisburg, Rogers got on a company phone and called the Brick Office at Enola and was informed that the No. 602 crew was ordered for the P-14 with steam power. Wartime demands kept the electric motors on high-class freight, with some of the modified P5's used in passenger service. We caught the bus over the Susquehanna River to Enola. Across the road from the Brick Office was Ungers Restaurant, where most of the crews ate. When we finished a huge Pennsylvania Dutch meal, Rogers said to the waitress, "Fix us a Jersey steam engine lunch." When she returned, she had a sack containing six assorted sandwiches, slices of pie, and some fruit.

I looked at the lunch and said, "We'll never eat all of that." Rogers laughed, and crews sitting near our table smiled. How little I knew about the Enola-Jersey City freight pool!

We walked over to the Brick Office, signed the register, and walked down to the engine service area. On the ready track was M1 6805. I climbed into the 4-8-2's cab, and Rogers handed up the grips and lunch bag. He said, "Check all supplies and get your fire ready, and then set the lubricator (which was a hydrostatic). Gimme the oil can." He was all business as he oiled around and inspected. Then he climbed back in the cab, opened the firebox doors, and examined the crown sheet and everything else, explaining to me as he did. He said, "O.K., now get your fire ready." I pushed the heel forward with

the blower on full, then ran the HT Standard, slowly watching the stack so I wouldn't have trouble with the local smoke-eater. Rogers moved down the outbound engine track and spotted the tender to top off the coal pile. Then I topped off the water.

With cylinder cocks hissing, we moved through the spring switches and down the departure yard lead and stopped behind two double-headed L1 2-8-2's, which Rogers said was a Port Road man. Our conductor climbed into the cab and gave Rogers the list of pick-ups and set-offs. Then he turned to me and said, "Are you a new fireman?" I replied, "Three months."

Instead of getting mad, he said, "If you have any trouble, the head brakeman will be in the doghouse; ask him, and he will give you a hand because he's a good man." I thanked him as he got off.

We moved to the head of the yard and reversed to our train, coupled up, and then started to pull east. I opened the stoker valve, and she raised the safety valve at 250 pounds. Rogers said, "Don't waste water." We pulled up the grade toward Lemo Tower, then stopped. Rogers saw the puzzled look on my face and called me over to the right side. He pointed to a signal box high on a catenary pole and said, "We are working with the green light. After they drop the hack off the ramp and couple up, the conductor will give us four greens to apply, then four to release the brakes; two long greens and we leave town."

While we waited, he explained how to fire an M1. He said, "This is a Standard HT stoker, which is a mechanical stoker. When someone uses the term automatic stoker, as applied to a steam locomotive, they don't know what the hell they are talking about, because if you are not on your toes at all times you can really mess

things up." He returned to his seat and said, "Two long greens, kid, and keep her hot because I'm going to give her the meat."

On sand, she started the 75 cars up the grade to Lemo Tower, which displayed a clear signal the same as the cab signals. She was a good steamer, and I had to back off on the stoker valve to keep her from popping off. Rogers stood up, reached overhead, and opened the feedwater heater valve. He shouted to me, "Use your injector once in a while and keep the deck and coal pile wetted down." We were now rolling along at a good pace.

I noticed that the water in the glass on my side was getting low. At Goldsboro, Rogers came over and hollered, "Keep your injector on and wide open, because this feedwater pump is not a helluva lot of good and don't let her pop off." He took a sheet of paper out of his bag and wrote a message; after blowing the whistle to get the block operator's attention at Cly, he threw it wrapped in a fusee to the operator, who was now on the ground. He said, "We'll get it fixed at Columbia or we will get another engine."

We crossed over the river, and, after passing Shocks, he eased off on the throttle trying to catch up on water. At Lake, he put the blower on and shut off. We rolled to Cola where he applied the automatic and stopped with the slack bunched at the home signal.

Two mechanics from the small enginehouse at Columbia were waiting with tools and a short ladder. Rogers got down and told them that the feedwater pump was no good. They climbed up and, after a few adjustments, which consisted mostly of a few good blows with a heavy hammer, declared, "It's working fine now." Rogers got back on the engine and opened and closed the valve a couple of times. The men on the ground beamed and shouted, "She's O.K. now!"

In the time that we had been there, an L1 2-8-2 had coupled to the hind end to push us to Gap, Pa., because we were picking up 17 more cars at Dillersville. Rogers made a brake test for the pusher, and after two westbounds passed, the home signal went to medium clear. Rogers eased the throttle out, and the 6805 started to bark. He looked over at me and said, "Keep her hot, kid, it's all upgrade, and I

Pennsylvania M1 4-8-2 No. 6987 heads a freight toward Enola Yard in July 1955. DON WOOD.

hafta work her hard." I kept looking at the water glass. Rogers said, "Put your injector on and leave it on. I think that damned pump stopped again." At Mountville, there was a little over an inch of water in the glass. Rogers eased off slightly, and we just made it to Dillersville without stalling.

After we stopped, leaving room for our pick-up, there was about a half inch in the glass. Rogers hit the ground with the coalpick and hammered on the pump, which made it start again. I kept the injector on during the entire pickup of 17 cars. When we coupled back to our train, we had half a glass of water. Rogers got down again, and when he returned to the cab, said, "Well it's working O.K. again, so, if we can make it to Thorndale we can get another engine there." He went to the phone and called the DS in Harrisburg and explained the problem. He climbed back into the cab and said, "We'll get another engine at Thorndale."

He watched the home signal, and after a passenger train left Lancaster station, we got the signal to follow. Then he called in the flagman. He said, "Knock off the injector or she will work water. He eased the throttle out, but after we moved a short distance she slipped.

I quickly opened the butterfly doors so the fire wouldn't get torn apart. She was a good M1 and only slipped once. Then she dug her heels in and started to really wheel the heavy train. The lollypop helper on the hind end was shoving hard because on the curves I could see the heavy cloud of smoke from his exhaust.

Passing Leaman Place, Rogers shouted to me, "Put your gun on again— the pump must have stopped again." Now I was really getting scared. I kept thinking about the I1 which had blown up at Bradford Curve. Rogers hooked her up a couple more notches, but upon approaching Ebys Curve the water was just bobbing in the bottom of the glass. Then he started to use the gauge cocks, mostly the bottom one. I could hear the safety valve sizzling and made up my mind that if she blew off, it was time for me to unload. We were going too fast to jump, but my route would be over the coal pile to the doghouse with the head brakeman. We topped the grade at Gap and Rogers eased the throttle off, but not fully, just enough to keep the water level raised. The water was now bobbing in the bottom of the glass.

Rogers gave me a relieved look and said, "We're coming to Atglen, son; get ready to scoop water." I positioned myself, and when he tooted the whistle, I dropped the scoop and took the entire pan. The distant signal to Park was Approach, so he brought the train to a stop at Park's home signal.

The head man went to the wayside phone, and when he returned said, "There's an M1 coming west running backwards, and he will change engines with us."

While we waited, I ate another pot-roast sandwich and said to Rogers, "When we get into Jersey, I'm going to quit this job."

He smiled at me and said, "John [not 'kid' or 'son'], I think that you will be making a mistake. You seem to like the job, and you are a good fireman willing to learn. You will have bad trips and good ones but more good than bad." I didn't answer, but I felt better.

The relief engine stopped alongside of our cab on No. 3 Track. The engineer swung over into our cab and said, "Wait until I look her crown sheet over." He opened the firebox doors and made a thorough examination. After he was satisfied, we handed our stuff over to the relief fireman. I swung over and looked around the cab and said to Rogers, "What the hell kind of engine is this?" He laughed and said, "This is an M1 with a Duplex stoker and a short tank for passenger service."

We moved through Park interlocking and reversed to our train. While pumping up the air, Rogers explained how to fire an engine with a Duplex stoker. After the brake test, the head man came back from the phone. The home signal went up to clear, Rogers blew the flagman in, and we started to move. The Duplex stoker was much noisier than the Standard HT, but the 6910 was a good steamer. When we reached 50 mph, Rogers reached over and put the blower on, making sure that I had seen his movement, and then shut her off. We rolled down Parkesburg Hill and stopped at the coal wharf at Thorndale, taking on coal and water, while Rogers looked her over. The 6910 was a good engine: good riding, strong, and a good steamer. She wheeled that heavy train up the Philadelphia & Thorndale Branch, then the Trenton Branch, where the hog law (16 hours) caught up with us at Morrisville, Pa.

While riding the company jitney to Trenton to deadhead home, Rogers said, "You stick around, son; you'll be O.K." I did and retired after 38 years of service.

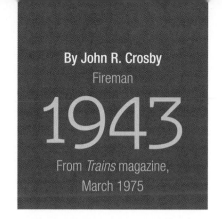

By John R. Crosby
Fireman

1943

From *Trains* magazine,
March 1975

Second engine 28

The 55th Street enginehouse foreman doodled the date on his desk pad—*8-14-43*—as he dialed the extension of the Movement Director downtown.

"Charlie? This is Sam. Just want to let you know that the 6110 we had marked for 28 today ain't going to be ready. The cold-water pump went to hell, so we had better figure on going with a couple of K's. I've got a pair of good ones ready—5471 and 5352. How many cars are you figuring on 28?"

The metallic voice of the Movement Director came back over the earpiece informing Sam that it looked as though 28 would be a 16-car train. As Sam hung up, he mused that the boys on 28's power today would have their hands full. Then he busied himself getting his people alerted to the change in power.

The Movement Director also began to work on his part in getting the Pennsylvania Railroad's *Broadway Limited* out of Chicago and headed for New York. He called the 55th Street crew dispatcher and ordered two engine crews for 28. Referring to his crew sheet, the crew dispatcher noted that the engineer on the first engine

would be Pat McCormick, on the second engine Harry Adams.

At 11:45 a.m, the crew dispatcher went into the crew room, found Harry Adams, and gave Adams the call for "second engine 28, reporting 1:30 p.m." Harry volunteered to give the call to his fireman. With that chore finished, the crew dispatcher went up into the bunk room to wake up McCormick and his fireman.

A few minutes later Adams headed across the wide expanse of 55th Street or the "boulevard" as the crews called it and headed into Huffman's, where his fireman, Johnny Cooper, was eating either an early lunch or a late breakfast. Cooper was one of the younger firemen on the extra passenger list; but from information Harry had been able to pick up from other passenger engineers, Cooper had a good reputation for keeping engines hot. Adams found a seat next to Cooper, gave him the call for 28, and then ordered lunch.

As they ate, Adams commented that 28

probably would be heavy today and they would have their work cut out for them. Harry briefly mentioned 28's schedule of 2 hours 22 minutes for the 148 miles between Chicago and Fort Wayne. He added, "Pat McCormick is the regular man on 28, and you know how he always is telling the crew on the second engine that he doesn't want to be able to see behind the bulge in his tender because the guy on the second engine is pushing that hard." With that gem of wisdom, their conversation turned to the fortunes of the White Sox.

After finishing lunch, the crew of the second engine on 28 returned to the crew room and there they watched some of the freight boys play cards in a game that apparently never ended. Fresh crews always were coming in off runs, or getting up after resting, to take the places of those who went out on runs or went to bed. About 1:25 p.m. Cooper and Adams went into the locker room to dress for work.

They picked out their grips from the gas-pipe racks along the walls. Both grips were of the same style and size, specially designed to fit into the standard Pennsy seatbox. Both men began to dress in much

Pennsylvania K4 No. 5471 is shown at South Amboy, N.J., in 1956, 13 years after her run on the *Broadway Limited* described by fireman Crosby. The engine was built by Baldwin in 1923 and has just been repainted and undergone Class 3 repairs at Altoona Shops. DON WOOD.

the same fashion: large red bandanna pinned around the neck to keep cinders out; light-blue work shirt. Adams left his shirt collar open and standing up in normal position; Cooper tucked his under, in the style many of the younger firemen had adopted. Over the shirt went bib overalls. Adams wore a gray pinstripe; Cooper went for the standard blue denim. Both completed their outfits with white Kromer work caps.

When they were dressed, they headed through the enginehouse for the crew dispatcher's office to register in for duty. Both checked the bulletin boards for new notices and General Orders; then they signed the Crew Register sheet which certified that the engine crew of second engine 28 was qualified for this assignment, had been properly rested, and in general were pure of heart. The crew dispatcher gave Adams the passenger time slip which showed the date, train number,

engine number, location, and reporting time. Adams would fill in the other information needed to keep the Hours of Service inspectors happy and also provide the timekeeper with enough figures to ensure a full check on payday.

A few minutes later Pat McCormick and his fireman walked in and went through the same routine Adams and Cooper had just completed. McCormick's fireman was grumbling that this run would be about his last on the "high wheelers" because it looked as though on the next list he would be set up running and would have to buck the extra engineers board. He was not getting much sympathy from anybody, so he quickly dropped the subject.

McCormick checked to see what engines were assigned to 28. He commented to Adams, "We had the 5352 down this morning, and she is a good one. The driving boxes are a bit loose and she rides

rough, but that's about all that's wrong with her. So, young man, you have no excuse not to be pushing hard enough to put a bulge in my tender." To Pat McCormick, anyone under 60 automatically qualified for the title of young man.

Both crews walked outside to get their engines. The lead 4-6-2, 5471, had been cleaned up by the roundhouse forces; and since it was just three days out of a monthly inspection, it looked fairly presentable. No. 5352 was another story. It was covered with almost 30 days of dirt and grime from more trips between Chicago and Crestline, O., than the boys at Altoona Shop would like. These days during World War II there wasn't much time for steam cleaning the running gear and washing down the tender flanks, to say nothing of polishing the bell or graphiting the smokebox.

Both firemen went up the gangway first while their engineers handed up the

The Pennsy liked to double-head K4s Pacifics on heavy passenger trains. Here the second section of eastbound No. 76, the *Trail Blazer,* leaves Englewood Station in January 1941.
Paul Eilenberger; Harold Stinton collection.

grips, which were promptly stowed away. The firemen handed down long oil cans and baseball-size chunks of waste, and the engineers began to oil around. On the second engine, Johnny Cooper took a quick look into the firebox of 5352 and noted with satisfaction that the hostler had left him a good fire with a large bank of coal across the back. He then dismounted and went across to the icehouse for a 25-pound block of ice and a fresh can of drinking water. After he returned to the engine, he set down the water can, threw the ice up into the cab, then placed the water can on the deck. Back in the cab, he put the ice into the left tender bulkhead, then set the water can on top.

He began to check for supplies. In his seatbox he noted an ample number of fusees and torpedoes. On the backhead of the boiler were waste and cans of engine and valve oil. In the coal pile was a fairly decent shovel. This was a surprise; the good ones more often than not were taken by the Chicago Terminal firemen for use on their hand-fired H10's and B6's. On top of the tender, secured by a steel rod inserted through the handle, was the clinker hook; and in the right corner of the tender stood the shaker bar. Hanging from the coal gates were a coal pick and a slide puller. On the back wall of the cab were two lanterns—one with a clear globe, one with a red globe.

Cooper next turned to checking his side of the cab. First the injector; then most important of all, the stoker. He opened the firebox and noted that the corners on the distribution plate were beginning to burn off. This might present problems in putting coal into the rear corners of the firebox. He opened the five jets that regulated the flow of steam blowing coal into the firebox. They all were open. Last of all, he opened the round-handled valve that operated the two-cylinder Standard Stoker motor directly under the fireman's seat. The motor operated well. The cab vibrated while the two pistons churned back and forth, turning the conveyor screw that brought coal from the tender to the firebox.

Cooper went over to the water-scoop operating handle on the right side of the tender bulkhead and dropped the scoop. It was the engineer's job to see that the scoop went down and that the leading edge of it was not too badly bent. The engineer would pull up the scoop when he was finished with his oiling chores. Every so often someone would forget to do this, and the crew would start backing up with the scoop down. As long as you backed up, nothing much happened except a lot of noise. If the engine moved forward with the scoop down, the result was interesting.

By now both engineers had completed the oiling and inspection of their charges. Harry Adams came back into the cab and pulled up the scoop. He put away the long oiler and checked the position of the

The westbound *Broadway Limited* pauses at Englewood Station in 1933, prior to the train being streamlined in 1938. The heavyweight, clerestory-roof observation car carries the train's tail sign on its open rear platform. RAIL PHOTO SERVICE.

double-heading cut-out cock located below the automatic brake valve handle. He noted that the handle was set in the cutout position. When the handle was set this way, the engineer on the second engine had no control over the train brakes except for putting them into emergency. The lead engineer applied and released the train brakes. The man on the second engine had control over his engine brakes and could apply and release them at will. Adams watched the needles on his duplex air gauges as McCormick tested the air. When the test had been completed to the satisfaction of both engineers, Adams gave three quick blasts on his whistle and moved both engines back toward the water plugs amid clouds of steam and water from the open cylinder cocks. Each engine was spotted at the plug and its fireman filled the tender to its rated capacity of 11,000 gallons. Number 28's power was ready to back downtown for the train.

The uneventful trip from the round-house to 22nd Street took some 20 minutes. Adams worked his engine lightly so as to conserve water. Before leaving the roundhouse and filling the tender, Johnny Cooper had filled the boiler to near capacity in an effort to go as long as possible without putting on the injector.

At 22nd Street they waited until an eastbound Santa Fe passenger train cleared the crossing. On the point of the Santa Fe eastbound was 4-6-4 3461 still

carrying high its stack extension. Every so often one of those Santa Fe hoggers forgot to lower the extension before entering the low confines of Dearborn Station. This had caused considerable excitement before canopy cross braces proved to have more tensile strength than the stack extensions.

After the Santa Fe train had cleared the interlocking, the position-light signal changed from stop to restricting, and 28's power rolled slowly northward. As it passed the PRR's coach yard. Cooper noted a laboring B6 shoving 28's train toward Union Station. The signal at 12th Street was "stop" while the yard man made his move. Harry Adams noted up on 12th Street bridge what appeared to be a City of Chicago smoke inspector and passed this news across the cab to his fireman, who filed it away for later use.

After the yard move cleared, 28's power backed down to the mail track and coupled to its RPO car. Car inspectors coupled air and steam lines, and a check was made of the brakes. The engines pulled south to Polk Street, stopped for a minute for the tower man to change the route, then backed toward 28 track in Union Station and tied onto the *Broadway Limited*.

Both firemen noted with satisfaction that their engines were safely hidden under the confines of the Post Office building, and the day would be a good one for getting their fires ready without keeping an eye out for the smoke inspector. With a number of Pennsy,

Burlington, and Alton engines in the vicinity, no one fireman could be blamed for the cloud of smoke slipping out from under the building. Of course, sitting under the Post Office on a hot day was like sitting in a dirty sauna bath.

About 3:10 p.m. the car inspectors asked McCormick for an application of the train brakes and then walked back along the 16 tuscan red cars to check whether the brakes had applied and piston travel was correct. After they reached the rear car they blew four blasts on the communicating whistle, asking for a release of the brakes. Then they walked back to the engines, this time checking to see that the brakes had released. The inspectors informed each crew that they had 16 cars, all working, and left for another train.

A few minutes later No. 28's conductor came up to the head end, gave each crew a clearance card, and told them they had no train orders. The conductor, dapper in his passenger uniform, complete with white carnation in his lapel, did not spend much time in the heat and gloom of the south end of Union Station. He hurried back to the cool confines of an air-conditioned Pullman, where he had appropriated a bedroom for use as his office.

Johnny Cooper was working on his fire. During the trip downtown he had purposely let the steam pressure lag around 180 to 185 pounds. He had kept a light fire concentrated mainly along the sides and back of the firebox. Now as departure time approached, he took the clinker hook and shoved live coals into the dead spaces on the grates. He noted that the bank of coal along the sides and back of the firebox had coked through nicely. With the shovel he carefully threw coal up under the firebrick arch to get the brick hot and ready for the 3:30 p.m. departure.

As the fire increased in intensity, the steam pressure rose. By this time the water level in the glass had dropped to slightly less than half full; as the steam pressure neared the pop-off point of 205 pounds, Cooper put on the injector and cooled down the engine. At 3:29 p.m. both engine crews on 28 were ready to head east. After moving the reverse lever the full length of the quadrant a few times to blow out any water trapped in the cylinders, Harry Adams closed the cylinder cocks on 5352. Goggles came down and covered four pairs of eyes. That low ceiling under the Post Office left no place for cinders to go but down. At the appointed departure time of 3:30 p.m. both crews were ready for the proceed signal of two short peeps on the communicating whistle, but none came. Back along the platform, a few last-minute passengers off some late-arriving Western road connection were hurrying beside the flanks of the Pullmans. Johnny Cooper glanced at the steam-pressure gauge and noted the needle standing at 204 pounds. He had a half glass of water showing and he was reluctant to put any more in; but he could not allow the engine to pop, so once more he cooled down the engine.

After a seeming wait of hours that in reality was 2 minutes came the long-awaited two peeps on the communicating whistle. A few feet south of the pilot of the 5471, the two white lights of a position-light dwarf signal shifted from horizontal to vertical. In the lead engine, Pat McCormick opened his bell-ringer valve, then the throttle. On the second engine, Adams waited until he felt some motion; about the time he felt that the slack was taken up, he too opened his throttle. The *Broadway Limited* left Chicago at 3:32 p.m., exactly 2 minutes late.

On the left side of 5352, Cooper turned on the stoker jets and started the stoker motor. The coal came up from the tender, fell on the distribution plate, and quickly was blown to its appointed place in the firebox. The Pennsy never went in for frills such as jet pressure gauges, so its firemen adjusted the coal distribution by eye. The rule of thumb in doing this was to blow a walnut-size piece of coal about 2 feet beyond the firedoor presuming you had some coal of that size. Frequently, only dust came out of the tender.

The first half dozen exhausts of both engines sounded muffled. This was due in part to the low ceiling provided by the Post Office and in part to the fact that the steam moving through the throttle valve to the cylinders was not yet superheated enough to get rid of all the moisture. By the time the engines had moved out into the bright sunshine at Harrison Street, hotter and drier steam had worked its way to the cylinders, and the exhausts took on a crisper sound.

Cooper had wedged a piece of coal between the two halves of the Butterfly firebox door. This allowed air to come in on top of the fire and kept down the smoke emission; it also prevented the overturning of a light fire should the engine slip while it was moving through the numerous double-slip switches at the south end of Union Station. The stationmaster took a dim view of too liberal use of sand on his switches, so engine slippage

in this area was common.

As the train neared the 12th Street bridge, both firemen were aware of the seemingly disinterested smoke inspector, who was keeping a careful watch lest 28 darken the sky over the south end of the Loop. Standing near him were two railfans, complete with cameras, who were looking for smoke. They may have wondered why when they pointed their cameras at an engine, the smoke cleared up just as they pressed the shutter release button.

With the speed up to about 20 mph, Pat McCormick moved the big brass automatic brake-valve handle to the application zone and watched as the brake-pipe pressure showed a reduction from 110 to 100 pounds. The cab filled with the sound of escaping compressed air, and 28 began to slow down. When the exhaust stopped, Pat moved the brake valve back to running. As the pressure needle moved again to 110 pounds of trainline pressure, he complied with company regulations calling for a running test of brakes at the first available opportunity.

During the brake test, neither engineer eased off on the throttle. Adams kept his engine brakes from applying, and before long the train picked up speed. Nearing 16th Street, McCormick blew two long blasts on the K4's whistle; and up under the Air Line bridge, a switchtender flipped a fancy highball in return. The same procedure was repeated at 17th and 18th streets. Past 18th Street, the crews saw the signal at the south end of South Branch Bridge displaying a green over two reds. This would be the only color signal seen by the crew today, since they were back on PRR tracks. Both engineers dropped their reverse levers farther forward to compensate for the short hard pull from ground level to some 20 feet higher on the elevation toward Englewood.

Suddenly the second engine slipped, even though it was on sand. The hot coals in the firebox lifted and danced in midair in response to the sudden increase in draft. Adams was alert and half expecting the slip. He swiftly closed the throttle, waited briefly for the blur of drivers to slow down, then slowly reopened the throttle. Up in the front engine, McCormick felt through the seat of his overalls the faint run in and run out of slack as the second engine slipped and quickly resumed pushing.

The engines rattled and bounced over the numerous diamonds at 22nd Street and complied with the 15 mph limit until

the tail of the last Pullman cleared the interlocking. On sand, and urged along by a heavy throttle and approximately a half stroke on the reverse lever, No. 28 accelerated. As it did so, both engineers came back toward center with their reverse levers. You ran these beasts by ear, and the sound of the exhaust told the experienced man what was going on. Of course, some engineers were a bit hard of hearing, and their engines worked harder than others. Nothing was wrong with the hearing of any member of 28's crew today, and passing the White Sox park No. 28 picked up speed to about 45 mph.

Past 41st Street, the grade dipped slightly and 28 was moving along at 60 mph. Nearing 47th Street, McCormick applied the brakes for the 45-mph curves around 55th Street Yard. On the second engine, Adams kept his engine brakes released; but as the speed dropped off, he eased in on his throttle. No sense working too much throttle and pushing McCormick around the curves at too high a speed. These curves were the favorite checking points for road foremen and trainmasters making speed compliance checks.

South of 55th Street the approach signal for the Rock Island crossing at Englewood came into sight. The three amber lights were leaning from left to right at a 45-degree angle, indicating approach—translated into speed, 30 mph. McCormick waited until the stack of 5471 passed under the signal bridge before slowing to 30. He released the brakes near 61st Street with the speed near 15 mph. The eastbound home signal at Englewood is difficult to read because the Englewood elevated structure partially blocks the view. Today 28's crew did not have to guess at the signal as they saw the last car of a south bound Rock Island commuter slowly moving across the PRR mains. When the commuter had cleared, they could see the silhouette of the operator pulling and pushing on the levers in the tower. Just after the split-rail derail had closed, the signal jumped from horizontal to vertical. This was the last time No. 28 would see any indication except a clear signal on its trip to Fort Wayne. The clear signal had shown just about the time 28 had come to a complete stop, and now both engineers really pounded their engines for the short hop to Englewood Station.

The lead engine stopped opposite a small sign reading "16" nailed to a post set into the ground along the south edge of the tracks. This showed McCormick that the last car was standing clear of the Rock Island tracks and there would be no delays to homeward-bound commuters.

The station stop took only 2 minutes. During this time Cooper shut off the stoker and checked his fire. The bank in the rear had about burned out, and the rest of the fire was as level as a pool table. The firebrick was glowing with heat. Since the distributor plate was not doing the job of blowing coal into the back corners of the firebox, Cooper elected to throw four or five scoops of coal into each. As he completed this self-appointed task, the communicating whistle peeped twice and 28 was ready to leave Englewood, 4 minutes late.

Two gauntleted left hands simultaneously opened throttles while the right counterparts opened sander valves. As 205 pounds of live steam per square inch forced its way past the valves and down into the cylinders, 5352's pistons began their task of moving back and forth. The exhausts of 5471 and 5352 started off synchronized, but because of minute differences in driver diameters, wheel slippages, and valve settings, the exhaust rhythm grew ragged and separated. Then slowly the exhausts joined again to one apparent set. This leave-taking of a station with two good engines flinging their exhausts to the high heavens was an experience most crews enjoyed whether they admitted it or not. This was about the only time they would hear the individual sounds of the engines, since once the machines were up to speed and sound ran together and turned into one loud roar.

Cooper glanced ahead and noted a mile away a smear of smoke that indicated the passage of the New York Central's *20th Century Limited.* The NYC boys had left without waiting for 28 for what often was a race to the Indiana line. The officials of each railroad frowned on these races, at least for the record, but no one ever had heard a general manager say anything about running away from the competition. All ideas of the race vanished quickly, because one of the Central's J's with a mile start could not be caught unless he broke down.

Cooper's thoughts were rapidly brought back to the second engine of No. 28 by increasing vibrations denoting an increase in speed. The line is uphill out of Englewood heading east, and neither engineer moved his reverse lever too far back toward center until the top of the grade at Grand Crossing. The Illinois Central's multiple mains were well below

28's wheels, but years before this had been one huge grade crossing. The old-timers told some horrendous stories about delays, waiting for all the IC commuter trains to clear.

No. 28's passage of Grand Crossing took but a few seconds, then the combination of downhill track and two well-tuned engines lifted speed to the 70 mark. A cloud of pigeons rose from the bridges at River Branch Junction when the bridge vibrated with the tread of the train. Just before passing the west end of Colehour Yard, McCormick applied the brakes for the 55 mph speed restriction for the curves around the yard. Since 28 was late, he did not make as heavy a brake application as normal and 28 strode by the yard a wee bit over 55—say, in the neighborhood of 62 mph.

Beyond Colehour came that smelly stretch past the refineries and chemical plants of Whiting. As the sky darkened with the smoke from the Indiana Harbor steel mills, 28 slowed once to 45 for that city's speed restriction. When 28 was out into the brief spell of open country between Indiana Harbor and Gary, the throttles came out and the block operator at Clarke Junction tossed a half-hearted highball to the engine crews.

Just west of the South Shore Line's overpass, McCormick slowed No. 28 to 45 mph for the trip through Gary. As 28 neared the Gary station a number of people walked out in the mistaken belief that the *Trail Blazer,* No. 76, was arriving. Nearly 4 minutes late, No. 28 was passing the station on 76's time. McCormick had expected this surge of passengers, and he violated Gary's prohibition on whistling to let the people know that this train was not stopping anywhere until it reached Fort Wayne. The tower operator at the Michigan Central crossing at Tolleston had the plant lined up, and 28 held its slackened pace until it cleared Virginia Street. The throttles were opened and hopefully they would be left open with the passage of the last speed restriction to Fort Wayne.

Once again the line was uphill, at least until east of Liverpool Tower. Neither fireman had difficulty checking the color of the smoke coming from the stack of his engine, since the smoke was being lifted well above the stubby stack before starting to drift away. Each stack showed a light-gray haze, indicating a good fire with maximum superheating. Number 28's whistle warned the good citizens of Hobart that the *Broadway Limited* was coming and come it did, with the sounds

of hitting the Elgin, Joliet & Eastern crossing carrying for some distance. Both engines were in full stride. The postal workers in the RPO car sensed that peculiar feeling transmitted through the couplers and draft gear of steam power accelerating: a gentle back and forth motion that told these experienced rail riders they were moving without their ever taking their eyes off the addresses on the letters they were sorting.

About a mile east of Hobart, the PRR tracks converged with those of the Nickel Plate and the two lines ran parallel almost to Valparaiso. Near Wheeler, 28 passed the cabin of an eastbound NKP hotshot of mostly reefers in various shades of yellow and orange. Passing the charging 700-class engine providing the source of energy for these reefers did not take long, and Harry Adams could hear its exhaust over the roar of the two K4's. That Nickel Plate man also was in a hurry to get to Fort Wayne. Down the track, the approach signal for the Grand Trunk Western crossing changed to clear as the operator lined up his plant for the PRR train. The tower was operated by Grand Trunk men, and they tended to give preference to any eastbound GTW train working up the short steep grade on the line at this point.

No. 28 bounced over the single-track diamond at the Grand Trunk crossing and almost immediately passed the Porter County Conservation Club building—or as some people called it, the Porter County Conversation Club. The speed of the train was about 80 as the overhead bridge at the west end of Valparaiso was passed. At Valpo, as the Fort Wayne Division men called the town, an old-fashioned "strong-arm" turntable handled the turning of locomotives assigned to the two Chicago Dummies and assorted locals that worked out of the place. If the engine was spotted with its weight balanced on the table, only a couple of men were required for the job. If the load was unbalanced, nearly the entire town population was needed. Once past the station, 28 entered a long S-curve leading first right and then left. Along the second half of the curve was the local lovers' lane. At night engine crews equipped with strong flashlights were privy to interesting sights. But 28's crew had little time for sightseeing today.

Cooper checked his fire as the pressure dipped to 200 pounds. He noted that the hard pull of the exhaust, plus the burned-off condition of the distribution plate, had let the fire get thin in front of the firedoor and in the corners. This was allowing cool air into the firebox and causing the drop in steam pressure. To counteract this, he got out the shovel and manually put coal in the corners of the firebox while he cut down on the amount of steam blowing coal forward. By the time 5352 hit the long straight stretch leading to Wanatah, the pressure was back to 205 pounds.

Passing Wanatah, with its water plugs and coal dock, No. 28 was covering 5,280 feet in 42 seconds. This 85 mph speed was 5 over the limit set by Special Instruction 2702 in the current timetable. Nobody ever bothered to use the 80 mph speed limit as an excuse for not making running time, though, since the man in the brick building on Clinton Street in Fort Wayne would politely but firmly inform anybody who could not make time that plenty of others could, and would you please bid in a yard engine someplace. So the Fort Wayne Division passenger crews operated their trains by what the timetable required as running time between block stations. If that required an average of 85 mph, so be it.

Near Hanna, 28 passed a westbound freight train and each fireman got up from his seat and stood behind the boiler. Somewhere along the freight, a chunk of coal flew off a hopper car and shattered Itself against the heavy screen over the front cab window on the left side of 5352. Without the protection of the screen, the cab would have been filled with pieces of shattered safety glass. Only one piece of something falling off a passing train was necessary to make believers of those who were too lazy to get up off their seats.

A mile east of Hanna, the speed of 28 began to drop from 88 mph to 60 as Pat McCormick drew off some 15 pounds of trainline pressure. Each fireman moved from his seat on the left side of the cab to a position directly behind his engineer and stood on the bouncing apron between the right rear wall of the cab and the front corner of the tender. Cooper looked over Adams' shoulder and noted a marker post coming up. As the cab passed it, he moved the water-scoop operating lever backward and 28's power began replenishing its demand for water from the Davis track pans. When the scoop dug into the water, a spray flew out from under the tender. The more spray, the less water was being picked up and dropped back into the half-empty tender. From the looks of the operation today, not too much water was being wasted. When the lead engine was halfway down the pan, its fireman dropped the scoop. By splitting the length

of the track pan between the two engines, each engine was assured of some water. However, once the lead engine dropped the scoop, little was left for the second engine. When the marker post indicating the end of the pan neared, each fireman in turn raised his scoop; and 28, having replenished its need for water, picked up speed.

The water-level indicator on 5352 was not working; for that matter, when the indicators were working, they were not too accurate. So Cooper started back over the coal pile to check the water level. He set the stoker operating valve at a point that should take care of the coal demands while he was out of the cab. With an engineer such as Adams, a fireman did not have to concern himself about the stoker setting; Adams would regulate the valve if necessary. Not all engineers would extend that courtesy. Some hard-nosed individuals would sit on the right side of the cab while the fireman was gone checking water, and if the stoker-operating valve vibrated shut they would not even bother to open it. When the fireman came back he would be 15 pounds of pressure off the mark. Sometimes he never got the pressure back.

Clambering over the coal pile, Cooper loosened small avalanches of coal and raised a considerable quantity of coal dust. He groped for the handhold on top of the tender slopesheet and pulled himself onto the flat water portion. Here there were no handholds; and with the tender doing a jig, the task of maintaining his footing became a matter of prime concern. Cooper moved back in a semi-crouch until he reached the lid covering the tender manhole. He opened it and noted that the water level was up to the top rung of a ladder that went down into the murky depths of the tank. This would be more than enough to get them to Fort Wayne; how much the lead engine had picked up was now of prime importance. He slammed the lid and reversed his route back to the cab.

Cooper glanced up at the steam-pressure needle and noted that it still was sitting at 205. He shouted in Adams' left ear, "Top step." Adams nodded an acknowledgment, then looked forward toward the cab of 5471 just in time to see McCormick turn around and give an "O.K." sign. Adams returned the sign and added a highball, and both engineers knew they had enough water to make Fort Wayne. While this was going on, Cooper pulled the squirt hose from its receptacle and, in a vain attempt to cut down on the

coal dust in the cab, sprayed water on the coal pile.

By the time this job was completed, 28 was passing through Hamlet. Just before 28 crossed the NYC's Kankakee Branch and rattled the windows in Hamlet Tower, Adams pulled out his Hamilton 992-B watch and noted the time: 4:47 p.m. No. 28 was running 3 minutes late. This information was given to his fireman in a bit of classic railroad pantomime. Adams held up three fingers and then moved them down to his ample backside. Had 28 been 3 minutes ahead, he would have pointed to his head with his fingers. With his watch still out, Adams checked the speed between the next two mileposts. Moving the mile took 43 seconds—just a shade over 83 mph. He put the trusty Hamilton back into the watch pocket of his overalls, then dropped the reverse lever forward a few notches to overcome the steady pull of gravity as the long uphill grade toward Plymouth began to slow 28.

From Milepost 398 at Hamlet to Milepost 384 at Plymouth, eastbound trains contended with 10 miles of ascending grades. By Pittsburgh Division standards, this grade, averaging out to slightly less than one-half of 1 percent, was almost level track; but with 16 cars hanging onto the tender and the timetable allowing 13 minutes to move 14 miles, there was little time to spare. As the reverse levers were moved forward slowly a notch at a time, the valves were feeding larger and larger amounts of steam into the cylinders. This led to the burning of more coal to evaporate more water, which called for more water into the boiler; and the more cold water put into a boiler, the more heat is needed in the form of coal.

For all of the trip to this point, the left injector had been sufficient to keep a respectable water level over the crown-sheet of 5352. Now, one injector simply did not have the ability to supply the demand for water; the water level in the glass dropped until only an inch was showing. Adams caught Cooper's eye and then pointed to the injector handle on the right side of the cab. Cooper knew he was being warned that soon it would be necessary to put on the second injector. With the infusion into the boiler of two relatively cold streams of water, keeping a K's steam pressure needle at 205 pounds became a problem. One thing about Adams, thought Cooper, he gives you warning when he is getting ready to put on the second injector. Some engineers seemed to delight in trying to catch the fireman unaware and slip on the second injector. In some circles this was referred to as "two-gunning."

At Donaldson, Adams put the right injector to work. He left it on until the water level had climbed a half inch and steam pressure correspondingly had dropped to 200 pounds. He shut off the injector and watched the pressure climb back toward 205 pounds. The engine was not being worked hard, so Cooper was able to shut off his front jets and let the pull of the draft in the firebox move the coal forward. Just before 5352 topped Donaldson hill, Adams once again put on the right injector to compensate for the forward surge of boiler water since the front of the boiler would be a bit lower than the rear. When he had a good solid inch and a half of water showing, he shut off the injector. Had anyone been clocking 28 at this time, he would have noted that its speed had dropped to 71 mph.

Number 28 moved down the hill toward Plymouth, picking up speed with every turn of the 80-inch drivers on the two K4's. The engineers began to come back on their reverse levers. In the eastbound siding sat a freight train, which the dispatcher had safely tucked away for the passage of the "fleet." The freight had been in the siding for almost 2 hours, and if it was lucky it still had an hour to go before there was a big enough hole for it to head east.

When 28 passed Plymouth Tower, the operator was on the ground giving the train an eyeball inspection. He was careful to stand well back from the track so that any errant chunk of coal would not find him a likely target. When those tenders jostled over the NKP's Michigan City Branch and the PRR's South Bend Branch, some coal usually bounced off the coal piles. Up in the cabs, both engineers checked their watches and noted that 28 still was running 3 minutes late. But the situation was looking good. Both engines were steaming well and were willing to run as fast as their engineers desired. Ahead was 64 miles of track to Fort Wayne, and most of it was good running ground. If everything went well, 28 should pick up a minute or two over the 25 miles to Warsaw. The timetable allowed 23 minutes over that distance.

The bouncing over the two diamonds at Plymouth had loosened the coal on the slope sheet of 5352's tender, and as coal slid forward the dust got thick in the cab. Cooper pulled out the squirt hose and wet down the coal pile. He sat down and as he looked out his cab window he noted that the mileposts, road crossings, and small

towns were passing in a blur. Near the thriving community of Etna Green, covering the distance between Mileposts 368 and 367 took 37 seconds. No. 28 now was moving at 97 mph.

The cloud of smoke laid down by both engines drifted across U.S. Highway 30, causing the cautious automobile driver who was lucky enough to have gas in this wartime period to slow down until the visibility improved. Both firemen noted that only a few drivers made a halfhearted attempt to race; the longest challenge was only about a half mile. Both crews were well aware of the speed of their engines. This was conveyed to them by the banging of the apron covering the gap between the cab floor and the tender floor, the rattling of everything on the engine, the roar of the stoker jets, the singing of the injector, the whistling of the breeze through cracks in the cab floors, and the sensation at every switch that the engine had jumped off the rails. Conversation was impossible; no wonder so many of the older engineers were a bit hard of hearing.

West of Warsaw, a sweeping left-hand curve gave both firemen a good chance to look over the string of Pullmans trailing their power. Cooper looked across the cab and gave Adams a highball signal and mouthed the words, "All black." Adams got the message. Cooper also stuck his head out the cab window for a couple of cursory sniffs to determine if anything was running hot on the engine. He smelled nothing out of the ordinary. Both engines reluctantly negotiated the curve, seemingly determined to jump over the superelevated south rail. There was no smooth motion, simply a series of jerks as the flanges caught and were forced to turn Instead of heading for a convenient cornfield.

Passing through Warsaw, the PRR's mains crossed a number of streets at grade. Some of these were but a few hundred feet apart. On 5471 Pat McCormick did not attempt to blow the standard crossing signal of two longs, a short, and a long for each street. No. 28 was moving at more than 90 mph, so he simply blew a long grade-crossing signal and repeated it a couple of times until he was past the last crossing. The block operator was talking to the NYC dispatcher when 28 rattled every window in the building in a vain attempt to blow it down. He noted the time of passage as 5:22 p.m., and when he had finished talking to the Big Four, he called the Fort Wayne dispatcher to tell him that 28 now was only 2 minutes late.

By the time the block operator had

finished his call, 28 had passed well out of sight around the curve along the north edge of Winona Lake. Pat McCormick once again was busy with the whistle as he let the autos heading for the beach know that he was coming, and coming hard. Most of the locals had an ingrained respect for the speed of the "fleet" in this area and took no chances testing the strength of a K4 pilot.

Once again 28 was back on straight track climbing the hill toward Pierceton. A noticeable darkening had taken place in the smoke coming out of both stacks. No good fireman likes to make smoke, but this day both men had no option since 5471 and 5352 were being worked hard. Of consolation was the fact that the engines had stokers; not too many years earlier these engines had been hand fired. The grade was topped at Larwill, and both engineers came back toward center with their reverse levers. They did not touch the throttles; both men were content to let the engines run as fast as they would.

The approach signal for Vandale Tower loomed from the brush as 28 rounded a gentle curve. The three amber lights were leaning at a 45-degree angle from left to right, indicating approach. The operator had been slow on lining up the route for 28. Just as McCormick reached for the automatic brake valve, the signal went clear. One of the mysteries of life to any engineer was how the towerman could wait to clear a signal until the engineer either had just begun to apply the air or was reaching for it. McCormick took his hand off the brake valve and blew for the Whitley County Poor Farm crossing. Five seconds later, passing Vandale Tower, he gave the operator a toot on the whistle to express his displeasure at the near miss. The operator, as they usually do in this type of situation, was standing out of sight behind the corner of the tower.

Once again McCormick blew one long grade-crossing whistle for the three streets of Columbia City. Then he pulled out his watch and noted that 28 had picked up another minute on schedule and had covered the 19.5 miles from Warsaw in 14 minutes. Back in the dining cars, the white-jacketed waiters also were aware that time was being made up as they balanced trays of food and made certain that the coffee cups were not as full as normal.

For the last lap into Fort Wayne, No. 28's speed stayed above the 90 mark, varying slightly in response to the ups and downs of the grades encountered. Some 4 miles west of Fort Wayne, PRR's mains dipped under the NKP bridge. Johnny Cooper wondered

Pennsylvania's fleet of 400-plus K4 4-6-2s were the mainstay of its passenger fleet from the late 1910s through the end of the steam era. ALEXANDER MAXWELL.

where that eastbound hotshot was. The way those 700's ran, the hotshot would be along soon. Three-quarters of a mile from Junction Tower, McCormick moved the automatic brake-valve handle into the application zone and drew off 15 pounds of brake-pipe pressure in a split reduction. For the first few seconds the retardation force was hardly felt, but as the brake shoes got a good bite on the wheels, the speed slackened. To assist in the slowdown, Adams did not hold off his engine brakes and he eased off on the throttle. As it was, 28 went past Junction at 50 mph, a bit over the legal 30 advocated by the timetable Instructions. With a clear signal, good track, and the brakes working well, no harm was done. Most important of all, 28 was back on time. Looking back along the train, Cooper saw blue brakeshoe smoke and pinwheels of sparks around every wheel.

McCormick released the brakes as 28 neared the Broadway Street viaduct. The firemen busied themselves getting ready to be relieved. They dug out their grips, loosened the shaker bar locks, turned on the blowers, and checked their fires. As Harry Adams closed the throttle of 5352 to drifting, the safety valves lifted. Cooper grinned to himself; it always was good advertising for a fireman to come into a station with a clear stack and the pops open. He checked his fire and noted that it would

need some shaking down but otherwise was in excellent condition, with no clinkers. His relief should have no complaints.

As 28 passed the west end of the Fort Wayne station platform, the two firemen were climbing over the coal piles and onto the backs of the tenders. McCormick had slowed the train to 15 mph and had released the automatic, but he held on the engine brakes as he spotted the engines for water. On the second engine, Adams had closed the throttle and was ready to assist in stopping, if need be. McCormick's eyes were on the water-plug marker. As his cab neared it, he turned on the sanders and, with a few more pounds of brake-cylinder pressure, brought 28 to a smooth stop. Up on the tenders, the firemen opened the tank lids and swung around the spouts of the plugs. Each tender would take 9,000 to 10,000 gallons to fill.

The outbound crews also were busy. The engineers walked around the engines, dropping a bit of oil here and there, and feeling the drivers for any signs of overheating. The relief firemen were stowing their grips and shaking down fires. Car inspectors were checking the train, and roundhouse people were busy with their grease guns.

By the time the tenders were almost full, the passengers had been loaded, the train had been inspected, and everybody

was in place and ready to go. Number 28 sat waiting until the inbound firemen had filled the tenders, closed the tank lids, and swung away the water-plug spouts. As the spouts moved around, the communicating whistle blew, the first of two peeps. By the time Cooper descended the back of the tender, the second peep came followed by sounding of the bell on the lead engine. After a 5-minute stop, 28 left Fort Wayne—still on time.

As the Pullmans slid by, the engine crew of second engine on 28 walked slowly down the station platform. A few curious passengers noted these men in their work clothes, with their smoke- and coal-dust-stained faces, almost black except for two white circles of skin that had been covered by goggles. The second engine crew caught up with McCormick and his fireman. Pat remarked that they had had a good run in spite of the fact that the lead engine had been forced to pull 16 cars and a dead engine. Adams countered with a reminder that he damn near had broken the lead engine's tender in two because he was pushing that hard.

No matter; when you have brought 16 cars 148 miles in 2 hours 18 minutes, somebody was pushing hard, and somebody was pulling hard.

By Harry Hall
Locomotive Servicing

1940s

From *Trains* magazine,
July 1982

Do not procrastinate

Certainly the readers of *Trains* have heard the klunk-klunk-klunk made by flat spots on a pair of car wheels as a freight train rolls down the track. The noise made by flat spots is much greater at slow speeds and does more damage to the rails.

Car wheels that have slid a distance great enough to make flat spots 1½ inches long should be removed and turned in a wheel lathe. This is time-consuming and expensive, causing a delay in arrival at the car's destination. Management takes a dim view of flat spots, and enginemen who cause flat spots by improper operation of locomotives and trains are subject to censure.

Santa Fe 4-4-2 No. 1485 was on a break-in trip from Amarillo, Tex., to Boise City, Okla., after receiving Class 5 repairs. Running time was moderate to allow the engineer time to frequently inspect the main and side rod bearings as well as the driving boxes (driving axle bearings located in the frame). After the engine's arrival in Boise City, I made a careful inspection of it after the crew had gone off duty, paying particular attention to the new driving wheel tires for any flat spots. New tires are "soft"; the steel in them is not as hard and durable as it will be after several hundred miles of service. It is *very*

easy to put flat spots on new driver tires! Further inspection revealed that the air-brake piston travel with the brake set was only 2 inches. It should have been at least 2½ inches (and preferably 4 inches) to apply less braking power on the driving wheels. Instinct and training dictated, "Change that piston travel to 4 inches—now!"

I didn't, and that was mistake No. 1.

It would have been difficult to adjust the brake piston travel since the locomotive was not over a pit in the roundhouse. The job could be done after taking water and fuel oil. Besides, I tended to be a little on the heavy side, making the job even more difficult. Good excuses.

Mistake No. 2.

Vegetation was growing along the rails, as you can see in my photo below. These were Russian thistles, better known as tumbleweeds. They grow to a diameter of 2 feet or larger, and in the fall they break away from their roots and are blown by the wind for miles, scattering their seeds across the Southwest prairies. Along this particular track their growth was such that they almost covered the tops of the rails, causing an oily, slick surface.

I got up into the cab, released the brakes, and started to move the engine to the water crane at about 10 mph. It was necessary to stop and throw a switch to move into the water crane track. I carefully applied the engine brakes and—wouldn't you know—the brakes locked and we went sliding down the track like an old hog on an icy pond! The Russian thistles had made the rails as slippery as if they'd been coated with cup grease! I thought we would never stop. And all of this at low speed. But finally we did stop, and I descended to see what damage had been done. Wow! All four driver tires had beautiful blue spots at least 2½ inches in length, which is a Federal ICC defect.

Mistake No. 3.

The toolshed didn't even have an air-driven emery wheel (which would have been a poor method to remove flat spots from steel tires). And there was no tire-turning lathe closer than Albuquer-que. But that did give me an idea: why not turn the wheels and work out the flat spots?

I got back in the cab and moved the 1485 backward about a quarter mile. Then, moving the reverse lever to forward motion, I opened the throttle with a quick movement and started the drivers to spinning on the thistle-covered rails. The engine barely crept along since there was scarcely any traction. I occasionally opened the sanding valve to expedite the turning process.

I made three passes over the track, being very careful not to heat the tires, which would have caused them to expand and move on the wheel centers, which would have caused much trouble. Careful inspection now failed to find any flat spots. True, the tread was worn a little—but who would know about that? So, who says you can't turn tires in place on a locomotive?

Moral: Do not procrastinate. Do the job right even if it is more difficult!

Judicious use of spinning drivers on slick track, with some sand added, was not the preferred method of removing flat spots from wheels—but it worked in a pinch on this Santa Fe 4-4-2. Harry Hall.

By C. Raymond Besheres
As told to Mark S. Womack
Dispatcher

1940s

From *Trains* magazine,
September 1985

Six trains
at Winsted

As a Nashville, Chattanooga & St. Louis train dispatcher during
World War II, we were moving heavy wartime traffic with the
timetable and train-order system.

One day I was working a relief
assignment as dispatcher on the Chattanooga Division between Nashville and
Chattanooga—in those days, such relief
assignments permitted the regular
dispatchers to have one day off each week.

On this Sunday morning I was
working first trick on the "north end," the
87 miles between Nashville and Cowan,
Tenn. This was single-track, automatic-
block-signal territory, except for the first 4
miles between Nashville and Glencliff,
which was double track and was operated
on a manual-block system. From Nashville
south, the stations involved were, in
sequence: Glencliff, 4 miles; Murfreesboro,
32; Winsted, 37; Fosterville, 45; Bell
Buckle, 51; and Wartrace, 55 (see the

schematic on the facing page). Glencliff,
Murfreesboro, and Wartrace were open
train-order offices ("T-O" on the
diagram). There was no train radio in
those days, but there were wayside
telephones in wooden booths which train
crews could use to contact the dispatcher.

When I came on duty at 7 a.m., the
third-trick dispatcher told me that a
derailment had occurred between
Fosterville and Bell Buckle. Among the
trains on the road was Extra 654 North,
led by a 2-8-2 carrying that number, in the
charge of Conductor A. H. Crossland and
Engineer F. C. Freeman. It was in the
siding at Winsted, with no orders on
which to move. The derailment had
caused traffic to become even more

congested than usual, and even though
Extra 654 North was beyond the derailment, it could not move because No. 4, a
northward first-class passenger train (an
unnamed Atlanta-Nashville local), was
overdue at Winsted, being held south of
the derailment, at Wartrace. Number 52, a
northward fast freight, was also at
Wartrace, and No. 6, another northward
first-class passenger train (the Chattanoo-
ga-Memphis *Lookout*), would soon be
joining them at Wartrace. There were also
several southward trains superior to Extra
654 North which were overdue at
Winsted.

First No. 45 was standing just north of
the derailment, waiting for the wrecker to
clear the main track. Second No. 45 was at
Murfreesboro. First and Second No. 55,
both oil trains, were by Glencliff, and
Second No. 55 was carrying green signals
for a following section, as there would be
four sections of No. 55. All these

Class L-1 Mikados handled a great deal of the heavy wartime freight traffic on the Nashville,
Chattanooga & St. Louis. Here No. 619 rolls into Dickson, Tenn., in pre-war days.
Louisville & Nashville Railroad.

southward trains were freights.

The wreck was cleared up enough to allow traffic to move, and the train handling the wrecker outfit and First No. 45 were about to get in the clear of the main in the siding at Bell Buckle for Nos. 4, 6, and 52. Division Superintendent J. W. Tucker, standing at my desk, asked me how I intended to move Extra 654 North away from Winsted. I told him I intended to send the extra an order in care of the engineer of Second No. 45 from Murfreesboro, giving the extra a meet with First and Second No. 55 at Murfreesboro, right over all other southward trains to Glencliff, and to run ahead of Nos. 4 and 6, Winsted to Glencliff. (Since trains ran on a manual-block system between Nashville and Glencliff, the extra would not need a train order to run ahead of No. 52, which was a third-class train; Rule 85 permitted an extra to run ahead of a third-class train.)

Mr. Tucker said, "No, let's not do that. It's O.K. to run the extra ahead of No. 4 and No. 6, but don't give him a meet with First and Second 55, just give him a good stiff wait on First and Second 55 at Murfreesboro, and the extra should make it without delaying those trains." (A wait order has a time on which the train being waited for must clear; a meet order has no time factor.)

"All right," I replied, "but if the extra doesn't get away, we will probably have a big saw at Winsted." A "saw" (or "saw-by") is additional maneuvering because a siding is too short to clear all the trains to be met.

I began to issue the necessary orders, dictating them by telephone to the operators at the stations. I met Second No. 45 with Nos. 4, 6, and 52 at Fosterville, and put Nos. 4, 6, and 52 in the siding at Winsted for First and Second No. 55. I also sent the necessary orders for Extra 654 North to leave Winsted; these orders to be taken to the extra from Murfreesboro by the engineer of Second No. 45.

In due time, after Second No. 45 had had time to run the 5 miles from Murfreesboro to Winsted and let Extra 654 North out, Aline Isbell, the operator at Murfreesboro (and wife of a conductor), reported the extra in the block. Mr. Tucker, in hearing her report on the dispatcher's loudspeaker, exulted: "Great! See, everything is going to work out fine!"

In a moment he turned to leave the office, but Aline's voice again was heard over the speaker: "Raymond, the block indicator has cleared up; Freeman has lost his nerve and backed in at Winsted." Mr. Tucker exploded: "Well, I won't interfere anymore; you will just have to get out of it the best way you can!"

Actually, it would have taken some time for the extra to pull out of the siding and for the flagman to restore the switch to the main track and reboard the caboose. Engineer Freeman sincerely thought, no doubt, that he lacked sufficient time to run to Murfreesboro, stop at the south switch and head in, and clear First No. 55 as required by the rules. Anyway, when he backed in at Winsted, it changed the picture.

Remember, Nos. 4, 6, and 52 had a meet with First and Second No. 55 at Winsted, but this meet order had been issued with the idea that the siding would by then be clear, Extra 654 North having gone. Now, the extra was still in the siding, and Nos. 4, 6, and 52 were away from Wartrace, the last open office for those trains before meeting First and Second No. 55.

Conductor Crossland had come on the telephone at Winsted after his train had backed into the clear, and he and I discussed the situation. He sent his flagman southward to flag No. 4 in the event there would have to be a saw. The saw would have required First No. 55 to pull south of the south switch at Winsted, toward the standing No. 4, that train having been stopped short of Winsted by the extra's flagman. Second No. 55 would then squeeze in on the main behind First No. 55's caboose, until Second No. 55's caboose had cleared the north switch at Winsted. Then Extra 654 North could depart, the flagman of that train having been recalled. After the extra left, Second and First No. 55 would back up to let Nos. 4, 6, and 52 into the siding. If the Winsted siding would not hold all three of those trains, First and Second No. 55 would have to pull to and fro until all three of the northward trains had cleared the siding at the south end. This would have caused more delay to all the trains.

Thanks to Providence, First and Second No. 55 barely cleared between the switches at Winsted, making the saw unnecessary. As soon as Second No. 55's caboose cleared the north switch, Extra 654 North departed. Before long, Nos. 4, 6, and 52 had pulled through the siding at Winsted, past First and Second No. 55, and after No. 52 cleared at the south end, First and Second No. 55 resumed their progress toward Chattanooga.

So, after a long wait at Winsted, Extra 654 North was again on its way to Nashville . . . but still would have to contend with Third and Fourth No. 55, No. 95 (The *Dixie Flyer*), and No. 91 (a mail train) before reaching the double track at Glencliff.

The 654 was a loyal and capable old girl. She and her sisters did a magnificent job in handling the extremely heavy traffic on the NC&StL during those hectic and often agonizing times.

In 1944, after this Winsted incident, the installation of Centralized Traffic Control (CTC) on the single-track portion out of Chattanooga Division gave us added flexibility in moving the trains.

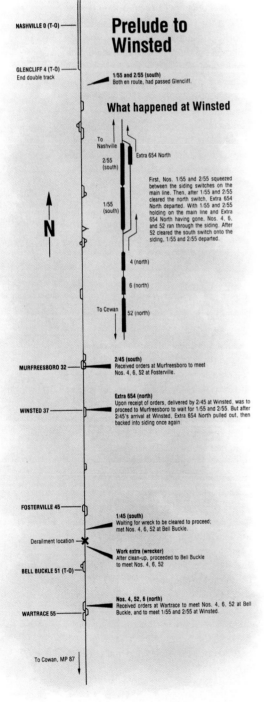

Prelude to Winsted

NASHVILLE 0 (T-O)

GLENCLIFF 4 (T-O)
End double track

1/55 and 2/55 (south)
Both en route, had passed Glencliff.

What happened at Winsted

To Nashville

2/55 (south)

Extra 654 North

1/55 (south)

First, Nos. 1/55 and 2/55 squeezed between the siding switches on the main line. Then, after 1/55 and 2/55 cleared the north switch, Extra 654 North departed. With 1/55 and 2/55 holding on the main line and Extra 654 North having gone, Nos. 4, 6, and 52 ran through the siding. After 52 cleared the south switch onto the siding, 1/55 and 2/55 departed.

N

4 (north)

6 (north)

To Cowan

52 (north)

MURFREESBORO 32

2/45 (south)
Received orders at Murfreesboro to meet Nos. 4, 6, 52 at Fosterville.

Extra 654 (north)
Upon receipt of orders, delivered by 2/45 at Winsted, was to proceed to Murfreesboro to wait for 1/55 and 2/55. But after 2/45's arrival at Winsted, Extra 654 North pulled out, then backed into siding once again

WINSTED 37

FOSTERVILLE 45

1/45 (south)
Waiting for wreck to be cleared to proceed; met Nos. 4, 6, 52 at Bell Buckle.

Derailment location ✕

Work extra (wrecker)
After clean-up, proceeded to Bell Buckle to meet Nos. 4, 6, 52

BELL BUCKLE 51 (T-O)

Nos. 4, 52, 6 (north)
Received orders at Wartrace to meet Nos. 4, 6, 52 at Bell Buckle, and to meet 1/55 and 2/55 at Winsted.

WARTRACE 55

To Cowan, MP 87

A million miles-plus in the uniform of George M.

By William Moedinger
Pullman Conductor

1940s

From *Trains* magazine,
February & March 1970

A few years ago, *Trains* Editor David P. Morgan admonished all of us "who recall and rejoice in the old order to renew acquaintance with the orthodox passenger train as often as we can . . . while we can."

Heeding the middle-aged sage's advice, this youngster, along with wife and son, boarded the Pennsylvania's *Broadway Limited* early one evening for a brief and perhaps final rendezvous with overland travel via the steel rail and flanged wheel. Although our train was westbound, we were not really concerned with where we were going, or with how quickly we got there. We sought only the satisfaction of riding all day long without being warned to fasten our seat belts, the pleasure of eating three leisurely square meals a day aboard a railroad dining car, and the opportunity to crawl between the crisp, white sheets of a Pullman berth at the end of each day. For the rest of the family, it was an experience enthusiastically described at the end of the trip as "the only way to travel." For me, it was a happy reunion with the wonderful world of two decades ago.

For more than a dozen years, beginning in the mid-Forties and ending on the eve of those twin transportational catastrophes we now recognize as the jet and the Interstate, I roamed the length and breadth of the United States aboard the finest the railroads had to offer when what the industry had to offer was fine indeed. Which is to say, I went Pullman during the final years of an era that concerned itself as much with the going as with the getting there.

In a sense, those years were the fulfillment of a dream I had cherished since my first transcontinental automobile journey back in Depression-ridden 1932. Regardless of what Detroit claimed, that bone-shaking experience convinced me that the automobile was a long way from being the ultimate in civilized travel.

Those long dusty miles once and for all allayed some doubts I had acquired relative to the superiority of rail travel in general and the Pullman version in particular. Sometime in the distant future, I promised myself, should time and funds become available, I would embark on a Pullman tour that took me coast to coast and border to border.

I was never one to dream small, and I'm afraid that as the years slipped by my dream grew wilder and wilder; so wildly improbable, in fact, that I doubt I ever expected even token fulfillment. Quite accidentally, however, while I was walking down Philadelphia's Filbert Street one dismal Saturday morning I noticed a large sign in the Railroad Retirement Board's office window. Railroad workers were desperately needed. Inquiry revealed that the pressing need was mostly for dry-land sailors: shopmen, electricians, and clerical workers.

As I prepared to leave, visibly unimpressed and disappointed, the Federal-man-of-job-opportunities casually mentioned that The Pullman Company was hiring men to be trained as conductors. As I turned back from the door, he seemed inclined to dismiss any further mention of the subject. In fact, he was almost apologetic that this bit of irrelevant information had passed his lips. After all, it was a job that entailed weeks away from home, not to mention endless miles of railroad travel from coast to coast and border to border. To an unmarried railfan with an insatiable thirst for train riding and a mild distaste for his means of gainful employment, this revelation was tantamount to an announcement of the discovery of another Mother Lode out there along the banks of the inky

Schuylkill River, where the Pullman employment office was located.

One month later, with passes in hands, another candidate and I boarded the *Representative,* an early-afternoon Pennsy express for Washington, D.C., bound for a two-week training session for prospective Pullman conductors. There a dozen of us from scattered points along the Eastern seaboard from New York to Jacksonville learned the meaning of a crash training program. Days were spent in classes conducted by a veteran Pullman inspector who had spent his prime as a conductor in regular service on the *Havana Special* in its plush days when it ran through to Key West, before the disastrous hurricane of September 2, 1935. Six nights out of the two-week period were spent making student runs with experienced conductors.

For my first student assignment I drew the Washington-Rochester (N.Y.) sleeping-car line which operated over the Pennsy as far as Canandaigua, N.Y., and the New York Central from there into Rochester. Between Washington and Harrisburg, Pa., I padded along after my mentor, Conductor Dean, as he collected tickets, issued cash-fare checks, disposed of a case or two involving duplicate sales (a situation that plagued all Pullman conductors in those busy days), and assigned space to passengers without advance reservations. Even though our train had changed directions at Baltimore, the whole business of conducting seemed elementary to me; and I suppose I fairly exuded self-confidence.

After leaving Harrisburg, where there had been considerable sleeper swapping, for which this junction was famous, Conductor Dean extended his diagrams and suggested I have a go at it. In the next half hour the established order of sleeping-car operations degenerated into mild pandemonium within the normally quiet aisles of the northbound *Dominion Express*. The transition from seats to berths was something with which I hadn't

Troop trains were a common assignment for author Moedinger through the 1940s. Here the commanding officer gives the Pullman conductor a travel requisition order in a drawing-room-turned-office in 1943. PULLMAN COMPANY.

reckoned, and I began to experience that phenomenon about which instructor Woodward had warned us. I kept losing my sense of direction, causing me frequently to work back in the direction whence I had just come and to awaken persons who had retired to ask them for their tickets a second and sometimes even a third time. I went from one car to the next without being aware of it and, in so doing, entered a Rochester passenger on the Canandaigua diagram.

And then I made my first cash sale. "It's good for ten bucks," the man promised, if I could get him a drawing room. No problem at all; the very top diagram on the pile had an empty DR. The man neglected to mention that he was Buffalo bound, and the promise of 10 dollars erased from my mind all such insignificant details as

destination and an extra half first-class fare required for a DR. Fortunately, as porters took their calls that night they discovered they had a passenger here and there whose destination didn't coincide with that of the individual car.

Conductor Dean appeared on the scene just in time. He wisely suggested that I retire, preferably out of sight, before the situation deteriorated further and a general passenger uprising ensued. Sensing that I suspected that I hadn't executed the job in the finest Pullman tradition, he assured me that the situation was not beyond repair and that I had not committed the unforgivable. I had not managed to get the sleepers off the track. Conductor Dean further encouraged me by declaring that I would improve in time; there wasn't any other way for me to go.

The hypothetical situations in the classroom became realities on the road, and the unheard of in the class often turned out to be commonplace on the train. On my third student assignment, a round trip between Washington and Cleveland aboard Baltimore & Ohio's Washington-Cleveland *Night Express*, a scantily clad female of provocative dimensions attempted to open the vestibule doors and jump from the speeding train. Thwarting her efforts toward self-destruction, my instructor for the trip remained unruffled through it all, then returned to writing up his diagrams as though nothing had happened. "After you've had a bad trip or two, you won't mind these little interruptions," was his wry comment.

Although for the most part our student

runs were limited to overnight scheduled trains on which the sleeper operations were known as "line" runs, considerable classroom attention was directed to special military moves known as "Mains." We were warned of the necessity for strict secrecy regarding these moves and accordingly were fingerprinted for the FBI files and were issued an ID card bearing a vague likeness and a right thumbprint.

Inspector Woodward concluded the two-week course with these words of wisdom: "Get hold of the biggest suitcase you can possibly carry."

During those busy years the average Pullman conductor bucking the extra list could exceed the normal travel expectancy of an average lifetime within the space of a few short months. Not only were these the last years of full flower for the Pullman way of travel, they also were the years of the Pullman troop train. Actually, less than one quarter of my million-plus miles as a conductor was logged aboard troop trains; but this unusual and now almost extinct species of the American passenger train was the open sesame to a personal and intimate acquaintance with many of the famous names that swelled the *Official Guide* of that day to nearly 1,500 pages crammed with passenger schedules.

Unlike the railroad conductor, who was confined to one or two divisions all his life, the Pullman conductor had a scope of operations that embraced virtually every railroad system and mile of track capable of supporting the weight and physical dimensions of the standard gauge sleeping car. Even so, a Pullman conductor occasionally found himself traversing branches of questionable capacity, and quite obviously the railroad had not dispatched those ponderous 12-wheel cars without some misgivings. Vividly I remember deadheading on standard sleepers into a remote military installation along the Eastern shore over a branch so fragile that the railroad dispatched a mobile crew to follow us with all the paraphernalia necessary, short of the big hook, to retrieve us from the marshy loam in the event that what passed for track suddenly disintegrated beneath us.

I never made a precise tally of the number of trips that comprised my wandering years; hasty calculation at this point establishes their number well in excess of 2,000. There were short overnight assignments, such as the 114-mile round trip on the Reading between Philadelphia's famed Reading Terminal and Bethlehem, Pa., where

sleepers bound for Rochester, Buffalo, and Toronto were turned over to the Pullman conductors of trains headed for those points over the Lehigh Valley Railroad. Many trips fell into the long-distance category. A typical example of this was the *Crescent Limited* assignment between New York and New Orleans. It required four days and four nights, including the 24-hour layover in New Orleans, which most extra conductors recall fondly as a night of uninhibited revelry in the old French Quarter, followed by a day of recuperation in the old Monteleon Hotel. Most memorable in my book were those protracted journeys, consuming two or three weeks, that added 10,000 or 12,000 miles to my Pullman travel diary. Frequently, in one swoop of transcontinental proportions, a single junket renewed my acquaintance with 25 or 30 states.

My second assignment after being enrolled on the conductors' roster of the Philadelphia district officially introduced me to the world of the Pullman troop train. My train was typical for the day; it consisted of 12 tourist sleepers and 2 U.S. Army kitchen cars. The latter were cut into the consist three sleepers from each end, so that each one comfortably served six sleepers. Except for numbers instead of names and the absence of the prominent clerestory bubble—the hallmark of the standard air-conditioned sleeper—the tourist sleepers outwardly looked little different from the standard variety to the untrained eye. Inside, the difference was readily apparent. Austerity was the keynote. There were no lower-berth ventilating fans, and all carpeting had been removed. Not one of the cars had an outlet for electric razors, which was to cause me to scurry uptown during a brief layover in Harrisburg to purchase one of the safety variety. The general decor, from berth lights to the all-metal washstands and dental bowls, indicated that these 12-wheelers were the real veterans of the Pullman pool. Some of them had been outshopped as standard cars by Pullman's Calumet works back in 1910. As new cars were constructed through the years, these older cars lost their names, were assigned numbers, and entered the tourist pool.

Parked alongside other passenger equipment in Penn coach yards adjacent to the Pennsylvania's 30th Street Station in Philadelphia that memorable morning 26 years ago, my first troop train scarcely could be described as varnish. Beneath the accumulation of roadbed and stack grime,

the Pullman green was indiscernible. For the previous 16 months since Pearl Harbor, these cars had been on the go day and night. Rarely had there been time for so much as a token exterior washing. Exterior housekeeping was largely the responsibility of whatever railroad the sleeper was on. Interior housekeeping, on the other hand, no matter where the car happened to be, was the sole responsibility of The Pullman Company. And since good housekeeping was an inseparable part of the Pullman tradition, the cars were immaculate. Floors had been scrubbed and painted; walls and ceilings had been wiped down; and the upholstery had been shampooed. The inside windows shone, and washrooms and toilets were spotless. No one in the armed services ever rode a dirty sleeping car if The Pullman Company could possibly help it.

The assignment involved a 106-mile deadhead move to New Cumberland, Pa., just across the Susquehanna River from Harrisburg, and an in-service move from the Army induction camp there to Starke, Fla., the Seaboard Air Line's station for Camp Blanding. I had previously selected a drawing room near the center of the train (adjacent to a kitchen car, of course) and had instructed the porter of that car to put up a table for me. As I was about to sit down at the table I felt the GG1 up ahead stretch out slack. My very first troop train was easing out of the yards.

This, oh, railfan, was that magic moment that comes but once in a lifetime, that fleeting instant when you stand on the brink of an adventure you know you will remember forever. As that mighty GG1 picked its way through countless yard switches, and the 6-wheel trucks of those tourist sleepers in tow squealed through tight curves that led to a great main line beyond, I knew I was embarking upon one of the greatest railfan excursions the world would ever know, one to make my wildest dreams of yesterday appear picayune.

Rolling west behind one of the fleetest units of electric motive power ever to grace the head end of a passenger train, I had the comforting feeling that my 30-year-old sleepers could keep up with anything anybody's motive power department chose to couple on the head end. Except for the chatter of a worn buffer plate, or the occasional vibration of some minor component such as a vestibule trap door, these cars were as solid as the day they were outshopped. Planned obsolescence and calculated minimum life were never a part of the Pullman scheme.

I admit that I had been a little

disappointed when I picked up the assignment. The daily assignment sheet, posted in the conductors' room at the end of each sign-out period, revealed that the extra conductors immediately ahead and after me had drawn mains to Fort Ord, Calif., and Fort Lewis, Wash., respectively. However, what appeared to be a round trip of approximately 2,000 miles of four or five days' duration ultimately developed into a 10,599-mile trip lasting 24 days . . . and an appreciation of inspector Woodward's advice concerning the large suitcase.

Troop movements frequently involved interesting and rare combinations of railroads and routes over which no interline passenger service prevailed. Often these moves included lines over which there was freight service only. Always, however, they utilized reasonably direct routes—unless instructions involving a change of destination were received en route. I mention this because a San Francisco conductor who hired about the time I did spent 42 days on a Navy Main before the train reached a boot camp that could accommodate the men. At each camp the Navy authorized a change of destination, hoping the men could be accepted at the next point. After 42 days that Main turned out to be the whackiest train in the Navy.

On the other hand, a conductor's return to home base was generally a circuitous, protracted adventure consisting of many individual assignments and devious routings; for regardless of a conductor's destination, the need for his services was universal. Pullman conductors were in short supply all over the country.

My fear of being deadheaded directly home was unfounded. The in-service move via Pennsy; Richmond, Fredericksburg & Potomac; and Seaboard consumed approximately 40 hours between New Cumberland and Starke. My return to Philadelphia (albeit I passed through it three times in the process) took 22 days and 8,500 miles. It sent me west to Denver, Colo., south to New Orleans, north to Providence, R.I., and south again (this time on the Atlantic Coast Line) for a second visit to Jacksonville, Fla. Meanwhile, I acquired a riding acquaintance with 13 railroads new to the pages of my travel diary.

Fortunately for the company, Pullman conductors were not subject to the 16-hour law. So the fact that a conductor walked into one of the 70 district offices or agencies throughout the United States,

disheveled and decrepit, with evidence of a 3,000-mile assignment clearly visible on his shirt collar, was of no consequence to the local signout clerk if he needed conductors, which he usually did. (If one of Pullman's roving inspectors caught the conductor with a dirty collar, it was another story, however.) To the average signout man, the very fact that a conductor walked into his office under his own power was sufficient evidence that he was physically fit, available for duty, and anxious for another transcontinental assignment.

My first five weeks with The Pullman Company, including the two weeks of training, gave me some insight into what the future held. I traveled 13,000 miles over 18 railroads and enjoyed the comforts and amenities of 10 name trains, including such prominent ones as Atlantic Coast Line's *Havana Special,* Louisville & Nashville's *Piedmont Limited,* Burlington's *Exposition Flyer,* and Santa Fe's *Centennial State.*

Those first five weeks on the road were like a shakedown cruise. Two weeks in the classroom did not produce a full-fledged Pullman conductor. This was the period of trial and error, with more of the latter than the former. Have you ever tried catching a train lugging a suitcase that weighs almost as much as you do, with another small suitcase tucked up under the same arm, while in the other hand you are carrying a paper plate which holds your breakfast and a paper cup of steaming coffee? With every step a little of that coffee overflows the cup and gradually soaks your plate and weakens it, so that when you finally catch up with your train and are about to step aboard, victorious, the whole business collapses, spilling hot coffee, scrambled eggs, bacon, and a blob of butter on your uniform—the only one you have with you. That happened to me on my first trip in the Atlanta yards. I knew the train was scheduled to split there, but I had taken up quarters in the wrong section. By the time I collected my belongings, the switching crew had made off with my section. My antics in trying to catch the Courtland (Ala.) section that sunny spring morning must have resembled an old Keystone Cops production.

But all of this was only the beginning. The troop train and I were to see much of each other during the next decade.

Life aboard a troop train could be pleasant for a railfan Pullman conductor. The very nature of the business and the type of equipment precluded the degree of

luxury found aboard the big name trains, but for me the troop train had much to recommend it. Once you picked up your passengers at the point of origin, you could close out the earnings diagrams (one for each sleeper) except for the date and hour of arrival at destination, set up the porters' rest periods, and generally dispatch the myriad details and bookkeeping chores incident to the business. Barring an emergency, from there on out you were free to enjoy the fascinating business of railroading on the move.

Morning, noon, and evening inspections of your train from end to end provided the necessary physical workouts. Remember how a five- or six-car walk to the diner, pushing and pulling open those heavily sprung end doors, sharpened your appetite? Well, inspection of a 12-car train translated into physical action meant opening 48 end doors, 12 electric locker doors, 12 linen locker doors, and 24 toilet doors. Including two kitchen cars, the inspection stroll was equivalent to a half-mile walk.

The troop kitchen car, an integral part of virtually every military move, was just what the name implies. It resembled an elongated box car with six rectangular windows along each side, end doors, buffer plates, diaphragms, and high-speed trucks. The wooden-sheathed interior was fitted with a battery of coal-burning ranges, a coal bin, a long waist-high worktable, and a hinged metal-lined locker for ice and foods requiring refrigeration. Each mess crew provided its own pots, pans, tubs, cutting utensils, and assorted culinary accouterments. At speed, the inside of a kitchen car sounded like a rolling boiler factory; the rattling, banging cacophony made conversation below a shout impossible. Some servicemen insisted that this ear-splitting commotion somehow became a part of the culinary creations emerging from these rolling kitchens. Be that as it may, dinner aboard the troop cars, although it was not to be confused with the Fred Harvey cuisine aboard the *Chief,* was nourishing and made up in quantity for what it might have lacked in variety and style. After all, what epicurean treats did Fred Harvey ever concoct from the meat and potato stores normally available to the average mess sergeant?

For me, the troop kitchen car had one especially desirable feature: a sliding center door which, when it was open and the built-in safety bars were swung into position, provided a grandstand from which to enjoy railroading on the move.

A Southern 4-8-2 leads a Main (troop train) movement near Craggy, N.C., in August 1944. The train is en route from Knoxville, Tenn., to Asheville, N.C. One of the distinctive troop sleepers is cut into the consist (third car in the train). W. FRANK CLODFELTER.

This vantage point, like the open baggage-car door of the present-day railfan excursion, was a satisfactory substitute for the divided vestibule doors normally found on standard sleepers but not on the tourist cars. What's more, it was a nice place to hang around as mealtime approached.

Unfortunately, the military took a dim view of cameras, so it was impossible for me to record any of the railroad sights witnessed from the open door of a kitchen car. The more memorable sights would have made lively additions to my 8mm film library started back in the mid-1930s.

Never will I forget the glimpse, from the open door of a Southern Railway Main en route from Chattanooga to Courtland, Ala., of Nashville, Chattanooga & St. Louis Railway's Nashville-bound *Dixie Flyer* canting into a long graceful curve on parallel tracks a short distance west of Chattanooga, with one of those handsome J-3 class skirted 4-8-4s on the point. It was a scene that lingered in the mind and made you forget that the beef stew that evening wasn't the best you'd ever tasted. Whenever the consist was long enough to merit two kitchen cars, I always tried to set up headquarters near the rear one. This

was the railfan Pullman conductor's 50-yard line, affording the best view of his own train.

The sport of railroading from the open door of a kitchen car was best in the West and the South, where single-track railroad prevailed. Multi-track Eastern main lines at speed presented a problem. Nothing could disrupt the mess crew in the preparation of a meal like the rumpus of a speeding steam express blasting in the opposite direction past an open kitchen car door. In the East, doors usually were kept closed or open just a crack. One notable exception to the closed-door

policy was on the Pennsy's New York division between Stelton (Camp Kilmer), N. J., and North Philadelphia when a Main train would be paced by another passenger train, quite frequently a *Clocker,* on the adjacent track. Engineers never race, they say, but the two trains would seesaw back and forth for what seemed miles on end, especially between Stelton and Trenton, until one of them either got a restrictive signal or slowed for a station.

Watching a train speeding in the same direction on the next track produces a strange sensation that invariably causes one to lose all sense of motion and direction. When the kitchen car would parallel the dining car on the other train,

some interesting pantomime often developed between the two dining establishments. Horseshoe Curve offered another exception to the closed-door policy because of speed restrictions, and rarely failed to put on an action-packed performance for those of us at the open door. Most troop trains were triple-headed between Altoona and Gallitzin, a circumstance that was a show in itself; but the whole Pittsburgh division often co-operated by scheduling three or four other trains that were in view as our train negotiated that engineering feat.

On freight-only divisions, or where there weren't enough passenger crews to go around, freight crews normally manned the trains. For me, this was the signal to step back into the caboose and offer my services to the freight conductor in unraveling the mysteries of the multi-coupon passenger ticket. Freight crews were experts with waybills, wheel reports, and all phases of the physical aspects of railroading, including the treatment of hotboxes and the replacement of punctured air hoses and broken coupler knuckles, but a passenger ticket stumped many of them. For my assistance the conductor usually invited me into the cupola, a very pleasant place to ride. The view is superb, and there's very little slack action at the end of a passenger consist.

Union Pacific cabooses were my favorites. I got the feeling of being up there, and the ride over the Blue Mountains of Oregon, a region where passenger crews invariably were in short supply, was spectacular. New York Central cabooses never were high on my list; cupolas were too squatty. Nevertheless, something about a ride in the cupola over the railroad's Newberry Junction-Lyons freight-only line, through the depths of Pennsylvania's Grand Canyon and across the spidery steel trestle atop New York's renowned Watkins Glen, gives these low-crowned cabooses a warm spot in my memory.

Every Pullman conductor was issued a thick book of rules dealing with almost every situation or contingency, from proper attire to the reporting of unusual incidents. After the first six months of service most conductors believed there was no such thing as an unusual incident aboard the cars. No mention was made in the book about engine cab riding while on duty or deadheading; so I assumed that this type of activity was left entirely to the discretion of the individual conductor. Therefore, purely in the interest of better service, and as an ambassador of good

will, I forced myself occasionally to ride a grimy engine cab. On rare occasions this was in a ballast-scorching high-wheeler on a stretch of fast high iron, but usually it was in a nondescript Consolidation probing its uncertain way through the weeds of some branch or short line leading to a military installation.

The all-time peak of Pullman troop travel came in the second half of war-torn 1945, after the necessity for redeploying troops from Europe to the Pacific Theater of war caused the Office of Defense Transportation to order the removal of sleeping cars from all regular passenger runs of less than 450 miles so that these cars could be used by the military. Effective July 15, 1945, approximately 900 standard sleepers were transferred from scheduled civilian service to the troop pool, and the formidable task of moving the military from the Atlantic to the Pacific swung into high gear.

Pages of statistics would be required to recite Pullman's part in moving the armed forces during this period. *Trains* Publisher Al Kalmbach reported in the September 1945 issue that the week ending August 3, a typical week for that period, saw 726 organized troop movements in Pullman cars. Now, a troop movement was not usually just one train. In the same report Al noted that a single troop movement of 31 trains had required 331 Pullman sleepers and 41 kitchen cars.

Those were busy days. From July 21, 1945, until the following January 21, I traveled 66,000 miles, completed 87 assignments that introduced me to 22 railroads I had never before traveled on, and had the time of my life.

When I was picking up an assignment, I liked to speculate on what it held in store. Usually the initial assignment from a conductor's home district indicated little. For example, one of many assignments from Fort Dix, N.J., to Camp Shelby, Miss.—normally a 3,078-mile round trip—developed into a 10,689-mile tour that lasted 18 days, gave me a riding acquaintance with such uncommon common carriers as the Georgia Railroad and the Charleston & Western Carolina Railway, and treated me to a protracted off-the-beaten-track excursion over New Haven's Brewster-Poughkeepsie freight-only line to Maybrook, N. Y., thence on Erie to Chicago, Santa Fe from there to Stockton, Calif, via Espee's Tehachapi Loop, and Espee for the 49 final miles from Stockton to Camp Parks.

An assignment sheet listed, among

other things, the names and numbers of every car in the consist; and it always was pleasant to find a sprinkling of names among the numbers. This meant that the cars were standard and in all probability air-conditioned and equipped with a reasonably good set of batteries. During this period, some pretty fancy standard cars were being used in troop service, and these compensated for those glorified box cars officially known as troop sleepers which then were being outshopped by the various carbuilders to cope with the transportation emergency.

Upon arrival in Seattle, Wash., after a cross-country journey from Indiantown Gap, Pa., in one of the new three-tiered troop sleepers, a crusty veteran who had fought the Germans and now was being transferred to the Pacific Theater of combat vowed that he would return to even the score with the culprit who had designed that instrument of torture. In all fairness to the designer and the builder, it should be noted that the gentleman had made the 3,201-mile journey in a troop sleeper that had four flat wheels.

I never could quite understand, though, why The Pullman Company allowed its name to appear on the sides of those rattletraps. In a day when Pullman was a household word that stood for the finest in everything, applying the name to the sides of a windowed box car struck me as sacrilege.

For every bad car, however, there were innumerable good ones. That very same evening I picked up a Main at Interbay, Wash., a troop embarkation point just outside Seattle, bound for Southern Pines, N.C. There wasn't a troop sleeper in the consist. All of the cars were standard, most of them air-conditioned, but the pieces de resistance were four 10-section, lounge-observation cars of early vintage. How many travelers have journeyed in an all-Pullman train with four brass-railed observation cars?

In anticipation of troop service, most of the heavy wooden furniture had been removed from the lounges, and these sections of the cars looked bare and uninviting. To the imaginative and enterprising element aboard, those vast unspoiled virgin floor spaces posed an opportunity for some serious games of craps. For three nights in a row, into the wee hours, the dice rolled and the favorite gambling sport among the military flourished aboard four rolling casinos.

Until Japan surrendered in September 1945, we worked westbound and

deadheaded eastbound. Since Pullman berths on regular trains were scarce, we usually deadheaded home on the equipment in which we had made our westbound in-service movement. The equipment from two or more westbound moves would be consolidated into a single eastbound train consisting of 20 or 30 deadhead sleepers, carrying those porters who needed transportation to their home districts and an Eastern district conductor who was in charge of the move.

Deadheading on equipment was quite satisfactory to me, for it had all the implications of riding a private train with one exception. Both The Pullman Company and the railroads involved made scant provision for feeding the Pullman crews in transit. Train crews ran their division or two and were finished; but the Pullman crews, to whom a division was simply another milestone in the direction of home, were at the mercy of the division dispatcher, who invariably insisted he could not delay a deadhead movement long enough for a meal except, of course, at some remote siding miles from the nearest restaurant at three o'clock in the morning.

To prepare for an impending transcontinental deadhead ordeal, I would contact the train commander of the westbound in-service move, who often was anxious to unload any leftover food before arrival in camp. Troop train rations usually were well calculated in advance, and any commander who arrived at destination with a surplus of food was suspected of not having fed his men adequately.

Train commanders generally were down-to-earth men. Most of them had been through the mill and were sympathetically co-operative to our problem. Occasionally a punctilious officer liked to let us know that he lived by the book. "Every bit of food has to be turned back or accounted for," emphasized one Captain, as a Main rolled down the west slope of the California Sierra through the just-awakening community of Dutch Flat, about an hour from our destination at Planehaven. All explanation of what the Pullman crews faced on the return deadhead to Philadelphia fell on deaf ears. Finally in desperation, and as a parting gesture, I informed the Captain that we would arrive within the hour and that I would be up to see him before that time for his signature on the "Damage to Equipment" form. Three windows, I explained, had been broken by his men between Council Bluffs and Denver and had been replaced during the service

layover in the Mile-High City two mornings earlier. Upon opening my compartment door three-quarters of an hour later to pick up the necessary forms, I was confronted by a mountain of cardboard cartons stacked in my room. In those bulging containers were several hundred thick sandwiches. The Captain had seen the light. I suppose it was a coincidence that the small case containing my inventory of Pullman reporting forms was at the very bottom of the tallest pile.

Those sandwiches, believe it or not, provided sustenance for 29 porters and myself during the ensuing journey from Sacramento to Omaha. During those three days my train of deadheading sleepers made but one meal stop. This was at Emigrant Gap, Calif, shortly after daybreak the first morning, where the whole crew, including the engineers and firemen, trooped into a trackside beanery converted from an old coach. The Chinese proprietor spread before us a breakfast of ham and eggs and all the butter we could possibly spread on accompanying toast and hotcakes. For the remaining 71 hours, the Pullman crew faced sandwiches, and sandwiches only, at meal times. To this day I have no hankering for another Spam sandwich.

By early 1946 the transportation crisis had reached its peak, and from then on the emergency eased considerably. On March 15 all restrictions were lifted on sleeping-car operations under 450 miles. Even though The Pullman Company was hiring conductors as rapidly as possible, an acute shortage of conductors still existed in the Philadelphia district as the older men returned to regular jobs on reinstated civilian services. Gradually supply caught up with demand, and months of 100 hours of overtime became part of the past.

The eight or nine postwar years were the most enjoyable and rewarding of my career. As a nation of travelers, we were still committed to terra firma, and the railroads were pulling out all the stops to persuade postwar America to keep its feet on the ground. They faced the future with confidence, and they manifested that spirit with orders for new passenger equipment virtually unprecedented in the history of the industry. Almost before the smoke of battle had cleared away, carbuilders found themselves swamped with orders for new passenger equipment. Within three months 1,244 cars were on order. In spite of a capacity for producing 4,500 new passenger cars annually, car manufacturers were unable to keep pace with orders, and the backlog continued to grow for several years. Finding a carrier, even among the smaller roads, that hadn't contracted for at least some new cars was unusual. The larger carriers placed single orders for sleepers, observations, and mid-train lounges that ran into the hundreds. Orders for entirely new streamliners involving four or five complete trains were common.

I can sympathize with those today who lament the passing of the orthodox passenger train and the proud Pullmans that were an inseparable part of every respectable consist. Nothing, nothing whatsoever, in the realm of overland travel has been invented whose accommodations can remotely approach the comfort and luxury of a Pullman car, whether it be one of the standard open-section 12-wheelers or one of the postwar all-room versions. And those who insist that the industry has done nothing to perpetuate rail travel simply do not know what they are talking about. All one has to do is spend one nostalgic evening perusing a decade or so of postwar *Trains* magazines for an appraisal of what an optimistic industry was doing to sell the public travel by rail.

Obviously, the big-name trains received the streamlined, all-room creations emerging from Budd, American Car & Foundry, and Pullman. The secondary trains, in turn, inherited the heavyweight 12-wheelers and the prewar lightweights. The secondary castoffs entered the Pullman pool, which in those happy times comprised thousands of sleepers. Consequently, the Pullman conductor of a postwar military move often found himself in charge of a consist that provided a degree of luxury found only in the extra-fare category less than a decade before. What's more, the railroad dining car replaced the kitchen car increasingly as the months went by. Air-conditioning, deactivated during the war because of the shortage of refrigerants, was ordered turned on. Army regulations no longer required two men to a lower. The troop train was becoming first-class.

When military installations were closed down after the war, the conductors' rosters in the districts serving those camps were decimated overnight. Philadelphia fared well, though. Fort Dix, Indiantown Gap, and numerous lesser military posts in the area remained active. The Philadelphia conductor was fortunate in that his district served an area that generated a considerable volume of charter business, which helped to take up slack during the lulls in military activity. Service clubs, fraternal organizations, and numerous industries accounted for many a chartered move out of the district. Two organizations in particular, the Philadelphia Orchestra and the University of Pennsylvania's famed Mask and Wig Club, were annual customers—the former several times each year. In the years immediately following the war, there was so much of this business that conductors from other districts frequently were brought in to ease the shortage. A tour with the Philadelphia Orchestra or with the Mask and Wig Club usually lasted two or three weeks, but an all-Pullman transcontinental tour sometimes took a conductor away for a month or more.

The end of the war also brought back the seasonal train, which in the realm of the Philadelphia district meant the famous *Bar Harbor Express* and the seashore trains to Atlantic City. Operating on a triweekly basis, the *Bar Harbor* always carried two regularly assigned conductors, for on board was the cream of Philadelphia society. Usually the train ran in one section to Portland, Maine, where it split, with the main section going to Ellsworth and a smaller section to Rockland. The first trains of each season were filled with housekeepers, cooks, maids, butlers, gardeners, and other domestics being dispatched north to prepare the summer mansions for the arrival of their employers around the first of July. All went ahead except, of course, the chauffeurs, who did not depart until they had safely installed their employers aboard the train at the appointed time; then there was an interstate parade as they raced those custom-bodied Rolls-Royces north on Route 1 as fast as machinery and law allowed. Their masters were not ones to be kept waiting. Actually, they were nice people—not the folksy type, of course, who were concerned that they would miss the bargain sale of soap chips at their local supermarket the following Wednesday, but sophisticated travelers who conducted themselves as passengers should. They knew how to tip when the occasion warranted too. The *Bar Harbor Express* was one of the few trains in the nation whose consist could reasonably be expected to include a private car or two, particularly one of those from the Pullman pool available to individuals and corporations on a daily basis.

Much of the seashore business was in parlor cars, which were always next to the engine eastbound. These were the years of the K4's, and it was fascinating to stand inside the front end door (no one in his right mind ever stood on the front platform with steam on the point) watching that tender bounce and sway and the rear pair of wheels slide from side to side as flanges challenged guard rails and frogs on the 45-mile fast stretch between Haddonfield and Absecon, N.J. To me, there will never be a jet that travels half as fast as those boardwalk-bound flyers as they blasted through Hammonton, Egg Harbor, and a dozen other on-line rural communities, with their whistles shrieking to the accompaniment of tinkling crossing-gate bells and six-wheel trucks pounding worn joints embedded in the paved street crossings. When the dust had finally settled, everyone knew that the *Sea Breeze* had just passed through town.

At one time or another Atlantic City played host to nearly every major fraternal group's annual convention. The largest gathering of them all, the national convention of the Order of the Mystic Shrine, brought in so many sleepers and lounge cars that trains of them had to be deadheaded back to Philadelphia for storage until the convention broke up. When the assembly finally ended and the last all-Pullman section headed west across the New Jersey marshes, the Philadelphia district was without an extra board. Not an extra conductor was left in town.

As the annual winter lull approached, common practice was to transfer to one of the neighboring districts such as Washington & Pennsylvania Terminal in New York, commonly known as PT. PT's seasonal business came in the winter, just before Christmas, when the Florida trains were put on. PT probably operated more big name trains than any other Pullman district in the country. *Broadway Limited, Spirit of St. Louis, Crescent Limited, Florida Special, Orange Blossom Special,* and *St. Louisan* were but a few. Late in the spring, when the Florida trains came off, we would transfer back to our home districts. To those of us from the Philadelphia district this meant reacquaintance with the troop train and transcontinental travel in the grand manner.

Although after the war railroad diners had replaced the kitchen car to a great extent on troop trains, there were many times when dining car availability was extremely tight. Possibly with this sort of contingency in mind, the armed services developed gasoline-fired units that could be used in either the conventional kitchen car or virtually any railroad baggage car. This circumstance led to one of the most memorable episodes of my entire Pullman career. With dinner over, the mess crew was engaged in cleaning up inside a Pennsy turtle-roofed baggage car. They had removed the gasoline burners from the ranges and were cleaning them and spilling considerable fuel in the process. The wooden floor became saturated with gasoline, and the inevitable spark from a cigarette set off the whole business. Despite the conductor's repeated skirmishes with the signal cord, no response came from the man at the throttle. Fanned by the wind through the open doors, flames spread rapidly through the car. We were westbound on the Northern Pacific between Livingston and Missoula, Mont.; and on we rolled down the mountain to Helena in a flaming baggage car. Masking their faces against the leaping flames, the mess crew managed to close the sliding doors. Then fire extinguishers from the sleepers brought the conflagration under control. A soaking by the Helena fire department completed the job.

Relations between the Pullman conductor and his passengers usually were very pleasant, but the annual advent of Daylight Saving Time occasionally strained the most cordial of dealings. The most frustrating experience of my career was trying to explain to a lady passenger when we would arrive at Princeton Junction, N.J. Her watch was on daylight time and my watch and the time table were on standard time. All my attempts at explanation only confused both of us. Then, out of nowhere, I was struck by one of those brilliant ideas that come only to the drunk and the desperate. Her watch showed 30 minutes past the hour. "In just twenty-seven minutes," I said, beaming triumphantly, "we will arrive at Princeton Junction."

"Conductor, is that standard or daylight saving time?"

One experience that belongs in the believe-it-or-not category occurred late one night on an eastbound main rolling through the Oklahoma panhandle between Tucumcari, N. Mex., and Liberal, Kans. The climax to the incident came when the train went into emergency, just as I was crawling into my berth. The locomotive and tender, an express refrigerator car, and the 19 sleepers ground to a halt on that clear mid-November night without that smashing jolt which usually accompanies a front-end collision.

According to the enginemen, a few minutes before an unstable individual,

resembling a sailor, had suddenly appeared in the cab, as if out of nowhere, and announced that he was about to take over the throttle from there on into Kansas City. When the engineer made no attempt whatsoever to relinquish his post, the sailor, to further emphasize his intentions, brandished a heavy orange-colored wrench he had appropriated from the equipment locker of one of the sleepers. Facing the possibility of being scalded to death should the sailor accidentally fracture the water glass, the engineer threw his train into emergency, and he and his fireman set about collaring their assailant.

It had all started 3 or 4 hours before when the train made a lengthy layover in Tucumcari to service the sleepers and to replace three Espee diners with two from the Rock Island. This gave those so inclined an opportunity to go uptown and restock their inventory of liquid refreshment. Suitably needled by a group of Marines and amply fortified with Tucumcari booze, a lone sailor set out to achieve the impossible dream. Reaching the head sleeper presented no real problem, but the rest of the journey required a rare combination of reckless courage and Divine protection occasionally afforded the inebriate. The feat was one few experienced brakemen would care to try. It meant climbing the end ladder on an express refrigerator car moving at passenger-train speed, negotiating the narrow catwalk atop the roof of that swaying car, climbing down the ladder at the forward end, jumping from the end sill of the car to that of the tender, climbing the tender ladder, and crawling the length of the tender top before dropping down into the cab. When the Main finally reached Kansas City late the next afternoon it was met by nearly every official agency, military and civilian, known to man. By that time, however, the culprit was sheltered in anonymity. Even the Pullman conductor wasn't certain just what had happened.

Someone once asked what train I most disliked. I can't say that I ever disliked any train; but the train I least liked to work was the New York-bound *Clocker* due out of Philadelphia at 8 in the morning. Tuesday traffic was the heaviest, and 150 passengers were a typical load in the four straight parlors and the parlor-buffet-lounge. Approximately half of those aboard were either cash fares or pass riders. Known simply as Two-Oh-Two, it covered the 76 miles (75.9 if you want to be fussy) between North Philadelphia and

Newark in 69 minutes; so there was time for little more than the barest civilities. More than once I found myself collecting a fare or two on the Newark platform. On occasion when there was an unusual number of pass riders, I would be completing my lift as the train emerged from the Hudson River tubes at the entrance to Penn Station.

My favorite train, you ask? Now there's a tough one. Katy's streamlined *Texas Special,* Espee-Rock Island's postwar *Imperial,* Baltimore & Ohio's *National Limited,* Lehigh Valley's *Maple Leaf,* Mopac's *Colorado Eagle,* Union Pacific's *Portland Rose* ... all are, or were, trains I like to remember. That wonderful scenery from the windows of the *Olympian* between Spokane and Deer Lodge; those midnight snacks (on the house) aboard the *Pittsburgher's* diner, featuring literally crocks of Wisconsin's famous Kaukauna cheese; breakfast of ham and eggs, with a short stack of pancakes, aboard Rio Grande's *Prospector* as it descended the snow-blanketed western slope of Utah's Wasatch Range ... all of these memories re-create glimpses of transcontinental travel in the grand manner.

But my vote, I believe, would have to go to Great Northern's *Oriental Limited.* It was reinstated a couple of years after World War II and lasted for about four years, until the railroad's *Empire Builder* was re-equipped for a second time and the *Oriental Limited,* sporting the flagship's original lightweight equipment, became the *Western Star.* Although the reinstated *Oriental* was by no means an accommodation local, its 57-hour schedule, in spite of quite a few more stops than the *Empire Builder* made, permitted a leisurely pace reminiscent of the prewar years.

Its normal consist east of Spokane, where the Portland sleepers were picked up, comprised six sleepers and an observation-lounge-buffet-section car. Another sleeper, en route from Great Falls to St. Paul, was picked up at Havre, Mont. There wasn't a single postwar 8-wheeled streamlined sleeper in the train. All were the durable pre-'31 products of Calumet, altered and upgraded through the years as travel habits changed. Nothing more conducive to overland travel in the grand manner has ever replaced those magnificent 12-wheelers.

The scenery, although it was not quite up to the Milwaukee's, was outstanding. From 7:30 in the morning until approximately the same hour in the evening, between Spokane and Cut Bank, Mont., the view from the enclosed observation

Soldiers of the U.S. Army's 35th Division board a cars at Camp Robinson, Ark., on December 18, 1941, less than two weeks after Pearl Harbor. The era of the troop train had begun. U.S. ARMY SIGNAL CORPS.

was varied and beautiful. Rivers, mountains, tall stands of towering tamarack along the north bank of the Kootenai River, and finally the high plains east of Glacier Park helped to stimulate one's appetite for those superb meals in GN's diners. From apple juice, through those giant baked potatoes, to that extra-large wedge of freshly baked apple pie, GN dining car meals took a back seat to no one's, not even Santa Fe's Fred Harvey cuisine.

I never once worked the *Oriental*. My frequent presences aboard it were simply as a first-class deadhead, which meant that I had the run of the train without any of the work or responsibility.

Most troop trains arrived and unloaded early in Seattle's King Street station, and the 12- or 13-hour layover there until the *Oriental's* departure that evening at 9:30 soon became a boring ordeal. The panacea was to appear in the district office there as soon as it opened in the morning and request a pass and permission to ride the *Cascadian*, a daylight coach train between Seattle and Spokane. Not only did this beat wandering the streets of Seattle all day long, but the *Cascadian* carried a reserved-seat observation coach with an honest-to-goodness brass-railed observation platform. For a mere 75 cents one was sure of a permanent seat over the 330

miles, which included GN's electrified section through the 7.79-mile-long Cascade Tunnel. What's more, after a five- or six-day westbound trip, spending the night in a Spokane hotel was welcome. Early the next morning I would board the *Oriental* for those 1,850 leisurely miles to Chicago.

By the mid-Fifties, a considerable slice of Pullman business already was in the hands of the airlines. The Philadelphia district, not a large one as Pullman districts went, had lost at least a dozen conductor jobs, including those to Washington and Erie, and the Pittsburgh parlor-car operations. Troop train movements were tapering off drastically as Fort Dix moved more men by air. The jet was still more than two years away, but the implications of its ultimate effect on long-distance travel, and the Pullman business in particular, were frightening. My final decision to leave Pullman came early in 1956 when I learned that the Pennsylvania Railroad was not going to renew its parlor-car contract with Pullman at the expiration of the present one in the fall. To the Philadelphia district this meant the loss of four regular jobs on the *Clockers,* as well as countless extra assignments to Atlantic City.

Before turning in my keys and other company-owned property, I indulged in one more assignment, one that took me over the Reading, the Lehigh Valley, and the Canadian National to Toronto.

Thus ended a personal railfan excursion which had lasted something over 12 years—a coast-to-coast, border-to-border travel extravaganza that added up to nearly 1.25 million miles, including the approximately 175,000 deadhead miles between my home in Lancaster and whatever district out of which I happened to be working.

Since December 31, 1968, the Pullman conductor and the Pullman porter have been a matter of history. On that date the great Pullman Company discontinued operating sleeping cars and only maintained and serviced such equipment. An operation that two decades earlier involved sleeping cars in the thousands dwindled to only a few hundred. On August 1, 1969, this service ended too, and The Pullman Company closed its doors in the U. S. (sleeping cars continued to be operated by Pullman in Mexico).

In the United States, the word travel has become sterile, meaningless. And the end of overland travel via the steel rail and the flanged wheel may be a whole lot closer than some think.

Iced and airless at Cascade Summit

By Steve Woodson
As told to R. Storia Hewitt
Engineer

1940s

From *Trains* magazine,
July 1982

My assignment on that icy winter night was helper duty. I was to handle a 4200-series cab-forward articulated, doubleheading Southern Pacific train 19, the westbound *Klamath,* from Oakridge to Cascade Summit, Ore. (Yes, I know that Cascade Summit is south, rather than west, of Eugene, but in SP railroad talk there is no north or south—only east or west. Here on the Oregon Division, all traffic headed for San Francisco is westbound, and vice versa.)

It was a real winter night. Although no snow was falling in Eugene, incoming trains emerged from the mountain gorges plastered with white on the leading edge of every car. Forty-five miles up in the middle fork of the Willamette River valley, at Oakridge, it was snowing. You did not have to be told that above Oakridge, the higher you got, the deeper the snow and the colder the temperature would be. At Abernathy, a lonely siding 4.1 miles west of the summit, the snow was 80 inches deep. At Cascade Summit, elevation 4,840 feet, the temperature was below zero, and Odell Lake was completely frozen over.

Following my orders, I deadheaded to the helper terminal at Oakridge, boarded a Mallet (as we called even our simple 4-8-8-2's) fresh from the roundhouse, and coupled to the front of train 19, which had 18 cars.

To complicate matters, a trainmaster was riding in the cab with me. The *Klamath* had been late the last five days in a row, and San Francisco HQ wanted to know why. As an extra man, I never knew in advance what kind of a situation I would step into.

Why was a Mallet needed to help this train over the Cascades? At Oakridge, the grade stiffened to 1.05 percent. From Oakridge up Salt Creek, then up the steep shoulders of the Cascades, through tunnel after tunnel, for 43.7 miles of steadily rising track on a grade averaging 1.6 percent, with tangents as scarce as hen's teeth, plenty of power was needed for a heavy train. If that wasn't enough, we would have to make a number of stops, for No. 19 was kind of a milk train. The baggage cars carried way freight, and people got on and off at every little burg.

Worst of all, there would be a number of unscheduled stops this night to drop off and take on extra crews engaged in snow service. When the snow became too deep for the regular section crews to clear, the passenger trains brought extra help. Relief crews had to be dropped off at nine isolated sidings up in the snow belt: Prior, McCredie Springs, Heather, Wicopee, Fields, Frazier, Cruzatte, Abernathy, and Cascade Summit. These men would dig snow out of switches and light switch heaters (and relight them when passing trains snuffed out the flames).

Our customary practice on the long ascending grades from Oakridge to Cascade Summit was to use the independent, or engine, brake only for holding the train after it stopped. As usual, I did not employ the engine brake when I headed into the west siding at Cascade Summit. We stopped at the water column, where the road engine took on water before departing.

As the trainmaster waved good-bye he said, "San Francisco ought to be happy. We got her on time today." He dropped off, aligned the switch into the wye, walked the length of the engine, uncoupled us from the road locomotive, gave me a highball, and realigned the switch after we had cleared. The fireman and I would now wye our engine, re-enter the siding, take on water, and eat at the company restaurant before setting out light back to Oakridge.

We had done our job, keeping the train on time in some of the worst conditions the Cascades can hand out. I patted myself on the back—too soon. Old Man Winter struck where I never suspected.

The wye track went uphill, dead-ending in a tunnel. The reason for that is that there is no level ground at Cascade Summit; there is only a shelf of rolling, forested terrain between the shores of Lake Odell and the nearly vertical slope of Lakeview Mountain. The tunnel was just long enough to hold a Mallet. Before entering it, I slowed down as usual to let the fireman off at the end-of-wye switch, which he would throw as soon as the tender was past. I did not need to apply the brakes to slow down; I simply had to close the throttle as we were on an ascending grade.

After the fireman dropped off, I opened the throttle for enough push to get us over the final rise into the tunnel, where the track leveled off. Then I closed the throttle, rolled toward the end of the tunnel, and applied the engine brake. For the first time since leaving Oakridge, I was using the independent for stopping rather than standing.

Nothing happened! Unknown to me, the brake rigging had iced up while we had been climbing the mountain. Since the rock wall at the end of the tunnel was coming up and we were not slowing, I had to act fast. I "cleaned the clock" (made an emergency brake application) and still nothing happened!

If there had been clear track ahead, the brake might have taken effect, but the rock wall was looming up. I had no desire to hit solid rock at any time, even less now because the cab, with me in it, was at the leading end of the locomotive. I remembered seeing a cab-forward which had

A 4200-series cab-forward is cut in behind a 4-8-4 to double-head Southern Pacific's *Overland Limited* upgrade out of Colfax, Calif., in April 1950. Engineer Woodson's adventure happened on a sister locomotive following a similar double-heading job. A.C. KALMBACH.

sideswiped a freight car. Outside, the cab was only slightly out of line. Inside, there was little damage. But the cab had tipped enough to break a superheated steam pipe and three men—engineer, fireman, and head brakeman—had died. I had to stop!

I threw the engine into reverse and jerked the throttle wide open, but I was too late. If I had had 6 feet more, I could have stopped the engine short of the track-end bumper. But the engine hit it—not severely, but sharply enough to break off the pilot. Along with the pilot went the dirt collector, which we usually referred to as the air separator. This collector, about the size of a gallon can and located beneath the cab and below the main air reservoirs behind the pilot, was a fixed casting with a removable sump which filtered dirt, water, and other foreign matter from the compressed air before it reached the reservoirs. When the collector broke off, all air from both sides of the main reservoir pipe escaped to the atmosphere air from both main reservoirs, from the distributing valve, and from the main reservoir to the automatic brake valve. As a result, all air-operated equipment on my engine—bell, air horn, whistle, air-actuated feed valves, air-powered reverse—was instantly disabled.

At the moment I could not detect the full extent of the damage; I did not know that the dirt collector was gone, but the air gauges' sudden drop to zero told me trouble was afoot. Now, the engine's valve gear was in reverse and the cylinders were loaded with steam, so the engine started backward too rapidly for the fireman to swing aboard. Alone in the cab, I had no brakes, no reverse, and no more than a few seconds to do something—if there was something I could do! This leg of the wye was less than four city blocks long and descended on a grade of 2 percent or more.

I had closed the throttle, but the engine was rolling free toward the side of the *Klamath,* which was just starting out but going slowly as its engineer made a running brake test. Unless I did something, some Pullman passenger was going to find a Mallet's tender in his berth. I could see No. 19's lights winking by as its cars dinged over the switch. Eighteen cars make a long train anyway, but now it seemed miles long,

I knew that the Mallet was designed so that its reversing mechanism would drop into forward gear in case of mechanical failure, but would it drop soon enough? Air was probably trapped in the dead cylinder, holding the piston and links in place until it bled away. The only way to

determine whether the shift had taken place would be to open the throttle. If the engine stopped, the problem was solved. But if the shift had not taken place, I would accelerate even faster toward No. 19. Even as I was deciding not to gamble, a solution occurred to me: the steam reverse! If I could find that valve, which cut steam into the normally air-actuated power reverse, I could stop.

Now, it can take minutes to find the right handle when you face a row of seldom-used valves located in an out-of-the-way place. When I'd been a fireman, I had never seen an engineer use the steam reverse valve; as an engineer, I had never used it.

There was a row of look-alike round valve handles on a long bar near the cab roof (see the photo on page 56), each identified with a small metal tag—but the tags were hard to read in the dim light, and one or more might be missing (after years of service, they weren't as clean and pristine as the ones in the photo).

Because the steam reverse was usually used only in an emergency, the company had been fitting it with a distinctive X-shaped handle painted yellow. Complications: If the reverse valve had been removed for maintenance, a worker might have installed an ordinary round

It can be tricky to quickly find the correct valve on the backhead of a large steam locomotive like this Southern Pacific 4-8-8-2. A small tag below the valve at top partially obscured by a pipe reads "Power Reverse Steam." Southern Pacific.

valve in its place. Or if the packing on such valves near the cab roof had leaked, and steam had condensed, dropping hot water down the crew's necks, a disgusted engineman might have seized a wrench and overtightened the packing nuts.

It was my good fortune that the reverse valve on my locomotive had an X handle and opened easily. I turned it, shifted the reverse lever in forward gear, and opened the throttle. The engine slowed and stopped, a few car-lengths from the moving train.

But I had no brakes. The engine headed back uphill until I closed the throttle. Then it rolled back. I cracked the throttle again and it started back up. All the while, No. 19, car by car, was passing

over the wye switch. Finally the train cleared. I moved back uphill to pick up the fireman, who was still standing at the wye switch to the tunnel mouth and wondering what was going on.

You're wondering why he had not tried to board before? He hadn't tried, and had been wise not to. Remember, all this took place at night on a track walled by packed snow not less than 8 feet high; his safest position had been in the cleared area around the switch stand. Once he was aboard, I moved the engine to the siding switch; he walked along the running board and across the tender (to avoid the snowbank), then descended the tank ladder to align the switch to clear us into the siding.

Before we could leave the engine

untended to get a much needed meal and rest, we had to tie it down, once I had released all steam pressure by opening the four cylinder cocks. In the absence of engine brakes, we tried the tender brakes. But we couldn't budge the chain because of a frozen mass of oil and dirt. We found a pile of 18-inch cord wood used by the cook for his kitchen range and wedged the drivers front and back more securely than if we'd used chains, which we didn't have.

I called the dispatcher from the eating house to report my disabled engine. He wanted me to proceed to Oakridge. You don't go 44 miles down a mountain on a steam reverse! The packing could blow, causing loss of all control. I am a second-generation Dutchman when someone asks me to do something out of order. "Hell no! I won't go!" We couldn't seem to get through to each other.

I hung up the phone on him. I knew it would ring again. It did. The DS had gotten the roundhouse foreman at Crescent Lake, 10 miles east, to work on the problem. I told him the piping was intact, not bent; he could bypass the dirt collector with a union and two pieces of pipe. He collected the material, rode over in a motor car, and soon had us fixed with air pressure. My fireman and I rode the engine back to Oakridge without further incident.

I could easily have been fired or at least temporarily taken out of service.

Some time before all this happened, a road foreman of engines had undertaken a program of telling all engineers in his jurisdiction about the steam reverse valve, urging them to familiarize themselves with its location and use. As it turned out, he was later promoted to trainmaster and was the same man who had ridden my cab up to Cascade Summit that night. When he asked me about my accident, I told him the whole truth, including how the steam reverse valve had enabled me to avoid a bad wreck. He said if only one person had heard his advice and prevented an accident, why it was all worthwhile.

He told me to button up about the bunged-up pilot and he would take care of it. I did, and he did. The only reason I can tell the story now is that he has crossed the final Summit.

Delivering EMD's locomotives

By W.A. Gardner
Locomotive Instruction

1940s

From *Trains* magazine,
November 1980

Over the years, the duties of the instructors Electro-Motive Division (EMD) sends to a railroad taking delivery of new locomotives have changed gradually.

But there have been drastic differences, too. No longer is it necessary to literally teach the engine crews how to run a diesel ("This is the throttle. It has eight notches plus a shutdown position. When you pull it toward you, the engines go faster. Here is the horn cord, the headlight switch, the transition lever, the generator field switch."). The job has evolved mainly into one of reporting troubles back to the plant, helping in correcting the problems, obtaining needed parts or instructions, and generally being helpful. In retrospect, I think I liked it better in what we older folks call the good old days.

One of the most interesting assignments I had while working as an instructor for EMD was in the fall of 1946—my very first one on my own, following a training period. I had just joined EMD after a stint on the Pennsylvania, where I had helped put in service PRR's first E7 passenger diesels (see "A Reputation For Reliability" in the January 1979 *Trains*). My first solo EMD job started inauspiciously with instructions to go to Mechanicville, N.Y, on the Hudson River about 10 miles north of Troy, to assist in placing one 1,000-hp switcher in service on the Boston & Maine.

The locomotive and I arrived about the same time, and after the usual preliminaries—fuel, water, oil, sand, etc.—the unit was put to work on the Mechanicville hump. That doesn't sound too exciting, and for a few days it wasn't. The hump did have one unusual characteristic, though, for the entire yard was downgrade toward the hump, with the result that the speed of the cut you were humping had to be controlled, not with the throttle but with the brakes. Five to seven cars ahead of the unit had to be coupled with operative brakes to give enough braking effort to do

the job. A gentle nudge would start the cut rolling, and from then until the last six or seven cars were actually on the hump incline, fancy brake-valve operation, not fancy throttle-handling, was in order.

After almost a week of this, I was informed that the unit would be taken out of service for two days in order to apply cab signals so it could be used on the main line as a pusher from Mechanicville to Hoosac Tunnel, Mass. A test trip was announced for the day following the cab-signal installation, and I got to ride along, although there hardly was room.

The road foreman of engines, the assistant trainmaster, the assistant shop superintendent, and the air brake supervisor all showed up. We crowded in, barely leaving enough room for the poor engineer to operate, but he managed it. We pushed a train being pulled by a four-unit FT up to the tunnel, and I began to wonder why we were there. No one paid the slightest attention to what our locomotive was doing all the way up—all the conversation was about the best places to go hunting and fishing and similar railroad-oriented topics. We reached the tunnel soon enough, stopped, and cut off: the train went on. After a short wait for the operator to line the switches, we crossed over to the westbound track and headed back for Mechanicville. Strange test, I thought, but fortunately not out loud.

As soon as we started downgrade, all hands came to attention, writing notes in little books that suddenly appeared. Mileposts, speed, use of air, curvature all were carefully observed and recorded. Several observations ("Feels okay so far." "No problem here." "Rides good.") were expressed aloud. After allowing the speed to gradually rise to 45 mph, the maximum for the locomotive, there came general

agreement that the ride was good and the speed safe. Now I found out why we were testing. The older 1,000-hp switcher the railroad had at Mechanicville had been used in this manner, as a helper, when it was new, with no problem. As it grew older, however, it took longer and longer to get home after a push since the crews claimed it was unsafe to run at 45, then 40, then 35, and finally 30. At this point it became unreasonable to use it as a pusher since it was gone from the yard too long. This test had established that it was indeed necessary to shop the older unit and go over its trucks; since the new unit had done so well (as the old one originally had), it was obvious that there must be something wrong—like maybe five years of wear!

No one knew how many helper trips the older switcher had made to induce the wear that was found (and duly repaired), so I never was able to equate the wear to miles.

The switcher job had not quite descended to the boring stage when things suddenly livened up. Oh, I frequently had to take time out to watch one of the Delaware & Hudson's Challengers pull a train into Mechanicville yard, or to view its poppet-valve Pacific snort out of town with the northbound local, but when several more instructors arrived with the news that six new F2's were on their way from La Grange, we got busy. One and two at a time, the three A units and three B units (Nos. 4224-4226 A and B) got there and were prepared for service. This procedure took two days each, which sounds like a long time until you consider that the preparation included a complete Simoniz application. The B&M was proud of its road units' appearance and kept them spotless. One of the previously delivered 15 F2A's (4250-4264) was coupled to each of the new A-B pairs to make an A-B-A combination, and they were put to work between Mechanicville and Boston.

One of author Gardner's first assignments for Electro-Motive was helping place in service a group of Boston & Maine F2's. A trio led by 4226 heads through Bellows Falls, Vt., in 1952, six years after they arrived on the railroad. HOMER R. HILL.

The F2 model was a 1,350-hp successor to the FT and produced only in 1946. It was new to all of us on the assignment, and consequently we decided that we would start off with two men on each trip until we learned the F2's secrets. Misery loves company.

While events would dictate that we would not have much time to admire the scenery, we began our first trip on a perfect day for that. A crisp, clear atmosphere produced the right conditions for viewing the bright yellow and red leaves of a legendary New England autumn. This was one of the best.

The first few miles out of Mechanicville yard on the B&M are either level or only slightly upgrade, so a diesel could easily accelerate its train above the first two transition speeds and hold it there for 18 to 20 miles. The grade then increases enough so the speed is pulled down to 17, 16, or 15 mph on the steepest part. The summit is in Hoosac Tunnel.

This meant that, between the yard and the tunnel, the engineer had to make forward transition twice and backward transition also twice. Transition switching, remember, has been an automatic feature on diesel locomotives since the late 1940s, so today's engineers, even experienced ones, may not know what you are talking about if you ask them about making transition manually. The engineer knew when to make transition by watching his

ammeter. The forward transitions add shunt to the traction-motor connections the first time and change the motor-generator connections from series-parallel to parallel the second time. This allows the use of full engine power at all speeds without overloading either the motors or the generator.

On that crisp 1946 autumn day, our engineer on the three-unit F2 went through all the proper motions at the right times, according to the ammeter indication. He closed the throttle two notches, moved the transition lever to the next notch, and reopened the throttle. The forward transitions were made with no problem, but when the back transition was called for, no power contactor switching could be heard, and the ammeter came right back to where it had been when the throttle was reopened. Something was wrong, dangerously wrong. If we didn't find the problem quickly the main generators would be badly overloaded and we would lose power to the point where we no longer could pull the train.

The problem turned out to be relatively minor. A relay that was supposed to release when back transition was called for had not done so. With a light tap from a screwdriver handle, it obediently, if belatedly, opened, and transition took place. The power contactors barked a little louder than usual, since the throttle was wide open, but nothing grounded and we

were still rolling.

Later on the trip we had a similar problem with the forward transition when an interlock on a contactor refused to do its job even though it looked fine. This not only prevented forward transition but made it impossible for the generator field contactor to close again, resulting in a complete loss of power on that unit.

All this left little time for admiring foliage, since it now became obvious that every time transition was made, in either direction, a tour of the units was imperative to be sure they all were running in the proper connection and making power. Since the profile on that B&M route is a series of ups and downs, we made several such tours. Oh well, it was getting dark anyhow and the trees would still be there next trip. They were, and they stayed worth watching for a couple more weeks.

When we got to Boston we asked if there were any spare relays of the type giving the problem. To no one's surprise, there were none, so we had the same routine to go through on the return trip. The relays did not always fail—only about one-third of the time, but that still meant we had to look each time. We also called Mechanicville and suggested strongly that the shop men carefully check this circuit on the other units before dispatching them.

Our return trip was not too different than the eastbound run. About every third or fourth time the relay would fail to open, and the old screwdriver-handle treatment was administered. Seldom did all three units get through a back transition without one of the two new units giving trouble.

As we entered the East Portal of Hoosac Tunnel, the sky over the mountain was beginning to look threatening, and when we came out of the West Portal it was like running into a car wash. I have never seen it rain harder or keep it up longer. The crew told us we had passed wayside signals without ever seeing them; cab signals are very comforting under these conditions.

About 6 or 7 miles west of the tunnel, where the eastbound grade reaches its maximum ascent, we passed a two-unit diesel with a train on the upgrade. There was considerable disagreement in our cab over whether the engines were running or not, but there was no question that the train was stopped. Our fireman, who was closest, said the engines were running full speed. The other instructor and I exchanged sour looks, speculating that the same relay trouble we had had also had taken place on the other units and was either unobserved or had not been corrected in time.

Upon our arrival at Mechanicville, our worst suspicions were confirmed. The eastbound train had stalled on the hill with the locomotives' engines running full speed, and both main generators were badly overheated. If the shop personnel had previous doubts about our reports of parallel relay trouble, they were now dispelled. Our units had new relays installed in about 4 minutes, even though a quick test showed them to be working.

The other instructor and I hung around until the other two units were brought back and, sure enough, both generators were throwing solder from the commutators and one was grounded. Both would have to be replaced. One of the relays still was stuck in the closed position, although by this time our story needed no further confirmation.

Why hadn't the two instructors on the other train been able to prevent such a mishap? It turned out both of them were on their very first trip and had not had even a quick tour of an F2 to familiarize them with it. Obviously it had not been planned that way; they had been called to ride two different locomotives, each in company with an experienced man, but the veteran who was to have gone on the first train had been delayed en route to the yard by his bus being in an accident.

My remaining time on the Boston & Maine could not match the start for excitement, but it was enjoyable. I was called one evening late for what promised to be a dull, routine trip: two units with a light train for Greenfield, Mass. We were supposed to bring back some empties needed badly in Mechanicville. Four or five hours, even with an hour or so at Greenfield, should do it easily, I was told. The trip to Greenfield went without incident, but on arrival there I found that we (the units and I) were now going up to White River Junction, Vt., not back to Mechanicville—this in spite of the units being due for their monthly ICC inspection the next day. At White River Junction I learned the next destination was Springfield, Mass., and then on to Boston. One crew made that run with a 5-hour layover in Springfield, where the locomotive was parked in the New Haven roundhouse.

The New Haven facility there was all steam at the time, and the B&M crew, having been there before, knew what to expect of the New Haven's hostler. As we approached the turntable to put the units in the house, the engineer called to the fireman to not allow the hostler up in the cab. I asked how come, and he told me, "If he ever gets up here, he'll have everything so covered with grease we'll never get it clean again."

By this time the fireman and hostler were arguing the point, with the fireman winning easily on account of having his foot in the hostler's face.

"Why can't I get aboard?"

"Because you're a fire hazard."

We put the units in the house, set the hand brakes, shut the engines down, locked the cab doors, and went to bed until time to leave for Boston. The fireman was right, incidentally; how that hostler dared get near a firebox on a steam engine, I don't know.

One of John L. Lewis's many coal strikes was called while we were still on the B&M assignment, and things changed drastically and quickly. The three new F2 sets had small steam generators so they could be used in passenger service if necessary, and since the weather was not really cold yet, these units were adequate for the fall climate. So all three sets were moved to Boston, where they were assigned literally to more trains than they could handle. Some of the schedules were such that if you arrived in North Station, Boston, on time, you already were late for the next departure. The incoming train had to unload and be pulled back by a switcher, and the units had to run across the Charles River bridge to be turned and fueled, then backed onto the next train. This added up to at least a 45-minute delay. The object, however, was to save as much coal as possible for those runs which had to be steam-powered, and it worked. Many trains were late, but none were canceled.

We even pulled commuter trains with the F2's. Two units, an A and a B, pulling two open-end wooden coaches (the Ambroid prototype) would be laughed off anyone's model railroad as unprototypical, but I assure you it happened.

My final run on the B&M was on a student special the Sunday night after Thanksgiving from Boston to White River Junction, stopping at all the college towns along the way. I cannot recall how many stops we made, but it was several and the train was long. With only two units, we set no speed record, but no one was late for class Monday, either. We came back on a milk train leaving White River Junction after 3 a.m. This was a daily scheduled train, and it stopped at most stations and at several places that really were not stations, just a car-floor-height platform along the track at a country crossroad. There would be from two to six milk cans (the kind that sell for exorbitant prices today as antiques) on each platform. We would stop; the train crew would load the cans; and off we'd go again. As we approached one of these platforms, the engineer rolled down his window and with his left hand on the brake valve, stuck his head out to watch for the trainman's signal to stop the open car door next to the platform. We had gotten down to maybe 10 mph when he pulled his head in, released the brakes, and opened the throttle. It seems the old platform had sagged under the weight of the milk cans and leaned toward the track far enough that we hit it, giving the units a milk bath along their right side and making it completely unnecessary to stop there anymore.

If you deduce that I liked the Boston & Maine, you are right. Its equipment and right of way were kept in first-class shape; the crews were well-trained, careful, and conscientious. They were probably the most knowledgeable about the locomotives of any crews I have been in contact with on any railroad, and they were far and away the best mountain dynamic-brake and air-brake handlers I have observed. The B&M did not go broke because its train service and maintenance people were not trying.

Following his Boston & Maine assignment, Gardner moved south to help deliver F3's to the Southern Railway. Here No. 4144 leads an A-B-B-A set on a long freight train. E.P. DANDRIDGE, JR.

My next assignment was an almost complete change of pace in all respects. The railroad was the Southern; the location, Chattanooga, Tenn. The locomotives were F3's, not much different than F2's except for horsepower rating, and like the three B&M F2 sets, they were equipped for passenger service. Unlike the B&M's, though, these Southern F3's had large steam generators in all units and a gear ratio allowing higher speed; they did not have dynamic brakes. Assigned to passenger runs in all directions out of Chattanooga, to Cincinnati, Bristol, Tenn., Birmingham, and New Orleans, the F3's for the most part displaced Ps-4 Pacifics. Two units, usually an A-B combination, were used on most trains, with an occasional A-B-B set if the train was unusually long and heavy. The cab units could not be used singly or with just another A unit, though, because only the B units carried water—the entire supply being in a large round tank in the front of the locomotive where the cab was located on an A unit.

Almost all of the men who had been on the B&M with me were moved to the Southern, where we were joined by others from various previous jobs and by several newly hired men. Those of us from the

B&M turned out to be the only ones with experience on F units, so we got the training and orientation jobs at the start. We looked the units over as they arrived and were put in service and were delighted to find a new type relay, very substantial looking, in place of the one that had given us transition problems on the B&M. It lived up to its appearance, never giving us any trouble. With the exception of one or two contactor coil burnouts and three governor failures, these F3's did an excellent job the entire time we were on the Southern. Our old friend the troublesome type relay was still with us in other applications, but fortunately none of these were critical and when one failed it was merely an annoyance until it could be replaced.

Unfortunately, the same could not be said of the steam generators. These were a new design that the manufacturer had labeled type "OK." He could not have been more wrong in his choice. A set of automatic controls, intended to make it possible to simply push the start button and stand back and watch it run, was installed. These would work for perhaps a half hour without giving trouble. The system was complicated and difficult to understand and, therefore, to trouble-

shoot, so the first trouble usually led to overcompensation of something else that really was all right, with a consequent failure there too. The end result could be operating the steam generator manually, which was difficult at best, or, at worst, a complete failure, which meant a substitute locomotive had to be found quickly. For the five or six weeks it took to analyze and correct the boiler trouble, the "retired" Ps-4's remained quite busy.

We had had the same steam generators on the B&M F2's, although in a smaller size, and they had performed flawlessly. Apparently what was a reasonably good, if complicated, design had been overpowered by the increase in size plus the necessity of producing them in large quantities quickly. The plant had built 50 units for Southern and 16 for the Santa Fe with no letup, and the steam generator people just were not ready to go that far that fast.

At the time, Southern's passenger traffic still was running well over capacity and the equipment was in need of maintenance with which wartime operation had interfered. The result was that a passenger train seldom made its destination on time and frequently didn't even leave its point of origin on time. The track speed limits were slow, seldom over 55 mph, with several stretches of 35 mph owing to sharp curves. If the track speed limit didn't interfere, freight trains did. This was principally a single-track railroad, operated on train orders and automatic blocks, and it was not unusual to be carrying orders to "Run one-half hour (or 1 hour) late" because of congestion on the railroad. When you were called to cover a particular run, part of the routine was to be informed how late the train was running.

Most of the engine crews had little or no diesel experience, and indeed, some of the road foremen were not much better off. There were several things to be learned at once, and few of them were able to absorb all of it quickly. The first lesson that seemed to come very hard was that when the diesel throttle was closed for a station stop and the brakes applied, this action had to be taken considerably before the point where they were used to doing it with a Ps-4. Most engineers learned this lesson after having to whistle out a flag and back up a train length or so to the station once, but some of them repeated the same mistake three or four times. They always pointed out, loudly and vehemently, that they had applied the brakes just as hard, and at the same place, as they had done for years; they couldn't seem to understand that a 250-ton roller-bearing diesel did not offer the same resistance as a steam locomotive with the throttle closed.

Only once did this develop into what could have become a dangerous situation. Just beyond a station there was a grade crossing with another railroad, and a slow freight was crossing in front of us. The road foreman had his hand on the brake valve, ready to use emergency, but didn't have to—by about 30 feet.

The second lesson that came hard involved the automatic train stop the Southern utilized. To pass a yellow or red wayside signal, the engineer had to hold down an acknowledging switch in the cab, while a pickup device on the locomotive passed over an inductor mounted near the signal. If he did not do so, there was a penalty brake application which could not be released in time to avoid a complete stop. The pickup shoe on the diesels was on the first journal box, while on the Ps-4's it was on the rear box of the front tender truck—a difference of from 2 feet ahead of the engineer's location to maybe 8 feet behind him. Invariably they would wait too long the first time, and we'd be treated to an undesired stop, sometimes a little rough if the speed was low. Again, a few

had to have more than one lesson before they got the message.

None of these incidents made the changeover from steam to diesel any more pleasant, but as the steam generator problems came under control and the engineers learned to remember they were running a diesel, there came improvement in maintaining schedules. The dispatchers learned that just because other train movements had delayed a train a half hour or more, it was not essential to put out an order to keep it that way. If they would allow the train to make up the deficit, most of the time it could. The schedules were slow for the available power, and it was not hard to gain back even a half hour if need be, provided another train did not get in the way.

Things got positively dull for awhile, but one incident livened things up, at least for a few minutes. One of the other instructors had an assignment out of Atlanta one afternoon, and when he arrived at Terminal Station and boarded the locomotive, which was already on the train, he was surprised to find no one else around. The engines were idling, but the steam generators had not been fired up, or so he thought. What he subsequently found out, to his dismay, was that he had arrived only seconds after the fireman and the road foreman, who, after several unsuccessful attempts to fire up the steam generators, had gone off seeking assistance. The engineer was on board, but he and the instructor never did see one another as they both walked around the engine rooms apparently on opposite sides.

The instructor knew the steam generators should be running since departure time was close, so he went through all the proper procedures to start one of them. Not knowing of the previous attempts, he did not realize that the bottom of the firebox was full of sprayed-in fuel that had not ignited, apparently because the men had neglected some small but vital step in the procedure. The instructor did everything correctly, unfortunately, for the steam generator lit and almost immediately thereafter exploded as the fire he had started ignited the pool of fuel. The boiler's jacket blew off, the stack blew up high enough to hit the roof of the trainshed, and black, oily smoke rolled up the stairs into the passenger station. The instructor wound up with a black face, but he wasn't hurt and the damage was not extensive, for the train departed only a little late. But a valuable lesson had been learned—never

fire up a steam generator without first looking inside with a flashlight (not a fusee) to make sure the inside is dry.

Winter was fast approaching, so naturally the next move I made was north (it always seemed to work out that way, north in winter, south in summer). The Chicago & North Western was about to get some F3 A units it intended to couple to FT's to make three-unit sets, replacing the former four-unit FT's. As the B&M had done, North Western had discovered that four units was just too much for many trains, and some terrain, even when it was flat as on much of the C&NW. The units were put in service at Clinton, Ia., and each time two F3's were ready, an FT set was cut off, split in two, and an F3 put with each half. The sets ran between Chicago and Council Bluffs, Ia.

The North Western crews were no strangers to diesels, having had not only the FT's but several varieties of passenger units for a number of years. So it took the crews only a short time to become familiar with the minor differences between FT and F3 controls, and they were off and running. The fireman was the biggest beneficiary, since the F3 took care of its own cooling problems. It had electrically driven cooling fans in the roof which were automatically started and stopped by engine cooling water temperatures. On the other hand, the FT had hand-controlled shutters and fans, belt-driven from a gearbox driven by the engine. As the engineer demanded more power, the engine needed more cooling, and the fireman had to manually open shutters and clutch in one or both fans, as needed, to keep the engine at the right temperature. When the engineer shut off, the fans had to be stopped and the shutters closed to keep the engine from getting too cold. On a subzero day, he had to be fast on his feet to adjust three or four units quickly after the engineer shut off to keep the radiators from freezing. He didn't always make it, either. The North Western had applied air cylinders, temperature controlled, to the shutters and was experimenting with air cylinders to control the fan clutches, but the latter was not yet successful so the firemen still were getting their exercise. The only complaint from them was that when the F3 was in the lead, they had to walk through it to get to the FT's.

On this job, we instructors got to see some really high speed freight-train handling. North Western's track was in excellent shape, and with no grades

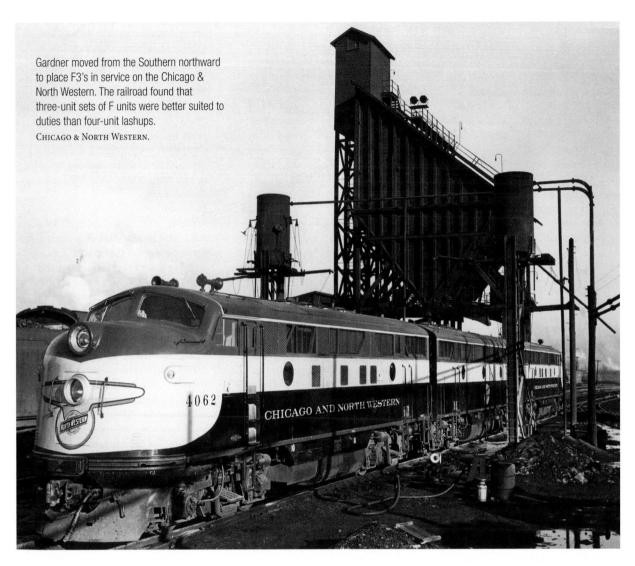

Gardner moved from the Southern northward to place F3's in service on the Chicago & North Western. The railroad found that three-unit sets of F units were better suited to duties than four-unit lashups. CHICAGO & NORTH WESTERN.

worthy of remark, it was not difficult to get a train well over 50 mph and frequently over 60. The one exception was if a heavy cross wind was blowing across the flat prairie country. It was amazing to me how much increased drag such a wind would cause to a train, pulling the speed down perhaps as much as 10 mph. Usually the wind would die down or stop at dusk, and train speed would pick up instantly.

This main line of the North Western was a double-track railroad with many passenger trains, C&NW then being the eastern connection for Union Pacific's Overland Route. Fortunately for freight trains, the varnish was bunched into a relatively brief period, so the name of the game was speed and to keep far enough ahead of any following passenger train so the dispatcher didn't put you in a siding for it to pass. If he did so, you seldom were able to leave before three or four trains passed, and no one enjoyed looking at the same scenery for 2 or 3 hours, especially when the scenery wasn't really worth a first glance (prairie and communication

line poles soon lose their attraction). The dispatcher tended to call freights only if he thought they could get to the end of the division ahead of the passenger fleet, and unless you ran into bad luck you usually could make it. I was never stuck with a long wait in a siding, but some of my fellow instructors talked about theirs, caused by a stuck brake or burst air hose.

One day I found out that EMD put a pad between design and actual requirements. I was aboard an F3 in Clinton on the way to the yard to pick up our train when the electric fuel pump, which keeps the engine supplied with fuel, lost its motor in a cloud of evil-smelling smoke. Clinton did not have an F3 pump motor but did have a complete pump and motor for a yard switcher. With some misgivings, we applied it to the F3, wondering if it would be able to keep up with the demands of the 16-cylinder engine (it was intended to supply only a 12-cylinder one). We had no trouble, and when I left the C&NW five or six weeks later, the small pump still was running.

While I was on this job in the early part of 1947, one of the blizzards frequent to the part of the country came along, taking down several miles of line wires as well as interrupting power supplies to many of the smaller communities. Several days passed before all the damage could be repaired, and in the interim there were long stretches of main line where the cab signals were inoperative. Since the North Western had no lineside signals between interlockings, this meant you had to cross the inoperative sections at no more than 15 mph or suffer a penalty brake application. This was an inconvenience that annoyed everyone, but the line which ran south from Nelson, Ill., to Peoria and St. Louis had a worse problem.

This line still was being operated with steam engines, mainly hauling coal north and empties south. It was a single-track railroad with only one long passing siding, about halfway between Nelson and Peoria. At the siding was a water tank where the steamers normally filled their tanks, in both directions. After the storm, the power that ran the tank's pumps was out for several days, and it wasn't long before the crew of a steam engine on a northbound train found the tank empty. They had enough water to make it to Nelson running light, so they left their train in the siding and did just that. The next train, a southbound, found the same amount of water in the tank—none—but also found no siding on which to leave the cars. With little choice, the crew left their train on the main and ran light to South Pekin, the terminal near Peoria, while they still had enough water to do so. The net result was a plugged railroad.

I got the assignment of going with the diesel sent down to unsnarl the mess. By the time we got there, both trains had been sitting in the cold wind and blowing snow for about 24 hours, so they were down to ambient temperatures (about 5 below in bright sun, 15 below at night). Our orders were to bring both trains back to Nelson. We coupled onto the train on the main, and had a long wait to get the brake pipe charged, then pulled the train north clear of the siding. We then coupled to the train on the siding. It was just getting dark, and we had a real fight to get the air to the rear end. Air hose gaskets are prone to leak when they get very cold, and these were very cold. We pumped air into that train for over an hour before the conductor was satisfied that the dangerously low pressure we had at the rear end was all we were going to get and we might as well try to start up. Needless to say, with the cars as cold as they were and the blowing snow piled up around the trucks, it was not an easy start. We slipped down and had to take slack several times before all the cars started, and we made it back to Nelson but set no speed records. No one really cared about that, since we weren't at all sure we were going to be able to make a normal stop at all, owing to the leaky train line. But when it did come time to stop, we found it remarkably easy. The engineer shut off, and that train literally stopped before he could reach for the brake valve. That was a hard-rolling train; it never did warm up.

We were making Clinton our headquarters on this assignment, and one bright, cold day I got a call to deadhead to Chicago to bring a unit west. The next eastbound train was the *City of Denver,* so I took advantage of my pass with "cab privileges" stamped on it to hitch a ride on one of the old long-nosed *City of Denver* units. Aboard, I found that a prudent person did not leave the cab while the train was at high speed or when the throttle was wide open, since the combined velocity of the train and the cooling fans caused at least a 100-mph wind speed in the engine room. This, plus the low outside temperature (between 10 and 15 above zero that day), resulted in a wind-chill factor in the engine room that must have been somewhere around 30 below zero—very uncomfortable and probably dangerous.

The engineer told me a story as he braked for the 35-mph curve at West Chicago, and I was happy he related rather than demonstrated it to me. The Streamliner trains were equipped with an early type electric brake system. When the engineer wanted brakes and moved the automatic brake valve handle to application position, he could get as much, or as little, brake as he desired on the entire train instantly, and simultaneously on all cars. Release was just as fast and easy—no waiting for the train line to exhaust, no sequential application from front to back, and no delay to recharge the train line when releasing. All this combined to make train-handling a pleasure—when it worked. There was a little box on top of the brake valve with a steady green light proclaiming all circuits were intact. A red light replaced the green if anything interrupted the circuits, warning the engineer he had to throw a changeover valve and go back to ordinary automatic air operation.

About three trips back, the engineer said, just as he moved the valve to apply the brakes for that West Chicago curve, traveling at 70 mph, the green light went out and the red light came on. He knew he was in trouble. By the time he had the changeover valve thrown, the curve was behind the train instead of ahead of it and he had violated the speed restriction by about 100 percent. Fortunately, no damage was done except to the dignity of a few passengers when they found themselves plastered to the side bulkhead for a few seconds. Electric brakes never did become widely used, and this problem may have been a principal reason.

Spoiling the stories about north in winter and south in summer, my next assignment took me to Tucson, Ariz., for an F3 delivery to the Southern Pacific. We covered the run between Tucson and Lordsburg, N. Mex., which was mostly straight and only mildly hilly, with a couple of tough grades. The worst was at San Simon (san si-MOAN), Ariz., where helpers were required even though we had four-unit sets of road engines. I don't recall, if I ever knew, what the SP classed the helpers, but they were small, low-drivered Ten-Wheelers. Usually, two helped all trains both directions, since the route was down into the valley and up to the other side, no matter which direction you were going.

On one westbound trip, we had stopped, picked up our helpers, and started up the hill. Our low speed and high current told us the helpers not only weren't helping but maybe even had their brakes on. What the helper crews didn't know was that the chief road foreman of engines was aboard. He was a pleasant enough man when you were helping him, but it was also easy to see that he could be very tough if you weren't on his side. After instructing the engineer to stop and wait for him at the top of the hill, he dropped off the left side as we swung into a long, easy right-hand curve.

About the time we had moved another train length, and undoubtedly coincident with the time he swung aboard the first helper, there was all kinds of commotion from the rear end; steam and smoke high into the air, much exhaust noise, and a remarkable pickup in our speed. I could only guess at the conversation between the road foreman and the helper crews, for the chief had very little comment when he rejoined us, saying only something to the effect that there were now at least two engine crews who from now on would help when called for helper service.

Owing to traffic of this immediate postwar period, motive power of any kind was scarce, and when I got into Lordsburg one night I thought I must have made a wrong turn somewhere for there in the SP engine terminal was a Boston & Maine Berkshire. It turned out the SP had purchased 10 when the B&M got the F2 diesels I had helped put in service. It was quite a sight to watch those SP crews, who were accustomed only to oil-fired steam engines, try to make those Berks perform on the low-grade coal which was the only kind available there. The B&M engines seldom ran without a steam failure. Some later were converted to oil, I believe, although I never saw any.

One night I thought I was going to be a close-up witness to a head-on collision, but fortunately it didn't quite come off. We were headed west out of Lordsburg with orders to meet an eastbound at a station where there was a three-track, double-ended siding not long enough to take our train in one piece. We had just left about half our train in one of the tracks

A four-unit set of F3's heads a solid train of refrigerator cars on the Southern Pacific near Alhambra, Calif. The almost-new engines wear the original "black widow" paint scheme in this 1949 view. DONALD SIMS.

and were drifting up to the mainline switch, waiting for our almost-novice brakeman (he was making his third trip) to throw it, when the signal just beyond the switch went red, indicating the eastbound was getting close. The other half of our train still was back on the main, but too far back to affect the eastbound signals. The eastbound man, with an AC cab-forward articulated steam engine on the front and another helping on the rear, had a rather short train and was coming up the hill fast. Our brakeman, instead of waiting to flag the eastbound down, unlocked and threw the switch for the siding. Our engine crew hollered their heads off for him to throw it back, but he was too far away and the steam engine noise was too loud for him to hear us. The crew and I departed the diesel cab without further delay. The brakeman lit a fusee and patiently waited until the approaching train's crew could see it. When they did, they applied emergency air, and the stop was made with a few feet to spare. I don't think I've ever heard such an expert chewing-out as that brakeman got from both engine crews simultaneously.

From the SP, my next job, on the Erie, was a study in contrasts. We delivered 12 F3 units (the road's first strictly for freight service), four-unit sets numbered 706-708, in November 1947 to Marion, O., and the railroad ran them from there to Salamanca, N.Y., and back. In those days, the Erie

schedule still included several passenger trains, and since it was an all double-track railroad with few passing sidings, the objective was to run a one-speed railroad. The freights were run fast enough to get from one division point to the next without having to go in the hole for a passenger train, and we therefore covered about twice the distance as we had on the SP in the same time.

Riding along one night with one of the more experienced road foremen in the cab, I got a strange question from him. He had been around diesels longer than I, so when he asked me "Say, how do you drain water out of one of these things?" I could reply only by asking him what was back of such a question, since I was sure he knew well how to do that elementary chore. Then came what he really was asking.

"Oh, sure," he said, "I know how to drain one when it's standing up like this one, but what do you do when it's laying on its side and it's 10 below zero?" It seems someone had had a severe lapse of memory while running a four-unit FT the winter before, and had tried without success to take a 35-mph curve at 65. The fireman had been back in the engine room and the brakeman in the rear cab, so no one caught the engineer's error until it was too late and four units lay on their sides on top of what had been a small depot. Fortunately, it was the middle of the night and no one had been in the station, and the crew suffered only minor injuries. The

road foreman had been called to go drain the units before they froze up.

He solved the problem when he found a fire axe, cutting off all the hoses he could find. When the water stopped running out, he went back home, washed up, and went to bed. He had barely gotten back to sleep when an irate engine house foreman woke him up, wanting to know why he hadn't drained the cab heaters, which had frozen and burst. The road foreman was indignant. "Can you imagine that," he asked me. "I save four $20,000 engines, and he beefs about four lousy $30 cab heaters." The prices he quoted were about right for the time; they unfortunately no longer apply.

That same road foreman asked me and any of the other EMD men to watch for a practice he knew was going on, telling us that if we saw it to lecture the engineer in the strongest possible terms since it was a bad practice and very dangerous. A couple of trips later, I saw it. When the engineer got aboard, he went down into the unit's nose, got a fusee, and wedged it between the dead-man pedal and a projection on the brake valve so he no longer had to keep his foot on the pedal. I gave him the lecture, using the reasoning the road foreman had told me. The road foreman had pointed out that someday someone would forget to remove the block and it would end up in the rear cab when the set of units was headed the opposite direction without being turned (normal procedure).

The head brakeman usually rode the rear cab, and if that man accidently pushed the rear end doubleheading cock open with his foot, things were going to get serious the first time the brakes were needed. As fast as the engineer drew off air from the train line to apply the brakes, the rear cab brake valve would then charge the train line back up and there would be no brakes. This reasoning made no noticeable impression on the engineer other than to observe that the road foreman must have talked to me, and we left town.

The usual procedure at Meadville, Pa., a fuel stop, was to leave the train in the yard and proceed up a slight grade for about a half mile to the fueling station, where the incoming crew would get off. A hostler would move the units through the fueling process, the new crew would board, and the units would return to the train. On this trip, we stopped, cut off the train, and ran up to the fueling station. Just before we stopped, I left the cab and was walking around the engine rooms, looking things over. I felt the units stop and almost immediately start up again, in the opposite direction. Right after that, I heard someone yelling, so I stuck my head out a side door of the third unit, where I was, to see what was going on. We were rolling back toward the train at an ever-increasing speed, and the yelling I had heard was the engineer, who was running down the track after the units, trying to catch them and losing the race. By the time I realized I was alone on the locomotives, got to the cab, and applied the brakes, there was a disturbingly short distance to our train. It seems the engineer had forgotten to apply the independent brake when he got off, and with the deadman pedal held down by the fusee, which he also had forgotten, the units simply had rolled back down the hill.

After I stopped the units, the engineer, of course, caught up to them, badly out of breath and very red in the face. He climbed up, grabbed the fusee, and threw it out the door as far as he could. When he finally got his wind back, he shook his finger under my nose and yelled, "I'll never do that again, but not for the reason you gave me. I've got a better one!" He did, too.

One final incident worth talking about occurred during my job on the Erie. Coming west one night, we arrived at the B&O crossing (at grade) in Akron. B&O controlled the crossing, so the Erie board was always red, and this time was no exception. Our engineer had anticipated this, approaching as slowly as possible

consistent with getting a little run for the grade to be climbed just beyond the crossing. He waited as long as he dared with his left hand on the brake valve before applying the brakes, hoping the towerman would give us a board before we had to stop, and, just as the engineer predicted, the green came almost as soon as he started the brake application. He hollered at the fireman, "Should I try it?" and when the fireman responded, "Why not," he released the brakes. The danger now was that since only a very light reduction had been made before the release, it was possible that some of the brakes would not release fully and we'd wind up with dragging brakes.

The fireman and head brakeman both watched the train carefully as we crossed the B&O diamonds and started up the grade, on which the track curved to the left. About halfway up the hill they announced together that there was fire under the train, about 15 cars back—at least one car with sticking brakes. The engineer waited until we topped the short grade and made a heavy reduction, and then released again. This pulled our speed way down but did not stop us. Further inspections of the train, made on both sides, showed nothing out of line, and we thought we had it made.

Then up ahead, we saw a train-order board displaying "Stop." The Erie had position-light signals, the same as those used by Pennsy and N&W for all purposes, installed on the same mast with about every third block signal. These were controlled manually by the dispatcher, and their indication took precedence over the block signal indication. It was one of these that halted us.

After we came to a stop near the signal, the head brakeman walked to a phone box next to the signal, and after talking to the dispatcher for a few minutes, hung up and started back. As he did, the train-order signal went to "Proceed," and the engineer called in the flagman. Before he got the brakes released, however, and even before the head man had finished his explanation of the conversation with the dispatcher, the train-order signal went to "Stop" again. (The conversation revealed that a crossing watchman had reported dragging brakes. The brakeman responded that we knew it and had fixed it.)

The brakeman, muttering under his breath, took off once more for the phone, and the engineer whistled the flag back out. The brakeman returned from this conversation, saying that another watchman had reported we had torn up all

the boards at his crossing, and the dispatcher said no matter what we thought we had done to overcome the problem, we were to inspect the train before proceeding. The signal stayed at "Stop" this time.

Taking off toward the rear of the train, the brakeman made his inspection, and I went to the rear cab's fireman's seat, from where I could see him, the train being on a gentle curve to the right. It was just getting daylight, and I saw him go back about 15 cars, where he did a double-take look under a car, then got down on his hands and knees for a closer look. He got up and waved to the conductor, who was approaching from the rear. When he arrived, he repeated the brakeman's act, and there followed some pointing and arm-waving. Both men then came to the engine to talk.

It turned out that the lead right-hand wheel of an old refrigerator car was only about two-thirds there, one-third having left the train. This had apparently happened while the brakes were dragging, the heat either starting or aggravating a crack in the wheel. The brake beam and shoes had caught in the gap left by the missing portion, torn loose from the hangers, turned with the wheel until they jammed against the car floor, then stopped the wheel from turning. The missing third was now on top of the wheel and a 7- or 8-inch flat spot, caused by the wheel sliding, was on the bottom.

The conference, of course, concerned "What do we do now?" Consulting the employee timetable revealed there was an industrial siding about 3 miles farther west, with switches at both ends. The plan was to cut off behind the cripple, drag it carefully into the siding and leave it, then return to the rest of the train. The dispatcher was consulted and agreed.

The conductor asked the engineer if he could run s-l-o-w. I suggested taking three of the units off line to make it easier, and the engineer replied, "Yeah, why didn't I think of that." After gently backing up so the coupler pin could be pulled, the rest went easily, and it was just a matter of time—a lot of time—before our train was together again and we were off and running, everyone congratulating themselves and each other that we hadn't filled an adjacent field with our train.

On subsequent trips, I noted that the crippled car we set out sat in the siding for about three days, then was gone. A highway truck had been dispatched to replace the car's damaged truck, and a local freight picked up the car. After the SP incident, this was as close as I had come

Delivering several four-unit sets of F3's on the Erie led to an interesting question regarding draining water from a wrecked engine before it froze. It also resulted in a near-wreck involving a car with a broken wheel. S.K. BOLTON, JR.

and wanted to get to being involved in a wreck.

I didn't know it, but my locomotive-delivering days were coming to a close. After one more job, my assignment would change. My last delivery job was on the Delaware, Lackawanna & Western. It had received five A-B-A sets of passenger F3's, 801-805, just before Christmas 1947 and was of course in a hurry to get them in service for the forthcoming holiday traffic surge. They were to be used between the Lackawanna end points of Hoboken, N.J., and Buffalo, N.Y.

Some people undoubtedly know it, but I'll bet most don't, that the Lackawanna had the greatest variation in grade per mile of any standard-gauge line in the United States. Putting that another way, there were more ups and downs than you could see anywhere else, and on a relatively short railroad. You were either struggling to maintain speed on an upgrade or braking hard on a descent. The F3's had dynamic brakes, which were put to good use.

Dynamic brakes, incidentally, bring to mind a story having nothing to do with this F3 delivery except the railroad. About three years later, the Lackawanna bought some E8's for the same passenger service as the F3's, upgrading their better trains' equipment at the same time, but for some reason elected to not opt for dynamic brakes. This may have been because dynamics cut down the steam-generator water capacity since an extra water tank could occupy space taken by the dynamic brake equipment. Passenger service started to decline about the time the E8's went into service, though, and as the trains got shorter and lighter it became necessary to use the locomotive brakes more and more on those hills and the Lackawanna ended up with an epidemic of thermal cracked wheels that caused a lot of research into wheel metallurgy before it was solved.

Back to the F3's, which was a fairly uneventful delivery until one week just before Christmas, when (you readers who lived in that area will know what's coming) it began to snow, and snow, and snow.

When the snow stopped, the wind blew and temperatures turned very cold. New York City was tied up tight, Buffalo was buried, and everything in between looked all the same—white.

The Lackawanna kept on running, but not on time. Drifts would be plowed out only to drift shut again in a few hours. Water hoses froze, and it would take hours instead of minutes to water locomotives and cars. Big chunks of ice gathered around the slightest steam leak on a train, and sometimes those big chunks would break off, damaging something (usually the steam connectors between cars). When that happened, we stopped at the next station and hoped people there could fix it, since not only was it uncomfortably cold for passengers behind the break point but a real mess if a car froze up, which didn't take long in that weather.

An unusual occurrence happened at Hoboken on the night the snow was at its worst. I was riding in from the engine house with the engine crew, and just as we came out of the short tunnel leading to the station, we could see a switcher laboriously putting our train together. All the lights on the signal bridge where the station tracks begin to fan were red, so we stopped and watched. Every time a switch was thrown, it had to be swept out first so the points would go over all the way. The switcher finally finished and went off to other chores, but all the lights stayed red. The crew remarked that we ought to get a yellow so we could go in and couple to our train, but nothing obvious happened.

After sitting for perhaps 10 minutes, the fireman got up and put on a heavy jacket, went into the engine room and got a broom, and climbed down. The engineer and I watched this curiously, but nothing was said until after he was gone, when the engineer said, "Wonder what he's up to." We could see the fireman, about 15 feet ahead of the locomotive, poking around in the snow with the handle end of the broom.

After a couple dozen exploratory pokes, he seemed to find something, for he reversed the broom and started sweeping. In due time (the snow was about 4 feet deep), he cleared away enough snow so we could see a dwarf signal. It was yellow! He plowed his way back to the cab, and the engineer said he should have told him what he was up to, for he would have helped. The fireman replied that he wasn't sure the dwarf signal was there and didn't want to make a fool of himself asking for help in finding something that did not exist.

Gardner's last job for EMD was delivering sets of passenger-service F3's to the Lackawanna. Here a three-unit set from that delivery is pulling the *Twilight* at Morristown, N.J., in the early 1950s. HOMER R. HILL.

The snow was deep all the way to Scranton that night, deep enough so the pilot was plowing it up constantly, throwing it in all directions. It was impossible to see wayside signals—all you could see was blowing white stuff. The cab signals, useful at any time, were especially comforting that night, for without them we would have had to slow to a crawl so the blowing snow would not interfere with observing the signals. The constant attempt to look through the snow made me dizzy and after a while I had to stop looking. When we got to Scranton, I asked the crew if they were similarly affected and both of them admitted they were, but they had said nothing thinking they were becoming ill and not wanting to worry their partner.

When the snow stopped and it turned cold, a new problem cropped up—frozen controls on the steam generators. I got a good taste of this on a trip from Scranton to Buffalo. We were about halfway there when the sun went down, and the temperature with it. This was our first experience with the new steam generators in cold weather, and it was not good. The automatic controls were almost all mounted up high on the machine, close to the blast of cold air that the engine and radiator fans were sucking in through the side screens. Since they were actuated by steam pressure and water level by means

of small steam and water lines, it didn't take a strong current of 10-below-zero air long to freeze them up. That was the end of automatic control.

Manual operation had to be resorted to, with the fireman taking charge of the lead unit and I the rear one. This maneuver kept the steam supply up where it belonged, but since we were not nearly as responsive as the automatic controls were, we used a great deal more fuel and water—particularly the latter. It became obvious we were not going to make Buffalo on our water supply, as planned, so a message for help was thrown off at the next open office and we made an unscheduled stop for water at a little town up the line, where a crew of men had been alerted to man the pumps. That got us to Buffalo, but the same action was required on the return trip.

Scranton shops, of course, knew of our problem, and by the time we got back the men there had made up some wind-shield sheet-metal plates to cover the controls and were preparing to apply steam tracer lines to the control piping. These were simply copper tubing wrapped around the pipes to be protected, after which both were wrapped with insulating tape. Steam was allowed to flow through the tracer lines all the time, keeping the control lines warm enough so they would not freeze even when there was no flow through

them. Things settled down to normal after that, and of course it never got cold enough again to really matter. One of Murphy's laws probably covers that, too.

The Lackawanna job was my last delivering locomotives, and I was scheduled to start on an office job when it was over. It was an interesting time to be on such a job, for most railroads had little experience in diesel operation and maintenance then, and many unexpected problems showed up. Operating and shop crews had yet to learn how to get the most out of their new equipment, and many of them were yet to be convinced that steam was really gone forever. There were a few dull moments when things went so well there wasn't much for us to do, but not nearly so many as the moments when the choice of what to do first had to be made.

After my Lackawanna job, riding on locomotives for me would be for specific purposes, such as looking for the answers to a known problem, and more often than not on locomotives that had been in service for some time. The job was just as interesting, but in a different way. Fewer surprises took place, as the problem area usually was well defined before we started, but frequently the answers would come from unexpected sources.

But that's another story.

The mud hop— dark passageways, moonless nights

By W.M. Adams
Yard Clerk

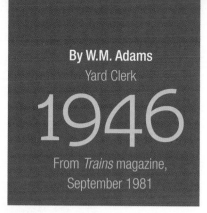

1946

From *Trains* magazine,
September 1981

"The waybill reads Pee-Mickey [Pittsburgh, McKeesport & Youghiogheny] 90099, not 90999, so just step out there and verify it." The "step" is a good hundred yards away through a cold, driving March rain.

You are trying to "set" No. 72, also known as the Meat Train, and the outbound desk clerk has refused to take your train check. You argue with him a little. "Well, it's nothing but an empty home-route gon—what's all the big deal?"

"Waybill reads 90099. I'll hold the bills until you verify it, or would you rather talk to the GYM?" Having no desire to talk to the general yardmaster, you struggle into your G.I. raincoat, pull on your gum boots, and take off. Delaying No. 72 is just not done, at least by a lowly "mud hop." At the very least, you would expect to get a dressing down by the GYM or a scathing note from the chief clerk; worse would be an invitation to join in a function in the office of the assistant superintendent. Such functions were to be avoided. No refreshments would be served, and the bulk of the conversation would be with you and about you, and little, if any, of it would be complimentary. L. W. Baldwin, long-time president of the Missouri Pacific, had decreed that clerks' work was "unproductive," and so the fewer on the property, the better he liked it.

A yardmaster could misfigure, an engine foreman could put out a bum "tab" on a cut to be handled, a dispatcher and his minions could mishandle train orders, but let the 5 a.m. report show a redball freight train delayed for waybills, and all hell would break loose. At least, that was the way your old-time yard clerk saw it.

Your old-time yard clerk, or mud hop, is just about a thing of the past in today's computerized-railroad scene. No more does the yard clerk stand out on the lead with a switchlist and a No. 1 pencil trying to keep up with a pair of hard-working yard goats. No more does he fight rain or sleet or hail or snow, trying to keep his switchlists legible enough so he can read them to the inside desk clerks who assemble the waybills and prepare other documents they needed to run a train. No more does he, soon after a moonless midnight, have to traverse dark passageways littered with offal and steel bands and twisted wire and broken boxes, with who knows what lurking behind the next dismal turn, checking all the cars in the industries in a designated portion of a large terminal. (Well, he did have his lantern for protection, if need be; a full arm swing with a heavy lantern could be very discouraging. Really, although there was plenty of imagined terror, there was little actual danger, for in over 30 years' experience, I can recall only one instance in our area of a yard clerk being assaulted and robbed.)

Such car-checking, at least on the Missouri Pacific, is no longer necessary. Or let us say it is not done, having been superceded by an elaborate system working out of a computer in a manner an old-time yard clerk would have scornfully referred to as "radio checking." In theory this system is workable and, once the machinery is paid for, cheaper, for you eliminate a host of car-checkers. Mr. Baldwin would be ecstatic!

Thirty years ago, we might—just might—have two or perhaps three "no-bill" cars in our hold tracks at North Little Rock, Ark. (A no-bill is a car separated from its waybill, a car you have to hold until the missing papers turn up or a copy of them is furnished by a reliable source.) Today, no-bills are a way of life. I will say that the computer, provided it has not "crashed," will give you the billing instructions on a mishandled car in a matter of seconds or minutes. I suppose today you can work out a 50-car track of junk as quickly as we dug up the running dope on just a couple of cars in 1946. Progress.

All the brainwork of mud-hopping on the Missouri Pacific at North Little Rock 35 years ago was carried out in a dark, gloomy, wooden structure built in 1872 just west of the crossing of the old Little Rock & Fort Smith and the Cairo & Fulton Railroads, both of which had been part of the glamorous old St. Louis, Iron Mountain & Southern, absorbed by the MoPac in 1917. In this old, high-ceilinged

structure were the haunts of the general yardmaster and his assistant, the desk clerks (inbound and outbound), the wheel clerks, and the chief caller. The latter had as his or her assistant a callboy (who might be three-score years old), and this pair summoned trainmen and switchmen to their duties (enginemen were tolled off by the engine dispatcher a half mile to the west at the roundhouses). Off in his own bay-windowed office was the telegraph operator. Everyone shared a common room, although the chief caller was fenced in in his corner.

Just in front of the building was the double-track main of the Arkansas Division, as well as the high line to the roundhouses. Well over a hundred engines, mostly coal burners, passed this spot every 24 hours, so to say it was dirty was putting it mildly. At the bottom of the office hierarchy was Henry, the porter. Henry was always busy but actually did little more than sweep floors and empty spittoons and wastebaskets several times a day. Had he tried to wash the windows he probably would have been cited for a formal investigation.

Today, in this era of winking, blinking supercharged computers housed in a sterile, air-conditioned office, with the hired help in comfortable, overstuffed chairs, and with drapes on the windows and carpets on the floors, it is hard to visualize the stark simplicity of a yard office 35 years ago. The only reasonably modern items in it were a row of teletype machines and a plentiful supply of telephones. Where we now find late-model photocopy machines that digest more than 150 cartons of paper every month, there was the gelatin copy table. If you wanted extra copies of a wheel report or switch lists, you made them out with an indelible ribbon or pencil, then went over to this monster and reproduced your works of art. You might get a dozen legible copies.

The shanties on the yard leads contained little more than a shelf-like desk built against a wall, with a "dummy" telephone and headset for the clerk and a regular phone for the yardmaster. Both phones had an amplified buzzer on the outside wall so that the GYM or the outbound desk clerk could summon you

from afar. A stove and a couple of chairs, along with a moss-covered coffee pot, completed the furnishings. The decor was plenty of grime. Outside was a bench for the switchmen to catch their breath on and, if "on spot" for any length of time, to whittle on.

It was an unwritten law, at least on the MoP at North Little Rock, that no one, and I mean no one, occupied a yard clerk's chair when he was away. You might be gone for an hour checking up on your rails, but when you came in, your chair and your phone would be waiting for you. The GYM and the outbound clerk probably were both looking for you, wondering what took you so long—you were always behind.

As yard clerk, you had to work with various engine foremen, and a contrary, hard-bitten foreman could make life miserable for you. The good ones would give you a "tab" on what they were handling, and most of them would give you their list when they finished working a cut. You had to check cars moving 15 or more mph regardless of weather, so oftimes you would just put down the

Here's how the Missouri Pacific's Hole Yard lead at North Little Rock, Ark., looked in March 1921. The Fort Smith crossing is in the foreground, with the yard office at right and shops and roundhouses in the distance. MISSOURI PACIFIC; COLLECTION OF CLIFTON E. HULL.

numbers and finish out the lists by referring to the one the foreman was using. Otherwise, you would have to take off down the tracks and match them up the hard way.

On the MoP, we had "hard" switchlists that would take considerable moisture, but when you had one of those toad-strangling downpours, you would slip over to the car inspectors' shanty and dip your lists in a bucket of kerosene. As you can imagine, this made for a greasy, smelly mess, and the initials and numbers you would write down would be faint almost to the point of being illegible. But, bring the lists inside, separate them, and let a little heat get to them to dry them out, and they became perfectly legible! Then all you had to do was get your hands clean. I often wondered how mud hops on really hard-weather roads, say the Bangor & Aroostook, got the job done.

Your old-time telegraph operator has been held up as a model of perfection in the art of penmanship, but most of your old mud hops didn't do so badly either. And your mud hop did the bulk of his writing on a narrow, thin board, usually while walking briskly or while cars were sailing by, in all kinds of weather conditions not conducive to neatness. We did have one old yard clerk, known as "Lightning," at North Little Rock who turned out an almost illegible scrawl. He was left-handed, but that was probably not the reason. I dreaded following him because I just could not decipher his scribblings, and when I was called to relieve him, I would show up early to check his lists so I could at least partially understand what he had put down. In spite of his dismal writing, old Lightning was always up with the engines and never missed a car. His numbers and initials were always right; your only problem was figuring them out.

In the interest of speed, mud hops abbreviated cars' reporting marks. At North Little Rock, we used AT for ATSF, E for Erie, F for SLSF, M for CMStP&P, and W for Wabash. When I went to work and found out how much this simplified car-checking, I wondered why they hadn't gone a step further and used P for Pennsylvania and S for Southern, both well-known lines with large quantities of cars. Yes I tried to put the P's and S's in use and was promptly slapped down by the older heads. I'm still trying to figure that one out.

I am sure all roads had at least one character who allegedly had a photographic memory and could stand on the lead, watch an engine hammer out a cut, and then go in and bring his tracks up to date from a built-in human computer. We had a couple of these mental giants on the MoP, and I served under one in Texas. I was told about his reputed ability when I arrived in the Lone Star State, and I was suitably impressed, but unfortunately I never witnessed this amazing talent. At the time, he was a general manager and I remember him chiefly for his propensity to ask a staggering number of what to me were unrelated and unanswerable questions.

At North Little Rock, the two red-hot yard-clerk jobs were the Hole Lead and the Locust Street Lead—they kept you tripping over your tongue. We had a job on the south end of the Hole Yard that was on-again, off-again; if business fell anyplace on the railroad, the job would be pulled off and the lead job would work both ends and the middle. Luckily, the yard was built on a sweeping curve, so you could take a short-cut back and forth across the chord when you were really in a hurry.

I worked the south end now and then, when the job was on, but didn't really care for it because it was so dirty. The shanty was just across the main tracks from the coal chute, cinder pits, and roundhouses, and at any one time there would be 30 to 40 engines pouring out their pollutants. Some present-day environmentalists would have had palpitations if they had had to even drive by what we took for granted 35 years ago.

Conversely, the north end of the Locust Street Yard was a lonely place a good mile and a half from the heavy, or south, end and could only be reached by walking or riding a switch engine. I worked this job frequently and liked it. You could, within reason, set your own pace, and on the 11:30 p.m. shift you got to see (and hear!) the *Sunshine Specials* in six or more sections tearing the night apart. Coming south, these magnificent 16-car trains would have just left the Tie Plant curve after having braked from 75 mph or faster down to the legal 60 for the curve, and the old hoggers would have the trains stretched out. The big 5300-series Mountain type would be chuckling, the oil fire flashing, sparks still rimming all wheels of the dark green Pullmans. The northbound 'Shines would be working from right down in the corner with a wide-open throttle getting up to maximum speed. Usually the firemen would start "dusting" (sanding) their flues at about the Cotton Belt connection, a short distance south of the shanty. Black smoke would be erupting from the stacks in greasy waves. All sections were identified on the back by bravely lit red-and-gold tailsigns. My wife still insists I would have paid the Missouri Pacific just for the privilege of witnessing this spectacle every night.

It was a sad night when diesels took over and very nearly was my last one. The first time No. 2 came out of Little Rock with diesel power, I was working the north end of Locust Street and had been down around the curve. I was returning between the two main tracks when No. 2 came around the curve behind the new engines, which were, of course, relatively silent. I did some scrambling and cursing. Sure, the "figure 8" headlight was working, but my back was to it. That encounter may be the reason I never fell head over heels in love with diesels.

In 1952, the Hole Yard was abandoned for classification; it now is the site of MoPac's welded-rail plant. Locust Street Yard was expanded to 30 long tracks, and a fine brick yard office was built. The new building didn't make life much easier for the mud hops, though; it took several more years of technology to get them out of the mud. In 1961, an ultra-modern retarder-classification hump yard was placed in service at North Little Rock, and today when you make any required car side-checks you drive to the scene in an air-conditioned company sedan! Sure, you walk the cut, with a walkie-talkie strapped to your hip in case the YM wants you. But no one is crowding you; you have all day. Today anybody can walk a rail and check it, or so it would seem, although if you listen to a hump-engine fireman swearing while trying to sort out one of these "easy money" checks, you will wonder.

Your old-time mud hop learned the job on his own time and longed for enough seniority to (1) hold down an inside desk job and (2) hold down a daylight job anywhere. Today, with sophisticated machinery at his fingertips to keep records on cars and trains, the railroad clerk has been fished out of the mud and dried off. Instead of being a semiskilled worker, sort of an educated laborer, he is a craftsman. On the Missouri Pacific, every new Transportation Department clerk, regardless of previous experience, must take a nine-week detailed training program in St. Louis and at his home terminal. And, they're paid a weekly stipend to go to school! I wonder what Mr. Baldwin would think.

"Fireboy, we don't fit through that bridge."

By Lloyd Arkinstall
Fireman

1940s

From *Trains* magazine,
March 1977

I'm reminded of an incident which has always led me to marvel at the hypercaution on the part of compilers of special instructions in employees' timetables.

On this particular day on the Pennsy's New York Division 30-odd years ago, I had been ordered to fire the westbound Waverly hump job. C1's were used on this job: The 8-wheeled switchers were huge barrel-chested brutes with, as I recall, some 78,000 pounds of rated tractive force. Their main- and side-rod structure was so massive that the counterbalancing very nearly reduced their driving wheels to what seemed to be slab discs. Their stack resembled a sawed-off ash can, and their cylinders might have come off the fat end of a marine compound.

It was an occasional practice to use them in pusher service in boosting road jobs out onto the main. The road job, usually with an M1 4-8-2 on the head end, would come in from either the Meadows or Greenville over the Bay Line with perhaps 75 cars and would pick up a string of possibly 50 more at Waverly. In situations of this sort, the hump job would be sent out to couple onto the rear of the road cabin, with the switcher cutting out his double-heading cock. On signal, the C then would push the slack up against the train and wait for the road engine to pull. The outgoing route was upgrade and was more involved with turnouts in the Lane interlocking than a spastic snake. The C1's exhaust in normal yard use was kind of a deep husky chuff. However, once the C1 was under way behind the road job, that exhaust took on a chesty operatic boom which, temporarily at least, gave the yard crew delusions of grandeur.

On this particular day, we accomplished the routine I've described; but the man at the head end must have been having his problems, because at the hind end we were blasting away and still didn't have much of a swing on the train. We pushed farther west than I had been before in a switcher.

We had shoved through the McClellan Avenue girder bridge and on past the coffin works before the flagman finally came out, closed the angle cock on the hack, and signaled us for slack so that he could get the pin up with the cutting lever. Once cut off, we of course went into emergency on the brakes and ground to a stop. I slid down, ran around to the front, closed the angle cock, and returned to the cab. I noticed that my engineman had taken out his employees' timetable and was riffling through the special instructions section.

After jogging back to the yard limits, we halted at the approach to the McClellan Avenue girder bridge, for no apparent reason that I could discern. My engineman held up the employees' timetable almost like a testament.

"Fireboy, know something?" he said. "We don't fit through that bridge." Well, he put the timetable back into his seatbox reverently and, throwing all caution to the wind, we proceeded home.

Authority assumes many guises. In the military, stripes and uniform insignia keep the pecking order vertical. Around a railroad installation in the Forties, spotting middle management was a far simpler if less definitive sport. Back then, from spring to fall, the appearance of a Panama hat on the horizon would send crews scurrying for their safety rulebooks and calendars.

Safety calendars were issued monthly, and each day was suitably keyed to some particular canon in the safety rulebook. (The recurrence of a safety rule on the calendar was determined by the rule's pertinence. A frequent repeater might read, "The use of the foot to adjust coupler-knuckle alignment on a car in motion is prohibited"—a rule which struck me as a pillar of wisdom.) The man in the Panama often employed the safety-rule-of-the-day query as an opening gambit with crewmen. When so approached, even senior enginemen complied with the query readily enough, for the Panama hat signified an Assistant Road Foreman of Engines.

Not all old enginemen responded according to script, however; some crusty shellbacks, crowding the pension age, would bristle when asked the safety-rule number for the day and would snap, "All of 'em!" Now such a reply put the interrogator on a bit of a spot, for the Assistant RFE, being an engineman himself on detached duty, in all probability had fired at one time (and perhaps not too well) for the rebellious patriarch. The Assistant RFE usually withdrew with one last menacing frown at the veteran's grinning fireman.

One prominent wearer of the official Panama—and one not to be cowed by such as the foregoing—was Assistant Road Foreman MacLeod. I recall MacLeod on one warm spring afternoon, standing in the doorway of the Waverly pit foreman's office, longing for an employee safety transgression to set aright. At the time, I was firing the engine-change job, which shuttled serviced engines out to three-trick yard jobs. The pit, which nestled in the lee of the eastbound hump, contained in addition to the actual ash pit the coaling chute, the sand house, and three or more ready tracks. The pit trackage, since it was in a slight depression, required an engine to brake a good deal on entry from the inbound lead. My engineman, who had recently returned to duty after a long hospitalization from a collision which had killed his fireman, would usually remain in the crew room until I had livened up the banked fire, set the lubricator, loaded ice and drinking water, checked the fire tools, inspected the flagging equipment, and finally lined up the railroad.

As frequently was the case, the H9 2-8-0 I had readied was blocked by another locomotive, this time a freshly hostled L1 Mikado facing my engine on the same ready track. Acutely conscious of MacLeod's unblinking surveillance, I threw the switch lining up my ready track with the inbound lead. I then boarded the heavy Mikado, made an impressive show of checking clearances from both gangways, turned on the bell, and took the Mike, with cylinder cocks hissing, lumbering back up the slight incline onto the lead.

Once again I dismounted—being sure to climb down in company-approved fashion facing the engine rather than sliding down the tank grab iron—and realigned the railroad for another ready track almost directly in front of the Panama hat. Ringing the bell, and with a commendable show of vigilance, I eased the L1 forward down the incline. I applied the independent brake in ample time—but nothing happened; the brute was slowly accelerating toward the tank of a C1! A wild swipe at the automatic brake dumped her; but alas, too late. Our fetch-up against the 0-8-0 rivaled the climax of the "Anvil Chorus."

In the ensuing silence, broken only by the soft trickle of coal sifting over the coal gates behind me, I centered the Johnson bar, returned the automatic brake handle to the running position, reapplied the gummed-up independent, and with reluctance climbed down to examine our pilot. The opposing coupler knuckles had mated like a fraternal handclasp and, but for a bit of displaced grime, all was sound.

Since I had to walk directly past MacLeod to enter the crew room, I hitched up my overalls and braced myself for a pungent stricture. MacLeod stood with what appeared to be a fistful of pasteboards until I drew abreast, then rasped from beneath his Panama, "Fireboy, have you this month's ticket to the Brotherhood Women's Auxiliary Raffle?"

"No, but I'll take three!" I blurted cravenly.

To this day, the origin of the term "dunnigan"—meaning a trackside shack or shelter—eludes me. These dunnigans were

"The hapless motorist panicked, reversed, roared back out from under the gate, and collided with two other cars before coming to rest."
Illustration: Lloyd Arkinstall.

mostly crude lean-tos or dugouts, but there were all sorts of variations. Muldoon, the engine cutoff man at Rahway Junction, N.J., had a little foul-weather cubicle that practically required his getting into the prenatal position to enter. At Waverly yard, the car knockers had made an elongated three-sided hutch down by the "time bein'" track. The open side, away from the prevailing wind, looked out on a "salamander," or fire barrel. On winter nights, the bulkily clad car knockers huddling in the glow of the fire barrel would resemble Van Gogh's Borinage miners. The dunnigan up on the summit of the hump nearby was company built and was snug enough. In it the hump brakemen nurtured a 24-hour poker game like the eternal flame. Moreover, for the warm summer months, the more enterprising of the car droppers had fashioned themselves an adjacent roofed patio from 4x4's and corrugated sheet metal. This they humbly christened the Coconut Grove.

But the dunnigan of all dunnigans, without peer, was "Stifler Tower" on the Greenville (N.J.) yard waterfront. It was an elegant structure in which a tall man could stand erect providing he was wearing a low-crowned hat. And it was constructed almost entirely of old refrigerator-car doors, which, of course, made it a monument to insulation. Its interior appointments were strictly luxury caboose, from stove and icebox to the cushions. It had been built and had been added to over a period of years by Tiny Stifler, an old yard conductor who lived in nearby Greenville and who from time immemorial had conducted 194C, the midnight trick of the departure yard makeup job. Some waggish trainman with a bent for handicraft had fashioned a Pennsylvania keystone tower nameboard and carefully lettered STIFLER on the Tuscan-red board for "Stifler Tower," naming it after Tiny, the elderly builder.

Tiny had two life drives: playing the horses and collecting junk. Shortly before midnight every evening, with the regularity of the solar system, old conductor Tiny could be seen shuffling across the Garfield Avenue bridge and into the yard towing an empty child's express wagon. With the changing of the crews, Tiny would hoist his empty express wagon onto the pilot of the waiting H9 and the new crew would clank off down the yard toward Stifler Tower and the night's work. In the morning light the process would be

reversed; only this time Tiny would shuffle across the Garfield Avenue bridge lugging a heavily laden wagon. It was his gleaning of the evening.

The years passed, but Tiny's zeal for junk collecting and horse playing never diminished. The junk collecting had been quietly rewarding. However, the horse playing was another matter. Tiny's winnings had always been trifling and sporadic. Finally one day an incredible long shot, upon which he had banked a sizable sum, came in. But this proved Tiny's final undoing. For the bookie from whom he was to have collected his princely sum dematerialized. The traumatic effect of this incident sent poor Tiny round the bend, never to return. I often wonder if Stifler Tower still stands and if some latter-day wag substituted the intertwined-noodle emblem of the PC for the dignity of the Tuscan keystone.

Before the Penn and the Jersey Central had dieselized their power on the New York & Long Branch Railroad, there were track pans at Branchport, N.J., which was between Little Silver and Long Branch. However, these were fair-weather rigs that had no provision for heating. Consequently, with the nearing of fall freeze-up, the pans were drained and shut down. There were standpipes at both Long Branch and Red Bank. By the mid-Forties, all the Penn K4's assigned to the Long Branch were equipped with the 11,000-gallon tanks. Winter trains on the Long Branch for the most part ran light in consist, with the exception of the Sunday evening New York-bound jobs, on which they would really hang a train.

On one bleak and cold January Sunday evening, I was working the northbound 788 out of Bay Head with my regular engineer, Ralph Eastman. Ralph had the reputation of being a slick runner. Now to the casual listener, "slick runner" may have a flip sound; however, at the time it was praise indeed. It meant that an engineman could get the maximum performance out of an engine with maximum economy of steam. His valve cutoff was always reasonable, which endeared him to firemen. And it goes without saying that he was at one with the air brake. Since we had a heavy train and were going straight through to Rahway, Eastman decided to play it cozy. He told me we would take on a rod or two of water at the Red Bank plug. (At the time, we used to measure the tank content roughly by the relationship of

the water to the horizontal stays in the tank. Since three of these usually were visible from the open manhole, we'd say we had a top, middle, or bottom rod of water. Of course, because of the displacement of the coal bunker, the lower rod readings were considerably greater in quantity.)

We left Bay Head on time and kept so all the way up the coast. Somewhere in the vicinity of Elberon snow began to fall heavily, and it increased in intensity as we went north. The plug at Red Bank was at the north end of the platform, so situated that when you had the tank perfectly spotted, a part of the engine was just abreast of the gearbox of the crossing gate. Since the plug swiveled horizontally, a spot had to be perfect or the plug would foul on the high bunker of those 11,000-gallon tanks. Eastman set her down right on the spot first try. I went up over the coal, which by now was covered with snow; opened the manhole cover; and pulled the plug around. From my high perch, I had a good view of the crossing and the street below. The snow looked thick and wet in our headlight beam ahead. Through the half-opened coal gate I could see Eastman below puttering with the fire, good fellow that he was.

I was watching the plug when suddenly above the blower hiss from the stack I heard an odd scraping sound. I looked ahead, and there in our headlight and directly in front of our pilot was an automobile two-thirds across the rails in front of us, with the crossing gate resting on top of its roof. This chap had slid under the gate; the gate had followed the contour of his hood up the streamlined windshield; and by the time he had got stopped, the gate was at rest over the passenger compartment. I could see Eastman's head out of the cab window avidly watching this unique sight.

But the fun wasn't over. Looking up through the wreaths of steam at the awesome bulk of our front end, the hapless motorist panicked, reversed, roared back out from under the gate, and collided with two other cars before coming to rest. I swung the plug clear and slid down over the coal into the cab to find Eastman in a state of jubilee. For years, he had been conducting a verbal vendetta with motorists over grade-crossing incidents on the Branch, and this was his night to howl. He went up Middletown Hill like Bastille Day, with the stack making a joyful sound.

The indestructible locomotive—the E7 experience

By J.W. Hawthorne
Motive Power Superintendent

1940s

From *Trains* magazine,
January 1979

When Editor David P. Morgan asked me to write about my experience with Electro-Motive's E7 diesel locomotives on the Central of Georgia and the Atlantic Coast Line, he opened the floodgates of nostalgia about more matters than simply locomotive design.

My shock came when I realized that not only are the glamorous E7's an endangered species rapidly approaching extinction, but that both of these railroads have been absorbed into large systems, the Central into the Southern and the Coast Line into the Seaboard Coast Line.

Now, the E7's were probably my favorite unit of motive power, and not only because they were so very good. On my own little Central of Georgia they were a touch of elegance and a part of that railroad's last desperate effort to make it on its own.

I became Central's Superintendent of Motive Power on January 1, 1945. At that time all of our freight and passenger trains were powered by steam locomotives with the exception of an every-third-day streamliner, the *City of Miami*. And although we were the proud possessors of 22 diesel switchers, the bulk of our yard

The *Nancy Hanks II* approaches the station at Macon, Ga., on its exhibition run behind brand-new E7 No. 808 on July 9, 1947. WALTER M. PHARR.

work was performed by steam engines. We were, to all intents and purposes, a steam-powered road. With the exception of eight Lima-built 4-8-4's delivered in 1942-1943, the Central's fleet of locomotives was far from modern, although some of the larger engines had been equipped in company shops with cast-steel cylinders, mechanical stokers, feedwater heaters, etc.

The last years of World War II had wreaked havoc with this motive power, since shortage of manpower and scarcity of material did not permit adequate maintenance. This condition was aggravated by the fact that a fleet adequate for normal peacetime traffic had been pushed to the limit handling wartime demands. I recall many nights in the engine houses at Macon and Columbus, Ga., when we hoped against hope that an inbound engine on a southbound manifest could be turned in time for a northbound extra because no other operable power was available. On one occasion I took the wreck train out with a switch engine to avoid stripping the roundhouse of its last

good-order locomotive. The yard engine's tender had very little coal capacity, but fortunately we were able to take coal from the tank of a passing train's engine before we were forced to shut down.

The passenger service on the Central was handled predominantly with Mountain-type engines, filled out as needed with Pacifics. Owing to the heavy service, engines which had not been fitted with cast-steel cylinders often dropped out with cracked cylinders and frames when we could least afford to lose the motive power.

The Central of Georgia at that time operated far more passenger service than the average railfan may realize. Of a total of 6.5 million train-miles operated by the Central in 1945, 2.5 million were passenger train-miles. Interline name trains were handled between Atlanta and Albany, Ga., and between Birmingham, Ala., and Albany. Additionally, passenger service was operated out of Macon, Ga., to Savannah as well as to Dothan, Ala. Diesel power thus had an exceptional opportuni-

ty to achieve success. Plans were being formulated to operate two new streamlined passenger trains—the Atlanta-Columbus *Man O' War* and the Atlanta-Savannah *Nancy Hanks II*—so it was easy to convince management that eight E7 units should be purchased, one each for the new trains and six for general passenger service.

In due time the new trains and the motive power arrived, and diesel maintenance facilities were constructed in Macon. Taking advantage of Macon's central location on the railroad, we were able to relay seven units with one spare by cutting in a fresh, fully fueled and serviced E7 on every train when an inbound unit needed fuel, service, or maintenance. This procedure paid off for the Central with a period of almost flawless performance. Whereas under steam-engine operations we could rarely reach 100,000 miles between engine failures, diesel locomotives achieved five times this mileage as a commonplace record. Delays formerly occurring daily for coaling and watering

Two new Atlantic Coast Line E7's pose with a train of lightweight fluted stainless-steel passenger cars shortly after delivery in 1945. The ACL would eventually acquire 20 E7's. ATLANTIC COAST LINE.

steam engines, shooting rods with grease, cleaning ashpans, etc., vanished from the 8 a.m. operations report.

It was Central's policy to avoid loading its diesels to the breaking point, and our train speeds were limited to 70 mph by rail weight and track structure. These factors, along with an adequate time allowance for servicing and maintenance, kept the Central, at least until I left the road, from experiencing the difficulties with E7 locomotives I was later to find on the Atlantic Coast Line.

I must add that personnel on the Central adapted to dieselization in a remarkable way. The supervisors and the men went far beyond the call of duty to render the new power a success. Even the oldest of the group were enthusiastic over the freight (EMD F3) and passenger diesels, and this attitude certainly added to the record of E7's on that road. As I told my people on leaving, they made me look so good that I was promoted right off the railroad.

I arrived at the Atlantic Coast Line's general offices in Wilmington, N.C., on January 1, 1949, and I soon found that I was in a different ballpark, and that this ballpark was in the big leagues. We had 189 diesel units supplementing a fleet of 619 steam engines, and all power was serviced right at the coal chutes and ready tracks. Diesel running repairs were done in roundhouse stalls equipped with raised platforms and jib cranes.

As far as Coast Line passenger units were concerned, I found a far different situation than prevailed on the Central in that ACL ran these diesels literally night and day with little time out for maintenance. Indicative of this, a Coast Line E6, the 501, accumulated 5,250,212 miles before retirement in April 1970, becoming the highest-mileage locomotive in the world, according to EMD.

Additionally, the railroad's passenger trains were long and heavy, and they were operated on extremely tight, fast schedules. Actually the trains were so heavy that

provision of stand-by steam engines as protection in case of motive-power failures, as provided on the Central of Georgia, was out of the question since double-heading would have called for more crews which were often not available on short notice. Furthermore, the train timings could not have stood the unscheduled stops for watering, coaling, and cleaning of ashpans of steam locomotives were we able to provide them. The Atlantic Coast Line was committed to diesel passenger trains—period.

The above, plus the fact that the Coast Line dispatched units on runs of 1,500 to 2,000 miles before maintenance compared with the Central's 100 to 400 miles, all contributed to problems I didn't even know existed when I left the CofG.

The E7 locomotives did not have the separately water-jacketed cylinder liners with which later EMD units were equipped, and leaking lower liner seals were a constant nagging headache. This problem was compounded by the earlier E units' cooling systems which, at least in our fast passenger service, was inadequate. To help the situation, we kept units idling as much as possible when out of service to maintain pressure on those lower seals and to avoid leaks created as assemblies and A-frames contracted.

Incidentally, EMD had greatly improved the E7 cooling system over that of the E6 locomotives on which the roof louvers had to be removed by ACL to increase air flow through the radiators. This left the engine room unprotected. When I made my first trip through an ACL E6 on a passenger train at high speed during a heavy rainstorm, I had a real thrill. It was somewhat like water skiing fully clothed in a hurricane!

The road attempted to keep abreast of the situation on both E6 and E7 units by replacing lower liner seals on one or two cylinders at each maintenance terminal. Frank Sineath, our Chief of Motive Power who was appointed to his job at the same time that I came to the railroad, started a program of resealing complete engines that was eventually successful in solving the problem. The high cost of this work, however, later forced us to equip all units with the separately water-jacketed liners.

During this same period we suffered many thrust washer failures, a problem also controlled by a replacement program.

Between seals and thrust washers, it seemed as though we would wear out the power assemblies simply changing them. In time (like 5 years) the units were all reworked and we settled down for a quiet breath.

During this time we were blessed with a powerful unit which would somehow keep running while being patched with everything from baling wire to paper clips and somehow get over the road with a heavy train on a tough schedule. The E7 design lent itself to patch repairs in a manner that later units with solid-state controls and sealed circuitry could never do. Undoubtedly this was for the best as a more sophisticated unit would have tied up the railroad as we moved toward complete dieselization.

For example, we found the CFK steam generators were simple to repair, and the regulating and control devices were easily adjusted and repaired by any normally careful and knowledgeable workman.

A great many parts of the E7's were common to freight locomotives such as the F7, combination locomotives such as the GP7, and also certain of the switching

units. Many entire assemblies were common to all this motive power, including traction motors (but not pinion gears), power assemblies, blowers, lube pumps, windshield wiper motors, voltage regulators, and many more. We took advantage of this commonality by establishing pools of such components, repairing the items on assembly lines in the heavy repair shop at Waycross, Ga., and shipping them to outlying engine houses for use in keeping badly needed locomotives in service. The failed or worn-out components were returned to Waycross for repair and replaced in the pool.

In time this system was extended to cover parts as small as injectors and as large as starting batteries, and the utilization of the motive-power fleet increased beyond any level envisioned by the most enthusiastic partisan of diesel locomotives.

Perhaps the average railfan does not realize the system under which steam engines had to be repaired. Since each locomotive was built as an individual unit at the builder's works and assembled from castings and forgings fitted to this single unit, there was little or no possibility that any parts would be found that were interchangeable.

On the Central of Georgia, as on any other Class 1 railroad, we had historically taken bad-order steam locomotives into heavy repair shops, dismantled them, repaired each part, and reassembled them all on the same track or in the same stall. True, we could repair air-brake equip-

ment, stokers, pumps, valve gear, etc., in supporting shops carrying such names as air brake room and pump room, but this was a small portion of the work needed to outshop a steam locomotive.

Now with the diesel, we were in possession of a unit of motive power which could have almost anything that went bad, excepting the carbody itself, replaced from a pool of spare parts. Naturally as hard-pressed railroad motive-power maintenance officers, we were quick to take advantage of this situation.

The result was motive-power maintenance on the assembly line—a breakthrough to modernity in the railroad industry!

However, we were not out of the woods with our local problems since the E7's were approaching the time when their cotton-covered varnished cambric wiring would give up the ghost. High-voltage as well as control circuit wiring failures became an everyday occurrence. We finally had to bite the bullet and initiate a rewiring program at our Rocky Mount (N.C.), Waycross, and Tampa (Fla.) shops during which the E7s' old wiring was all replaced with material having heavy neoprene insulation.

To a person unfamiliar with railroad motive power, my reminiscences might be misconstrued to indicate that the E7's were a constant source of trouble. But again, as in the case of the Central of Georgia, we must look at the job to which the units were assigned. On the Atlantic Coast Line

Atlantic Coast Line E7 No. 526 pauses in Miami in January 1965. The 20-year-old locomotive has had some body panels modified and its fuel-tank skirt removed, and is painted in the railroad's simplified black scheme. COLLECTION OF LOUIS A. MARRE.

Former Atlantic Coast Line E7 No. 537 was relettered for Seaboard Coast Line following the 1967 merger. The E7's ran out their final miles for SCL, as none continued in service by Amtrak. Seaboard Coast Line.

we operated a first-class passenger service complete with all the amenities. We had streamlined coaches and Pullmans, feature cars, an excellent dining service, and well-trained crews. Above all, we operated on expedited schedules with a reasonably consistent on-time performance. Without doubt, the diesels were responsible for much of this record because as a result of their use in locomotive consists of from two to four units, the failures we experienced with individual units seldom delayed trains badly.

The E7's were a large part of the fleet that handled such trains as the *East Coast Champion, West Coast Champion, Havana Special, Vacationer* (winter only), *Florida Special* (winter only), *Palmetto, Everglades, Southland,* and *Miamian.* Along with these trains there was short-distance handling of the *Dixie Flyer* and *Seminole.*

The great number of local and connection trains still available for diesel engine assignment after all the high-grade through trains were diesel powered left little time for the units to sit around ready tracks or in shops undergoing maintenance. As stated before, ACL's passenger

units operated around the clock, seven days a week, 365 days a year.

We experienced other troubles with our diesel operations, but these were either typical of the design (such as pollution at fueling stations and traction-motor problems) or a result of our lack of specialized service and maintenance facilities.

In the early 1950's we constructed diesel running repair shops at Florence, S.C.; Waycross, Ga.; and Lakeland, Fla., and converted our backshops to suit. Then as full dieselization became an accomplished fact in 1955, we tailored all of our mechanical department work to the peculiarities of the new power. As a result of this effort and the detailed planning that paralleled it, our E7 and other passenger-diesel problems diminished to a reasonable level consistent with the funds available to us and the needs of the service.

When passenger service started its long trek downward, finally vanishing into the bare bones of Amtrak, we foresaw the eventual retirement of the E7's. After discussions with the president and with

his concurrence in our maintenance policy, instructions were issued limiting all passenger motive-power maintenance to that necessary to preserve safety. Our people were told to concentrate E8 and later units on all assignments and to take E7 and earlier units out of service as they became unsafe, inoperable, unreliable, or in need of heavy and costly maintenance. This move was akin to turning a loyal friend out in the cold and was certainly unpopular with our operating officers who had come to look at the E7's as the backbone of our passenger fleet. The wisdom of the move, however, was made abundantly clear when Amtrak restricted its purchase of the railroads' diesel power to E8 and later model units.

As a final word, if it were to fall my lot at some future date—when a now-unknown form of motive power replaces the diesel-electric—to compose a eulogy for the Electro-Motive Division of General Motors, it would read: The Builders of the Indestructible E7 Railroad Locomotive.

End of the line: A Seaboard Coast Line E7 awaits its fate on the scrap line at Waycross, Ga., in September 1972. JESSE CONE.

A Georgia/ Alabama sleigh ride

By James E. Satterfield
Fireman

1947

From *Trains* magazine,
December 1977

Firing the *South Wind,* flagship of the Montgomery District of the Atlantic Coast Line, was no job for a greenhorn.

The position normally was in the hands of a regular fireman. However, on a foggy night in December 1947, I drew that responsibility and experienced as hair-raising a ride as anyone ever has had on the deck of a bucking steam engine.

Under the best of conditions, the 210.5-mile trip from Thomasville, Ga., to Montgomery, Ala. (see the map on page 83), would be one to remember. The line, although nicely ballasted and well-maintained, followed the terrain like a roller coaster, and the route lacked block signals.

The original portion had been built out of Montgomery as a narrow-gauge line to Luverne, Ala., by the Alabama & Florida Railroad. Deterred by lack of money, the A&F ran intermittently, and the Plant System moved north westward out of Florida and Georgia to claim the territory. The system absorbed the A&F, made a connection at Sprague, Ala., and standard-gauged the line. The segment from Sprague to Luverne became a branch line and to this day has been the only one abandoned on the old ACL Montgomery District.

When the line from Thomasville to Sprague was built, the economies of the day called for laying track with as few expensive cuts and fills as possible. The result was that a train was either diving down a grade at high speed or climbing up the other side. In such terrain, a fireman was lucky to live to an age that would qualify him for the right-hand side of the cab. Stokers later eased this somewhat, but in the early postwar years there still were quite a few hand-bombers around and the experience was, if not enlightening, at least conducive to clean living, since you were so exhausted at the end of a run that sleep was a necessity.

On the day before my *South Wind* trip, I had been called to replace the regular fireman on time freight No. 214. Firing one of the 2000-series 2-10-2's used on the district was not too hard a task. The fire usually was cleaned by a hostler at Dothan, and there normally was little trouble on these runs. With passenger trains, however, there was no stopping for such amenities, and if the fire was in bad shape when you boarded at Thomasville, you could expect to fight to maintain steam all the way to Montgomery. Any clinkers would have to be pulled with the tongs or just left alone if you did not have time between looking for order boards and grabbing hoops at 60 mph. The head "brake" would not be in the cab to help you; he would be back in the train somewhere, taking his leisure in his resplendent uniform, venturing out only when an uncalled-for stop occurred. On the freight runs you always could rely on the brakeman to throw in a couple of scoops or work on the clinkers if things got too tough. Not on this night.

Clyde Mann, my engineer, called me over and told me he was worried about our engine, the 1516. There had been trouble with her blower coming down yesterday. He said the engine was a little different than her contemporaries because when she last had been shopped in Montgomery, her cylinders had been made smaller in an experiment to save fuel. Crewmen had found that unless the reverse lever was well forward, a touch of the blower had to be used to maintain 210 pounds' pressure even when the engine was working. If the engineer tried to run her without the blower, the more notches he had to shove forward and the more likely he would tear up the fire. So Clyde told me he would run her light and for me to be sure to keep the blower on enough to maintain pressure. I could almost sense a coming problem as the sounds of a chime whistle blowing for the yard echoed through the night.

As we stood on the Thomasville platform, a vague shaft of light showed through the fog as 1516 eased her load of Chicago-bound passengers into the station. The time was 3:46 a.m., already 6 minutes after our advertised departure time. As we waited, a 1200-class eight-coupled yard goat trundled by with a silver-sided ACL coach incongruous with its purple striping for placement among the Tuscan red coaches. Climbing aboard, I crawled onto the tank and pulled down the spout to fill her to the brim. Our next water would be at Dothan, the only mandatory stop en route. We probably would have to take water again at Youngblood before we reached Montgomery, or perhaps at Troy if we were delayed anywhere. By this time the fog had settled in and visibility was barely a quarter of a mile.

I checked the fire; it looked nice and level with no clinkers. I added a scoop or two to the bank and checked the stoker valve. Crawling out on the boards, I checked the sand dome and lights. After pulling down the coal I was ready to go. In the meantime, the train had been reassembled and Clyde was waiting for the line pressure to build. Clyde yelled across the cab to tell me we would have a passenger stop at Troy. Finally at 3:55 a.m., 15 minutes late, we got the highball.

Clyde flipped on the headlight—it beamed into a completely white blur. Visibility now was virtually zero. Easing the Johnson bar forward about three notches, Clyde gently touched the throttle and we eased out of Thomasville station in a manner that would have made any district superintendent proud. There we were, bound for Montgomery over a roller-coaster railroad, with no visibility, on a schedule that called for no delays under the best of circumstances, and with a dumb greenhorn trying to fire what might be a faulty engine. All the elements were there for something to happen.

Easing her forward another notch as we cleared the yard, Clyde again touched

Atlantic Coast Line 4-6-2 No. 1516 rests at the railroad's Montgomery, Ala., shops in a far more tranquil scene than when leading fireman Satterfield's problem-filled nocturnal race through the fog. Ed Rutledge.

the throttle and 1516 set up a low-pitched bark. Cutting in the stoker, I eyed the water level as our speed passed 30. Our first order station was Pine Park, 7½ miles down the line. I hoped I could see the order board, let alone catch the hoop. We were doing 60 when we roared by the station. I leaned out of the cab hoping not to miss the order board, and I barely could make out the green as we shot through.

Clyde motioned to me that he was about to shut her off for the slow order over the Flint River drawbridge. This brief respite gave me the opportunity to ask him how he knew exactly where he was when he couldn't see 10 feet ahead of the engine. "I watch the ground just below the cab. I've been over this route so many times that I know by the way the engine acts just where I am." He allowed further that there were 38 ridges and dips along this part of the line between Thomasville and Dothan and that he knew every one of them. His green fireman did not and was scared as hell.

The schedule called for our first meet at Whigham, where time freight 210 was supposed to be in the hole. I could see the red order board as we approached and so crawled out on the step to grab the hook. I couldn't see 210. I grabbed the hoop, pulled the order, and threw the hoop to the wind. The order read, "NO. 11 MEET

210 AT BAINBRIDGE." We were late, and so was 210; our next station was Climax, and Bainbridge was 8½ miles beyond. At Climax, the ACL's 32-mile Chattahoochee branch wandered south to connect with the Apalachicola Northern at Chattahoochee, Fla. The AN had trackage rights into Climax, and No. 31, the AN doodlebug, departed Climax at the ungodly hour of 3:35 a.m. after connecting with ACL local 57. The ACL ran mixed trains at reasonable hours over the branch, but my experiences firing a hand-bomber of the 400-class on this branch constitute another story.

At Climax, the board was red. I clung to the rungs as I grabbed for the hoop. The "19" read, "210 WAIT AT BAINBRIDGE FOR NO. 11. NO. 11 MEET EXTRA 2005 AT JAKIN."

At Bainbridge, we were doing close to 60 when we hit torpedoes. Somebody had goofed. Number 210 was in the siding, but some 10 cars extended onto the main. Clyde hit the air and we gradually slowed, hoping not to disturb too many passengers. We hoped 210 would clear behind us and allow us not to stop, but it was not to be. We ground to a halt just short of the desperately waving rear brakeman. By now we were 20 minutes off the advertised.

Until this point I had been having few problems with the 1516. With just a touch of the blower, she had been steaming nicely. Clyde occasionally would get up and check the fire and nod his approval. Number 210 cleared the main and we headed for Dothan. As we swept through Jakin, Extra 2005 was where she should be.

Then, things began to happen with the 1516. The pressure began to drop: 205 . . . then 200, then 190. I eyed the stoker. It was working fine. The water level was alright. I checked the fire; a growing dull orange spot indicated that clinkers were building up. I shook the grates and eyed the fire. Clyde nervously looked in my direction. I grabbed the tongs, determined to pull out the clinkers and level the fire. "Leave it alone or we will be in trouble," Clyde yelled.

"We're losing steam," I retorted.

"I know we are," Clyde replied, "but if we try to pull those clinkers here we never will get the cold spots covered and we won't have enough steam to pull a sick nanny goat away from the feed trough."

"What are we gonna do?" I yelled.

"Let her ride and hope we make it to Dothan. With 150 pounds we are alright and you can clean her up while we're stopped there. Shut off the stoker and use the scoop. Spread the coal around and keep that damn blower on as hard as she'll go."

We raced through Alaga and Gordon. I was staggering all over the cab, occasionally missing the door completely with a scoop of coal. The deck was covered and Clyde was mumbling under his breath. I didn't quite catch it—I was too busy—but I am certain his comments had something to do with "greenhorns." By the time we reached Ashford the pressure was down to 180 pounds. Clyde had taken over the chore of watching for the order boards, but now there were only 11 miles to go to Dothan and a respite.

At 4:45 a.m. (Central Time), 19 minutes late, we rolled to a stop by the water spout in Dothan. As Clyde climbed down to talk with the conductor, he yelled at me, "Get that fire in shape, and for goodness sake shut down that blower a little. I can't hear myself think." Ordinarily the stop in Dothan was brief for water and to discharge and pick up passengers. But this night it took Clyde and me, with a hostler's help, over 10 minutes just to get the fire in order. Thus ended the first 91½ miles of the roller-coaster ride.

Whether we ever would get No. 11 out of Dothan became a debatable point. Clyde decided to take a hand to see if he could get the fire straightened out. I had inadvertently left the injector on, and steam pressure was down to 150 pounds when Clyde mounted the cab after checking the bulletin book in the depot. He grabbed the injector handle, turned off

the feedwater pump, and eyed me—his questionable fireman—with a baleful eye. I had been struggling with the tongs, and the deck was covered with clinkers. I had again shaken the grates, and his somewhat intemperate remark that I had dumped half the fire on the ground when I had shaken them left me confused. By this time the tongs were so hot that my new leather gloves were almost an integral part of the skin on my hands. Clyde turned the blower wide open and threw in a few scoops while I tried to level the fire.

By this time the conductor was cabside, raging. "What the hell is going on? Let's get this train outa here," he yelled.

"We're having trouble with the fire and we only got 160 pounds," roared Clyde.

"I don't give a damn if you only got 10 pounds, get this train moving," came the reply. Clyde dropped the scoop and reluctantly edged 1516 off as I worked feverishly—hands blistered, my engineer cursing, and me contemplating how much unemployment insurance I would be entitled to when I visited the Alabama Employment Service tomorrow morning.

We cleared the Dothan yard, and by some stroke of luck by the time we had passed Midland City, 10 miles from the Dothan depot, the pressure was climbing and it looked like maybe we would make it after all. Clyde opened her up, and the 60 mph speed limit went by the board on the fairly tangent stretch to Pinckard. The time was 5:14 a.m., and night still hovered over the foggy right of way.

As we slowed for the Central of

Georgia crossing at Ozark, I hung onto the ladder to grab the flimsy. My foot slipped as I reached wide for the hoop. I clung hard with one hand, trying to keep from falling; the hoop hung over my wildly thrashing left shoulder. Clyde must have heard my screams of terror, for I felt a strong arm grab my left hand and pull me back toward the cab.

I will never forget the expression on his face. It was one of disbelief. I could almost fathom his mind. How could he, a veteran engineer whose seniority on the line gave him the best and fastest run, be subjected to the likes of a green extra-board fireman who kept falling out of the cab, ruining the fire, and generally blemishing Clyde's otherwise spotless record? I would carefully avoid him for some time after this run.

The order read, "NO. 11, MEET NO. 57 AT TENNILLE. WAIT UNTIL 5:30 AM AT ARITON FOR EXTRA 2016." Besides these trains, we still had two regularly scheduled meets that were bound to be all screwed up by the time we reached Montgomery if the fog didn't lift and give us a break.

As we left Ozark I began to sweat. Ahead was Morgan's Curve. This double reverse curve called for cautious running. In March 1917, engine 434, a handsome Pacific under the guidance of Engineer Dick Morgan, had been a few minutes late with No. 57, the daily Savannah-Montgomery passenger train. It is not certain whether she hit Morgan's curve too fast or not; what is known is that she left the rails and spread No. 57 all over the landscape. Dick Morgan and his fireman, Brown Hunter, went to Glory, and the engine plowed a hole to the right of the track that later filled with water. To this day the spring created by 434 is filled with water, a reminder to all engineers on the Montgomery District that Morgan's Curve is not to be fooled with.

Clyde eased us through the curve with no trouble, however, and we overtook No. 57, which was safe in the siding at Tennille. Daylight was beginning to show in the east as we drifted to a stop on the downgrade at Troy station to allow a Florida reveler to disembark. Fog still shrouded the rails as we moved away from the station, and the old bugaboo of the 1516 came to haunt us.

The blower pipe broke. Steam pressure began to fall. I yelled at Clyde, but he was aware of the problem and said we would try to fix it when we stopped at Youngblood, 7 miles from Troy, for water. When we eased under the tank at Youngblood we were down to 180 pounds and the cab was

The *South Wind* arrives at Montgomery, Ala., on June 6, 1948. The power is Atlantic Coast Line 4-6-2 No. 1533, which didn't receive the cylinder modifications given to the 1516.
F.E. ARDREY, JR.

filled with smoke. Clyde crawled out on the boards while I pulled down the spout to fill the tank. Five minutes later, he still was fiddling with a series of pipes and valves which were alien to me when the conductor came stumbling through the cindered right of way and queried, "Just what in the hell are you two monkeys doing with my train? Let's get the hell outta here. Old man Duncan is going to eat us alive as it is." Clyde shrugged his shoulders, and off we shuffled in the hope that we could make the last 44 miles before we were out of steam.

Daylight was full on us by this time. We were 55 minutes late, and we still had two trains to meet, drag No. 522 and time freight No. 209. They normally were scheduled to meet us at Ramer, but the "19" we picked up there indicated the dispatcher had held them both at Day Street Yard in Montgomery, apparently wondering just what was going on with No. 11. We swept through Sprague with the pressure at 180 pounds and falling.

At Sprague, Ten-Wheeler 996 sat on the siding awaiting her morning venture down the Luverne branch. I was tempted to tell Clyde to switch engines. Maybe the reliable old Ten-Wheeler could haul the *South Wind* into Montgomery with a little steam left over. The thought passed as I worked frantically with the scoop (I had given up on the stoker) as the pressure continued to fall. Coal covered the deck and we were down to 160 pounds as we roared through Snowdoun at 60-plus. The grade was almost level from there to Day Street Yard, and if we could make it to there we could coast into the station. As we passed the yard office, we were carrying 150 pounds and I knew we would make it.

As we pulled under the canopied shed of the Montgomery station, the irate face of R.H. Duncan glared up at the cab. Fifty-five minutes late with the *Wind,* an unheard-of delay to his crack train. In addition, we had managed to delay almost every train on the line. Explanations were in order, and I could see a great deal of the problem being laid on the head of the greenhorn fireman. I calculated that my unemployment check would amount to $53 a week, and maybe I could hock my

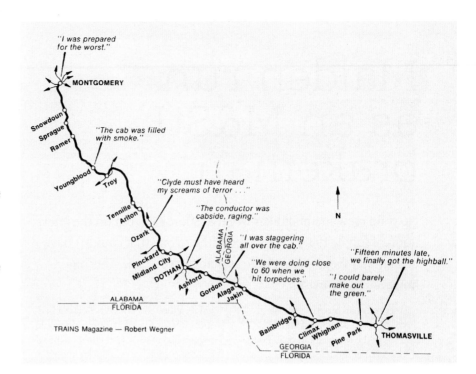

"I was prepared for the worst."

MONTGOMERY

Snowdoun
Sprague
Ramer

"The cab was filled with smoke."

Youngblood   Troy

"Clyde must have heard my screams of terror . . ."

Tennille   "The conductor was cabside, raging."
Ariton

Ozark   "I was staggering all over the cab."

"Fifteen minutes late, we finally got the highball."

Pinckard   "We were doing close to 60 when we hit torpedoes."
Midland City   DOTHAN   "I could barely make out the green."

ALABAMA
GEORGIA

Ashford
Gordon   Alaga
Jakin

ALABAMA
FLORIDA

Bainbridge   Climax   Whigham   Pine Park   THOMASVILLE

GEORGIA
FLORIDA

N

TRAINS Magazine — Robert Wegner

watch for something near a tenth of its value.

Mr. Duncan ignored me as I alighted from the cab. As I walked away I could see him waving his hands before Clyde and the conductor. I knew I could expect a call from the office the next day. Sure enough, the call came, and I was prepared for the worst. As I entered Mr. Duncan's office, he eyed me forebodingly. "Clyde tells me you did a good job under the circumstances," came the voice. I was both surprised and elated. "However," he droned on, "I am going to assign you to the yard, and maybe the dummy, until you gain a little more experience."

I was delighted until the next day when I looked at the 1434, the "dummy." How this 0-4-0 could move a box car, let alone two or three cars, was a mystery to me. However, the old dummy would run on a teaspoon of coal, and for the next 6 months I gladly rode her left side while we tended to the needs of the several industries on Coast Line's downtown, middle-of-the-street Montgomery trackage. I was then promoted to 0-8-0 1230, which had Joe Mitchell as permanent engineer and did yard and transfer work at Day Street Yard. Finally, eight months after the *South Wind* fiasco, I once

again was allowed out on the main line, where I remained until I returned to flying (which was my first love, but which in later years has left me with doubts as to whether I should have been a railroader or an aviator).

Clyde Mann and the *South Wind* are now blowing for the crossings in Valhalla. Seaboard Coast Line's Montgomery-Thomasville main line still is going strong with recently installed 120-pound welded rail, and a Chicago-Florida passenger train under the aegis of Amtrak, the *Floridian,* still plies the route. Day Street Yard is gone in favor of old-ACL-line trains using L&N's yard, but the great Union Station in Montgomery and its trainshed still stand, and the building is undergoing restoration in connection with a convention center being developed by the city.

Except for Amtrak's twice-daily calls, the place that once saw the likes of L&N's *Humming Bird* and *Pan-American;* the West Point Route's *Crescent Limited;* and the *South Wind* and the *Florida Arrow,* as well as trains of the GM&O and Seaboard, sits silent. The only steam whistle to be heard is on a new excursion steamer on the nearby Alabama River.

Maiden run as an M&StL brakeman

By Bob Lunoe
Brakeman

1947

From *Classic Trains* magazine,
Fall 2007

No train crew member likes to get a "short call," but on the afternoon of July 1, 1947, I was responding to one that couldn't have been much shorter: "Get here as quick as you can." This one, however, had a twist.

I recently had hired out on the fireman's board of the 11th and 12th districts of the Minneapolis & St. Louis, working out of Monmouth, Ill., 123 miles east of Oskaloosa, Iowa, and 62 miles from Peoria, Ill., the southeast end of railroad. During my rulebook examination, the trainmaster's eye had been fixed on my service letter from the Yosemite Valley Railway, where I'd done a little braking before the war. Would I agree to a trip braking once in a while, should the need arise? "Sure," I'd said, "if it's all right with the brotherhoods."

It must have been OK with everyone, for there I was on that beautiful afternoon, dressed like a fireman but carrying my old Justrite lantern and on the way to begin my maiden trip as a brakeman on the road whose initials most everyone pronounced "Em and Saint Ell." (Its two most common nicknames were "the Louie" or "the Saint L.")

Our train that evening would be 96's extra, which had already arrived in Monmouth. I could see her two engines slowly drifting down the roundhouse lead heading for the cinder pits, where they would be cleaned up and made ready to take over when we got back from Peoria in the morning.

Inside the yard office was the smiling agent, Ed Connor (whose crew problem I had just solved), and my conductor, a Mr. Mitchel, who somehow failed to reflect a similar level of confidence and relief. Too bad, I thought—it's me or nobody!

After signing in and reading the orders, conductor Mitchel briefed me on what he wanted done when we got to Maxwell, at the top of Kickapoo Hill, M&StL's entry into the Illinois River valley. Kickapoo Hill was more than 4 miles long and at its steepest was rated as a 2 percent grade, although I always believed it had spots steeper than that. Our train would require about 10 or 12 retainers to be set up, after which we would telephone the folks down at the Bartlett Yard office to let them know we had arrived and ask if they had any special instructions for us.

After conductor Mitchel's "words to live by," it was time to go to work, which meant getting the engines off the hot track and onto the train.

Our power that evening was a pair of 2-8-2's, the 607 with "Kink" Barr as engineer and the 626 with Harry Wells as engineer and Leon Fernald as fireman. Both engines glistened like new pennies, and as I walked past the 607, its fireman (whose name I can't remember) was running the stoker without the distribution jets working, in order to fill any unseen holes in the fire around the stoker pot. On the 626, Leon's scoop could be heard scraping on the apron as he was filling his back corners as high as he could. It was clear that on this trip we would be in good hands.

The engines were in the wrong order, so they would have to be taken out one at a time. While walking out to the cinder pit switch to line it back so we could get by, I gave Harry a casual come-ahead sign; as a new man I had to appear "cool." Now, the 626 had an unusual pilot, in that in addition to an abbreviated flue-bar "cow-catcher," it also had full switch-engine footboards. So, as the engine approached, I simply stood just outside the rail and let it scoop me up. That was the wrong thing to do, for that engine stopped like it had hit a brick wall. I looked up and there was Harry, hanging halfway out the window. In a shrill voice you could hear over half the town, he told me that he didn't give a damn how they did things where I came from, if you're going to work with him, you did not ride on the front of his engine! Good grief, I thought, what a grouch. I knew he was right, but where had my idyllic summer evening gone? This could be the beginning of a long, slow trip.

After backing him up in the proper manner and making the joint, I went back to get the 607. As she rolled by, the two grinning comedians in the cab asked, "Did you meet Harry yet?" The engines were coupled together without any further ado, and after completion of the air test, I climbed up into 607's cab and waited for Kink to pump off the brakes. Then we would be off.

Monmouth, 17 miles west of Galesburg, was quite a railroad town back then, as trains departed in seven different directions, although one was the semi-abandoned old Rock Island Southern. First we would cross the Chicago, Burlington & Quincy branch to Rio, then the CB&Q's double-track Chicago-Denver main line. When those two Mikes went pounding across the Q, plus all the whistle-blowing, it was clear that no eastbound M&StL train ever left Monmouth quietly.

The trip east went without incident. We took water at London Mills and coal at Middle Grove, and I set up about 10 retainers at Maxwell. Soon we arrived at the Bartlett yard office, and despite our being almost 12 hours behind schedule, a satisfactory departure for counterpart No. 95 was possible.

Not only possible, but necessary, for 95 was to have a long cut of hot cars off the Illinois Central destined for a fast trip up to Minneapolis and then on to Washington state, probably on the Great Northern. These movements were referred to as "ore trains," and while I never knew what kind of ore was in those sealed boxcars, my guess was bauxite from Jamaica. Although these cars didn't rate a "spike all switches" treatment, before the night was over, I would flag down M&StL's hottest train, "sacred cow" No. 20, to give the right of way to our humble consist. Such was the emphasis that headquarters in Minneapolis placed on a no-delay trip for these ore trains.

The first hint of a problem surfaced when we pulled up to the yard office on Peoria's south side—no cars from the IC! Serious worry didn't set in until our two Mikados were ready to go and there was still no sign of the delivery.

When all hope for a satisfactory connection had just about faded away, someone came running out of the yard office and said the IC was on the way over. That was when the "old heads" got together and came up with a "Plan B."

It went something like this: Both of our engines would go out and wait on the main line, and as soon as the delivery engine could get out of the way, we would back down onto the train and wait for the Alco RS1 yard engine to tie on with a "fill-out" cut of cars and our caboose. Then, after our air test, we would be off, with the diesel pushing as well. As soon as we arrived at the top of Kickapoo Hill, I was to cut off the lead engine, the 607, while we were still on the move. We would then go flying, light-engine, across the nearly straight and level track to Cramers. There I was to disembark from the engine at the depot and continue, on foot, for about a mile and flag down No. 20. Harry would bring our train over from Maxwell with just the 626, which would be no problem.

"Look at the time we'll save," they all said. "What could possibly go wrong?"

Well, I could think of a lot that could go wrong, but who would pay attention to a brand-new brakeman with only half a round trip seniority to his credit? Good or bad, that was the plan, and we would soon be sitting out on the main line waiting for the IC to show up.

We didn't have long to wait, and as soon as they got out of the way, we backed down onto the train. The slack ran in on us in practically no time—the RS1 had done its job, and an air test could be made. No. 10, the local freight, would wait for us up at Maxwell so we didn't have to worry about them. Soon we were ready, and with a couple of toots from the 607, we were off.

Now, we'd been standing around quite a while, and there was a lot of condensation in the cylinders to get rid of, but after blowing it out for about 100 feet or so, Kink and Harry kicked off their cylinder cocks and then commenced to really "bat

the stacks off" those two old girls. I may be exaggerating a little—after all, I was hyped up, since a lot of this ad hoc plan depended on a flawless performance from me—but I don't think I've ever heard two engines being worked any harder than those two old Mikes. The cannonading was unbelievable. Even a North Western 2-8-4 drifting light down Radnor Hill on its parallel line as we began to attack Kickapoo gave us a little whistle salute. About a half mile from the top, Kink motioned me over and suggested it might be wise to get ready to cut us off. The big show was about to begin.

My climb up and over the 607's coal pile proved to be a bit more difficult than I had anticipated. The "Saint L's" rebuilding program of the late 1930's had raised the side sheets of the tenders to well above the eave line of the cabs. This didn't leave much room for anyone to squirm his way through the gap between the cab roof and the coal boards on the front of the tender. I can still feel that cab roof overhang scrubbing my skinny backbone.

My next cause for pause was the size and shape of the coal pile. An extra ton or two had been taken on in order to make it possible to highball the coal chute at Middle Grove. In the dark it looked like a mountain—well over the tops of the stacks and already trimming itself by vibrating much of the extra coal over the sides. To cross this semi-fluid mass upright was out of the question. A hands-and-knees approach, and right down the middle, seemed like the best way to go . . . and it was, until I got just short of the slope sheet when first the front truck, and then the rear truck, ran over a series of diesel-wheel burns in the rails. The vibrations were unbelievable, and I wound up down on the top of the tank near the manhole cover, all covered with wet coal.

Spitting out coal, I made my way down the tank ladder. I was soon draped all over the front of the 626 trying to reach the angle cock, which on a steam engine is seldom if ever at the top end of the air hose. Finally, with both angle cocks turned, I caught Kink's eye and let him know I was ready when he was.

As we approached the Maxwell phone booth, Kink looked back again and I gave him a little highball with the lantern. To my surprise, he responded with a one-handed pin sign. Now, there was no doubt that the two engines were at the top of the hill, but the balance of the train most definitely was not! I couldn't believe he wanted me to cut us off this soon, not

until he gave me a lot of slack so I could get the pin. Well, I thought, he's got the whiskers, so I immediately pulled the pin and then nodded my head rapidly up and down. Off we went like a scalded dog.

Back on the 626, things immediately changed! Its exhaust tempo decreased abruptly, and it had lost its sharp bark—it was more like an extended "woof" now. I also imagined I heard someone shouting unkind words at us. Turns out, the crew back on the RS1 thought we'd hit a truck!

My climb back to the cab over 607's coal pile started out easily enough, but after passing No. 10's side-door caboose, the combination of our speed and the rough yard trackage put that top-heavy tender into such a series of ups and downs and side-to-side gyrations that even a hands-and-knees crossing of the coal pile now seemed much too risky. So I went "on your belly like a reptile," as the old saying went. Fate was kind, and while I was getting up from where I landed on the apron, Kink asked me, "What happened back there? You look like hell."

"Wet coal, and I think we cut off too soon," was my reply.

"He would've whistled," Kink said.

When the yard-limit board went flashing by, we must have been doing over 40 miles an hour . . . and still gaining. Now, those old Mikes had only 59-inch drivers, and even at those speeds the rods and valve gear were all spinning around at a fearsome rate. One look out the window at that whirling blur convinced me that the brakeman's front seat was not a good place to be should something come flying off—better to stand over the stoker grate and brace myself on the throttle fulcrum.

"Don't worry," reassured old Kink, "think of all the money you're making." Well, doubleheaders did mean double pay for the brakeman.

We arrived at Cramers much sooner than any of us had expected. I purposely did not look at my watch, for I didn't want the facts to influence my response if I was asked about the event later. Suffice to say, we'd arrived at Cramers, on the passing track and in good shape, so I hit the ground running with my "stop 'em stuff" for No. 20 in hand.

I didn't get very far, though, for in the dim light I stumbled on the butt ends of some grade-crossing planks and down I went—fusees, torpedoes, and my lantern, all over the roadway. As I picked everything up, my thoughts flashed back to California and old George Hanners, who always said, "Don't ever run, you'll

Mikado No. 627, a 1921 Alco (Brooks) locomotive that author Lunoe fired to conclude his memorable workday, charges toward Peoria with a hot freight in a publicity photo.
MINNEAPOLIS & ST. LOUIS.

fall and crack your head open." Lesson learned.

After that, I walked with resolve for almost a mile until I heard the distant sound of a diesel horn blowing for a grade crossing. Soon there appeared a glow in the sky followed by the brilliant beam of the headlight. It was time for me to light up as well, so I busted one of my fusees and made ready with a couple of torpedoes. I didn't want to "wash him out," just slow him down enough for me to climb aboard, so I made slow and deliberate "easy" signs, followed by several little wrist-action "come-aheads." He responded with a couple of ever-so-short toots—he had gotten my message.

Number 20's engine that night was the 147, a quite new three-unit EMD F2 (numbered, as the Saint L did in those days with its diesels, for its month and year of construction or acceptance), and I swung aboard as it came by. I announced that I was "flagging for 95," trying all the while to make it sound like I'd done this many times before.

That didn't fly.

"Well, look who we got here," said the hogger, little Freddy McMahon, one of the oldest engineers on the entire railroad. The real surprise came when he told me, "That was one of the best jobs of flagging I've seen in a long time." Of course, Freddy instantly became my favorite engineer, but I told him he should check with Harry Wells before making such a sweeping statement.

Aside from being scared half out of my wits by the explosion of several torpedoes I'd placed strategically close to where I'd drop off the 147, I was feeling good about everything, and all the time we'd saved. Soon Harry arrived, and I climbed aboard the 626. In no time at all, we were on our way.

The remainder of the trip over to Monmouth was uneventful, with one

exception. In town, as we clattered across the CB&Q branch to Rio, which ran behind the Saint L's roundhouse, the question arose: Where were the two engines that would take over to continue on to Oskaloosa? Still on the hot track, it turned out.

And, as before, they were short one man and as before, there was agent Conner! "Bob," he shouted to me, "I need you to go west, firing!"

I complained that I did not have enough time left. But as a brakeman, he explained, I'd been released from duty while the two engines were being serviced in Peoria, and I could at least get to Brighton, Iowa. There, No. 10 would deliver another fireman, a Mr. O.F. Watkins, who would take the ore train on west to Oskaloosa, while I deadheaded behind on the train engine.

It was apparent that I couldn't get out of going, so before long, there I was, firing for Fred Lathrop on the 627 heading west to Oskaloosa. I was so tired I could hardly stay awake, and I was hungry enough to eat a skunk. What a way to wind up my maiden trip braking, I thought. What did these folks do before I showed up?

There were a lot of fine people on the M&StL, and Kink and Harry were among the best. Old Kink was the "instant friendly" type, and, while Harry took a little more time to cultivate, I later fired for him on many occasions and always regarded him as a friend. Why else would he have given me his prized photo of Chesapeake & Ohio 2-8-8-2 No. 1550, the locomotive he ran from Peoria to Monmouth when it was being delivered to the Union Pacific during the war?

Even though the M&StL considered 2-6-6-4's before the War Production Board assigned it FT diesels instead, let no one say articulateds never operated on the Minneapolis & St. Louis!

Running the Big Rebels

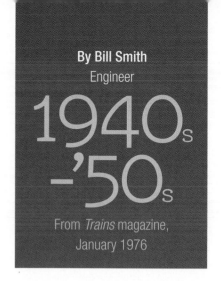

By Bill Smith
Engineer

1940s -'50s

From *Trains* magazine,
January 1976

One fall evening in 1940, my father took me down to Union Station in Jackson, Tenn., to see something very different. It was called a "streamliner."

Two other streamliners had been on display in Jackson before going into regular service: the *"Little Rebel,"* as it was to become known, which had been introduced by the Gulf, Mobile & Northern and was running from Jackson to Mobile and New Orleans; and Illinois Central's *Green Diamond,* which was in service up north. Neither had been anything quite like this new train. The new train was Gulf, Mobile & Ohio's *Gulf Coast Rebel.* It was made up of five rebuilt cars, and up front was a new kind of diesel locomotive numbered 270. We learned later that the locomotive was an Alco-GE DL109* rated at 2,000 horsepower. Number 270 was one of the first three such units built and certainly was one of the most beautiful in its red and silver paint.

Engine 270 and its sister unit 271 were to pull trains 15 and 16 between St. Louis and Mobile for the next 17 years. These refurbished *Gulf Coast Rebels* had been preceded by the smaller ACF-built, Alco-powered motorcar sets which later operated between New Orleans and St. Louis as trains 1 and 2. Because of the difference in the sizes of the equipment, the trains became known to the GM&O crews who operated them as the "Big Rebel" and the "Little Rebel."

The focal point of the new train, of course, was the locomotive. I noticed first the whistling sound that came from the 270's two engines as they idled. Then I noticed their seemingly odd firing order. I later learned that all Alco 539-series turbocharged engines had these characteristics. I have never ceased to be amazed at the reliability of those turbochargers. They were fitted with friction bearings and operated at over 10,000 rpm under load. Even more amazing was the 1-3-5-6-4-2 firing order of the engines. One needs to stand above the exhaust of one of these engines under full load to really appreciate the odd staccato that is produced. I often wonder why those engines did not break their crankshafts.

The sounds of the 539 engine are distinct and unmistakable. One cold morning in 1966, I was sauger fishing at Pickwick Dam on the Tennessee River when a towboat, pushing hard, came up the river. No one had to tell me whence came those sounds—McIntosh & Seymour were talking.

In addition to having air horns, the 270's (as well as the 350-series power cars of the *Little Rebels*) were equipped with sirens. They were used mainly to frighten cattle off the tracks and were removed in later years. The most noticeable feature of Nos. 270 and 271 (and later of No. 272) was their air horns. They were the most beautiful I have ever heard; very few locomotives were equipped with that type of horn.

After World War II, for reasons unknown to me, the horns were replaced with Nathan Air Chimes. I think those two types of horns, plus the Westinghouse single long-barreled air horn, were superior to and more desirable than most of the horns used today. I have been saddened to see the long lines of stored GM&O and IC E units sitting at Paducah with silent air chimes. The chimes could well be used on rebuilt Geeps and on other locomotives.

The DL109 was an underrated locomotive. The engines were good and the GE electrical equipment was superior. The DL109 often is compared to later-model Electro-Motive E units, which is unjust. The DL109 did have some troublesome characteristics, such as manual radiator shutters (later converted to automatic operation) and exhaust manifolds that leaked, releasing permeating fumes. Only a few people could properly set the governors on the 539-series engine. When the governors were not set right, the engine would vibrate violently, as any engineer who has run a yard locomotive equipped with a 539 will verify.

The Alco 539 engine is one of the most reliable, trouble-free power plants in existence. When one was pulled from a GM&O S2 for overhaul after eight years of service, the prime mover was found to have all rings on one piston, only two rings left on another piston, and no rings at all on four of the pistons; yet this engine had continued to operate around the clock.

I have never heard of a turbocharged six-cylinder 539 engine that actually produced the rated 1,000 hp. The 539's usually produced 940 to 960 hp after overhaul. This was more favorable than unfavorable, because these 539-powered locomotives did not slip their wheels as

---

All of the Alco-GE 2,000-hp A1A-A1A 539-engined passenger locomotives styled by Otto Kuhler were initially known as DL-109's. Later paperwork from Alco has refined the designation numbers for separate locomotive orders. The initial Rock Island engine, 624, was a DL103B; GM&O 270-271 were DL105's and 272, built later, was a DL-109.

Alco's distinctive pre-war DL passenger locomotives were styled by industrial designer Otto Kuhler. The diesels also featured a distinct sound, with a pair of 539 engines—the post-war PA's had a single 244 power plant. AMERICAN LOCOMOTIVE CO.

did some PA's and E's. The 270's had good balance and maintained their footing with much heavier trains than they were designed to pull. Most engineers agree that they would rather operate a locomotive with more weight and less power than one with more power and less weight. Of any locomotive I can recall, the 270's gave me the best ride; the 900's (SD40's) run a close second.

During the war years on the GM&O, a single DL109 often pulled 9 or 10 cars. Paul Kilzer, one of the best engineers ever to sit on the right-hand side of a locomotive, says he cannot recollect any train failure caused by a 270 during the seven years he worked on the *Big Rebels*. The units did occasionally limp in on one engine, though, and their train-heating boilers gave a small amount of trouble.

Number 272 was delivered in 1943, 2½ years after Nos. 270 and 271; 272 was bought to be used on the odd set of conventional coaches on 1 and 2. When 270 or 271 was being tested or overhauled,

272 was used to pull the Big Rebel. Both 270 and 271 had raised rear rooflines to conform to the configuration of the streamlined heavyweight cars used on the Big Rebel. This distinguished the units from 272 and all other DL109's.

As did all Alco-GE units, the 270's could run above their top-rated speed. The 270's and the 290-class PA's were geared for 85 mph but could easily run faster. I remember an engineer and a diesel supervisor telling me of doing 107 mph through Pinson, Tenn., one night running No. 16 with a 290 and a 270 towing 10 cars. The General Superintendent was aboard the last car.

Dewitt Coppedge, another fine engineer, recalls clocking 110 mph with 270 and 271. They were pulling 12 cars detouring on the Frisco, and the Frisco pilot took the controls in a successful attempt to meet the time on a wait order. Coppedge had the distinction of acting as a dining-car steward on the first run of the *Big Rebel* and a fireman on its final run.

It should be pointed out that Alcos would run faster than EMD's with comparable gear ratios. On several occasions when an EMD trailed an Alco in a lashup, I observed the EMD "light up" and make noises like a tilted pinball machine after exceeding the maximum geared speed, while the Alco continued to accelerate.

The M-40-A brake valve on the 270 series was well liked by both engine crews and machinists. The independent brakes were the best I encountered. The engine had to be shifted only once, from series to parallel, at about 25 mph. It accelerated slowly to transition and then picked up considerably. After the GM&O's 2,000-hp, 290-class PA's and 280-class Baldwin passenger units were delivered, 270 and 271 ran together most of the time. The DL109's later were equipped with adapters to enable them to be run with PA's and FA's. When a 270 trailed a 290 and shifted, you could feel a lunge against the lead unit.

Its paint and glory faded, Gulf, Mobile & Ohio Alco DL No. 271 rests on the Indiana Harbor Belt at LaGrange, Ill., on its way to scrapping for trade-in credit on new EMD locomotives in September 1963. Jim C. Seacrest.

For comparison purposes, consider the ratings of GM&O's passenger units over Alto Pass in Illinois, before they required a helper. A 270 was rated to pull seven ears, a 290 eight cars, and a 280 nine cars (when the units ran at all). The Baldwins had good engines but something was almost always wrong with their electrical systems.

After the Big Rebels were discontinued in 1958, the 270's were used frequently on work trains and sparingly in freight service. Occasionally they were used on locals. The DL109's worked better with Alco freight units than did the PA's because the DL's did not slip as badly. But by that time, parts for the 270's were hard to come by, and maintenance on the units declined. The last several years of their existence they mostly sat around at Iselin Shop in Jackson with their paint peeling and lettering almost invisible. When they ran, they belched enormous amounts of gray exhaust from low-grade fuel oil. The last time I saw a 270-class engine in freight service, it was trailing an FA and three E B units. The DL was 271, working hard up Jackson Hill, headed for St. Louis for use there on a work train.

E units might have done a better job on the *Big Rebels,* but I don't think so. South of St. Louis, the GM&O was virtually an all-Alco road, and the maintenance provided at Iselin, St. Louis, and Mobile made the 270's among the best-conditioned locomotives operating anywhere.

They were kept well tuned and spotless. And even after they were painted in the Alton colors, their good looks were not diminished. I cannot recall a 270 ever having been involved in a serious accident, which speaks well for the locomotives and for the crews who handled them for millions of miles.

One spring morning in 1962 my phone rang, and chief crew caller Bob Arnold asked me if I would go on the branch local. This was a 49-mile run from Jackson to Dyersburg, Tenn., on the old Birmingham & North Western (sometimes called the Beer & No Whiskey) where GM&O founder Ike Tigrett got his start. This track was a portion of the Tennessee Division out of Jackson, and J&O District men were not required to go. But we usually did.

I reported to the Iselin Yard office and picked up my orders; I could hardly believe my eyes. A clearance card and one train order read, "ENGINE 270, WORKS EXTRA, JACKSON TO DYERSBURG AND RETURN, WITH RIGHTS OVER ALL TRAINS," The order was normal, since our train would be the only one on the line. But a 270 and its six-wheel trucks on 65-pound kinked rail with no slag? This hilly railroad was run "wide open" uphill and "brake on" downhill. The standing (unofficial) order was, "Never look back before you look ahead, or you might get your head unscrewed by a low-hanging limb."

With a little concern and a lot of

conviction that 270, train, and crew would end up in a swamp or a soybean field, we backed the 5 miles to Bemis Junction and began our adventure. My apprehension turned out to be that and nothing more. The big Alco hung onto the small rails as we made our way to Dyersburg, cautiously turned the locomotive on the old wye, and returned without incident.

On the return, we stopped at the outskirts of Jackson to let the 3:59 p.m. yard engine take the hole in the L&N west-side interchange. The GM&O track across the bottomland to Bemis was straight and had just been tamped, lined, and dressed. We had 11 or 12 cars; I opened the throttle and "let her out" until we reached 65 mph before shutting off and rolling uphill to Bemis Junction. With her black smoke lying back, dirty white flags flapping, and paint peeling. No. 270 reminded me of an old "four stacker" destroyer making her last torpedo run under a boiling smokescreen in rough seas. This was surely one of the last runs of a 270-class unit because soon they were towed off to La Grange as trade-ins on GP30's.

Gone are the GM&O's splendid trains, the pretty hostesses, and the gracious locomotives with sirens, odd-sounding engines, and trombone whistles. Another chapter in the history book has been closed, and all that is left is memories.

Wreckmaster's moon

By Lloyd Arkinstall
Fireman

1947

From *Trains* magazine,
October 1982

Even in repose, the Waverly, N.J., hook was an awesome machine—coal black and unadorned by corporate symbol (with just a simple PENNSYLVANIA on her underframe), she hunkered massively over her banked fire on a shopyard track coupled to her drab gray wheel, tool, and crew cars.

When, infrequently, a shop man checked her fire, soft coal smoke would curl lazily from her stub stack and steam would issue from her injector overflow. But for the most part—silence. Hers was a waiting game.

The raucous shopyard Klaxon wrecker call would explosively shatter this brooding idyll, as it did on a crisp, full-mooned evening in the fall of 1947. The nearby Hunter Street produce yard's H9 Consolidation was hastily commandeered into wreck-train service. Firing it provided me with a welcome respite from my plodding yard drill and practically guaranteed a box seat at some monumental dislocations.

After topping off the tank at the 20-track plug, we were hustled through a reverse move by the switchman, and backed down against the hook and its gray entourage.

With my fire ready, I stood in the right gangway in quiet conversation with my engineman, Joe Carlton, watching the unhurried mustering of the wreck train crew. The big hook was aroused, her smoke lofting high and slowly diffusing in the moonlight. Shortly after the squatty heroic figure of the wreckmaster boarded the crew car, our young conductor came forward with the orders: "We're going first class tonight. Hunter will main line us off the Ought—watch your speed, the hook's boom is leading!"

My engineman, muttering to the general effect that he had been conversant with crane boom special instructions before the conductor was housebroken, ripped off four shrill freight-whistle screeches and almost instantly received a baroque highball from the Waverly 5 switchman's yellow lantern. Hunter Tower's dwarf low home signal beckoned our grim little train onto No. 1 main.

Song pluggers, from the 5-string banjo era to the present, have hackneyed the harvest moon practically out of orbit, but it would require the collaborative effort of Thomas Wolfe and Stephen Foster to capture the magic of a full autumn moon framed between the cab roof overhang and the coal gate, pacing your trailing smoke plume.

So went our 10-mile lope to Harsimus Cove; the H9 steamed like a fallen angel, and the hook rode like a Pullman heavyweight. Shortly after booming under Journal Square's resonant Bergen Avenue arch, we crossed the double-track trestle over the New York Central's interchange onto the western extremity of the Cove's long elevation. Finally, at the Henderson Street crossovers, we ran around our train and shoved the hook up to the derailment. The lead engine of a pair of P5 box-cab motors had climbed the rail about four car-lengths east of the Henderson Street Tower. The derailment had obviously occurred at a slow speed while lifting an empty hopper drag east, for though canted, the P5 had not strayed far from the rail.

Old Tom Shawn, the catenary boss, had, of course, de-energized the overhead. With the hook in position, our engine, which was still hotter than a crew dispatcher's prospects in the hereafter, was abreast of the tower bay. To keep her from popping practically into the towerman's bullhorn, I had bottled her almost out of sight and left the firedoor open.

Usually, unless a wreck was of apocalyptic proportions, the top operating brass would hotfoot their lieutenants to the wreck site—accounting, in this case, for the presence of Assistant Road Foreman of Engines MacLeod at the Cove on this almost lyrically beautiful fall evening. Across the Hudson, the illuminated mass of lower Manhattan looked for all the world like the product of a Hollywood special-effects studio. However, the beauty of the night was lost on the studiously important group of middle management clustered around the dark, silent, slightly canted lead locomotive of an endless band of empty Berwind-White hoppers destined for Enola. All but a few hundred feet of the trip remained, for the motor had strayed from the rails at the yard's throat just short of Henderson Street Tower.

In a simpler, pre-computer era when only miners and structural steel workers wore hard hats, some corporate maverick defined "camel" as a horse designed by a committee; equally disastrous results can follow divided authority at a big hook lift. Our wreckmaster was an impressive specimen: His heavy arms probably only appeared to hang to his knees from a body as broad as a boxcar door, though he was barely 5 feet in height.

When under derailed equipment, directing the arrangement of blocking, he scuttled in a crab-like fashion. His unique talent, however, was an uncanny, computer-like faculty which constantly sensed and evaluated balance, stress, probable direction of topple or collapse, cable purchase points, hook boom elevations, and the minute-to-minute whereabouts of his crew members. In any critical maneuver, his command was absolute. Operating Department heads could huddle on grand strategy, but final implementation commands issued from the wreckmaster alone. His hand or lantern signal became an extension of the hook operator or engineman.

Fortunately, most brass respected the absolute nature of this time-honored custom, and settled for spectator roles and authoritative body English. One flagrant nonconformist to this tradition, though, was Assistant Road Foreman of Engines MacLeod. To Mac, who fancied himself as an action-oriented, take-charge type, passive roles did not come easily. Unlike the power director's relaxed representative, old Tom Shawn (whose presence lessened the likelihood of mass electrocution), MacLeod, as if drawn by some magnetic force, would visibly wind up practically breathing down the wreckmaster's bull neck. An even less ingratiating foible was his insistence upon carrying a regulation trainman's electric hand lantern at night emergencies.

Our safety valve still buzzed and feathered as Joe and I watched the purposeful shuttling between tool car and derailment of the wreckmaster's muscular gnomes, laden with oaken blocks, rerailing frogs, choker cables, spike mauls, and sundry tackle. Since the hook and its service cars were between us and the derailed motor, details of the rerailing strategy were all but obscured from our view, and since the wreck site primacy of the wreckmaster was in effect, MacLeod's self-assertive need to chew out somebody was becoming almost organic.

His normally ruddy complexion would flush to Tuscan red when his low choler threshold had been crossed. Since we were the only potentially vulnerable motive-power targets in the immediate area, we abandoned as counterproductive the idea of strolling forward for a better view.

Although never entirely out of harm's way, MacLeod had avoided a collision course with the wreckmaster, who studiously ignored him, but there was always Mac's hand lantern upon which we fixed almost hypnotically. So far, he had used it only for illumination.

Even though the derailment briefly paralyzed the Cove, the lift itself was obviously a routine chore, for, once squared away, a few short bursts of the hook's chuckling, rapid-fire exhaust, and the wayward motor was back on the iron. In the cab, our sense of letdown was acute; here we had been pumped up in anticipation of a titanic confrontation which seemed to be slipping away.

Both out of consideration for the towerman and to avoid MacLeod's censure, I had kept the pops seated by letting the fire wane, secure in the

knowledge that the coked-up reserve in the rear of the firebox could be shoved forward and blown hot in very short order. Obviously, with the motor rerailed, our services would soon be required to couple the hook to the motors and pull them away from the train, for relief power in the form of an M1 4-8-2 from the Meadows enginehouse had quietly nudged her huge tank into position just clear of the crossovers.

A cut was made between motors and hoppers, followed by the wreckmaster's back-up signal to drill the slightly scuffed juice jobs into the clear. His lantern had barely begun a very gentle close-in come-ahead signal when MacLeod's restraint finally caved in, prompting him to swing a lusty go-ahead with his lamp! With an outraged bellow that carried from the stockyards to Pier F, the wreckmaster scuttled wrathfully up to the offending official and spewed an incendiary torrent of Anglo-Gaelic profanity, point blank, at about the level of Mac's cigar-filled breast pocket. One particularly telling point was his explicit threat to dispose of the Assistant Road Foreman's lantern in an unspeakably earthy manner. MacLeod gave ground under the onslaught, tripped backward on a stray piece of blocking, and landed ponderously on his official rump in the moonlit ballast.

My engineman was convulsed. He pounded on his armrest, wracked repeatedly by gasping, shoulder-shaking gales of laughter—his abandon was total.

As the eye of a hurricane magically transforms fury into calm, such was the effect of MacLeod's slapstick prat fall, for even as the ARFE struggled to his feet, fanning cinders from his trousers, the wreckmaster, without a backward glance, redirected his attention to the work at hand. Which, of course, was to repeat his gentle lantern come-ahead to couple the wrecker to the motors. My engineman, still shaken by spasmodic seizures of laughter, made the coupling while I hastily started knocking my fire back in shape.

Perhaps the marathon laughing jag had undermined Joe's throttle cunning, for his first attempt to lift our train and the motors up the slight grade resulted in the H9's slipping and erupting like a Roman candle. Fortunately, I had the firedoor open. which prevented at least part of the firebox's contents from going into orbit. The wildly spinning drivers had barely come to rest when a truculent voice below

the right gangway loudly demanded to know our steam pressure. There below, hands on both grab irons, bifocals glinting ominiously in the firelight, was MacLeod who, minutes earlier, had made a legendary ass of himself.

Steam pressure, or its lack, was strictly a motive-power matter, and MacLeod, infuriated by his humiliation in full view of his peers, was seeking relief—and what better way than to loudly tear the packing out of the nearest engine crew, namely us!

"Steam pressure?"

I knew that if I claimed full working pressure, he would clamber aboard, check the gauge, then really go to work on me, so I truthfully replied, "One ninety."

"Then get the other 10 pounds," he rasped as he released his hold on the grab irons and, still clutching his controversial lantern, strode aggressively toward the relief M1 to harass its crew on general principles. It was MacLeod's passionate belief that mankind's noblest achievement was the work ethic; motherhood, July 4th, and the Interstate Commerce Commission paled by comparison. Man was flawed, prone to indolence and sloth—particularly firemen—and it was Mac's mission to discipline the wayward. What's more, he enjoyed hell out of providing this service!

Smarting under Mac's cheap shot, I lunged into my work and, foolishly, produced considerably more than the deficient 10 pounds of boiler pressure, for during the remainder of our stay the H9 screamed like a banshee.

We took our leave via the Cove loop, Exchange Place, and the elevated light-engine track to Waldo Tower, which nestled, damply, in a rock outcropping near Journal Square. Looking back over the low tank, I saw that the towers of Manhattan were darker now, as charwomen and night people extinguished lights upon finishing their custodial rounds.

Crossing the Hackensack River passenger span, we cut through the funnel haze of a tug passing directly beneath us; its mast light seemed almost within reach. As we accelerated down the West bridge approach, I rode the seatbox, watching the eccentric crank tirelessly chase the back end of the main rod, and the counterbalances flash in unison in the moonlight like a precision drill team.

It had been a good tour of duty, and by morning, news of MacLeod's fall would enliven many an Enola coffee break—the crew of the relief M1 would see to that!

"A truculent voice below the right gangway loudly demanded to
know our steam pressure."

Illustration: Lloyd Arkinstall.

Tales of EMDs, Alcos, F-Ms, and Baldwins on NYC

By Harold B. Crouch
Mechanical Engineer

1940s

From *Trains* magazine,
January 1986

An old adage claimed that only 5 minutes were required to find the trouble on a steam engine but 5 years to fix it, whereas with a diesel-electric locomotive, it took 5 years to find the trouble and 5 minutes to fix it.

I spent 25 years working with steam, electric, and diesel-electric locomotives on the New York Central, and the following are some tales from that career. The time I was riding the locomotives as a diesel inspector was the summer of 1950, just before I went to Dunkirk, N.Y., to work on the Bituminous Coal Research coal-fired gas-turbine locomotive project.

One day, one of NYC's two four-unit FT locomotives—Nos. 600/2400/2401/1601—was towed into a roundhouse on account of being inoperative. The master mechanic called his diesel supervisor and requested he investigate. The supervisor returned to report that the units were operational once again. The master mechanic then asked what the difficulty was and was told that all four ground relays had tripped. He said that didn't mean anything to him—what had the supervisor had to do? When told that four buttons had to be pushed, the M. M. exploded: "If I tell headquarters that

the locomotive could not move because four buttons weren't pressed, I'll be the laughing stock of the railroad!" Yes, there was a lot to learn.

An F3 was reported to be flashing the main generator, so it was connected to the load box at the Collinwood Diesel Terminal in Cleveland. The shop's general foreman, Sid Morse, was standing alongside the generator while it was under full power. Just as he stuck his head out of the carbody air filter opening (through which the generator leads passed) to check the voltage on the load box, the generator flashed over! For a moment, it seemed as though Sid would come right through that small opening! The generator was changed out at once.

The F3's and F7's were equipped with a relay called VI, or transition relay. Often this relay would stick, thus transition to parallel would not occur. On these occasions, it was common practice to grab the door behind the fireman—leading to the engine compartment—and slam it

shut a couple of times. The resulting vibration would usually jar the relay enough for it to pick up, enabling a successful transition. Good running time could then be made, but this was rather hard on the door and its hinges.

The early EMD's were notorious water leakers. The difficulty stemmed from the fact that the little rubber grommets which sealed the water passages between the cylinder liner and cylinder head would get out of place during assembly, or had been accidently omitted. With the water-pump pressure greater than the air-box pressure, water would enter the cylinder and go out the stack as steam. (A diesel-steam locomotive?)

During a freight engine test of burning No. 6 oil on the River Division up the old West Shore to Selkirk, N.Y., we had one of these leakers, F7A No. 1759, as the third member of our consist. Although the expansion tank was overflowing upon departure from the North Bergen (N.J.) engine terminal, by the time we were near-

ing Kingston, N.Y., the water was just bobbing in the bottom of the gauge glass. We told the engineer that we would have to stop and get water for the unit before the hot engine alarm sounded. The head brakeman said there was a water hose in the baggage room of the Kingston depot, coming up. The engineer slowed the train and, as we neared the end of the station platform, I jumped off, brought the hose out to the unit (the hose was a long one for watering coaches), stuck it on the "pineapple," put a few inches of water in the tank, returned the hose, and got back to the cab … all with the train still moving slowly. When I gave the engineer a highball, he looked at me and said, "But I thought you wanted to get some water for the unit." When I said that we had already gotten it, he shook his head in disbelief, but began to notch out the throttle. We made it to Selkirk with a little water to spare. The unit was taken out of service and given an overhaul.

Train 27, the *New England States,* came

Multiple road locomotives, including EMD Geeps, Alco FA's, and Alco PA's, pause for servicing at New York Central's West Detroit engine terminal in the early 1960s. J. David Ingles.

into Syracuse, N.Y., one evening whistling for relief because of ground relay trouble on the 3500, the lead unit of its A-B-A passenger-service F3 set (3500/3601/3501), one of two such on the NYC. I didn't take any exceptions upon inspecting the main generator and electrical cabinet, so the traction motors were to be next. About this time, the steam-generator water tank overflowed, making a small pond under the unit, so I inspected the No. 4 traction motor first. The trouble? A brush pigtail had broken off and was striking the motor frame, so I quickly twisted the offending pigtail around one of its neighbors and replaced the cover.

To make sure everything remained in good order, I took a ride west. It seemed like every time I donned a clean set of work clothes, the locomotive on the first train through would have ground relay trouble, making it necessary to inspect traction motors, and I'd come out looking like that New Haven steam hostler at the joint Springfield, Mass., roundhouse whom the Boston & Maine crews would not let board their new F units (see W. A. Gardner's "Delivering EMD's Locomotives" on page 57).

It so happened that a road foreman of engines had been on hand at Syracuse when word of No. 27 having difficulty was received, but he had gone west on a preceding train, No. 41, the *Knickerbocker,* as scheduled, getting off at Rochester. When we arrived at Rochester, he came up to 27's cab and, upon learning that the units were in good order, asked that I come over and check the depot yard goat No. 807, an old Alco high-hood unit. The locomotive wouldn't pull itself, let alone any cars.

Upon checking the throttle switch, I noted that the exciter field relay was picked up, and so I inspected the exciter. On these early units, the "order of the universe" was reversed—i.e., the main generator and exciter were in the forward nose of the unit, while the radiator compartment was next to the cab. On checking the exciter, I found the insulation missing and the leads badly burned. I recommended that the unit be taken out of service and sent to the Rochester enginehouse for repairs.

I recall Buffalo Central Terminal for a couple of incidents. One night No. 68, the *Commodore Vanderbilt,* a through passenger train from Chicago, came into the Terminal with ground relay trouble on one engine in its pair of E7's (an A and a B), each of which was equipped with two

12-cylinder 567A engines. I inspected the main generator, electrical cabinet, and traction motors and could find no problems, so the Syracuse Division crew was told they would have to make it on three power plants instead of four.

The train departed, but shortly the yardmaster called to say that No. 68 had died at Depew, N.Y. This is near the site of today's Amtrak Buffalo station, so you know the train didn't get far. About this time a mail and express train, with a steamer on the head end, was leaving, so the engineer was swung down with a stop signal, and he took me out to the disabled train.

It is a bit disconcerting to see a big train stopped on the main track with no sound anywhere and only a few lights here and there. Upon entering the cab, I found a road foreman of engines had preceded me. He had found that the 80-amp control fuse had blown, thus shutting down the fuel pumps on the two E7's. Going back to the B unit, we put in the control fuse from there, only to have it blow also. Obviously, we had a bad low-voltage ground (as distinct from the high-voltage ground mentioned earlier). Hence, the jumper cables between the units were pulled down; fortunately, the fuse held, so the two engines in the B unit could be restarted. The hostler's control was then cut in, and the units were moved away from the train.

About this time the road foreman, who had gone to secure a relief locomotive, reappeared, and he took over. Later at the East Buffalo roundhouse, we found one of the fuel pump motors on the A unit had gone to ground, thus blowing the fuse. Shortly before we arrived at the round-house with the lame E's, a centipede tender of a steam locomotive had gotten away and was resting in the turntable pit—it was just one of those nights!

On another night, after No. 25, the westbound *20th Century Limited,* had departed Buffalo in good order, my co-worker Henry Norton and I went up to the Terminal restaurant for a midnight snack. We had just placed our order when an announcement over the PA system requested that a diesel inspector come to the east end of the depot. I told Henry I would go down and see what was wanted and would be right back. It turned out that the units on 26, the eastbound *Century,* were having ground relay trouble. I didn't find anything wrong during my inspection, but to make certain, I stayed aboard them as far as Syracuse. The trip went smoothly; apparently a traction motor had flashed over and the carbon dust had been

knocked off, so the unit settled down. The next evening, when I saw Henry, he said, "I thought you were coming right back last night. When you didn't, I had to eat your order as well as mine. I'm still full."

The Central's passenger diesel fleet was maintained at Harmon Electric Shop, 33 miles out of Grand Central Terminal, where third-rail electric motors were changed out in favor of diesel or steam power to Albany and beyond. When a new or overhauled engine was applied to an E7 at the shop, the locomotive was load-tested on the load box, then coupled to another unit for assignment on a regularly scheduled train. On these occasions, it was customary for someone to go along and change the lube oil suction strainers when the lube oil pressure in the newly installed engine went down.

One night I drew this assignment, departing Harmon on No. 67, the *Commodore Vanderbilt,* on time with back-to-back E7A's. A road foreman was along, deadheading to Albany, so he rode the cab while I kept an eye on the new engine. Shortly, the road foreman came back looking for me, saying the crew couldn't get the wheel-slip light in the cab to go out. It only took a minute for me to ascertain that the No. 2 power plant in the lead unit was in trouble. I checked the electrical cabinet but noted nothing unusual. Then it dawned on me that I had seen the unit on the drop pit that day receiving a new pair of wheels and traction motor in the No. 4 position. Apparently the traction-motor leads had been incorrectly coupled, thus causing the wheel slip. So the power plant had to be left off-line.

About this time, the lube oil pressure on the new engine began to go down, so I checked with the road foreman. He asked if I thought the pressure would hold until we had negotiated the curve and grade through Poughkeepsie. Luck was with us; it did. After we passed Hyde Park, the new engine was shut down, and I changed out the lube oil filters ... in a hurry—that lube oil is hot stuff! Despite having only two power plants on line, our train speed only went down to 60 mph with a 16-car train! That's the Water Level Route.

Just before any passenger power was dispatched from Harmon, a group of laborers would clean the cabs and engine compartments. The laborers had grown accustomed to the hostlers moving the units around and so would keep on with their work. One evening a hostler took a pair of E7's over to the ready track, and a laborer was busy as usual. The engine crew came aboard and saw the laborer, but said nothing. Shortly, the train was on its way to Albany. Back in the engine room, the laborer finally realized that the engines had been under power for a long time, so he went up to the cab. There, he learned that he was halfway to Albany already, with all his personal effects—including his railroad pass—back at Harmon.

At Albany, the engine crew steered him to the stationmaster's office, where arrangements were quickly made with the conductor on the next train for his return. The next day, Shop General Foreman George Beischer remarked to me that perhaps we had better cut a stencil for the back of the laborer's overalls: PLEASE RETURN TO HARMON ELECTRIC SHOP.

One weekend when I was dead-heading home to Buffalo on train 35, the *Iroquois,* the train came to a stop near Jordan, N.Y., west of Syracuse. The conductor came in and said we had lost the main air reservoir pressure on the locomotive. I went up to the cab, where the engineer explained that the main air reservoir pressure suddenly started to go down, so he had decided to stop while he still had some air. I could hear a heavy flow of air emanating from beneath the cab floor. Going down into the nose of the lead E7, I found that a union fitting in the main reservoir line had come adrift, one leading to the pipe bracket for the 24RL automatic brake valve.

Getting under the cab floor of an E7 required a Harry Houdini, and the fitting was almost beyond reach, just at my fingertips, so I could not reconnect it by hand against the heavy flow of air. Fortunately, the fireman had a small wrench with him, so the next fitting downstream was disconnected and then the upstream fitting was able to be reconnected. This is one case where the "long arm of the law" would have been very useful. After I reconnected the downstream fitting, the main air reservoir pressure came up, the brakes released, the engineer whistled the flagman in, and No. 35 continued. I was just a little late getting home.

Such tales were not restricted to EMD diesels, of course, and not just to first-generation models. In the late 1960's, a GP40 was reported not producing its full horsepower. With the unit on the load box at the Collinwood Diesel Terminal, all we could get was 2,200 hp instead of the rated 3,000. Going over the electrical system with a fine-tooth comb, we did not find any problems, so the difficulty must be

with the prime mover, which wasn't pulling. The governor and fuel injector rack settings were correct, but still there wasn't enough horsepower. We finally discovered that the wrong fuel injectors had been applied. With the correct fuel injectors, the horsepower rose quickly.

Alcos were another breed of cat. One day a four-unit consist of FA's and FB's departed from Selkirk Yard outside Albany for the Boston & Albany route. Despite the engines really putting out with a full injection-pump rack setting, good turbo pressure, and main generators loading well, it was slow-going all the way up into the Berkshires. At Pittsfield, Mass., the train stopped to pick up and set out cars. While the switching was going on, the conductor came up to the head end to report that the train had 30 more cars than he had waybills for! This explained the slow performance—too much tonnage. Upon our calling back to Selkirk, the yardmaster exclaimed, "So that's where they are. I've been looking all over the yard for them!" A yard crew had put them on the wrong train.

Another time an FA1, 1035, came into the roundhouse at Selkirk with ground relay trouble. The foreman and hostler ran the unit back and forth, endeavoring to locate the cause of the difficulty. Becoming engrossed in their work, they forgot to look where they were going and—you guessed it—ended up in the turntable pit. The big hook did the necessary work to fish the unit out, and shortly it arrived at the back shop at Collinwood, O. Here it was lifted in the air to remove the trucks. When the unit was about 10 feet in the air, one of the legs of the lifting rigging slipped out, and the locomotive came down with a crash into the pit.

The locomotive was duly overhauled and furnished with a new unit-exchange 12-cylinder Alco 244 engine. Out in the fire-up shed, we undertook the usual break-in procedure. The last item to be checked was the overspeed trip of the engine, for which the machinist got out his tachometer while I brought the engine speed up with the potentiometer in the electrical cabinet. The overspeed trip went out at its designated speed, and the engine began to decelerate.

Suddenly there was a loud explosion, and the engine compartment filled with smoke—we had experienced a crankcase explosion. With the crankcase exhauster running, the engine soon cooled down—and we found that one of the temporary main-bearing lube oil filters had come

adrift. It was No. 4, the critical one, naturally. The damaged engine was changed out, and another overhauled one was installed and load-tested satisfactorily before the unit was sent back into service.

During Collinwood's first rebuilding of a 12-cylinder 244 engine after a Class 1 overhaul, a block of metal was required for an operation. The machinist went to get something and returned, handing it to me. Taking one look, I burst out laughing. Everyone present was mystified as to what the joke was—the "block of metal" was none other than a Walschaerts valve-gear link block from a steam locomotive. Somehow, it had escaped the scrap bucket.

Steam once helped with diesel repair. The early 244 engines were supplied with soft crankshafts and, in a Class 2 repair at Collinwood, had to have their main and connecting rod journals lapped in place. This brought up the question of how to drive the crankshaft. The shop crew obtained one of the big air motors that the boilermakers had used to drive the staybolt taps in steam locomotive boilers, and an adapter between the air motor and the crankshaft stub shaft did the necessary. With a valve in the shop air line, speed was easily controlled in both directions.

One day in 1950, when a pair of month-old PA2's (Nos. 4208 and 4209) were dispatched east out of Englewood, trouble developed on the lead unit, 4208. At Elkhart, Ind., someone did something, but it was ineffective, so the units limped on to Toledo, O., where my good friend and co-worker, Bob Ash, was stationed. He brought the units through to Buffalo, and I took them on to Harmon. These later units came equipped with a device called a multi-point shunter, which was supposed to keep the main generator output right up to the curve at all times and so improve performance. In this case, the shunter was stuck in the up position and could not be run down either electrically nor mechanically—it was solid.

So, our modus operandi on this trip was to accelerate the train up to about 35 mph, then request the engineer take the throttle down to Notch 1. We'd wait a few moments for the engine speed to drop off (hence the main generator voltage), then the transfer relay (TR) picked up manually. With a loud bang and a flash, the unit was then in parallel shunt, and we could make good running time. This procedure had to be repeated after every stop. Upon inspection after the trip, it was found that the manufacturer had forgotten to put any lubricant in the gear box of the shunter, so the bearings were frozen solid!

PA's on the *Century*? Yes, one evening PA1's 4201 and 4202 were dispatched on a second section of No. 25. We departed Harmon on time, and I stayed in the trailing unit to check performance. Upon going up to the lead unit, I saw that the RD-2 turbo was on fire. An accumulation of oil from the bearings had been ignited by the hot turbo. I grabbed a fire extinguisher and emptied it, but that wasn't quite sufficient to put the fire out. I went up to the cab for another extinguisher, and when the engine crew saw the fire, they were all for stopping and calling a fire department, but I told them to keep the train going. Most of the oil had burned out, so everything settled down, and the units went on through.

When New York Central received its 26 Baldwin shark-nose units in 1951-1952, it assigned them to the DeWitt Diesel Shop at Syracuse, N.Y., for maintenance. Here they received the same degree of maintenance as did EMD's and Alcos. But the Baldwins didn't like this—they wanted more, and since they didn't get it, delays and failures were widespread. After a change in management, the Baldwins finally got what they wanted: new pistons, cylinder liners, cylinder heads, turbos, the works. They then went out and did the job, but their operating costs went through the roof. Consequently, the Sharks were transferred to the Southern Region (the old Big Four), where heavy tonnage (coal) and low train speed (30 mph) were more suited to them. The Baldwins were luggers, not runners.

One time, a pair of Sharks did slip east of Collinwood. The Erie Division engineer at first refused to take them, but he gave in when he was told that a diesel expert—me—would be going with him. We left Collinwood yard at a full 625 rpm and ambled along at the Baldwins' usual gait. At Ashtabula, O., we had to slow down for railroad grade crossings, and the engineer elected to use the dynamic brake to slow the train down. Having slowed it down, he went from braking to motoring position, at which time the engine in the lead unit died. Knowing that any attempt to restart the engine would result in an automatic air-brake application, the engineer elected to try to keep the train moving to get the caboose clear of the crossings. This he was able to do, so I then went back to restart the engine. The engine rolled over and fired, but when the start button was released, it would die—low lube oil alarm. Since we had plenty of lube oil in the crankcase and no visible oil leaks, I reasoned that the difficulty must be with the pressure switch. The next time around, when the lube oil pressure came up, the armature of the pressure switch was manually picked up. It held. The engineer then pumped off the air brakes, whistled in his flagman, and we continued on to Buffalo without further difficulties.

Baldwin engines themselves contributed to another tale. The model 606 engine from 660-hp VO switcher No. 750 came into Collinwood back shop for an overhaul, its first since construction. Two machinists began dismantling the engine and eventually got down to removing the cylinder liners. After working two days, they got one cylinder liner out! Upon learning this, I suggested to the department foreman, Nelson Paulson, that he give the men something else to do while we had the machine shop make up a gadget to remove the liners. With a 50-ton hydraulic jack on top of the cylinder block and a 7½-ton jack pushing up from the bottom, the liners were popped out in a hurry—to the accompaniment of an ear-splitting screech as, literally, metal was torn apart, the liners being so badly rusted. The engine overhaul was duly completed—although it was practically a new engine, what with all the new material applied—and shipped back to DeWitt for reinstallation in the carbody.

Some time later, the same locomotive came in for a Class 1 overhaul. This time we had no difficulty with the cylinder liners, but out in the fire-up shed, exhaust smoke was noted coming from the engine air-intake filters. It turned out that the polarity of the starting leads had been reversed and the engine was running backwards. This was corrected, but when the main generator was connected to the load box, the prime mover ran hot. The shop general foreman, Harry Stonebraker, happened to see me and asked if I would stop by and see what the cause of the difficulty was. It turned out that the piping from the thermostat to the radiator fan air clutch had not been applied. When this was done, 750 was satisfactorily load-tested and put back in service.

Later still, in the early 1960's, this unit and sister 751 came in to Collinwood to be retired. The two engines were removed, overhauled, and sent to the NYC marine department at Weehawken, N.J., for

A pair of EMD F units have been taken inside for repairs at Toledo, Ohio, in July 1955. ERNEST L. NOVAK.

installation in diesel-electric tugboat No. 34. The tug originally had two old McIntosh & Seymour engines which had failed beyond economic repair, so the Baldwins were used to re-engine it.

After the tug was back in service, complaints came in that the Baldwins made so much noise that the skipper in the wheelhouse couldn't hear the bargemen's whistle signals. With my marine experience, I was elected to visit the marine department. There, I contacted my counterpart, who in ocean-going circles was known as port engineer, and we went down to the dock where the tug was tied up. I suggested that the exhaust stack be cut off at a 45-degree angle, facing aft, to eliminate the pipe-organ effect. This was done, and the noise was greatly reduced; anything further would have required a muffler of some sort. With the arrival of Penn Central, the marine department at Weehawken was closed and the tug sold. Its new owners once again re-engined the tug; the fate of the two Baldwin engines is not known to me.

Baldwin engines were tough indeed. A short line in Pittsburgh had a Baldwin switcher with a 606 engine which had failed, so the railroad asked Baldwin for a cost estimate to repair it. The Baldwin representative took one look and said it couldn't be done, trying instead to sell the short line a new unit-exchange engine. The railroad was reluctant and called the New York Central at Collinwood, asking what our charge would be to repair the engine. Going only on information over the phone, we estimated that the crankshaft would have to be reground, the main bearing caps closed in, and the main bearing bores line-bored for new bearings—all for an estimated $1,000, plus overhead.

Shortly, the base with its main bearings arrived, and what a sight! Both ends and each side were bowed toward the center like a saucer. The main bearing caps were wedged so tightly that they had to be cut in two with a torch to get them out. At that time, a large open side planer was available in the machine shop that would just take this base. When we started machining, we discovered that we were merely adding to the bow as the machine's ways were worn. So the job had to be taken down and the planer rebuilt to plane correctly.

Meanwhile, it was found that the crankshaft was scrap material because of heat checks, so the short line had to purchase a new one. Subsequently, the A frame was sent in and a skim cut taken off the bottom where it bolted to the base. We

then installed a thicker gasket between the base and A frame in order to maintain the required ³⁄₁₆-inch clearance between the top of the piston and the bottom of the cylinder head. The locomotive went back in service and ran for years before being retired.

The Baldwin 608-SC engines developed a history of piston upper-ring wear. In an attempt to reduce this wear, NYC carried out an experiment. An engine that had been sent in to Collinwood for overhaul from Beech Grove Shop at Indianapolis had two lube oil nozzles screwed into each cylinder, one on each side, the nozzles being connected to a mechanical lubricator driven off the camshaft of the engine. To facilitate the equal distribution of the oil around the circumference of the piston, a helical groove was cut in the cylinder wall—a groove from each nozzle.

When word of this construction got out, there were all sorts of predictions—crankcase explosions, fires, and mayhem in general. So when the engine was reinstalled in the carbody at Beech Grove, nobody would touch the start button until I arrived. When the moment of truth came, everyone seemed to have urgent business elsewhere. With lube oil in the crankcase, the cooling system filled, and fuel pressure up (to release the shutdown feature), I pressed the start button. The engine rolled over, fired, and quickly settled down to its normal idle speed. Since none of the predictions had developed, everyone's courage returned, and we went through the usual Baldwin break-in procedure . . . while I sat on the water pump discharge pipe adjusting the output of the lubricator and listening to the turbo do its thing. The unit went back in service, but our experiment didn't prove much, because the Baldwins were retired before any significant mileage could be attained.

The Hamilton T69 and T89 engines installed in the switchers and road-switchers produced by Lima-Hamilton at Lima, O., were another matter. It was an abomination of an engine if there ever was one; perhaps the less said, the better. Most of the time the engines would come to the Collinwood backshop with one or more connecting rods sticking out through the side of the crankcase, but several arrived in the form of a connecting rod bent like a pretzel with a polite note attached: "Please build us a new engine!" My opinion is that the crankshaft was improperly balanced, and the harmonic vibrations soon

destroyed it. After two of NYC's 16 road-switcher units, 6210 and 6211, came into Collinwood with damaged engines, an exasperated management decided to re-engine them. EMD 12-cylinder 567 engines, with D-4 main generators, were installed at Collinwood in 1955-1956. This made a good combination, and these two units outlasted their sisters by several years.

Originally, the Lima road-switchers hauled commuter trains out of Weehawken, N.J. Beginning in 1954 and gradually continuing through 1961, the units' steam generators were removed and ballast was added, and they were reclassified as freight locomotives. All but the two re-engined units wound up being re-assigned to transfer and yard transfer service in Cincinnati, and they stayed there until retirement in 1965-1966. The two re-engined Limas were assigned to transfer work between Root Street and La Salle Street Station in Chicago. With the coming of Penn Central, the Root Street facility was closed and the units transferred to Philadelphia for use at 30th Street Station. On a visit to 30th Street, I noted with interest that as the original electrical equipment had worn out or failed, it had been replaced with EMD material. The only original electrical items left were the reverser and, of course, the Westinghouse traction motors.

On the New York Central, the Fairbanks-Morse units were the poor relations of the locomotive family—they always seemed to be in trouble. The first two passenger-service Erie-built units, Nos. 4400-4401, never got out of Harmon station on their very first revenue run in 1949 but had to be cut off and a pair of E7's substituted. The Erie-builts were supplied with a copper bus bar between the electrical cabinet and the traction motor leads. In wet weather it was almost impossible to keep the ground relay reset. Many times the ground relay knife switch would be opened (thereby negating ground protection) and, with the engine control knob set at Throttle 2, an attempt would be made to dry the bus bar out. Sometimes this worked, but the solution in subsequent shoppings at Collinwood was to replace the bus bar with neoprene cable.

One evening at Syracuse, repair to an Erie-built was made quickly . . . and cheaply. Train 17, the *Wolverine,* came into the station behind two of the Eries, Nos. 4402-4403, whistling for relief. All the Mohawk Division crew could tell me was that there were no alarm lights and no alarm bells, but the lead unit was producing no power. Quickly, what is wrong and how do you fix it in less than the 5-minute station time?

I boarded the unit through the side door and noted that a monkey wrench, with its jaws opened about 1 inch, was on top of the sandbox. A 1,000-watt light bulb went on in my head. Quickly, off came the cover on the governor, and, upon unscrewing the fuel limit pilot valve cap, I saw two pennies. Now, it was well known that two pennies were not enough—three were required. Depressing the pilot valve to make sure it wasn't stuck, I added the third penny and replaced the cap and cover. I gave a highball to the stationmaster and road foreman of engines, who were standing on the platform. With the road foreman riding the cab, the train made up 17 minutes to Buffalo, and the units went on through.

On another evening two of the Erie-builts came into Albany from Harmon in need of help. As the train approached, all that could be seen was a moving dark mass. The headlight, number boards, and cab lights were extinguished. It turned out that the auxiliary generator voltage regulator was defective and the batteries were almost on their last legs. I blocked the regulator in to a reasonable voltage level, and the train departed; Syracuse was notified to check it upon arrival. This can't be done with today's solid state regulators.

New York Central had 19 FM H20-44 freight transfer units with the 10-cylinder (opposed-piston) 2,000-hp engine, and two of them, Nos. 7104-7105, came to Harmon Electric Shop for application of multiple-unit control. Arrangements had been made with the manufacturer to furnish the material; railroad forces were to make the application. The material was arriving spasmodically, so one day the shop general foreman, George Beischer, asked me to work up a sketch for the gangway between the units, as the material hadn't arrived and the date the units were due out of the shop was getting close. I did the sketch, and the boilermakers began to gather the material to construct it. A couple of days later, the material from FM arrived, so the boilermakers quit what they were constructing to apply the new material.

Late that day, I had an occasion to stop by the shop foreman's office, where the foremen were finishing their daily paperwork. When the boiler foreman, John Cassiday, saw me, he said, "Hey, Harold. I checked your sketch against the material that arrived from FM, and you were a quarter-inch off." Loud laughter.

I replied, "John, I've been working with you boilermakers long enough to know that when I put down a dimension you're going to be a quarter-inch off anyway." More laughter . . . and I ducked as John threw a pack of timecards at me.

Later, when these two units were leaving DeWitt Yard for Corning, N.Y., 7104 lost the string band on the main generator. A new band was applied, but the locomotive lost it on the next trip. So I received a call from the diesel supervisor, George Schryer, to come over to DeWitt and help apply another new string band, plus try to locate the cause of the difficulty. Another new band was applied to the generator armature and, with the unit on a pit, the bottom covers of the traction motors were re moved. By looking up at an odd angle, I discovered that the No. 2 traction motor had a large patch of insulation missing on one of the field coils. After the traction motor was replaced, the unit settled down to its intended operation.

Then came the FM C-Line 2,000-hp freight units, and with them trouble; NYC had 12 cab units and 3 B units in this series, Nos. 5006-5017 and 5102-5104. The piston crowns in the 10-cylinder OP engines all cracked. To get the upper pistons out required the removal of the upper crankshaft, a big job, so the out-of-service time on these units was horrible, to say the least. Finally in desperation, the maintaining terminal, West Springfield, Mass., set the fuel injection pump racks back a little on one unit and dispatched it without saying anything to anyone. The unit ran for some time without difficulty. However, the beans eventually were spilled, and it was back to Square 1 again. By then, though, the decision had been made to re-engine the locomotives with EMD 16-567C engines, performed at Collinwood in 1955-1957. The units then gave good service, although with a slight loss of horsepower (2,000 to 1,750), until retirement in 1964-1965.

Finally came the C-Line passenger units, with the B-A1A truck arrangement and the 12-cylinder, 2,400-hp engines, beginning with FM demonstrator units Nos. 4801 and 4802. The first time I went aboard these units, at Syracuse, I was left with the distinct impression that they were lemons. The eight production units that NYC subsequently received in 1952 (4500-4507) proved it. At first, the main generators had the cute trick of disintegrating, making it necessary to go in with a bushel basket to pick up the pieces. After much experimentation by the manufacturer, this antic was calmed down, but it was never really resolved.

Then the engines wore out. It was truly amazing how, in one year's time, the engines could be so completely worn out from the accessory end to the blower end, despite much out-of-service time for other work (compared with other manufacturers' units). After three years of messing with these units, NYC decided to re-engine them, too; 1,750-hp EMD 16-567C engines were installed at Collinwood. These units also then gave good service, although maintenance was hampered by the presence of the steam-generator water tanks in the engine compartment. Finally, the units were retired in 1966, although one was put back in service in connection with a superheated steam rail-cleaning device. They were mighty expensive locomotives.

Speaking of costs, using maintenance costs on EMD's as a base, Alcos were 1.5 times as expensive, Baldwins were 3 times, and FM's were 4 times—so you can see why the expensive units were the first to go.

In all our early discussions on the future of diesel motive power on New York Central, the conclusions were that we would end up with only EMD's and Alcos. Nobody considered that General Electric would get into the domestic market on its own, but as we have seen, GE came on the scene with the U25B and subsequent models, and Alco gave up, leaving GE and EMD as the sole manufacturers today. Though most of the early diesel units have been replaced with more modern ones, no doubt many tales will be told of escapades with them too.

Surprise! Tests held the operating end of the railroad together

By W. M. Adams
Trainmaster

1940s -'50s

From *Trains* magazine, March 1980

"If you see an engineer whittling, follow him—he's making a wedge to block out the deadman pedal!"

These were words of wisdom from a grizzled road foreman of engines to a newly sworn-in assistant trainmaster. A quarter of a century ago, the diesel was rapidly pushing aside the steam engine from the Atlantic to the Pacific, from Hudson Bay to the Bay of Campeche, and every engineer was losing much sleep trying to figure ways to overcome the deadman pedal, a device he thoroughly detested. Conversely, it was the bound duty of trainmasters and road foremen of engines to forestall these attempts to render inoperative a device designed to initiate an undesired application of the train brakes in the event the engineer was suddenly incapacitated (and did not slump to the floor squarely on top of the pedal!). Releasing the pedal gave a visual and audible warning and, if not promptly forestalled, caused a loss of power and depleted the train line completely. A brake shoe, a knuckle pin, a monkey wrench, or a ball peen hammer worked fine, but the favorite was a flagstaff with a wedge-shaped point whittled on it. It could be jerked out and stuck in the proper receptacle if the enemy was sighted, and hopefully no one would be the wiser

One evening back about 1956, I crawled up on the lead unit of train 173 in the Texas & Pacific's Lancaster Yard at Fort Worth. The engineer was one of my old-timers; I had several between 75 and 80 years of age, and this old boy was one of them and also one of the best. He always had the remnants of a cigar in his mouth, and when I opened the door behind him unannounced, he was getting ready to make a brake application for a service test with his left hand. But in his right was a Barlow knife and a nice wedge-shaped piece of pine. He looked up at me, his mouth dropped open, and the cigar fell in his lap.

"Tom," I said, "you can hold that pedal down a whole lot better with your foot." About that time the cigar burned through his overalls and he jumped up, flapping at his lap. His foot slipped off the pedal, and he busted his air. Tom pitched the chunk of wood out the cab window, and I told him to let it go at that, pump his air up again, and get on with his brake test.

An old-time, toe-tapping, hoe-down fiddler would never make a hoghead on a modern diesel locomotive. Start keeping time with your foot and bells will ring, lights will flash, you lose your train air, and people come running from every direction.—Bozo Texino.

One of the most, if not *the* most, important duties of a trainmaster, in league with the road foreman of engines and other division officers, is to observe the performance of duty and check the compliance with rules by all operating employees. When I was trainmaster for the Missouri Pacific, this ranged from merely checking a train register to see if the proper information was entered, to secreting one's self adjacent to the right of way and displaying, in one manner or another, signal indications of a nature not anticipated by the unsuspecting crews. These tests could be made by setting out fusees and torpedoes, by having a signal supervisor rearrange the signals, or in some cases, by simply waving a red flag. All tests had to be reported.

Mere observation tests were entered on a designated form, and, on the Missouri Pacific at least, a specified number of signal surprise tests had to be made each month by division officers and a concise narrative report rendered. Failure to make the tests called for censure. Failure to make an intelligent report called for censure; failure to—well, you get the idea.

The general manager dearly loved to sharpen his teeth on trainmasters, probably recalling the miserable time he had had as a trainmaster under some hard-nosed old curmudgeon schooled on 16-hour locals or unending nights bent over a train sheet. Of course, it helped if the trainmaster was conversant with the rules, and on the Missouri Pacific in the early 1950's we had a gnarled old fellow in St. Louis who made sure we knew them. Our general rules examiner wasn't happy unless he was trapping a green assistant trainmaster during the annual rules examination. Needless to say, we burned plenty of midnight oil preparing.

A boomer brakeman told me he knew the Book of Rules so well that every place he worked he had the rules examiners following him around.—Bozo Texino.

In my earlier years, nurtured by exciting tales in the old *Railroad Man's Magazine*, I had formed the opinion that all trainmasters and road foremen of engines were selected for being dense, and one and all could be outsmarted by the frowziest old freight conductor on the board—not to mention, of course, the engineer, fireman, brakeman, switchman, yardmaster, and the local agent! I cannot recall a story in this dearly beloved old publication in which the trainmaster or RFE got his just due.

And the superintendent was always pictured as a benevolent old gentleman who always upheld the brilliant conductor and belabored the slow-witted trainmaster. Of course, the kindly old superintendent had once been a trainmaster—bumbling or otherwise—and I have known some kindly old superintendents who could literally pull track spikes with their teeth.

One of the finest stories I ever read in *Trains* magazine was the personal experiences of the late Walter Thrall while working as a locomotive fireman on the Union Pacific during World War II. Thrall wrote that the UP was "notorious" for tests. To me, this is probably the reason the UP has always ranked high in the annual safety standings of Class 1 railroads, being many times winner of the coveted Harriman award.

Tests, as I quickly found out when I went out as an assistant trainmaster many years ago, were not only required, they

were necessary—they held the operating end of the railroad together. Quit testing crews and soon rules observance would deteriorate, and derailments, split switches, cornering, sideswipes, shove-outs, and other calamities would become routine. Tests, as I also found out in a hurry, were no laughing matter and oft-times became an onerous chore, sprinkled with not a little peril! But then, as has been observed, time and distance are great healers, and in looking back over a 25-year span, I can recall some light moments. Maybe it wasn't so bad after all.

The Book of Rules is always the "Book of the Month" on the railroads.—Bozo Texino.

I recall one night in Chidester, Ark., a whistle-stop community a few miles out of Gurdon on the branch line to El Dorado, when I was treed on a tie pile by an angry bulldog. I was thankful for two things: the ties were untreated; and the lady who owned the bulldog lived just across the street from the main line. She was awakened by the uproar and came out and called the dog off. She called me a few things, too.

Again at Chidester one fine night, the roadmaster and I put out torpedoes and displayed a lighted red fusee. When the engineer of train 275 made his brake application, the flagman pitched out a lighted red fusee to try to keep train 271 out of his caboose. This was in the fall of the year, and the grass and weeds were high and dry There was a brisk wind blowing, and the fusee took a bad hop—it took us something like an hour to put out the right-of-way fire.

One time the Bank of Chidester was robbed, and a few days later the boss trainmaster and I and the assistant trainmaster from El Dorado drove into the town in the middle of the night to work over Nos. 272 and 274. We had tested one of them and were parked on a side street more or less across from the closed depot, debating our further activities, when a car pulled up behind us. Nothing was done; no one got out—it just stopped. But when we started up, it started up, and when we stopped, it stopped. We drove around the block, and it stayed right on our heels.

It finally dawned on us that this was probably a very nervous constable. We thought about getting out and identifying ourselves but then decided this fellow might have an equally nervous trigger finger No one wanted to test his accuracy with a load of 00 buckshot, so we just eased into gear and departed Chidester.

Chidester was handy to Gurdon, and besides, there was a little drugstore in Gurdon with a soda fountain staffed by a waitress who whipped up a mean sundae.

The wear and tear on a hoghead's nerves is something awful, but I never let that derail my train of thought.—Bozo Texino.

On another night, the assistant trainmaster from El Dorado and I were stopped by an Arkansas state patrolman. He wasn't nervous, thankfully, for until we could identify ourselves he had a very large pistol with a very large muzzle stuck right under our noses. We had been in the little Gum Springs depot, which was closed at night, listening in on the dispatcher's telephone, trying to get a rundown on our trains. The trooper had observed us leaving the depot and was merely doing his duty—but then, so were we. When he holstered his Magnum, I thanked him for looking out after company property and headed for an open coffee shop to try to unjangle my nerves.

I suppose the chief occupational hazard for a trainmaster making tests in southwest Arkansas during most of the year was mosquitos. They snapped like feisty dogs, and a few hours on a windless night down around Fulton would leave so many welts that your wife would hardly recognize you when you finally drug yourself home. Little wonder that making surprise signal tests, or any other kind, for that matter, was not exactly my idea of fun. Well, one did enjoy the companionship and camaraderie with the other unfortunates you were out with. After shagging up and down the railroad for an afternoon and part of a night, a hamburger steak smothered with onions and a cup or two of black coffee in an all-night truck stop over on the highway tended to smooth out the rough spots.

One day the trainmaster, John Toler, nearly took me out of service for tying up and eating. I was at Gurdon, and he called me from Little Rock and advised that he and the signal supervisor were catching No. 7 to Malvern. I was to get off center and meet them there so we could make some tests. Number 7 was due out of Little Rock then, and I had to hump to drive from Gurdon to Malvern and make it on time. Naturally, I had no chance to eat. Now, No. 7 carried a diner, and they took advantage of it, so I just stood on my rights and got a bite to eat before we left Malvern. Toler wanted to go up to Haskell and test on the Rock Island crossing, but owing to the delay caused by my hunger pangs, we missed three or four trains—trains manned by crews long overdue for our attention.

One day I showed up in Little Rock, and the boss wanted to go over on the Hot Springs Subdivision and do some testing. We slipped out of the depot at Little Rock into a sudden downpour and ran to my car, way down in the parking lot only to discover I had locked my keys in the accursed Chevy! That brought on some cryptic remarks, but not nearly as pointed as those directed at me when we got over on the branch near Lonsdale and I was asked for some torpedoes and fusees. I didn't have a one; I didn't even have a red flag. Well, we started back to the highway, and I had a blowout; that ended our nefarious activity for the night. When we finally got the tire changed on that steep, rocky, rutted mountain road, we tied up!

Down in Texas one dark night, I ran my station wagon through a three-strand barbed-wire fence. I was following the directions of the roadmaster, and he couldn't see any better than I could. When I traded off the wagon several years later, it still had those cruel lacerations on it. I suppose I was lucky to be promoted and sent to Texas, or Toler might have cut short my career sooner.

If you don't know which is what or where is where, read Rule 108 in the Transportation Book of Rules.—Bozo Texino.

The average operating employee was of the opinion that tests were made for one purpose, to run someone off. This was just not true, and a trainmaster or other official who used, or tried to use, surprise tests as a tool to get at someone was a fool. Yes, I have known it to happen—we once had a hard-case trainmaster on the north end of the Arkansas Division who tried this at least once, and it bounced right back in his face. You cannot fire an employee without a formal investigation, and when something like this was pulled, the trainmaster became the star witness. And any good employee representative could, and would, tear you to shreds as a witness.

Whenever tests revealed glaring deficiencies in performance, they had to be handled, but in the vast majority of cases this could be done by just calling in the crew and talking to them. Most of the time, it was just a case of inadequate knowledge of the rules, not willful violation, and most crews welcomed a clear understanding of how to get over the road by the book.

A yardmaster found a student cowboy

switchman adjusting a coupler with his foot. He almost swallowed the kid whole and told him he should always use his head on the railroad as it was against the rules to kick a drawbar with your foot. The cowboy then butted the drawbar over with his head!—Bozo Texino

As I recall, during my service as an officer, we felt it necessary on only one occasion to conduct a formal hearing, and this was brought on by the conductor's bullheadedness. This particular crew had performed miserably on a surprise signal test. This was mostly due to lack of knowledge or desire on the part of the conductor—an extra man, by the way, and not one of our regular chain-gang men.

I remember the investigation vividly, since I had to be a witness—and for another reason. The head brakeman (who performed 100 percent, incidentally) was sitting next to me, and John Toler was in the witness chair relating just what had happened when this man turned to me and blurted out, "Why, he is telling the truth!" This employee had some 14 years' service and, possessing a perfect record, had never been in an investigation. It was apparent that he had really been pumped full of misinformation by older and "wiser" members of the crew. I don't remember the discipline imposed by the superintendent; nobody was fired, but I believe the conductor and engineer had to sign for some demerits. At no time during the investigation did the crew or their representatives allege any unfairness, but you heard that insinuation often, usually secondhand.

I do recall an incident that happened after I went to Texas in 1956 as a trainmaster. We had a turnaround local between Mart and Valley Junction, 59 miles, and it usually operated at night. The engineer was a rather wild-eyed and wild-haired character nicknamed Smokey. One day the division special agent had business in Mart and had his evening meal with my wife and me. I suggested we go out and make a few surprise tests, and he agreed, so we went in his automobile down to MA Siding between Mart and Marlin and put out torpedoes and displayed a burning red fusee. Old Smokey performed 100 percent, except that he failed to sound the prescribed whistle signal for a road crossing in the vicinity. This was really easy to understand; when an engineer is manipulating brake valves and throttle he just doesn't always think of the whistle.

I didn't send for Smokey, but he came into my office the next day just the same,

glared at me, and asked, "How did I do last night?" (This will give you an idea of just how secret tests actually were.) I told him okay, except for whistling for the crossing.

"Dammit," he said, "I knew you would find something wrong!" He went on, "You know that was an unfair test, don't you?" This I promptly denied and asked just how he had arrived at that conclusion. "Well," he said, "your car was in your driveway when I left town!" I lived on the main street of Mart, and I learned then that just about all crews when leaving on a run drove by my house to see if my blue-and-white Chevy station wagon was in the driveway.

I once fired for an old-time hoghead who always had an iron-clad alibi when anything happened on the road. When he took his pension, his record was as clear as a green block signal.—Bozo Texino

The old trainmaster's clerk at Little Rock was given to tipping off the crews when we tried to get out and make some surprise tests, and I often thought we spent more time trying to deceive him than we did in making tests. Actually, you just had to make two or three signal tests and everybody knew it anyway. At that time, radios were new, and we had no base station on the Arkansas Division; only the engines and cabooses were equipped, so the sets came in handy for the crews to tip each other off with no one being the wiser.

Now, this old trainmaster's clerk was also one to tipple, and the crews kept him well supplied with potables in payment for favors done or hoped for. One Christmas season, a north-end conductor slipped him a fifth of whisky, neatly wrapped up, in the office. It seems that several roadmen had already asked him out to their cars. He was feeling no pain, but when he started home that evening he accidentally dropped his gift on the floor of the trainmaster's office. The smell of vintage Scotch lingered for weeks!

I asked Toler why he put up with his man, and he allowed as how most of the high-ranking operating officers on the road had been trainmaster at Little Rock at one time or another and had done nothing about him, and he hated to be the hard-hearted goat.

A boomer once told me: "There's nothing against the rules on a railroad if you don't get caught!—Bozo Texino

I was breaking in a new assistant trainmaster down on the old "Jenny," as we called MoPac's International-Great Northern district in Texas, and one hot summer noontime I decided to test the Valley Junction-to-Spring local. This job worked out of Valley Junction on Monday down to Spring (20 miles north of Houston) and back on Tuesday, etc., and since Spring was merely a whistle-stop, the crew lived on the caboose during their layover. We had a bath facility rigged up at Spring and electrical connections so they had at least some of the comforts of home. Most of their work was around Bryan, and the usual practice before leaving there was to stop for a minute across from a large supermarket to stock the larder. Leaving Bryan, they usually cooked and ate en route to their next chores, ordinarily at Navasota, there being little in between save College Station just a short distance south of Bryan.

On this particular day I put my new assistant near the depot at College Station with a red flag and told him to hold them for a few minutes. I hid my station wagon and took cover in some scraggly mesquite trees where I could observe the actions of the flagman. I was curious to see what he would do, since the south yard limit board at Bryan would be just a few car-lengths to their rear and the possibility of their being overtaken by a following train was nil. They stopped—no problem, they were going perhaps 25 mph, maybe less—and the caboose paused directly across from my hideout.

The flagman was a big, good-natured fellow named Frankie Porterfield and nicknamed "Paddlefoot" in recognition of his more-than-adequate underpinning. Frankie fell off the caboose promptly enough, but instead of flagging equipment he was carrying a china cup. He looked back toward Bryan and then up toward the engine, and about that time the engineer whistled him in. Frankie waved a highball with the cup and boarded the caboose. Now, this struck me as being a slipshod way of railroading, and I hurtled out of my concealment and boarded the caboose. Royce Rogers, the conductor, was busy at the cookstove and graciously invited me to sit and eat. I declined the invitation and stormed up and down the caboose, calling their attention to this lackadaisical way of protecting their train.

"Porterfield," I said, "you could at least have carried a flag with you—protecting your train with a cup of coffee is a pretty sorry way of railroading."

Frankie looked at me and grinned.

"One fine spring evening we 'redded' all the absolute signals. Well, before we could pick up the signals, we'd gotten seven trains in our net." Ben Bachman.

"Here, boss," he said, shoving the cup toward me, "this isn't coffee, it's buttermilk!"

A brakeman fresh from the ranch who still wore one spur told the trainmaster that he used his cowboy hat to flag a hoghead instead of a red flag. He said if a hoghead was so old he couldn't see a cowboy hat, he sure couldn't see a red flag!—Bozo Texino

One fine spring evening we encamped at Clear Lake Junction, Ark., about 10 miles north (or east) of Texarkana. This was the start of double track leading into the Texarkana terminal, or the end of double track leading out of Texarkana, depending on which direction you were facing. We "redded" all the absolute signals; i.e., rigged them to display a "stop" indication. Well, before we could pick up the signals, we had gotten seven trains in our net. Probably the last four or five of them knew it was a test and not signal trouble. We also got censured again, and severely, by the GM for unnecessary delay of trains. We had caught, among others, such hotshots as No. 60, a transcontinental perishable connection; No. 65, which carried large numbers of auto parts for the assembly plants in the Dallas-Fort Worth area; No. 32, a remnant of the fine old *Sun-*

shine Special; and, as I recall, two of the *Texas Eagles.* A pretty good haul. We then went back up to Hope and hit the Nashville local when he got back to the main line. Then, weary of our duties, we tied up at the old Barlow Hotel for a late night, or early morning, rest.

Upon reflection, I suppose that the chewing out from the old man had had its purpose. Toler always said that if you kept on the crews for little stuff such as reading a newspaper on duty or stepping on a rail, they would soon get the idea you were really concerned about little things and begin to wonder just how hard they will get hit if they were found guilty of big things. I suppose it just boiled down to the simple fact that if you showed a concern and respect for the rules and safety and heads-up operation, the crews would soon realize that you wanted them to work safely and efficiently and that they couldn't come into an investigation and claim the trainmaster always looked the other way, or we have always done it this way, and so forth.

The Book of Rules is nothing but block signals on the road to reason.
—Bozo Texino

Remembering the Malleys

By Barry Anderson
Fireman

1953

From *Classic Tains* magazine,
Fall 2009

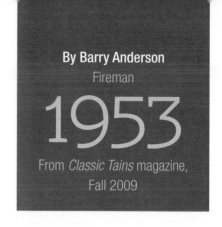

My love affair with Southern Pacific's cab-forwards began in the late 1940's, when I was a teenage railfan growing up on the San Francisco Peninsula.

I'd seen them occasionally in the mountains on family vacations to Lake Tahoe and trips north to Mount Shasta, but never "up close and personal."

Then, as hundreds of new F-unit diesels arrived on the SP, they began to displace the cab-forwards from their traditional stomping grounds. First, the older "flat-front" AC-4's, 5's, and 6's were bumped off the Portland and Shasta divisions and the Modoc line. Then the more modern AC-7 to AC-12 classes (excepting the AC-9's, which were rear-cab 2-8-8-4's built as coal-burners to work in New Mexico) were displaced from Donner and Tehachapi passes, showing up in increasing numbers on the Coast and Western divisions.

Many a warm summer night I lay in bed with the window open, savoring the distinctive whistle of an AC-powered freight heading up or down the Peninsula. Cab-forwards became regular power on the freights bound for Tracy by way of Altamont Pass.

Finally, in 1953 I became old enough to go firing. The Coast Division was still almost entirely steam, and firing promised high adventure. My first student road trip was the regular night extra for Watsonville Junction, called for 10:30 p.m. from Bayshore, SP's big yard just south of San Francisco.

I met my engineer, Denny Allison, at the roundhouse. With an "OK, kid, let's go; we've got a Malley tonight," we headed off for the ready track. (A note here: In the years I worked for the SP, I never heard the terms cab-forward, cab-ahead, or cab-in-front used by enginemen. We called them Malleys or by their number series—4100's or 4200's. Although SP's 2-6-6-2 and 2-8-8-2 cab-forwards of the 1910's were compound Mallets, these were retired or rebuilt as simple articulateds, and the 4-8-8-2 cab-forwards of 1928–44 were simple; nevertheless, the nickname Malley stuck to the end.)

There's a magic about a roundhouse alive with steam at night. The flicker of a firebox illuminating the darkness, black looming shapes quietly hissing steam, the pounding of air pumps breaking the stillness. And, there, huge in the inky night, stood our power, AC-10 No. 4243, its twin air pumps sounding that whistling phew-phew distinctive to all the AC's.

There seemed to be a bewildering amount to learn, but I couldn't have had a better teacher. Allison and his regular fireman were patient to a fault. As they showed me around, I tried to memorize everything they were telling me, knowing I'd be on my own soon enough.

We climbed to the cab and put our lunch and overnight bags in the seatboxes. With the head brakeman occupying the extra seat by the front windows, I'd be riding on the sandbox tonight. (All oil-fired engines carried a supply of sand in the cab to be tossed into the firebox periodically in order to clear the flues of oil residue.)

I noticed the fireman place his pint whiskey bottle full of coffee on the steam manifold to keep it hot. (Note to self: Obtain an empty whiskey bottle to carry coffee.) His preparations for the run continued: Set the firing pin to the spot-fire position on the firing valve. Drain the water glass and test the gauge cocks. Open the firebox door, kneel down and peer through the flames to check for leaking staybolts and soft plugs. Turn the tank heater on. Walk back and climb onto the deck behind the smokebox to check the lubricators on the air pumps and the feedwater pump. Climb up onto the tender, open the valve releasing air pressure from the oil tank (thus avoiding a faceful of Bunker C), check the measuring rod for fuel, and don't forget to close the valve to repressurize the tank. (Later that year I had an embarrassing experience forgetting to close that valve, resulting in no fire and a precarious trek along the running board at speed to close the valve.) Check the water level, supply of water treatment chemicals, and the electric marker lights. Light a white kerosene lantern and hang it from the hook on the rear of the tender.

Back in the cab, we hosed down the deck with the steam hose, then checked that the water pump and injector were working. We were running as Extra 4243 East tonight, so the fireman told me to insert the proper numbers in the drop-down indicator boxes and turn the classification lights to white. Lastly, give the engine a good blow-down to drain sediment from the boiler.

We soon left the ready track, picked up the head brakeman, and backed down to our train, a short 35 cars tonight, but we'd get more at San Jose. My first impression as we moved past Visitation tower, picked up our orders, and pulled out onto the main, was how out-in-front the cab of an AC was. Visibility was much greater than on any of today's diesels because there was nothing in front of the windows, just a straight drop to the tracks.

We made an uneventful trip down the Peninsula to San Jose Yard, took water (and pie at the popular beanery), filled out our train, and headed for Watsonville Junction as Second 938. One other impression from that first trip was just how big and robust these engines were.

When I got a chance to take over the firing, we were just passing through the spring switch at Coyote and starting up Morgan Hill. Denny Allison stood up and shoved the throttle toward the backhead (shorter engineers often handled the throttle standing up and facing backward because they could get more leverage than from a seated position). A roar from the firebox filled the cab. The fireman shouted at me, "Give 'er some juice!" Relying on my limited experience on switch engines, I timidly opened the firing valve, whereupon clouds of gas belched from the firebox as the fire became starved for oil. The fireman reached over and yanked the valve halfway across the quadrant, saying, "No, like this!" Next I opened the feedwater

valve, increased the atomizer, and turned off the blower.

With the increased draft through the firebox, it was time to sand the flues. Because the regular fireman and I were busy trying to keep the steam and water up, the head brakeman shoveled a few scoopfuls of sand through the firedoor peephole. Looking back along the boiler, I could see clouds of black smoke rolling across adjacent Highway 101.

After that first trip, I got to fire four more cab-forwards—Nos. 4196, 4287, 4211, and 4253—on my four days of student trips to the end of the division at Santa Barbara and back. Among my memories of that student week, Tunnel 6

Southern Pacific AC-7 No. 4165 pulls an extra freight near Mount Shasta, California, in January 1944. TRAINS MAGAZINE COLLECTION.

stands out. The raison d'être for the cab-forward was, of course, to keep the crew ahead of the smoke in the tunnels and snowsheds of the Sierras. That works well in theory, but it's a moot point when you're on the third and rearmost engine of a hundred-car train slogging upgrade at less than 10 mph.

I was making one of my student trips on the 4211, on this occasion the second helper on a heavy eastbound drag climbing from Santa Margarita to the top of Cuesta Grade on the Coast Division. As we coupled on ahead of the caboose, the regular fireman handed me a strange-looking sheet-metal cone with a hose protruding from it. "Here," he said, "You'll need this for Tunnel 6." As instructed, I soaked cotton waste in water from the drinking cooler, stuffed it into the cone, and plugged the hose into an outlet from the engine's air reservoir.

Enginemen are inveterate storytellers, especially when it comes to razzing a new fireman. As we started out of the siding at Santa Margarita, the fireman felt the need to relate in gruesome detail the November 19, 1941, tragedy of Chatsworth Tunnel on the Los Angeles Division. On that day, Extra 4193 West (a Malley) was working uphill through the 7,369-foot tunnel with a 96-car train. The engine stalled. Then, while trying to start, the train broke in two, setting the brakes in emergency. In the dense smoke and heat, the inexperienced fireman panicked, opened the firing valve, spilling hot oil on the track, which caught fire. The fire incinerated the two enginemen, the head brakeman, and 12 cars of cattle. Just the story to tell a green fireman heading into Tunnel 6 for the first time!

Our Malley was working hard all the way upgrade. We plunged into the 3,610-foot tunnel and were immediately engulfed in hot steam and smoke from the two engines ahead of us. Even with all the cab lights on, I could barely see the engineer. The sound of our exhaust bouncing off the tunnel ceiling was so deafening I couldn't hear the fireman as he shouted in my ear. Breathing cooler air from the respirator helped some, but not knowing how long we'd be in the tunnel was a terrifying experience I shall never forget.

I had the good fortune to fire many more cab-forwards during the next three years. With a four-wheel front truck right under the cab, they rode smoothly at the lower speeds of most drag freights. They would get up and move when called upon,

but the ride became considerably worse. On the long downgrade from Gilroy to Coyote, for example, we'd often reach 50 mph or so, but the ride got so rough you could hardly read the gauges for the bouncing.

The Malleys fired differently from rear-cab engines. The fireman's controls and gauges were located on the right-hand side of his position in an AC. At first, it seemed strange to fire sitting sideways with my back to the window, but it was much easier to keep an eye on the water glass and steam pressure and to look rearward to the light at the stack to check smoke density. You couldn't see the engineer (and thus change your firing settings in response to changes in throttle or reverse). Helpful hoggers would shout across the cab when they were about to make a move.

The forward windows provided terrific visibility, but that cab was no place to be if you had a grade-crossing accident. Another advantage was the quick access the head brakeman had to drop off and throw a siding switch.

However, having the cab in front was a distinct disadvantage when backing up, since the distance between the crew and the rear coupler was much greater than on a conventional engine. On one occasion, Roseville gave us the 4215 for what amounted to a local freight to Gerber via Davis on the West Valley Subdivision. I spent most of the day listening to the engineer's curses while wrestling the big engine into spurs and sidings as we dropped off and picked up cars at stops all the way up the valley.

None of the roundhouses on the Coast Division had a turntable long enough to turn a cab-forward. As hostlers, we turned them on the wyes at San Luis Obispo, Watsonville Junction, San Jose, and Mission Bay. On arrival at Bayshore, the hostler ran the engine the 5 miles up to Mission Bay, turned on the wye around Potrero Tower, and returned to Bayshore. Turning an AC meant at least one leg backing up with some 120 feet of engine and tender obscuring your view. Fortunately, I never had any accidents, but others occasionally ran through closed switches.

One of the distinct benefits for a brand-new railfan-fireman was that I had absolutely no seniority. All I could hold was the extra board and as the agricultural business (mainstay of the Coast Division) fluctuated with the various harvests, I found myself laid off more than once. Other divisions were hiring and I was

loaned out at various times to the Sacramento, Western, and Rio Grande divisions.

On the Sacramento Division, it meant the last chance to fire steam on legendary Donner Pass—The Hill. Four-unit F7's had already bumped the cab-forwards as road power between Roseville and Sparks, Nev., but the helpers were still nearly all AC's.

The cab-forwards were versatile locomotives, handling passenger, fast freight, and drags with equal ability, but they really came into their own as helpers over the Sierras. Their tremendous power came to the fore slogging upgrade at full throttle, sometimes at 10 mph or less.

The long, slow grind from Roseville up to Norden (only 85 miles) typically took eight or more hours including two water stops. Rear helpers were usually spaced 4 cars ahead of the caboose and another 11 cars ahead of that. Water plugs at Colfax, Gold Run, and Emigrant Gap were spaced so both helpers could take water at the same time. Typically, the rearmost helper was cut off first, then drifted back (with its four cars and caboose attached) to the downhill water plug. Next, the forward helper was cut off (with its cut of cars) and backed up to the upper plug. Those big tenders held 22,000 gallons and took as long as 15 minutes to fill. When both engines had satisfied their thirst, the moves were reversed and the train coupled up again. As with any helper operation, the rearmost AC began to start the train first, followed by the forward helper, and lastly by the road engine.

Uncoupling and turning the helpers in the Norden snowsheds was a rather complicated maneuver. The rearmost helper was cut off first, backed up to spot the caboose and attached cars, then backed through a crossover onto the covered turntable. Next, the forward helper shoved its cars back against the caboose, backed through the crossover, ran around the caboose, then shoved the rear 15 cars forward to a joint with the rest of the train. It then returned up the siding and backed onto the turntable. After turning, both engines took water, coupled up, and were off to Roseville on the westbound main.

The ride back to town was a piece of cake, especially if you were on the second helper. Nothing to do but set a spot fire, watch the water level, and relax. On one such Friday night trip downhill on the 4227, we stopped to pick up a section gang headed for town for the weekend. Ten or 12 of them crowded into the cab sitting on the deck and sandbox—a little crowded, but glad for the ride.

Keeping sufficient water in the boiler was always the prime consideration in firing a steam locomotive. Vivid photos of boiler explosions posted by the company on the walls of crew rooms were a constant reminder of what could happen if a fireman let the water get too low.

Cab-forwards carried their water just the opposite of a conventional engine. Working uphill, water ran to the smoke-box end of the engine—that is, away from the firebox crown sheet. For this reason, the AC's were banned from at least one line—over the Siskiyou Mountains between Ashland, Ore., and Black Butte, Calif.—because the grades were too steep to keep sufficient water over the crown sheet. Going downhill, the opposite was true. Water ran toward the front end and you carried water high in the glass, often nearly full.

The trickiest stretch of track on the Coast Division was the Guadalupe Subdivision, between San Luis Obispo and Santa Barbara. The subdivision had a roller-coaster profile, always climbing or descending. To compound the problem, the line ran close to the ocean and was often blanketed in fog. For a fireman, it was frequently difficult to know exactly where you were and whether you were heading uphill or down.

One of my first trips over this stretch was firing the "Smoky," a peddler freight that picked up and set out all along the line. The engine was the 4293 and we were running as First 916, called for 8 p.m. on a slow job that would take most of the night. Predictably, we encountered thick fog after picking up a string of reefers at Guadalupe. Visibility was cut to a few dozen yards. Green signals swam out of the fog, visible only when you were right on top of them. Soon I had no clue where we were and told the engineer. "That's OK, son," he replied. "I'll help you watch your water and tell you where it should be."

We spent a lot of time in the hole that trip, getting out of the way of a string of first-class westbounds: train 373, the hotshot *Coast Merchandise*; 95, the *Starlight*; and 75, the *Lark*. Sitting in a lonely siding with the headlight turned off, it was black out there beyond the flickering of the firebox on the tracks. All was quiet but for the whistling sounds of the air pumps. Suddenly, the signal ahead turned red, and out of the cottony fog the flashing Mars light of a Daylight-type 4-8-4 emerged, gave a couple of toots of his air horn to acknowledge our green signals, and slammed by with a lighted string of cars, then vanished into the fog. For me, that exemplified the romance of railroading.

By the end of 1955 the diesel invasion was in full swing and, except for the San Francisco commutes, most steam had disappeared from the main line. My last trip on a cab-forward was on the 4199 with train 403, from Tracy over Altamont Pass to Bayshore, an unremarkable five-hour trip. Had I known it to be the last, it would have been a sad farewell to a unique experience.

Southern Pacific 4-8-8-2 cab-forward no. 4203 works hard in pusher service on Tehachapi near Woodford, Calif., in August 1948.
REGINALD McGOVERN.

Love those diesels!

By A.M. Rung
Military Train Escort

1953

From *Trains* magazine,
April 1977

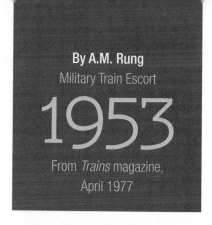

The current fuss about how dieselization will put the kiss of death on any interest the public has in railroads is amusing to me. You see, I once was a railfan before I went to work for a railroad and got rudely dashed in the face with some cold facts of life.

I was just out of the Army. I took a Pennsylvania Railroad timetable, picked out the highest-ranking official on it, and sent him a job letter. I got a prompt reply; he would be happy to see me for an interview next week. What else? I thought. I'm a railfan who knows all the answers, and I'll get things humming on that railroad. Despite this attitude, I was hired; and for the next three months I traveled all over the Pennsy system as a military train escort, acting as liaison between the railroad and the commanders of troop trains bringing GI's home.

Did I show the Pennsy a thing or two? You guessed it—I did not. A greener rube never entered the marble halls of the PRR's general offices in Philadelphia. But the railroaders were patient with me, God bless 'em; and while I was having the time of my life doing nothing but riding trains, I also began to learn some things about railroads.

At that time the Pennsylvania, now the largest diesel-locomotive operator in the world, didn't have a diesel to its corporate name. I was in ecstasy as I started my job. Just think of it: I would be riding Pullmans to fascinating places behind the sweet-chanting, handsome K4 Pacifics and M1 Mountains. That, my friend, would be really living. It was then that my education began. Remember those wartime train trips? I don't like to think about them either, and I'm sure the railroads feel the same way. All air-conditioned equipment was either in the normal consists of regularly scheduled trains (which were running in several sections) or in hospital troop trains. So if you rode a train as a GI, the odds are the trip was not one you would write about glowingly, especially if the train had a steam engine on the front

end. As a representative of a railroad, interested in the welfare and comfort of passengers, I found my love for the steamers quickly cooling.

The Pennsy's Horseshoe Curve is one of the outstanding scenic attractions in the East. I once accompanied a trainload of German prisoners of war around Horseshoe as they traveled west.

Some of the passenger trainmen on the New York-Altoona portion of the run were of Pennsylvania Dutch ancestry and spoke German. They reported that the prisoners believed Nazi propaganda that German bombs had rained destruction on the eastern U.S. As we traveled down the heavily industrialized corridor from New York to North Philadelphia they gazed in disbelief at the bustle they witnessed, and they became a bit less high-spirited than they had been at the start of the trip.

For the next 5 hours or so we sped through the beautiful farm country west of Philadelphia, and beyond Harrisburg we followed the lovely Juniata River valley toward Altoona. In late afternoon we climbed up to and around the magnificent Curve. It was then, I think, that the prisoners realized the full extent of their deception. They realized there had been no destruction at all to this country, parts of which resembled their own Rhine valley.

They soon fell silent and, as the bright glow of the steel mills in the Johnstown and Pittsburgh areas lit their faces, we could see that they had become thoughtful and looked tired.

But even the Curve's magnificent vistas are considerably diminished when soot and cinders from a brace of K4's or M1's are descending upon you like a soft

The clouds of smoke from double-headed steam locomotives illustrate a disadvantage to riding behind them—particularly with open windows. Here a "Main" (troop train) extra rolls east of Staple Bend, Pa., on the Pennsy. Several troop sleepers are in the consist. WAYNE BRUMBAUGH.

summer rain. One morning I walked through a troop train that had just climbed the grade out of Altoona. Most of the men still were asleep in the bunks of their troop sleepers (and may the guy who designed those dimly lit, flat-wheeled, prone-to-jump-the-rails monstrosities get his just reward in the Great Beyond). I cringed when I saw that the men were covered not only by GI blankets but by a thick layer of soot and cinders. It was painful to watch them awaken and wipe and spit the grimy mixture off their faces. No wonder many GI troop-train passengers decided to do their postwar traveling in the family auto.

It was in this period of my life that I developed for the giant GG1 electric a respect and affection I shall never lose. Many times I would wait through the night and early-morning hours at Potomac Yard across the river from Washington, D.C, in a rain of soot and cinders for military Mains (railroadese for troop trains) to arrive over a southern road. The Mains would always be late, sometimes as much as 16 hours. And they would limp into the yard behind one or two tired steamers which looked for all the world as though they had aching bunions (if locomotives could have such an ailment).

Then the greatest show on earth (for me) would start. Our GG1 would couple to the 20-odd Pullmans, coaches, troop sleepers, and kitchen cars. Slowly we would cross the Potomac River bridge, slip through the tunnels under the city, and continue up the freight route to Landover, our junction with the Washington-New York main line. Then the engineer would open the throttle. That's when I would enjoy walking back through the cars. The boys would jam against the windows, staring in disbelief at the landscape that whirled by at 80 miles an hour. We'd slip nonstop through the Baltimore tunnels and station, race across the flat Maryland meadows, thunder over the low-level bridge at Havre de Grace, maintain our high speed on the elevated trestles at Wilmington and Chester, and clock the 13 miles to Philadelphia's 30th Street Station in as many minutes or fewer. Then we would be on the New York Division, and our specials would devour the mileage so quickly that before the returning troops knew it, they would be peering through the windows across the Jersey Meadows for a glimpse of the Empire State Building.

When I saw what the GG1 electrics were doing on the New York Division, I knew the steam locomotive was through. And I was glad. If you stood on a North Philadelphia station platform on a Sunday night you gained the impression that everyone in New York had decided to come to Philadelphia for the evening and that all Quaker Citians had taken a notion to ride to New York.

Twenty-car trains rolled through that island-platform station like streetcars. Every train had standing room only and darn little of that. Pennsy was using every passenger car it had, albeit somewhat shamefacedly, in a masterful effort to transport everyone who wanted to ride. That's when the road's costly electrification, carried out during the Depression, really proved its worth. I have heard reputable persons say that the transportation job performed by the electrified divisions of the Pennsy helped to speed World War II to its conclusion. I agree.

Unfortunately, for a number of reasons the Pennsy's steam locomotives weren't up to performing the wartime transportation job with the ease the GG1s did. Although the steam locomotives were well cared for, the bulk of them (save for the Chesapeake & Ohio-pattern J1) were of 1929 vintage or earlier, and the brutal demands of wartime aged them much more quickly than normal work. Like most roads, the Pennsylvania literally had to rebuild its entire railroad after the war except for the durable GG1s. The PRR steamers may have staggered a little, and they broke down occasionally, but they did the job.

An alert military train escort considered several factors when assessing his assignment to a steam-powered train. One was the train's length. If it was short—fewer than 10 cars—he knew he probably was in for a fast ride. If he drew a train of 20 cars behind an M1 Mountain, his spirits sank for that meant slower running time and going in the hole for scheduled passenger trains as well as for fast freights or other Main trains.

With any train, there was the chance of a hotbox or mechanical breakdown. One summer day on a 20-car Main en route to Chicago, the trailing truck of our M1 developed a hotbox near Mansfield, Ohio. We stopped at a wayside phone, and the conductor called the tower. On a siding waiting for us to clear was a freight train, also pulled by an M1. We faced a wait for a relief engine, so I decided to have some fun with the engineer of the freight. I climbed into the cab and said breezily, "Well, Dad, we're gonna take your engine." The engineer, probably already exceeding

his hours of service, got red in the face, grabbed a wrench, and thundered, "The hell you are." Eying the waving wrench, I got out of the cab.

Another factor a train escort looked at was the type of equipment his train had. If the season was summer and the train was one of troop sleepers and tourist Pullmans, he was in for a hot, dirty ride. However, on the Pennsylvania, there often was on each train at least one Pullman with air conditioning. The PRR had the nation's largest pool of air-conditioned coaches and Pullmans, which gave troop trains a better-than-average chance to boast this kind of equipment.

There were three types of air-conditioned Pullmans: ice-cooled; steam-activated; and mechanically cooled. Steam-cooled was the most popular with train escorts, because when you connected the steam line and flicked a few switches inside the car, the air-conditioning unit would begin to function. The mechanical system was second choice because usually the unit contained the necessary Freon liquid and thus could be operated. The ice-cooled-type car presented a challenge. The Government had not contracted with the Pullman Company for ice, which is another way of saying that ice was neither supplied nor allowed. But many were the acts of piracy committed on station platforms, and I suspect that railroad management somehow looked the other way when a troop train snatched a load of ice from station ice trucks.

I heard on excellent authority about a certain military train escort, who shall remain nameless, who figured in one such caper. It was a scorching July night, and his 20-car Main was winding through the Pennsylvania mountains. On Main trains the custom was for the train escort and the Pullman conductor to share a drawing room. If there was an air-conditioned car on the train, that was where you would find the escort and the Pullman conductor. One of the niceties of the rulebook that was not observed was that the train escort was not to sleep. As the heavy main rounded Horseshoe Curve, the Pullman conductor told the train escort that the berths in the drawing room were ready and that he was going to turn in. In the drawing room, the Pullman conductor always took the lower berth and the escort the upper. But on this night the drawing room was in a non-air-conditioned tourist Pullman, and cinders were pouring through the room's screened window and onto the crisp sheets of the lower berth. When the train escort entered the drawing room he found the Pullman conductor asleep in the upper and clean berth. The escort, deciding he would rather sit up than sleep under soot and cinders, walked through the train.

One of the Pullmans, he noted, was equipped with an ice bunker. It was without ice, of course, but Pittsburgh was less than 2 hours away. Maybe that ice bunker could be filled. At Pittsburgh, the platform crewmen—especially those on ice trucks—had never seen a train escort in such good spirits at such a late hour. He joked with them, handed out playing cards (furnished by PRR to the train escorts for use by the troops), and was, in short, a mighty fine fellow. They agreed with him that the night was one of the hottest of the summer. There was an air-conditioned Pullman on the train that didn't have ice? Sure, they would be glad to put some ice in the bunker; in fact, they filled it.

The next morning, a wilted and outraged Pullman conductor entered the delightfully air-conditioned Pullman and acidly asked the train escort to sign a Pullman pass receipt, a formality Pullman conductors never observed with train escorts.

After three months of riding trains, I was brought into the passenger traffic department at Philadelphia, whose job was to sell the public on the merits of traveling on the Pennsylvania Railroad. Clubs, fraternities, business organizations, and labor and trade groups were solicited for their passenger business, which ranged from six people to a 10-car or 12-car train. You didn't sell these people on the melodic exhaust of a K4 or the soft patter of cinders. They wanted cool, clean cars and a smooth, comfortable, on-time ride.

To the delight of the passenger traffic salesmen, the Pennsylvania had begun to dieselize. New coaches and Pullmans and smooth-gliding diesel locomotives were being rushed into service on all principal

trains. But it was difficult to convince a lady of that if she had received the cinder treatment when she rode a non-air-conditioned coach last Sunday. It was tough to explain to a man who wrote to say he had observed that "your windows are now insulated with cinders."

Now all that is just an unpleasant memory. The Pennsylvania, like most other roads, is dieselized and air-conditioned. Passengers who get on the trains clean get off clean. And they get a smooth ride. A comment I heard one time when I was aboard the *Spirit of St. Louis* is not likely to be repeated. We were about 10 minutes out of Harrisburg when a businessman who was sitting next to me in the smoking room took his cigar from between his teeth and said, "This town we're coming into is Harrisburg. That's where the mountains start. They take off this electric engine and put on two steam engines. And all night long, the one 'gees' and the other 'haws,' and 1 can't sleep worth a damn."

Yes, my great romance with the steam locomotive had ended. It had been a romance with deep roots, for my earliest and happiest memories centered about the Pennsylvania Railroad and its noble steam locomotives. As a youngster on summer vacations in a Pennsylvania mountain town, I would arise early and run down to trackside to watch the *Rainbow Limited* glide around the east end of the Barre Straight Line and sweep past the small station. I would still be there at noon when the *Metropolitan* express would snatch the mail sack off the hook. Memories linger of the night local, with flames from its K4's firebox casting a wild orange glow into the stillness of the mountain night as the train barked across the stone-arch bridge and off into the great unknown.

The ringing clang of the drivers of a K4 as it coasted to a halt was music to my young ears. I drew the speedster's handsome outline on many a school pad,

for nothing in the world held as much beauty for me as a Pennsylvania K4. As I grew older I photographed them: Every Sunday I watched them. And just after the war, when a railfan in Utica, N.Y., said to me, "I really love steam locomotives. I could just put my arms around them and hug them," I knew how he felt, for I could remember. Now I get a thrill when I see a speeding, brightly painted diesel hauling a streamlined dome-car train, because such a train is a symbol of progressiveness, of advancement, and this is important. Now to me the sight of a steam locomotive is depressing.

My experience with the railroads and with *Trains & Travel* has brought me to the conclusion that public appreciation of the railroads is an important asset for the industry. Are we doomed to lose this appeal that seems to have become symbolized by the steam locomotive? Will youngsters of the future pay no more attention to a diesel-powered train than to a road-crushing highway behemoth? I am sure this is not to be the case.

I received heartening reassurance of it a short time ago. *Trains & Travel* has built a small model display for loan to railroads in Southern California, and this was exhibited during a recent hobby show. We had models of a steam engine and of a Union Pacific diesel on the layout. And what did the under-age-10 small-fry ask? "Will ya run the diesel, Mister?" Whether powered by steam or diesel, trains will never lose their appeal.

Editor's note: This article was written in 1953, when the diesel was decimating steam to the dismay of a majority of Trains *readers. Aware of their anguish, Kalmbach's West Coast sales manager (later vice president—public relations and advertising for Burlington Northern) drew on both enthusiasm and experience to explain why even his beloved PRR had gone off the coal standard. It was not published until 1977.*

By Ron Britzke
Track Gang

1954

From *Trains* magazine,
February 1976

The view from High View Tunnel

The New York, Ontario & Western Railway was mortally ill in the summer of 1954 when I went to work with the High View track gang. The "Old & Weary" had less than three years of its poverty-stricken history remaining. The handwriting was on the wall near the door.

I spent a grueling but happy six months in that golden summer and lingering autumn, wielding a shovel with a handful of dedicated veterans as we tried to keep the deteriorating track in a semblance of operating shape for the few freights that rattled past.

They talked often about the railroad's increasingly bleak future. Would the Government step in and save the O&W? Could fresh business or capital be found? "They'll never let it die," they assured each other. As their world crumbled around them, they looked the other way and worked harder.

Something of the love those longtime employees felt for the rickety railroad rubbed off on me, and I shared their disappointment—heartbreak for many—when the rusty old line went under in 1957.

Life was bittersweet in 1954. I had a freshly minted college degree, but the looming military draft made the future uncertain. I needed temporary employment and found it at O&W headquarters in Middletown, N.Y. A summer track laborer was needed at High View on the Orange-Sullivan county border in southeastern New York near my home.

I reported to the section shanty on a bright, hot June Monday, meeting a reserved—even dubious—reception from Jim, the grizzled veteran foreman, and Bill, one of two laborers on regular duty. The other hand, Jerry, was ill that day. Jim and Bill both had been with the O&W about four decades, and the railroad was the central force in their lives. Jerry was younger and had been on the gang 10 years.

Jim, Bill, and I wheeled out our ancient motorcar in a ritual that was to become familiar as the weeks passed. Jim would start the engine with a crank—an uncertain procedure, particularly in cooler weather. I never looked underneath at the power plant, but it obviously had few cylinders (perhaps only one) and fired at about every other milepost. The exhaust was deafening; and at every tenth revolution, a shattering backfire disturbed the tranquility of the weed-cloaked right of way.

Once this temperamental conveyance had warmed up, to the accompaniment of much fiddling with choke and throttle, we boarded and were off after Jim had called the dispatcher to get the whereabouts of the morning southbound freight. "Past the Manor at 5:23," he'd announce gravely to us. This meant the train had gone through Livingston Manor on schedule and we had time to run from High View down to Winterton, the southern end of our section.

At Winterton, we took to an unused siding next to a boarded-up creamery—symbol of a vanished source of O&W business. Eventually, the train would appear, usually with two or three F3 units trailed by too-few revenue cars. With the main clear, we'd proceed to the site of that day's work. It was mostly the same—raising joints.

Since the O&W was not ballasted on our section (or on most others), the procedure was simple. Bill inserted our big jack under a rail—one of several tasks he guarded with a jealous passion—and raised the track, exposing cavities under 10 or 12 ties on each side of the joint.

The foreman knelt about 50 yards up the right of way and sighted down the rail, gesturing until the jack was high enough. We filled in under each raised tie with cinders from trackside, tamping the fresh material with a downward stroke of foot on shovel. Then it was on to the next joint to repeat the task.

One day, as I watched a train approach and a line of empty Buffalo Creek flour box cars dancing like drunken sailors over a section we'd just raised, I remarked cynically to Jerry that I saw no visible improvement from our labor. He just grinned and I got a sour look from Bill. We went on raising joints and the trains stayed on the crooked, wavering rails, so maybe we were doing something productive after all.

It was sweaty, dirty work. The cinders raised clouds of sooty dust. The right of way was carpeted with a deep blanket of the black stuff—a legacy from countless passages of Consolidations, Ten-Wheelers, Camelbacks, and other steamers which preceded the O&W's small fleet of diesels.

Yet there was no drudgery in it for me and no reason to think about the process of labor. It was automatic, particularly after my muscles hardened. I recall working a section of track on the north side of the High View tunnel after lunch one day, letting my mind wander and being brought to reality in total disbelief as Jim ordered us to pack it in for the day. Three hours had passed like 3 minutes.

In retrospect, those days may not have been as enjoyable as they now seem through the mist of more than 20 years. But I can summon pleasant memories in abundance today . . . long-spanned gliders from the airport at Wurtsboro wheeling silently above us in the cloudless sky; the riotous racket of mating chipmunks racing through the dry leaves; the sun's first glow piercing the ground mist on a damp September morning.

And things were seldom dull on the O&W. There came a day when Jim, who was somewhat hard of hearing, knelt to re-sight a joint after we had raised it and removed the jack. A freight rounded the curve behind him. We called a warning. Engrossed in his calculations, he missed it. We waved with increasing vigor. He finally looked back. By this time, the train was fairly close. He retreated in haste and jerked his arm up and down twice as the engine passed—a signal for the engineer to blow the airhorn next time. The crew grinned down at us, but I gave the hogger a middle-finger salute, thinking that he damn well should have hit the horn as a courtesy to an aging man whose knees had long since lost youth's agility.

I had only one contact with an O&W train crew, and that was a memorable occasion during my third day at work. We were cutting brush near the High View station when a train crept out of the tunnel and stopped. The engineer and fireman climbed down and told us they had hit a rock in the dark, dank 3,856-foot bore. The prow of the diesel was scarred and a beam was hanging underneath.

I listened but took no part in the discussion that followed. I was very much a junior member of the O&W enterprise—summer fodder to be laid off when snow fell. I'd tried to match the pace of Bill and Jerry, stopping to rest only when they did; but my physical distress in those first days was obvious. It was commented upon frequently, particularly by the tireless, wiry Bill. I cheerfully admitted, when asked, that, yes, my ass was dragging, and, no, college was never like this. But in the first week, I was still a nonentity.

Voices in the huddle near the engine rose. "I wouldn't crawl under that damned thing for $10,000," Bill exclaimed, glancing up at the three F3's muttering like prehistoric beasts in the sunshine. Noting that the diesels and about half of the train were on a downgrade, Jerry agreed. The train crew expressed concern that the dangling beam would catch in a switch, but they weren't going to crawl around in the cinders.

A ready-made chance to be a hero! "I'll take a look," I volunteered in the calmest voice I could muster. Five sets of eyes focused hastily on me and I read astonishment in each. I wriggled between the pilot and the leading truck, passing a weak joke to Jerry before disappearing into Stygian blackness and monstrous diesel rumblings: "Wedge your foot in front of that wheel if she starts to roll." Luckily, the beam hung by a thread and I soon pulled it free. I sensed a reluctant respect in the manner of my fellow workers, which lasted only until my next

foulup at some trivial task which a degree in journalism did not cover.

After this incident, an enduring uneasiness remained with me the rest of my days on the gang. We went into the tunnel to clear out the fallen rock and found it about a third of the way through. It was the size of a tabletop. Fortunately the slab was 4½ feet wide and had dropped between the rails. Otherwise we and the train crew might have been waiting for the hook and wrecking crews from Middletown and Scranton.

Scanning that huge fall of slate, I recalled the crashing echoes from the wide-open exhaust of our motorcar against the tunnel walls. What if a backfire shook a big rock down from the roof? The car's canopy was one-eighth-inch plywood. Nothing ever happened, but the twice-daily trips through the tunnel held an element of suspense I could have done without.

The tunnel was also Jim's rainy-day work backup. We occasionally sharpened tools in the shanty during storms, but most of our implements were worn beyond a fine hone anyway. So we cleared rock from the tunnel ditches when it rained. The bore was only partially lined, and the brittle slate of the roof crumbled with monotonous regularity.

The yearly rockfall was substantial enough to require attention from the Scranton "extra gang" every winter. I met this crew once, when we changed a rail early in my stay. Most of the extras were young, and of Polish or Slavic extraction, I judged. They did their work with insolent expertise, drank Finkle's Tavern dry of beer during their overnight stay at Summitville, then moved on.

Late in the summer, we were ordered into the next section northward—Mountaindale—to help repair a lumber yard siding. We wound up almost needing repair ourselves.

With the motorcar showing a fine turn of speed. Jim whisked us down Mamakating Mountain to a rendezvous with the neighboring gang at Summitville Junction. As we entered the deserted, weed-covered yard, I spotted a switch lined against us. Assuming that Jim had seen it too, and was going to stop. I said nothing. A yell from Jerry broke the silence.

Jim, who ran the car with one hand on the throttle and the other on a huge brake lever, slammed on the binders far too late. As we slid at a brisk pace up to the closed switch, Jerry and Bill bailed out. Glancing at the switch stands, adjoining tracks, and

other impedimenta whizzing by, I stayed aboard with the captain. We hit the switch with a crash as the tools, Jim, and I bounced around the interior of the car. The ensuing silence was total.

Jim's embarrassment was evident, and he covered it by reprimanding the bruised Bill and Jerry for cowardice in jumping. Bill indignantly responded with a hair-raising apocryphal tale of a section hand who had failed to jump when a motorcar derailed and took a 6-foot pry bar through the groin—pointed-end first.

Thankfully, the Summitville-based gang had not yet appeared from an inspection trip up the Ellenville branch and we rerailed the motorcar with relative ease. We had everything shipshape when they arrived, and I soon dismissed the incident—but not the tale of the unfortunate gandy dancer and his pierced private parts.

Derailing a motorcar must be a rarity, but it happened again a few weeks later. Our foreman was nearing the end of a long career and he was tired. He overlooked another switch, this one on the passing track halfway up the northern side of the mountain. I saw it coming, yelled, calculated that we wouldn't stop in time, and stepped out away from the pointed pry bars.

This time there were no trackside obstacles. I landed on my feet at about 20 mph, took one gigantic running step, and plunged forward. As I glided toward a landing in the forgiving softness of the cinders, I looked up at Jim, Jerry, and Bill clutching whatever handholds were available. They looked at me, soaring in midair beside them. This time the cacophony of bouncing tools was almost drowned out by their raucous laughter as the car hopped to an ignominious halt and I picked myself out of the long furrow I'd plowed with my nose. Again, nobody was hurt.

The amusement died when we tried to rerail the car. This time we couldn't do it. A grim-faced Jim had to call for help on the track phone, and everyone from Middletown to Cadosia must have heard about our mishap. The Summitville gang tried without success to hide their grins as they helped to heave our conveyance back on the rails, but their nonchalance was not deceiving. It was a cruel blow for Jim. and I could read it in the tight set of his jaw.

Our section went up, down, and through Mamakating Mountain, so we worked in a sylvan setting into which the right of way almost blended. The O&W's

Nature quickly began to reclaim the right-of-way at High View Tunnel shortly after the New York, Ontario & Western was abandoned in 1957. This 1963 view at the south portal shows rails and tie plates gone and weeds encroaching upon the weathered ties. GEORGE WEIDNER.

efforts to keep the tracks clear involved some ancient scythes and a curious contrivance which loomed up one summer morning. It was a motorcar from Middletown, pulling a trailer. On it were perched a workman, a large tank, and a hand pump.

The gentleman in charge of the apparatus flailed away, and the nozzle produced a feeble stream which he aimed at the profusion of poison sumac in the ditches. Jim glanced with grim amusement as the apparition passed, then asked me, "What's in that tank, boy?" When I hazarded that it must be weed-killer, he retorted without elaboration: "That's liquid fertilizer." As the days passed. I saw what he meant. A few leaves turned brown at the edges, but the undergrowth mostly flourished. Apparently the cash-poor railroad had watered the stuff to stretch it. and the water more than offset the poison.

The High View station guarded a sunken, rusting side track which was all but hidden in weeds. I was surprised one morning to see a gondola parked there. I hadn't even been sure the switch worked. I peered over the side at a half load of new

ties, fragrant with creosote. It took Jim hours of agonizing just to decide which of the crumbling ties on our section needed replacing most. We could have used up the whole allotment within sight of our shanty.

This led to my only attempt at spiking. Bill was adept at it, smashing the spikes home with a few well-directed blows. Jerry wasn't bad either. I did most of the tie-shifting with a huge pair of tongs while they hammered.

One day I demanded to try it. Jim handed me our oldest hammer, worn with years of use and probably twice as old as I was. My first blow across the rail (I shunned the more cautious same-side approach) was a direct hit. I smirked as they goggled. The second shot hit the rail. The hammer head and half of the handle whizzed away into the woods like a scared pheasant, and my spiking career was spiked.

I was laid off briefly in August, collecting a graduation present from my parents—a British-built Triumph motorcycle. That transformed the 8-mile

trip to and from work. I swooped joyously over the undulating back roads between home and High View, lunchbox slung over my shoulder with a rope. I parked my shiny new beast in an empty shack which still stands at the mouth of the tunnel.

On the weekend before Thanksgiving, I was laid off for good and said farewell to my companions. Jerry and I had developed a warm friendship, and the taciturn reserve of Jim and Bill had thawed occasionally. Now it was over.

I was 3,000 miles away in Los Angeles, savoring trips to Tehachapi Loop and working in the motorcycle industry, when the O&W went under. But even before that, the High View gang had broken up.

Jerry quit soon after I left and went on to other things. Mercifully, Jim did not see the end of his life's work. He retired and died quietly six months later as the O&W swayed on the brink of oblivion.

Bill—fierce, square-jawed, touchy—stayed to the finish. Forty years a track laborer, he was proud of his many skills as only a man of little education and limited horizons could be. When the O&W died, Bill's light went out. A year or two later, firemen were called to High View one night and found the section shanty aflame. They put out the blaze and discovered Bill's body in the ashes.

What did it all mean? I stand at the gaunt, silent tunnel portal today and find no answer. More than 20 years have fled since I drove away from High View on that last icy November afternoon, and the past is as irretrievable as the future is unknown. The weeds finally won and the forgotten right of way is vanishing.

My thoughts are far away as a distant rumble intrudes. The morning southbound at the far portal? A change in engine pitch breaks the spell as a twin-stacked International Transtar heads down old Route 17 with a load that might have gone LCL if the Old & Weary had survived.

There is a small ache in my throat as I straddle the motorcycle which brought me to High View once more. A throb of power beckons me back to today, and the shadows of another time fade in the shimmer of heat waves along the highway.

How to be an Assistant Trainmaster

By W.M. Adams
Trainmaster
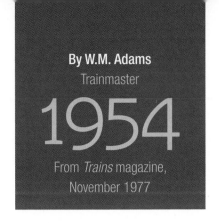
1954
From *Trains* magazine,
November 1977

"After riding a bucking steam iron horse for half a century, it's hard for the old hogheads to become high-octane engineers and get used to wallering in the giant overstuffed seats in the cab of a streamline diesel locomotive." —Bozo Texino, January 1948.

Near the end of a long, weary day in November 1954, I grabbed the irritating office telephone for at least the hundredth time, but my snarl quickly evaporated when I realized it was the general manager on the line. He brusquely informed me that I had been appointed assistant trainmaster on the "south end" of MoPac's Arkansas Division with headquarters at Gurdon, Ark., and that I was to report to the superintendent in the morning. I innocently asked if he wanted me to break in a replacement and was informed that anyone could work my job and to report as instructed.

I had no argument for that and so early the next morning I was sitting across from Mr. Treadwell. First, we made the acquaintance of the chief dispatcher and his minions, and then the boss gave me my formal instructions. "Go down to Gurdon," he said. "If you see anybody violating a rule, tell him about it." About then the road foreman of engines stuck his head in the door looking for someone to go over to Hot Springs with him to switch a strike-bound lumber company. The superintendent told me to accompany the RFE and remarked, "You will get your officer's seniority started off the hard way, as a scab."

So the RFE and I went down and caught No. 219 for Hot Springs, riding the cab of a big 8000-series Alco PA with veteran Claude Hatfield at the throttle. At Hot Springs, we spotted an empty boxcar at the lumber company and pulled one load, had a repast with the yard crew at a nearby beanery, and then rode No. 220 back to Little Rock.

By that time the trainmaster who I was supposed to assist had drifted back to town, so I made his acquaintance. He outlined some of the problems we had facing us on the south end, and they were legion. The most interesting one was the hasty elimination of all steam-powered trains and steam yard engines (the management was wild to dieselize, or so I gathered). John M. Toler had been trainmaster at Little Rock for about two months, but he was experienced. He had been assistant trainmaster at Newport, Ark., on the "north end" for a time and had recently returned to the Arkansas Division from the DeQuincy Division, where he had been trainmaster for about two years. I had been chief clerk to the assistant superintendent at North Little Rock for nearly two years and all my experience had been in the yard. My only road experience consisted of occasionally riding a passenger train to Memphis or San Antonio or St. Louis.

I had a lot to learn. I was reasonably well versed on the book of rules and knew a timetable when I saw one. I also knew trainmen's and enginemen's labor agreements fairly well, and a good thing this was true, since the favorite way for crews to break in a new ATM was to ply him with thinly disguised, hypothetical questions to try and trip him up. An ATM spent the first year or so on the job trying not to make a fool of himself.

The south end was an awesome hunk of railroad consisting of the Little Rock, Benton, Hot Springs, Gurdon, Norman, Delight, and Nashville subdivisions. The Little Rock sub was the main line, extending 146.60 miles between North Little Rock and Texarkana—a heavy-duty, high-speed main line with all operations controlled by signal indication and including 41.39 miles of double track (see the map on page 120).

Additionally we had 228.84 miles of branch lines including the 41.4-mile line through Hot Springs to Mountain Pine that broke off the main at QQ Junction, 25.77 miles south of Little Rock, and the 25.36-mile Nashville branch that left the main line at Hope, 113.1 miles south of Little Rock. The Hot Springs line headed right for the heart of the Ouachita Mountains, and although the branch was crooked and steep, it was laid with heavy steel on rock ballast and was protected by automatic block signals. The Nashville branch was laid with 65-pound rail on cinder or chats ballast and was subject to a healthy speed restriction.

Gurdon, 80.62 miles south of Little Rock, was the hub of the south end. Two branches diverged there. The Gurdon Subdivision extended 65.95 miles southeast to El Dorado, and while the line was not protected by signals, the track was laid with heavy rail on rock ballast. Beyond El Dorado this line was part of the Louisiana Division, intersecting the main line of that division some 77 miles away just out of Monroe, La. On the north side of the main line at Gurdon, the most interesting—and my favorite—branch line, the Norman Subdivision, angled off in a northwesterly direction for 59.64 miles to the mountain settlement of that name.

At PK Junction, 20.28 miles out of Gurdon on the Norman sub, the 5.52-mile Delight Subdivision took off to the west, crossed Antoine River, bisected a miniscule village of the same name, and went on to Delight, where it served a mammoth sawmill and a pole yard. Another branch off the main line extended southeast from Benton, 22 miles south of Little Rock, 44.37 miles through the tall and uncut forest to Pine Bluff. Sparsely settled and infrequently served, this branch called for little apparent attention from anyone, including trainmasters.

On any given day, we operated 18 regularly scheduled passenger trains, 14 redball freight trains, 11 locals, 3 traveling

A Missouri Pacific 4-8-2 rolls an 83-car freight train under the coaling tower at Gurdon, Ark., in 1952, shortly before mainline steam gave way to diesels on the division. JOHNNIE M. GRAY.

switch engines, and 10 yard engines, plus frequent extras, both freight and passenger. When I began working out of Gurdon, all mainline freight and passenger trains except for a portion of one local freight run were dieselized, and most runs had been so for some time. We operated a local each way between North Little Rock and Gurdon, and out of North Little Rock it was given an EMD GP7 while the counterpart out of Gurdon would have a steam engine, a 1200-class oil-burning Mikado. At the meeting point the engines would be exchanged and the 1200 would back up to Gurdon.

The Gurdon Subdivision to El Dorado, as well as El Dorado yard, had been handled by diesels since early October. The Hot Springs trains and the every-other-day local between North Little Rock and Pine Bluff via Benton were dieselized, as were two traveling switch engines at Malvern, 45.1 miles south of North Little Rock (and soon to be the scene of large amounts of grief for me). The 1200-class Mikes had just been bumped off the Nashville local when I went to Gurdon, so this left Gurdon yard, the Norman-Delight subdivisions, and the two yard engines at Hope still handled by steam—and the management suffering intense pangs every time one of the engines turned a wheel. I had my work cut out for me, make no mistake about that.

To compound my problems, the Government was building an Air Force base just to the northeast of Little Rock, and all of the aggregate for the runways and other works there was being dug out of the banks of the Ouachita River just below Malvern. This traffic was to the tune of about 100 cars daily, and we were also getting up to 30 cars of brick daily out of the three brick works adjacent to Malvern. All this called for handling into Malvern probably one and a half empties to each load billed out, and everything we loaded there had to be weighed. Little wonder we worked two traveling switch engines at Malvern.

The bulk of the cement used in this construction came from a site on the little Graysonia, Nashville & Ashdown Railroad at Okay, Ark., to an interchange with the MoPac at Nashville, and it required us to assign up to three GP7's every night to power the Nashville local. There we learned the hard way not to shove back with three GP's through a No. 6 switch against 25 cars of cement.

Toler expanded on the instructions issued by the superintendent. "Go down to

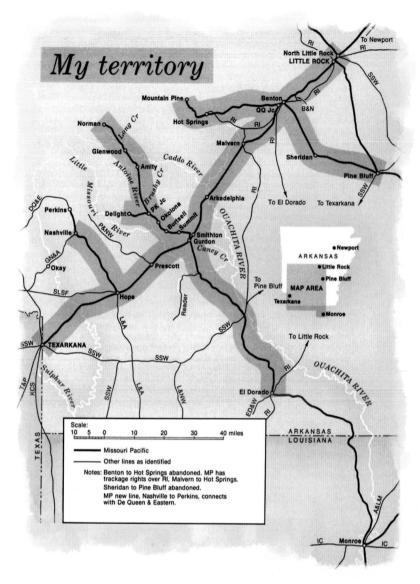

My territory

Scale:
10 5 0 10 20 30 40 miles

▬▬▬ Missouri Pacific
——— Other lines as identified

Notes: Benton to Hot Springs abandoned. MP has
trackage rights over RI, Malvern to Hot Springs.
Sheridan to Pine Bluff abandoned.
MP new line, Nashville to Perkins, connects
with De Queen & Eastern.

---

around to the various hired hands. How they knew me or when I was going to arrive was beyond me, and I often wondered what their reaction would have been if I had tried to sell them an insurance policy. I suppose they just kept a lookout for a tall, dark stranger with a new watch and chain and a general air of apprehension.

Actually, Gurdon was swarming with good, first-class railroadmen known on the Arkansas Division as "brush hogs" who relished their nickname. They liked to hunt and fish but would rack up their fowling piece or drop their fly rod at a word to take out a local or work a yard engine.

Weary by then from making executive decisions, I went across the street and engaged rooms at the old Ledra Hotel, unpacked my scanty belongings, and sought out the dining room for a repast. Frankly, my dauber was down and it would not have taken much to send me dragging for home with my tail tucked between my legs. Perhaps Toler anticipated this, for that night No. 822, the little passenger train from El Dorado, brought me a visitor, Conrad Brown, a tall, soft-spoken Texan who was assistant TM at El Dorado. Brown was a top-notch railroader, and our meeting was the start of a lifelong friendship; he cheered me up as best he could before having to catch No. 271 back to Union County. I turned in and spent the rest of the night listening to the windows rattle from the heavy exhausts of a hardworking switch engine. I later learned to sleep when the exhausts came hot and heavy and wake up when they stopped for any length of time. Actually, you soon learned to sleep in the daytime or any other time you could catch a wink. In those days a trainmaster's hours were from 12:01 a.m. Monday to 11:59 p.m. Sunday, and when you figured out your pay on an hourly basis you made almost as much as the old fellow who dried sand down at the coal chute.

Looking around the next morning, I found my office—a startlingly plain wooden structure on the wide station grounds just across the main line north of the depot. I shared the imposing premises with the roadmaster and a special agent (railroad policeman). The furniture was spartan; the most important fixture was a telephone equipped with a headset and a selector jack by which you could talk, as needed, directly with the Little Rock switchboard or the Arkansas Division dispatchers, or on the Arkansas Division

---

Gurdon and ride the locals and learn the crews," he said. This was on a Friday. Saturday morning I went to town and invested a goodly portion of my first month's paycheck for a Hamilton 992B "Railway Special" and a good stout chain—such timepieces being at that time required for the prompt and safe operation of trains. That afternoon, laden with responsibility if not with lucid instructions, I drove to Gurdon, my spirits going lower and lower with each mile I covered.

I parked in the lot adjacent to the yard office, noticing a steam engine switching on what I assumed to be the main line. The engine was an oil-burning Mikado, one of the old 1200's built back before World War I. The minute the engine foreman saw me, he stopped the whole works, and he came sauntering across the tracks and asked me if I was the new trainmaster. As far as I knew then or know now, for that matter not a soul in Gurdon knew me, but there was no use to deny

who I was. The foreman pointed to the cars he was handling; one of them was an old passenger coach fitted up as a maintenance-of-way bunk car and plainly stenciled on each end "REAR-END RIDER."

"Say," he hollered (right in my ear for the 1200 was popping off about then), "do I have to put this car next to the caboose?"

My perceptive answer was short and to the point. "Yes!"

I walked into the yard office and the agent/yardmaster didn't even wait for introductions. "Mister Adams," he asked, "do you want to run a gig to PK tonight? We have plenty of men and a 1200."

Now, not only did I not know what a gig was or why one seemed to be so desirable—I didn't even know where PK was. But my first executive decision had seemed to work so I used it again. "Yes," I sagely informed him.

That seemed to establish me as a man of action, if of few words, and the agent then took the time to introduce me

120

message line. All stations on the division except those on the Norman-Delight subdivisions were on the message line. You did not use this line for anything of a confidential nature because there could be, and probably were, up to two dozen people listening in on all conversations—especially when the TM was on the line.

The Norman branch had no such communications; the dispatching, such as was needed, was performed by telegraph—provided there were no trees down on the wires. If you wanted to talk to an agent up there you rode up on the local and called on him in person. You could drive your car, but the trip was long, roundabout, and rough, as paved roads were few and far between. It wasn't too hard to lose the local up there, and we did—several times.

My desk was covered with litter—well, correspondence and reports and speed tapes and cigarette butts—and I wondered when my predecessor had last been near the office. On top of all this accumulation was a letter addressed, "Mr. W. M. Adams, Assistant Trainmaster, Gurdon, Arkansas, PERSONAL." Stamped in the upper left-hand corner was the return address, "General Manager, Room 204, Union Depot, Little Rock, Arkansas." I was reasonably sure it wasn't a check but opened it anyway and found it to be merely a copy of a letter written to the superintendent taking him to task because apparently W. M. Adams had not participated in any signal surprise tests during the month of October. Since I had not been appointed to my new position until November, I thought this rather ominous.

By this time I needed some fresh air, so I took off down the main line toward the most prominent feature of Gurdon—a massive steel-reinforced concrete coaling station that served the two main tracks of the Arkansas Division, the lead track into the roundhouse, and, off its south side, the main line of the Louisiana Division (to us, the Gurdon Subdivision). At that time all steam power remaining in service had been converted to oil and the only portion of this facility being used was the sanding plant. I went farther and found the little four-stall wooden roundhouse, stuffed full of steam engines in all stages of repair and disrepair. Some were live but most were silent and cold, and there was little room for the diesels with which we had to work.

Entering the office, I met the garrulous old general roundhouse foreman—hat shoved back on his grizzled head, puffing on a gurgling pipe loaded with an especially pungent tobacco, and studying the engineer's call board as if daring it to

say something. Apparently most of the important decisions at Gurdon were made over a cup of coffee, so at the suggestion of the GRHF we adjourned to Earl's Cafe to get properly attuned. All I wanted from him was a little information—about engines and crews and the rip track and the wheel car and sundry other items coming under his immediate jurisdiction.

I got my information after several cups of coffee—as well as a lot of other information I did not seek, including how he would run the railroad if he owned it and what was wrong in general with the operating department and specifically with the young officials "they" found—from where he knew not—to run it, etc., etc., etc. At the time I was 35 years of age and feeling my years; this old boy was at least 30 years my senior.

Our big problem in dieselizing the south end was the Norman branch. The two yard engines at Hope were not too heavily laden. They switched the St. Louis-Shreveport Pullmans on and off trains 31 and 32, the remnant of the fine old *Sunshine Special* (but still carrying that name), and handled a fairly lively interchange with the Louisiana & Arkansas and the Frisco. We had to use steam there until more diesels became available, for there was no way to cycle with the Nashville local, the only one operated south of Gurdon. Gurdon Yard, where we worked three regular switch-engine tricks a day, was mostly steam but when and if more diesels arrived they could be cycled with various locals and through freights.

The Norman branch was another matter. This branch was a picturesque little railroad pieced together out of several logging lines built in the 1880's. North of PK Junction the line entered the gorge formed eons ago by the Antoine River, and in threading this canyon the track swung back and forth across the stream three times on truss spans which dated back to the original railroad. The bridges were incapable of carrying an engine classified on the Cooper's bridge-rating table higher than E-35. Leaving the river near the village of Amity, the line climbed over the ridge forming the watershed between the Antoine and Caddo rivers and crossed the Caddo just south of the town of Glenwood on another feeble bridge. A few miles north of Glenwood, the branch crossed Long Creek on another E-35 span. The lightest diesels then commonly used in road service carried a Cooper's rating of E-45, while the standard steam power for the Norman branch for many years—the

2300-class Ten-Wheelers—were classified at E-35. We had on hand at Gurdon the 2348, 2349, and 2389 to power the Norman local (actually the 2389 was out of service providing much-needed parts for the other two).

When I went to Gurdon, work was well under way in removing these stumbling blocks. Bridge gangs were busy installing new piers and abutments under the existing spans, and steel gangs in North Little Rock were rebuilding turntables picked up from outmoded facilities all over the system, tailoring them to fit the five river crossings between PK Junction and Norman. These new spans were moved into position, and when all was ready the old bridges were lifted bodily out of place and dumped into the watercourses to be fished out later and cut up for scrap. The new spans then were carefully fitted into place; all was done without delaying—well, too much anyway—the daily money maker on the branch. This work had been scheduled to be completed during the summer of 1955 but the dreamers in St. Louis could not stand further steam operation and had finally decided, some weeks before I was posted to Gurdon, to remedy the situation.

This is the way it was to have worked: EMD FT units 505-512 were assigned to redball freight trains 274 and 275 operating between Gurdon and Monroe, La. These trains, if on time, operated at night; No. 275 was due out of Gurdon at 7 p.m., and the northward No. 274 was scheduled to arrive at Gurdon at 2:30 a.m. The units, built in 1944 and 1945, were 1,350-hp machines and weighed in at 222,660 pounds, but it was decided that they could be used, paired, to PK Junction, where one would be set out and the remaining unit, even though classified as E-45, could operate to Norman and back provided an empty idler car was handled next to the engine.

Anybody could figure this out—you didn't have to be an inhabitant of the upstairs offices in the big city in Missouri. No. 274 was due in Gurdon at 2:30 a.m. and No. 881, the Norman local, was due out at 7 a.m., allowing over 4 hours to take the engines off, service them (diesels had to be serviced despite what some folks thought), and put them on 881. When 880 got back at 4:05 p.m. (according to the timetable) the operation would be repeated and No. 275 could be called on time at 7 p.m. Simple, wasn't it?

Now I don't know what 275 did after it left Gurdon, or what 274 did before it arrived—eventually—at Gurdon, for while that subdivision plus El Dorado Yard was theoretically under my somewhat shaky supervision, Toler had made an executive decision shortly after my appointment leaving everything on the Gurdon sub south of the yard limit board at Gurdon to Conrad Brown. I had been told not to worry about it.

The Norman branch I worried about, and worried and worried. Uncle Sam had built an impoundment on the Sulphur River not too far west of Texarkana. As a result, the water had backed up and covered the Cotton Belt main line, and Uncle had had to build a new railroad for the Cotton Belt. In so doing. Uncle was using the very best fill material—rock out of the foothills of the Ouachita Mountains dug from a newly opened quarry 5 miles or so north of PK Junction on the Norman branch. On a good day this outfit would shoot and load as many as 20 cars of rip-rap. From this quarry (chiseled out of a sheer rock bluff overlooking the Antoine River) to PK Junction, the track was on a slightly descending grade, and a 2300-class 4-6-0 with a tractive effort of 29,670 pounds could handle 18 to 20 cars of rock plus all the other freight gleaned from the hills to the northwest. The problem was in the final 20 miles to Gurdon. Starting right at PK Junction, the track climbed up over a ridge on a nearly 2 percent grade to Okolona, went down across a creek bottom through Burtsell, and then surmounted Maple Hill on another stiff grade—one heavier, if anything, than the Okolona ridge. Here the local would have a run on, and the little 2300, barking like a fox, would be making 35 to 40 mph when she started up the hill. If she was handling full tonnage and was lucky, she would be making 5 mph when she reached Summit.

A 2300 was rated at 1,000 tons from PK to Gurdon while a pair of FT units was rated at 3400 tons, so it was not hard to understand why the management wanted to set the 2300's aside. But, if you got the Norman local out of Gurdon on time (and that happened perhaps once a week, if that often), it took at least 12 hours to do all the work on the branch and get back to town. Plainly this would be late in the evening and No. 275 already would have been due out. The engines had to be serviced, for you could not and did not just run engines—even diesels—in on one train and out on another. Fuel had to be taken, sand had to be replenished, and certain ritualistic maneuvers cloaked in great secrecy by the mechanical department had to be carried out. Well, this took from 1½ to 2 hours with you prodding them all the

way. So 275 would be late getting out and this would start a chain reaction that would result in 274 getting into Gurdon at 8 a.m. or later (often it was high noon). Solution: run a 2300 and to heck with the diesels.

Luckily there was track room at PK Junction, so the 2300 could leave all the rock there and bring in the rest of the revenue. This is where the ubiquitous "gig" came into being, the gig being simply a PK Junction turn. Since the distance was less than 25 miles, you could operate two turns with the same crew in the same day for the price of one, if need be. For the gigs we looked to our 1200-class Mikes, for they could operate to PK Junction. They rated a hefty E-52 on the Cooper scale and so were not supposed to operate farther, even up to the quarry.

Soon after my arrival at Gurdon, in my inexperience or ignorance (depending on one's viewpoint), I instructed a crew to go all the way to the quarry with the 1276 and clean up the railroad. The engineer—nicknamed Speedy and for a reason—did not raise objection, and neither did the conductor. There was only one bridge between PK Junction and the quarry, a stout-enough looking steel-deck affair over Brushy Creek, but the next day the chief dispatcher called and whispered in my ear and I ran no more 1200's to the quarry. As I recall, when all the bridges later were strengthened or replaced and the new ratings issued for this part of the division, absolutely nothing had been done to this bridge, so it must have been in good shape. The 1276 made at least two trips over it with no ill effects.

We did use GP7's on the gigs if the units were available, and ofttimes on a Sunday when the local didn't operate we used a pair of the 505-class FT units. The management wanted to use anything but steam, and you could not blame the railroad for wanting to get rid of the 2300's, for the extra trains cost money and the general idea was to try to make money.

When tonnage was left up at PK Junction and a gig was run, it would hit Gurdon yard with 35 to 40 cars of rock, which all had to be weighed. This was more than our assigned yard engines could cope with, so an extra yard engine or, as we called them, "bums"—would be called. That would set everybody's teeth on edge right up to the 22nd floor in St. Louis.

We had problems with diesels besides the dismal lack of enough of them. In the first place, if we were lucky, we would get about one GP7 for every two steam engines, and a GP7 had possibly two-

thirds the tractive effort of one of the steam engines it replaced. People then would wonder why 50 cars of pulpwood couldn't be moved out of Gurdon on the local. In theory a diesel could work 24 hours a day, and so it could—footboarded in a yard. A diesel couldn't do it working a local for 10 or 12 hours before getting back to the yard. Toler told me later that when he had arrived back at Little Rock from the DeQuincy Division, the assistant general manager had said, "Here, take this one GP7 and dieselize El Dorado yard."

Worse, at that time enginemen just were not as knowledgeable about diesels as they are these days, and mechanical forces were little better. The old roundhouse foreman at Gurdon was about ready for retirement and was just hanging on until the last steamer was laid to rest. He was nicknamed "Happy." I never found out if this was because of his happy-go-lucky attitude or, as I sometimes suspected, because he was slap-happy.

We got along fine, up to a point. According to my notes, engine 4178, an EMD GP7, failed on No. 96 at Arkadelphia on Wednesday, January 5, 1955, delaying trains 7 and 8 and creating a lot of crackling conversation. Then she failed again on the 11:30 p.m. yard engine at Gurdon on Thursday, January 6, and when she was operated on an extra to PK Junction on Friday, January 7, she pooped out again. On Saturday, January 8, the accursed machine fell down again on No. 884 at Prescott, so on Sunday, January 9, old Happy and I had an executive session in Earl's Cafe (for crying out loud, Happy, warm up the 1215 or the 9773, I have 40 cars of rock to weigh!). Happy admitted that he was strictly a baling-wire and cold chisel mechanic who knew very little about diesels—say, just a little more than I. And since I knew absolutely nothing about diesels, we were in sad shape at Gurdon.

Diesel failures were the bane of an operating man's existence. With a steam engine, except for an outright boiler explosion or slipping the tires or something of that nature, you could usually at least limp into the clear. For that matter, you could go to the nearest farm and ordinarily find enough tools and help to get a steamer going, after a fashion. With a diesel you just stopped. You could—and I have known it to happen—have a four-unit lashup on a 100-car train of Texas grapefruit die on the main line and stay right there until a man drove all the way from North Little Rock and then fix the recalcitrant motive power with a

10-cent screwdriver. To me and Happy it was a whole lot easier to boil water than to produce volts and amperes.

In a last-ditch effort to dieselize Gurdon and its satellites, the MoPac sent me its BL2's. Built in 1948, the EMD's were rated at 1,500 hp, weighed 221,210 pounds, were pegged at E-45 on the Cooper scale, and carried numbers 4104 to 4111. They came to us from Kansas or Missouri (I don't remember which), and upon arrival they were promptly nicknamed "hermaphrodites." A BL2, being a bit lighter than an FT, could operate up the Norman Subdivision, past PK Junction with an idler car. By leaving one BL2 at PK and picking it up on the way back, we could just about handle all the rock off the branch the same day loaded. This made nearly everybody happy, especially the Corps of Engineers, who claimed to be falling behind in rebuilding the Cotton Belt's main line and alleged it was all our fault.

The BL2's were fine on a local. I was partial to them, for there was plenty of room in their cabs, and best of all, visitors could see where they were going.

On our GP7's, and later on the GP9's, someone at high management level decided on dual controls and then promptly negotiated a labor agreement which negated most of the desirability of that arrangement. Dual control stands, an engineer, a fireman, and a head brakeman filled up the cab and left little room for an ATM or anyone else. In retrospect, perhaps this is why the GP engines were favored—they kept the riff-raff back on the caboose. The head brakeman, sitting on a low stool in the middle of the cab, was ineffectual staring at the walls or at various instrument panels or at mostly nothing. He certainly wasn't looking his train over.

Although the BL2's were well thought-of on locals, they were heartily disliked—detested, really—in yard service. An engineer had to stretch pretty well out of shape to see his men on the ground, and the units loaded up so slowly that switching cars was akin to torture. We tried to keep the BL2's out of the yard and on the locals and on the Gurdon-Monroe redballs, but with our chronic shortage of power this couldn't always be arranged. We worked engines on the local to El Dorado, where they were supposed to switch three days before being rotated back. Every time we sent a BL2 there, back it would come the next day, and while at Gurdon I never did have any luck keeping one working in Union County.

One day, sometime after the steam engines all were deadlined, I was entertaining the trainmaster himself. We walked down the main line and crossed over to the Gurdon engine service facilities to see how much progress had been made in erasing all traces of steam locomotion from the property. Just before we got to the foreman's office, an irate engineer burst out, lugging a grip. Spying us, he strode up and confronted Toler and inquired if he might be the TM. He knew good and well who I was, for he had been force-assigned to the engineers' extra board at Gurdon some weeks before, even though his heart lay in a firing job on through freight out of North Little Rock. On one of the first trips he made out of Gurdon he had caught the Norman local with the 2349. He had had an extra fireman, and between the two of them they had managed to run out of oil and had left a train at Okolona that required a gig to bring to town. I had spoken to him at length about this fall-down, and I suppose he figured further conversation with me was futile.

Be that as it may, he bluntly informed JMT that he had been called for the 8:30 p.m. yard engine at Hope and if he got down there and found a BL2 he would lay off sick even though it meant tying up the job. I certainly wasn't going to interfere between him and John. After all, old John was THE trainmaster and made more money than I and had more experience. Besides, I wanted to see Toler in action, for this was mutiny; perhaps I could learn something.

JMT had his pipe pulling real good, and he just sorta grinned and remarked, "Oh, that's too bad. I sure hate to see you go to all the trouble to drive to Hope, for I just came from there and the 4108 is on the job and is going to stay. I suggest we just step into the foreman's office and I will have another engineer called. We will save you the trouble of laying off, sick or otherwise; just consider yourself out of service and I will have my office notify you when to report for a formal investigation on charges of insubordination. Understood?"

That was plain enough for even me to understand. The engineer looked at JMT for a minute and then allowed as how he was feeling better already and would be in Hope in time to keep from delaying the switch engine. But as he left, he threw this at John: "Goodness (or words to that effect), Boss, you sure get a crick in your neck working on those derned 'morfurdites.'"

As long as we are discussing the Hope

yard engine, let me go on record with the fact that the 9301—an 0-6-0 switch engine built by American Locomotive in 1920 to general USRA lines—was the last engine under steam on the Arkansas Division. She was working Hope yard, and on March 17, 1955, was run light to Gurdon, whereupon arrival her fire was killed, bringing down the curtain on more than 80 years of steam operation on the Missouri Pacific in Arkansas.

I was not through with her, though. When she arrived at Gurdon, Happy had her yarded on what was known as the Tom Watson track, a short spur just west of my office and adjacent to a city street. He then had one of his monkey-wrench experts disconnect the oil line between the engine and tender and leave the line down. Well, there were several hundred gallons of hot oil in the cistern and it drained out, down the street gutter eastward down a hill, and around into an underpass under the main lines a short distance north of the depot.

I had business in both Hope and Nashville that day, and on the way down by automobile I had met the 9301 gleefully backing up through Prescott. I returned to Gurdon the next day, and as I walked into the office, Hugh Shideler, the usually genial roadmaster, stormed all over me.

"Did you see my tires?" he demanded.

Why heck no; why in the world would I look at his tires? He then led me out the door and showed me what at one time had been rather attractive white-sidewall tires now grimy with residual oil. Hugh then explained what had happened and advised me to lay low for a day or two because the citizens of Gurdon were talking lynch. He had had to work a section crew overtime putting sand on the oil and trying their best to shovel up the worst of it.

Quite naturally this led to Happy and me having another heart-to-heart talk over a cup of coffee. I asked him just whatever possessed him to pull a trick like that—why not dump that oil in Caney Creek like they did all the rest (ecology at that time was just another hard-to-spell word). "Boss," he said, "I got news for you. Effective today, I am taking my pension."

"Happy," I said, "You have finally made me happy."

Happy was a fine old man and wasn't averse, even after he retired, to coming down and helping clean up sundry derailments that occurred from time to time. He was as much a whiz with blocks and jacks as he was a dud with diesels. We even used to get in a little bird-hunting and bass fishing. Happy shot an old L.C. Smith 12-bore double gun with barrels as long as the main rod on a 1200 and choked down like a rifle, but this did not keep him from claiming every feather that fell. He used to send me through the briar thickets: "You just work through there, boy, and I'll go around here." I don't know whether he figured I was dumb or agreeable, or perhaps he just liked to see me bleed.

Yes, I paddled the boat—I was younger and stronger, and all the while old Hap kept up a running commentary covering everything from how sorry diesels were to how to square the valves on a 6500-class Pacific, but all leading around eventually to the pitiful state of affairs prevailing on the railroad and wondering where in the world they dug up such dumb operating officials. He criticized everybody except Mr. Treadwell, our kindly, courtly superintendent. I felt that Happy dwelled on my antecedents a little more than necessary, but we still had lots of fun.

Happy's replacement was a cracker-jack diesel man who gradually trained the mechanical forces and enginemen, for all practical purposes eliminating most of the mechanical problems around Gurdon. But we still had some 21 steam engines stuck around on every inch of spare track and some tracks we well could not spare. They sat, silently rusting, until one day when I had an engine and crew available. I ordered an extra yard engine and had them all rounded up and dragged out to Smithton siding for storage until they were called in for scrapping.

Smithton siding's north end was about 2 miles north of Gurdon, and it lay between the main tracks; it was entered from the north end through two remote-controlled switches. The siding ended about 10 car-lengths north of the passenger station at Gurdon, and about halfway through the siding there was a pair of hand-thrown crossovers from both main tracks. The south switches also were hand-thrown. This siding was seldom if ever used north of the crossovers, but the south end was used as a setout and pickup track for southward trains. We lined these lonely old hogs up, more or less in weight order from the north, and left them up north of the crossovers. This location was pretty well out in the country with no houses nearby that I recall, but it was accessible from dirt roads.

The location, it later developed, was remote enough for a pair of former employees to go out and strip all the rod brass off the engines as well as the injectors, check valves, and any other parts made of brass except the bells. The bells were just too heavy for them to handle. This revolting situation was revealed some weeks later when it was decided the engines must be brought to North Little Rock to be scrapped. The master mechanic and a whole carload of experts rushed to Gurdon and finally decided to make rod bearings (you could not really say "brass") out of good hard Arkansas red oak.

Then one day a drag was called out of Texarkana with a three-unit hookup of the old Baldwin 200-class diesels and about 85 Gurdon cars. We lifted the Baldwins off the train and ran them up to Smithton and back down through the north end to the string of engines. There was a mechanical expert for about every three dead engines

The MoPac handled many loads of stone and gravel dug from near the Ouachita River near Malvern, Ark. ED WOJTAS.

and another pair driving a pickup truck loaded with "bearings" and lubricants and any other material that might be necessary. This pair followed the train as closely as possible on the adjacent highway and checked in at each station. A Form X train order was issued restricting the speed to 15 mph. There was a fairly heavy ascending grade through the turnouts at the north end of the siding, and I was afraid I was going to have to call on a yard engine to shove those old 200's out on the main line.

I don't know why I didn't ride that train. The road foreman of engines was aboard but as far as I can recall I never gave it a thought, and neither the superintendent nor the trainmaster issued any instructions to that effect even though it was customary for me to ride any special or unusual train. Until that time I had been so busy I had had little time to contemplate the fate of these fine old engines, and as much as I loved steam locomotives, I had had little time to mourn.

Vance Driskill, the roundhouse foreman, and I decided to drive up to Arkadelphia, 15 miles north, to see how they were doing. They were doing fine; there was no sign of trouble, but as they went clanking by, the realization of what was taking place struck me. If I didn't actually shed a tear, my eyes still were pretty moist all the way back to Gurdon. That was the last time I can recall seeing any Missouri Pacific steam engines, although about a year would pass before they all were finally scrapped. They were stacked up around North Little Rock by the dozens awaiting the torch. I had little if any business in North Little Rock, and I suppose I shut them from my mind.

Gradually all traces of steam operations were removed or smoothed over at Gurdon. The roundhouse, the turntable, the coal chute, two water tanks, a large fuel-oil storage tank, several water cranes—all were eventually destroyed or salvaged. Today's freight trains headed by massive, powerful diesels generating horsepower undreamed of a score of years ago charge through Gurdon unmolested, and while it is possible that the engineers and conductors were baptized in steam it is extremely doubtful if the remainder of today's crews ever saw or heard a hardworking steam locomotive.

"I railroaded when the callboy rode a horse, and if a fireman sassed a hoghead he was discharged on the spot. I fired eight-wheel passenger engines that would take three cars and go anywhere on the railroad and 10-wheel freight hogs that would pull six cars up a 1 percent grade at 3 mph. The passenger cars were heated with a stove and if you had a go-getting porter you burned up and if you had a lazy one you froze to death. Someone is always hollering that railroads haven't improved any. They have always stayed a long ways ahead of me, as I have never even run a streamline locomotive and have been a hoghead since '28. My trouble has always been keeping up with the railroads."—Bozo Texino, November 1947.

Recollections of a professional tour conductor

By Jim Neubauer
Tour Conductor

1950s

From *Classic Trains* magazine,
Winter 2009

A year-'round fixture on America's postwar streamlined trains was the professional tour conductor, a representative of one of the major tour-operating companies, which included American Express, Berry, Cartan, Cook's, and Happiness.

Although technically a paying passenger, the tour conductor was a professional traveler and a co-worker with the train crew. He took his meals with the crew after the revenue passengers had left the dining car, for he had to settle the bill with the steward. When he was deadheading on a train such as the *California Zephyr* out of Oakland, the train's stewardess would easily recognize him. (The suntan he'd be sporting from the *S.S. Lurline* voyages to and from Hawaii and two weeks on the islands helped, of course.)

If the tour conductor was traveling in coach with his tour party, the Pullman conductor often would offer an open bedroom for his overnight and "office" use. Usually, the tour escort was given a minimum sleeping accommodation—a lower berth on trains that had them, such as the CZ, otherwise a roomette or, if the train carried a Slumbercoach, a single room. For a good night's sound sleep, however, there was no finer accommodation than a lower berth in a heavyweight Pullman car.

Railroad tours predated the streamliner era by decades—they helped fill seats on the western railroads serving scenic areas. Union Pacific's Department of Tours, for instance, started in 1909, selling travel to such places as the North Rim of the Grand Canyon, Utah national parks, and West Yellowstone, Idaho. For the Eastern young lady wanting to see the West, UP escorted tours were a safe, desirable way to go. Soon other railroads entered the tour business: Santa Fe and affiliate Fred Harvey to the South Rim of the Grand Canyon and to Yosemite National Park in California; Great Northern to Glacier Park in Montana; and also Northern Pacific and Milwaukee Road to Yellowstone. The UP

every summer ran a tour train, the National Parks Special, departing Chicago midday on summer Saturdays, first on the Chicago & North Western as far as Omaha and then briefly, after the 1955 changeover, on the Milwaukee Road.

For three and a half years in the late 1950s and early '60s, I was such a travel professional, based in Chicago. During the three peak summer months, June through August, I was in the Chicago office for Happiness Tours, accepting client bookings from travel agents and sending escorts on the "Around The West" tours each week, with usually about 80 coach passengers. The similar "California Golden West" tour usually booked a similar number each week.

From September through May, though, I got to go on the trips. I averaged 35,000 to 40,000 rail miles per season. Sometimes I would arrive home in Chicago on a Saturday, empty the suitcase, do the laundry, and fill up the bag again for another two weeks on the road, beginning the next day.

Although there may be no explaining by doing, there is learning by doing. In this fashion, I became a tour conductor par excellence. There was no novice's trial run, and there was no briefing that would adequately prepare a new tour escort. Helpful prerequisites included being familiar with the art of the possible, a knowledge of geography, a photographic memory of people's faces and names and train schedules, and an understanding patience with people.

Especially patience.

A tour conductor is a tour business manager, as opposed to a "guide," who merely lectures and maybe drives the sightseeing bus. The process of becoming a tour conductor is perhaps best explained

by samples drawn from a composite tour. To begin, let's put ourselves aboard a streamliner at the end of a two-week tour.

Fourteen days ago I had left Chicago, armed with a little nervous tension, a sheaf of 32 names and 33 railroad ticket books, and waning confidence. Now, though, I am relaxed as UP's Domeliner *City of Los Angeles* glides along the last few miles of Milwaukee Road trackage into Chicago Union Station, concluding a "California Golden West" tour.

Two weeks! It has seemed an eternity for me. It also has been a pleasant interlude, but within the hour it will be over. Thirty-two names have become an identical number of individuals. The ticket books are empty. All that remains is arrival, the final handling of "the bags" (passenger luggage), payment to the Red Cap porters, the "green handshakes" (accepting passengers' tips), and fond farewells.

Oh yes, and the sore face.

The briefing sheets at the outset of the tour told me to "keep smiling." I did. Through two weeks I have smiled that confident smile, the one that says, "What, me worry? All in is control. I'm happy to have you as my passenger." Now I'm relaxed, although I'm conscious of extreme pain in my cheeks.

Two weeks ago, the checking-in ritual proceeded at Chicago's Dearborn Station on a Sunday morning prior to the departure of Santa Fe train 19, the *Chief*. A desk, set up in the concourse for just this purpose, was the rendezvous point. I greeted passengers, introducing myself and exchanging a pleasantry, and noted the number of bags each passenger had ("Limit two pieces of baggage"). I collected their transportation tickets, and a Red Cap carted the bags to their assigned cars, both coaches and Pullmans.

After departure, I held an introductory gathering in the lower lounge of the full-length dome car. Passengers were introduced to one another, and I outlined tour rules and regulations, making our guests feel they are in sure hands, safe hands.

"Good morning, ladies and gentlemen. I am Jim, your congenital—er, your congenial—tour conductor. [Polite laughter.] As this is Sunday morning, Illinois is dry [sighs] until noon, about the time we reach Galesburg. The bar will open then [aahs!] until we cross the Mississippi River . . . into dry Iowa at 12:55 p.m. [boos and catcalls]."

The tour is thus keynoted, with humor and the promise of good times. With the essentials completed (e.g., passengers are to sign their dinner check on the train with their names and that of the tour company), the tour conductor returns to his roomette and pouches the tickets for the train and Pullman conductors as the *Chief* leaves Joliet, Ill.

During the afternoon across Missouri and the evening across Kansas, I make conversation. I inquire as to the comfort of my charges, listen to tales of woe ("My wife and I are taking this tour to see if we can patch up our difficulties"), and answer such questions as, "How come Illinois has such black soil?" or "What kind of tree is that?" I am patient. I smile. I nod approval. I register dismay. I do what is appropriate. Above all, a tour conductor is a good, sympathetic listener.

The next afternoon at Williams, Ariz., our tour party detrains for the Grand Canyon. I direct my passengers to the bus waiting behind the depot, count noses, count bags, tip the Red Cap, and present the tickets to the bus driver. I count empty bus seats, knowing the capacity of the bus (39) and the number of passengers (32). I come up with seven. "Something's wrong;

it should be only six, counting a seat for myself," I say silently.

My patient smile hides the expletives, as I realize one elderly woman did not get off the train. A wire to the next station commends to Santa Fe's care the errant octogenarian; 40 hours will elapse before she can rejoin the tour. (I later introduce her to a fellow octogenarian, a male passenger who is going back to see his civil engineering work on San Francisco's Twin Peaks tunnels. They soon become "a couple.") I count people at each stop.

The tour conductor must be ready to comfort passengers who are reduced to tears upon first seeing the Grand Canyon. It really is spectacular. He must warn them of the effects of alcohol at the rim's 7,000-foot elevation. He must, on arrival at the Bright Angel Lodge or El Tovar Hotel, pass out room keys, count the bags, tip the bellboys, announce the sightseeing schedules for the morning East Rim drive, and the meal hours. He may recommend Fred Harvey's Irish Coffee and "El Diablo"—broiled tenderloin tips on a skewer with tomatoes, red and green peppers, and mushrooms. He must know that altitude combines with unfamiliar elements in drinking water to produce travel ailments variously labeled as "tourist trots" or "Montezuma's Revenge." His handy remedy is anything from paregoric to sympathy . . . and always, a patient smile.

He must be prepared for anything from a chipped anklebone incurred minutes before train departure to a serious injury. (A passenger once tripped on a paving brick at Southern Pacific's Merced,

Calif., depot while waiting for the *San Joaquin Daylight,* which meant I had to get statements from witnesses and the station agent to prevent a lawsuit and get medical attention for the passenger.) From time to time, the tour conductor must, for example, arrange single hotel rooms for the balance of the tour for a couple who have not patched up their problems.

Tour conducting has its rewards, of course. As in many instances, George Jue's Lamps of China restaurant in San Francisco's Chinatown gave tour conductors a free dinner for directing their party there. The price of dinner, of course, still shows on the expense account. The restaurant also paid a commission of 50 cents per dinner. The smart tour conductor used this commission to buy a round of drinks for his passengers. "George, will you serve my people cocktails with my compliments?" "Certainly, Jim." Casting his "bread" upon the "waters," the tour conductor smiles warmly, anticipating a better "green handshake" at tour's end.

Such were the myriad duties of tour conductors. Moreover, his care and feeding of passengers is almost a science— to enhance his tip potential, his commission earnings from additional sightseeing services, and his "knocking-down-on," or padding of, the expense account. Additional services which proved remunerative ranged from extra sightseeing trips to group photos to recommending "the better" (i.e., commission-paying) souvenir shops.

On a two-week "California Golden West" tour, all the "hot spots" were visited or ridden in their turn, according to the particular itinerary: Yosemite, San

Tour-group photos are a must. Here author Neubauer (crouching in front) poses along with his group at Grauman's Chinese Theater's Forecourt to the Stars in Hollywood during a 1958 tour. JIM NEUBAUER COLLECTION.

Francisco, Southern Pacific's *Coast Daylight,* Los Angeles, Hollywood, Disneyland, San Diego, and usually, the grand finale on the "Crapshooters' Special," Union Pacific's train to Las Vegas.

Now we are homeward bound, in Wyoming on UP's *City of Los Angeles,* and tonight is the farewell dinner in the private Gold Room dining area.

"Tomorrow morning we will arrive in Chicago. For our last dinner together, I suggest the baked Rocky Mountain brook trout or the prime rib. I had the steward put aboard extra supplies of California white and red table wines this morning at Ogden. They will be served tonight with my compliments." The tour manager

dresses for dinner every night, even while en route on board trains, by donning a fresh white shirt and a different suit and tie.

At Chicago Union Station, after tallying the proceeds from the green handshakes (legal tender ranging from 25 cents to $20 or more in the palm of my hand, as a gratuity), it is evident the tour conductor's patience has paid off.

After my break-in experience, I conducted more than California tours, escorting them nationwide . . . and beyond. One, the "Budget Tour of Mexico," went to our southern neighbor, and I escorted it several times during

1960-61. A November '60 Mexico tour is particularly memorable. To begin, at the Information Desk in Chicago Union Station on a Saturday morning, I introduced myself and let the station folks know I'd be checking passengers in and where I'd be receiving them.

I corralled a check-in desk on the south concourse opposite the gate from where Gulf, Mobile & Ohio train No. 1, *The Limited,* would leave for St. Louis. The "Budget Tour" was coach from Chicago to Nuevo Laredo via St. Louis and Missouri Pacific's *Texas Eagle,* then Pullman to Mexico City. Strange as it may seem, Mexico City is as close to Chicago as is San Francisco, and also in the Central Time Zone, to boot.

Out of Chicago, I had 31 coach passengers, with two more expected to join us at Springfield, Ill. At check-in, I met my passengers, collected their luggage and tickets, handed out tour literature, and made mental notes as to their identifying features. I directed them to the train gate, where as customary, a tour party had the privilege of boarding before the regular passengers. Railroad Transportation Notices ("TN's") had alerted station personnel, Red Caps, the coach attendant of our assigned car, the train conductor, and dining-car steward, and all were ready to receive us.

There was nothing else to do in the three-plus hours down to Springfield but chat with my passengers and memorize their names. When the couple joined us in the Illinois capital, I was able to walk them down the coach aisle and introduce them by name to each of the 31 Chicago passengers.

The transfer of passengers and baggage at St. Louis Union Station went with textbook efficiency. Some passengers stepped up to Slumbercoach rooms on the *Texas Eagle,* as I did. No. 21 carried a dining-lounge car to San Antonio, as well as a Planetarium car, as MoPac called its domes. Tour passengers signed their dinner checks, and after dinner I settled with the steward by filling out a form that went through railroad and tour-company accounting offices.

The border crossing the next evening at Nuevo Laredo also went without a hitch. Tour passengers were walked through the Mexican entry procedures, and we reboarded our train, now called the *Aztec Eagle.*

National Railways of Mexico's feature cars for us were Swiss-built: a first-class coach; diner El Comedor; and on the rear end, lounge-observation car Club Mexica.

A few new Budd lightweight cars are mixed in with older cars on Canadian Pacific's *Dominion.* This Dutch-door view shows the eastbound train entering upper Spiral Tunnel. JIM NEUBAUER.

All three were supposed to have run through from St. Louis, but possibly Missouri Pacific thought it bizarre to contemplate locking couplers with any such animal, so the trio remained south of the border. The train did carry a regular through 10-roomette/6-double-bedroom sleeper from St. Louis to Mexico City, but in Mexico, our group rode in standard heavyweight Pullmans, each with a drawing room and sections. Two of my passengers chose coach accommodations all the way and rode "up front with the goats and chickens."

Next morning leaving San Luis Potosi, we were on time. Our cars were at the rear of the train. I was enjoying the fresh air wafting in the open top half of a Dutch door with one of my passengers, a vacationing Chicago fire chief, when suddenly I had to tell him, "Hold on! We're on the ground!" As I looked forward, I could see the Pullman ahead going sideways to the direction of our car. Its truck had picked the point of a switch and toppled over a caboose on a side track. We lost two of the Pullmans and the rear lounge car in the incident. All passengers from the last three cars were moved forward to share the space to Mexico City, where our shortened *Aztec Eagle* arrived a couple of hours off the timecard. It was no problem for me to keep smiling, as things could have been a lot worse.

The dining-car steward had accepted the tour company's payment slip for last night's dinner and this morning's breakfast, but immediately afterward he told me, in fractured English, that he could not accept a payment slip for lunch and dinner because payment for the preceding tour's services had not come through. For once, I started to frown, for I had to ask my passengers to pay cash and get receipts for their eventual reimbursement.

Upon arrival in Mexico City, a representative from our Mexico office met our train, and our party transferred to the Premier Hotel. I told our local office folks what had happened with the dining-car steward, and on the return trip to the border 10 days later, there was no problem.

Our time in Mexico was memorable. We spent three nights in Acapulco at the Tampa Motel, where I had curried turkey on Thanksgiving Day. I also caught an 8½-foot-long Blue Marlin while deep-sea fishing (using sailfish tackle) with several other male passengers. We spent one night in quaint Taxco, then went back to Mexico City via Cuernavaca for five nights at the Premier Hotel.

Soon the day arrived to begin the return to Chicago. Back on NdeM's *Aztec Eagle,* running as First 22, observation car *Club Mexica* was again in our consist and the car's attendant told me a tale about what happened when the car came to its abrupt stop 10 days earlier. At the jolt, one of my female passengers riding in the car let out a scream . . . and the mirror hanging on the bulkhead broke!

The northward return trip was uneventful. During the brief San Antonio layover, some of my group hired a taxi for a quick look at the Alamo. On Saturday, the 15th day, a Missouri Pacific passenger rep was on board train 22, inquiring as to our welfare. Approaching St. Louis, he and I had breakfast in the diner, and I still have the MP tie-bar he gave me. Further, he assisted with our transfer to GM&O train 2, the *Abraham Lincoln.* In those days, MoPac was still very much a pro-passenger railroad.

Among tours out of Chicago I conducted were some going east, on New York Central's *Fifth Avenue Special* to Buffalo or *New York Special* via Welland, Ontario, to Niagara Falls, with onward movement on an NYC *Beeliner* (Budd Rail Diesel Car) to Buffalo and a connection with No. 50, the *Empire State Express.* Once on such a trip I met Rogers E.M. Whitaker, the noted *New Yorker* magazine writer (under the name "E.M. Frimbo") and worldwide rail traveler and "mileage collector."

After a few nights in the Big Apple (it was just called "Manhattan" then), the Pennsylvania Railroad took our tour parties to Philadelphia on train 115, the *Executive,* for a motorcoach side trip to Atlantic City and back, and then on to Washington, D.C., on PRR train 155, the *Embassy.* Once we rode the *West Coast Champion,* a through Atlantic Coast Line train to Florida, to the nation's capital.

October's bright blue weather made for an especially impressive time in Washington to watch the changing of the guard at Arlington National Cemetery and to visit the White House. The tourists were thrilled. Our return leg to Chicago was on board my favorite overnight coach train, Baltimore & Ohio's *Columbian.*

Illinois Central heavily promoted its service from Chicago to the Crescent City, especially for Mardi Gras, southbound on train No. 1, the *City of New Orleans.* On the Saturday morning before Mardi Gras, tour parties rode the train's first section. It was truly a party train, with live music and dancing in the lounge-observation car. On one tour I conducted, no one seemed to mind that our New Orleans arrival was late, except for the team of escorts who had to transfer the passengers and baggage to the Jung Hotel at 3 a.m. We all faced the next five days and four nights with a minimum of sleep.

Northbound on IC's *Panama Limited,* I would exit the lounge car at Jackson, Miss., and lower the bed in my roomette. When I would raise the window shade next morning, often I'd look out as we crossed the Kankakee River, slowing for the Kankakee station stop an hour out of Chicago. I would rush to the diner, have breakfast, and settle with the dining-car steward. At journey's end, the Pullman porters were well practiced in getting the bags to the Red Caps, whom I'd pay in Central Station.

Another Happiness Tours destination, although one I did not escort, was a weekly summer Saturday departure for South Dakota's Black Hills, on Chicago & North Western's *Dakota 400.* Happiness also offered Greyhound Bus tours there.

In my experience, the Santa Fe ranks without equal in keeping its trains on time. After the Winslow, Ariz., stop at 11:45 a.m. on No. 19, there were a couple of hours before arriving at Williams about 1:40, where we'd detrain for the Grand Canyon. The train's route description folder listed crossing Canyon Diablo at 12:24 p.m. With confidence, I could tell my passengers to look out and down for just a moment before we quickly soared over the deep, narrow canyon. It's not selective memory—I really don't recall any grievously late trains in the years I escorted tours, on any railroad.

Of course, schedule-padding occasionally contributed to such performances, as it still does today with Amtrak. For example, you could leave an hour or more late on Union Pacific out of Omaha and be on-time by Sidney, in western Nebraska, next morning.

One thing I do recall is that the Burlington Route and the Santa Fe set the standard for comfortable reclining leg-rest seats in the coaches. Union Pacific's coaches were more spartan, lacking such passenger amenities as carpeting, and its ACF-built domes had less forward visibility—not as good as Budd-built domes. Not that UP didn't provide nice memories. I just missed its steam era in my escorting years, but a colleague related to me how, departing Cheyenne westward with doubleheaded 800-class 4-8-4's up front, one could "see" each chug of the engines as the coffee sloshed a bit in the cups on the dining car's tables at lunch going up Sherman Hill. West of Laramie during the run across the Red Desert, no matter the motive power, we would see the mileposts go by every 40 to 45 seconds —and that was with heavyweight Pullmans riding on three-axle trucks with friction brass bearings!

On board Santa Fe's *Chief* one time, I had the privilege of meeting former President and Mrs. Truman. As new, proud grandparents, they were returning to Kansas City from daughter Margaret's back east. The President struck me as a benign, friendly person, the kind of grand-father whose lap a five-year-old would

climb into, but the message on the face of his wife, Bess, was less hospitable. On the next California tour I conducted, our party met President Eisenhower, who was just about to leave office, as he exited the dining room at the Sheraton Palace Hotel in San Francisco. "Ike" had just given a speech there.

The "Three Nations Tour" visited Mexico as an optional side trip from San Diego, and returned to Chicago via Canada: Victoria and Vancouver, British Columbia, and Banff, Alberta. It was all-Pullman, all-first-class, except for the coach-only daytime ride between Oakland and Portland, Ore., on Southern Pacific's *Shasta Daylight*. By then the SP was

becoming disenchanted with passenger service, but it still put on a good show with great trains—slow, but nevertheless good. One night leaving Los Angeles on the *Lark,* the steward in the triple-unit diner-lounge invited me to dinner . . . at 10 p.m.! I declined, instead sharing the lounge with my passengers until I looked out and realized we were already at Santa Barbara and I could see the ocean surf. The car still had phone books in the telephone booth, but the phone itself had been removed.

On this itinerary, Northern Pacific's 5 p.m. pool train from Portland to Seattle (a route shared with Great Northern and Union Pacific) offered great dining in a

Raymond Loewy-designed dining car. The NP's famous "Great Big Baked Potato" was the main menu feature, but the prime rib was also excellent.

Canadian Pacific's diners had subdued lighting, with the ceiling appearing as star-filled as the nighttime Canadian sky. Very elegant! Once, on the last tour of the summer season, we had an elegant next-to-last lap. Our cars were among the through cars switched off CP's *Dominion* (itself then a mix of heavyweight cars with a few new Budd lightweights), onto the Soo *Dominion* at Moose Jaw, Saskatchewan. On the rear, we had the train's usual Cape-series heavyweight bedroom-solarium observation lounge car, from which to rest our weary, scenery-surfeited eyes and enjoy the golden wheat fields, white grain elevators, and blue skies of the prairies.

Homeward bound, we clicked faithfully and diagonally across southern Saskatchewan, crossing into North Dakota with a border stop at Portal late in the day. Soo Line took us through the night to its Minneapolis hometown, where we were to make a breakfast-time connection with Milwaukee's *Morning Hiawatha.* At the time, the *Morning Hi* was combined with the *Olympian Hiawatha* from Seattle/Tacoma, and this morning, the train was late in arriving from the west. Milwaukee provided a make-up train, without a Super Dome lounge or a Skytop observation, but we were on time into Chicago.

My tour-conducting days ended in 1961 when I left Happiness Tours for another company; I was still in the tour business, but not in the field as I had been with Happiness. I had seen North American passenger service in its full, final, glorious bloom. I recall these days happily because they provide fond memories of rail travel. All those days on the road made the point that rail travel was the best way to see our beautiful land, and of course, it remains so.

Once in a while, I'll ride a train again, and as I go from the vestibule to my seat, I often catch myself turning on a conditioned-reflex smile.

Santa Fe's *Golden Gate,* a secondary Bay Area train, pulls into Merced, Calif., in May 1958 as author Neubauer's tour group prepares to board. The inset at lower right shows a Missouri Pacific coupon for three *Aztec Eagle* passengers riding coach. JIM NEUBAUER.

As the Centurys passed slowly in the night

By Chandler H. Mason
Tower Operator

1960

from *Trains* magazine,
November 1974

The year was 1961, or perhaps late 1960. I was working as a New York Central towerman on the main line at River Bridge tower ("RB," or just "Bridge," as we called it) in Buffalo, N.Y., 2.5 miles west of the passenger station. I had come on duty for the night shift, just in time to catch "the fleet"—the nightly parade of passenger trains in both directions.

There were Nos. 28, 14, 6, and 22 eastbound and Nos. 27, 15, 7, and 17 westbound, plus others whose numbers I have since forgotten. Three tracks, referred to as 2, 1, and 6, narrowed to two in order to cross the Buffalo River/ship canal where it winds among waterfront grain elevators and warehouses.

It was a pleasant fall evening, and I heard the depot operator announce that No. 25, the westbound *20th Century Limited,* was in the station. On the lines-west dispatcher's phone I heard that 26, the eastbound *Century,* was by Silver Creek, 30 miles to the west. Thus the stage unknowingly was set for an interesting night.

I became aware of commotion on the river a half mile or so to the west. Among the grain elevators I could see red and white lights flashing, and I could hear sirens. Apparently there was a fire somewhere upriver, so I called the dispatcher. "River Bridge. There's a fireboat coming up the river. Shall I let him through?"

The dispatcher made some calls.
"Depot, where's 25?"
"Hmm, he's about ready to pop."
"Bay View, where's 26?"
"By Angola."

The *Centurys* were scheduled to pass somewhere near Buffalo, and they usually were on time. About six minutes of slow running was required to get from the depot to my tower; the same amount of time of fast running was necessary to get there from Bay View, which was about 10 minutes from Angola at 90 mph, the *Century's* speed on lines west.

The dispatcher approved my opening the bridge.

"OK, get that fireboat through quick, and don't plug anything" (read Nos. 25 and 26).

So I put the drawbridge up and the fireboat came . . . but whoops—what was this other slow-moving set of lights emerging from behind the closest grain elevator? A big oil tanker, easing its way upriver! I hadn't seen the tanker because my view of the last half mile of river was blocked, and he hadn't made any noise. The fireboat came charging around the slow-moving tanker, hooted through the bridge, and forged upriver. The tanker captain, seeing the bridge conveniently up, gave a blast on his horn and kept on coming. Now, one thing that is not done is to drop a bridge in front of a boat—especially a big tanker once the boat is approaching. The fun began.

Depot: "25 is out." Bay View Tower: "26 on the bell on 2." The circuit board on track 1 winked on, and the bell rang: 25 was moving. Tower 29-A: "Train number 25 on track 1." The oil tanker gently maneuvered through the pilings.

Dispatcher: "River Bridge, how we doin' on that fireboat?"

I told him. But how does one explain to a DS that there is still 550 feet of a 650-foot tanker to be pushed carefully by a tug or two through a drawbridge? I explained. Swear words burned the wire.

Buffalo Creek tower (the next one west of me): "Here's 26 on 2, and you got an Erie puller on 6 with 30 cars."

Oh joy. Twenty-six, headlight on dim, coasted to a stop at the home signal on track 2. The engineer blinked the light a couple of times. The fireman, lantern in hand, hit the dirt and headed for a phone to find out what was up. Twenty-five ground to a stop east of the tower, eying No. 26 across 200 feet of open water. Suddenly I was very busy answering phones. The man on the aft rail of the tugboat waved a friendly greeting to me, and the long boat-tug combination finally cleared.

By the time I got the bridge down and locked and signals set (which took about three or four minutes) and the high green pulled on, each *Century* had been plugged almost 15 minutes. The DS was having a stroke, and both *Centurys* had Dutch doors full of blue-uniformed train men . . . all looking at me. How nice it was to be the center of attention.

That night I had many official visitors, from the trainmaster all the way to the division superintendent, wanting to know what was going on. The next day, I had to write what must have been a half-dozen letters of explanation.

So that night, the *Centurys* passed in front of my tower—at about 15 mph, their big 4000-series diesels wide open, the sanders tied down, and their engineers looking a bit grim as they notched their throttles up. How I wish I had had a camera to record the whole affair. But someone else would have had to take the shots—I would have been too nervous to do it.

Train 26, New York Central's eastbound *20th Century Limited,* pauses at Buffalo, N.Y., on its final run in December 1967. The river bridge of author Mason's story is just a couple miles west of the station. EDWARD J. JOSCELYN

By Ed King
Road Foreman of Engines

1960

From *Trains* magazine,
March 2001

Big tonnage

His name was Albert S. Tabor. He had thinning, iron-gray hair and a pair of steel-blue eyes that could freeze Tahiti. If railroads awarded combat decorations, he could have filled a dresser drawer, from his 40-plus years working his way up the ladder on the Norfolk & Western Railway.

He rose from brakeman in the Pocahontas Divisions coalfields to become superintendent of the Scioto (rhymes with "iota") Division at Portsmouth, Ohio. This part of the railway—which in 1962 stretched from Williamson, W.Va., northwest through the hub of Portsmouth, with lines to Columbus and Cincinnati—was the funnel through which all of N&Ws westbound coal poured: 2,500 loads a day. At that time, that was more gross tons in one month than many large railroads moved in a year on their entire system.

The "super" was known on the division as Bert Tabor, or Boss Tabor, unless he was actually present, when he was addressed only as "Mister Tabor." His background had imbued him with little tolerance for either college boys or anyone who had anything to do with an engine, and as I stood before him on December 1, 1962, in his office at the east end of the second floor of the Portsmouth passenger station, I represented both those groups. His boss, W.A. Noell, general superintendent, Western General Division, had plucked me from my comfortable assistant yardmaster job deep in a West Virginia hollow and sent me out to Portsmouth to be Tabor's newest assistant road foreman of engines. At that time, N&W promoted about half its assistant road foremen from engine service and the rest from other departments, the latter succession very, very rare elsewhere in railroading. In 1962, though, it was a long-established practice on the N&W.

After a couple of seconds of what he probably intended to pass for pleasantries, Tabor impaled me with those eyes and

said, "Boy, I want you to get out there and learn how to handle those trains." Although I was 26, it didn't seem like a very good time to object to being called "boy."

I was then ushered into the adjoining office to meet Otis Mullins, the rotund assistant superintendent of the division, who quickly and efficiently arranged for the lodgings I'd use for what would turn out to be three years in Portsmouth (I was a bachelor at the time). He also told me about a few of the unwritten rules. One of the slogans on the division was, "You labor for Tabor, or get your notice from Otis."

Having received my marching orders, I went down the hall to the road foreman of engines' office and made myself known to Quincy Goff, my new boss, himself an old Pocahontas Division engineer. After just a few more "pleasantries," Goff asked me how my interview with Boss Tabor had gone.

"Fine, I guess."

He then related his favorite Tabor anecdote, about an assistant road foreman whom the Boss encountered in the hall one morning. "What [train] are you coming back on?" Tabor had asked the unsuspecting ARFE. Goff laughed, "Heck, the poor guy didn't know he was going anywhere that day, much less what he was coming back on."

I got the message, and vowed I'd think fast if the Boss ever asked me that question. Then, looking for some words of wisdom, guidance if you will, about how to implement Boss Tabor's mandate, I asked, "Mr. Goff, Mr. Tabor told me he wanted me to get out and learn how to handle those trains. Do you have any suggestions?"

If I was looking for sympathetic understanding, I'd come to the wrong place.

"Yeah. I suggest you go do it."

Fortunately, my two fellow ARFEs—Ray Morgan, who'd been a Cincinnati District engineer, and Sid Wohlford, who like me had originally come out of the Motive Power Department—were considerably more helpful. "Start out on the Kenova District," Ray and Sid told me. "It's the easiest to learn to handle trains on."

The three mainline districts of the Scioto Division were the Kenova District, the Cincinnati District, and the Columbus District, known respectively as "the Tadpole," "the Peavine," and "the Valley" (see the map on page 139). The Tadpole extended from Williamson, W.Va., 73 miles down the Tug and Big Sandy Rivers to Kenova (named for the three states coinciding nearby), where it crossed the Ohio River, following the river for 39 more miles to Portsmouth. Geographical purists insist that the Tug River is actually the Tug Fork of the Big Sandy River, but N&W men knew it as the Tug.

Except for three CTC-governed single-track tunnels, each of which had 45-mph equilateral turnouts at each end, and some CTC on both mains in the Kenova area, the Tadpole was righthand, current-of-traffic, double-track territory all the way, with automatic block signals and center sidings. Only the 0.3 percent hump over the Ohio River bridge at Kenova kept it from being gently descending the whole way west.

Even with this little grade, the Tadpole was a good place to haul heavy trains. It had showcased N&W's finest power in steam, the Class A 2-6-6-4. Extreme curvature for the first 30 miles out of Williamson made heavy trains hard to accelerate, but the A's could regularly cover the 112 miles in less than 4 hours, non-stop, with 16,000-ton coal trains. Curvature limited train speeds east of

Kenova, but the limits west of there were 65 mph for freight trains and 78 for passenger trains. Kenova was also the site of a coal transloading terminal that consumed about 125 loads a day, which were backhauled from Portsmouth by rail and then barged up the Ohio River to the Pittsburgh area.

At Vera, just west of the Portsmouth passenger station, the line split. The Cincinnati District, or "Peavine," crossed the Scioto River and meandered west 97 miles to Clare Yard on the eastern outskirts of Cincinnati. Passenger trains, by 1962 down to just the *Pocahontas* and the *Powhatan Arrow* (POW-uh-tan) in each direction, went on west from Clare another 14 miles utilizing Pennsylvania and Baltimore & Ohio trackage into Cincinnati Union Terminal.

Norfolk & Western's competitor, the Chesapeake & Ohio, was fortunate in having a double-track speedway from Kenova that followed the Kentucky bank of the Ohio River through the railway's hub of Russell, Ky., to Covington, before crossing into Cincinnati. N&W's Peavine, on the other hand, went inland, using an old narrow-gauge right-of-way that was not only crooked but cross-drainage for numerous streams flowing into the Ohio, with several grades in the 1.4 percent range.

There were several little dips and humps—known elsewhere as rip-rap or hogbacks—that had proven to be real knuckle-busters. One of the worst, especially for coal trains, was the area through Sardinia, mid-point of the district and junction with the 19-mile Hillsboro Branch. This was Ray Morgan's native land, though, and he was a crafty old-timer who knew all the tricks. Like the rest of the division, the single-track, CTC-equipped Peavine was quite well-maintained, with nominal speed limits of 65 mph for passenger trains and 50 for freights, where the curves allowed.

The 95-mile, double-track "Valley" went straight north from Portsmouth up the Scioto River to Joyce Avenue Yard in Columbus. This was a beautiful piece of railroad. For the most part, curvature was not a problem, but northward coal trains (westward by timetable) had to conquer 9 miles of 0.3 percent grade from Chillicothe up to Kingston-Delano Hill. In 1962 there was a 35-mph speed restriction at the foot of the hill across the B&O diamonds at the passenger station in Chillicothe. As on the Tadpole, center sidings were prevalent except at Waverly, where there were two sidings between the

Albert S. "Boss" Tabor, superintendent of the Norfolk & Western's Scioto Division, had a reputation as a hard taskmaster.

main tracks. There was one 10-mile stretch of CTC-controlled single main track, between Waverly and Chillicothe. One nightly passenger train ran from Columbus Union Station 3 miles to Joyce Avenue, then south to Portsmouth; after making a connection with the Pocahontas in each direction, it returned to Columbus. Like the Tadpole west of Kenova, the Valley's nominal speed limits were 65 for freight, 78 for passenger.

Most Valley and Tadpole trackage was double track with automatic block signaling; there was little CTC on the double track. During the good-weather trackwork season, N&W naturally wanted to get the utmost production out of the maintenance-of-way forces. Therefore, it was necessary to take one of the mains out of service during the day so that track maintenance men and machinery could work uninterrupted. This meant that all trains had to use the other main to get around the work. On the N&W this was called "detouring," a term usually reserved for trains running on another railroad during an emergency.

Besides N&W's desire to closely supervise operations (a circumstance not often found in railroading today), another reason existed for the employment of three assistant road foremen of engines and two assistant trainmasters on the Scioto Division—handling the detours. During detours, the only train order that all trains would receive would simply inform them of the time and between which points, and on which track, the detour existed. The actual movement through the detour would be handled at

the scene by a supervisor—an ATM or ARFE on each end—and operators who would hand up the detour messages to the trains using a standard train-order hoop.

The engineering department maintained wooden shanties that contained seats, telephones, and stoves (sanitary facilities were behind that tree over there). A crane would unload a shanty at each end of the detour, a lineman would hook up the phone to the dispatchers' and message circuits, and you'd be in business. The N&W employed enough supervisors to have a detour on both the Tadpole and the Valley at the same time. Terminals at Portsmouth, Williamson, Columbus, and Cincinnati, incidentally, each had their own staffs.

When I arrived at Portsmouth, the N&W had been fully dieselized for two-and-a-half years. This had been accomplished with 8 Alco RS3's, 307 EMD GP9's (including 22 with higher-speed gearing for passenger service), 100 Alco RS11's and RS36's, and 40 Alco T6 switchers. (N&W's 1959 merger partner Virginian had dieselized before N&W acquired it, with all road units built by Fairbanks-Morse.)

These hadn't been enough to handle N&W's heavy traffic. Passenger-train dieselization was accelerated by leasing EMD E units from Atlantic Coast Line and Richmond, Fredericksburg & Potomac, and freight dieselization by leasing 30 GP9's from the Pennsylvania. The N&W followed up by quickly purchasing 48 EMD GP18's, then 44 GP30's in 1962, and 40 GP35's about a year later, plus 12 Alco Century 420's. All N&W diesels (except the passenger GP9's, which were red) were painted solid black, and all the road units had high short hoods. Some leased Bessemer & Lake Erie EMD F7's also spent time on the N&W. The ACL, RF&P, and PRR units had been gone for some months when I transferred to Portsmouth, while the F7's had just been returned to the Bessemer.

On the Tadpole, the N&W had still not found out just how many loads of coal the diesels could take to Portsmouth, but it was made plain to us that there was no car limit, either for loads or empty hoppers. In warm weather, 275-car empty hopper trains were commonplace. Usual practice was to put loaded trains of about 240 cars out of Williamson with three small Geeps or Alcos, or just two of the GP30's or '35's. That's right: Just two GP30's or 35's for, say, 22,000 tons of coal. (Nobody knew exactly what these trains weighed—N&W's

westbound coal was not weighed until it went over the scale at the hump at Portsmouth, which was why Kenova coal went to Portsmouth and was backhauled.)

This operation was successful mainly because the power was new, and the troublesome transition arrangements of the GP30's and 35's had not yet made their presence known. But the slipping! Well, most engineers found that their house keys would fit in the slot behind the sander levers to wedge them open so they didn't have to sit there and hold the lever open all day. Because of the big tonnages and the economical use of power, the Tadpole might have been that rarest of districts: uphill all the way from terminal to terminal, in both directions.

The Tadpole handled 2,500 loaded coal cars every day the miners went into their holes, and you couldn't hold the traffic back: It just kept coming. And every day you had to get 2,500 empties back east so more coal could come west. On top of all those black diamonds, there were four time freights and two passenger trains in each direction, and it was expected that coal or empties would not delay them. If a derailment occurred, the first priority was getting a main track open; cleaning up could be done later.

Portsmouth Yard was well equipped to handle all these loads, weighing, classifying, and pumping them out the other end toward Columbus or Cincinnati (or back toward Kenova). There were separate westbound coal and time-freight humps, but everything eastbound was handled in a flat yard.

On the Columbus District, Delano Hill was not a momentum grade, so tonnage was limited. Three of the "big" Geeps could get over the summit at Kingston with 210 loads at about 11 or 12 mph if it didn't rain (if it did, you sanded, jockeyed the throttle, and swore a lot, but usually you made it). This was a convenient figure, since the classification tracks at Portsmouth's coal hump averaged about 70 car-lengths, so the classification yard doubled as the departure yard. These tracks were equipped with yard air, so when they were full of cars, the carmen could couple the hoses to the brake systems to charge and pre-test them. The efficiency of this operation was indicated by the fact that 210-car westbound coal trains could be called an hour apart. A Valley crew could get its power to the yard, triple its train together, make a continuity brake test, and be departing just as the next crew was bringing their power down from the engine terminal. As on the

After doubling its train together at Clare Yard in Cincinnati, train 78 prepares to depart for Portsmouth over the Peavine in December 1959. Doubling the train blocked the Pennsylvania main line diamond at Clare. TOM SMART; COLLECTION OF J. DAVID INGLES.

Tadpole, 275-car empty trains were common on the Valley.

It very quickly became apparent to me that what Boss Tabor really ran was a conveyor belt—a very complex one, but a conveyor belt nonetheless. So I started riding trains on the Tadpole, trying to get to know the crews, the trains, and the railroad. I found the men to be very friendly and helpful, going out of their way to tell me things that, at that point, I had no hope of comprehending. For example: "You got to watch it in those single-track tunnels; every one of 'em is downhill westbound and you'll gain speed through them." Or, "You don't make a runnin' release [of the automatic brake] on them coal trains. If you set the air, you stop."

At that time, N&W "enjoyed" a Christmas rush of mail traffic, handled in either advance or second sections of the regular passenger trains. These would consist of one or two of the passenger GP9's and up to five or six mail and express cars, plus a rider coach which occasionally would be occupied by a revenue passenger.

Passengers eventually get hungry, and since there was no food service on these extra sections, at least one considerate conductor, Shirley Thompson, provided a remedy. Thompson took it upon himself to arrange for box lunches to be put aboard his westbound middle-of-the-night Second No. 3 (the westbound *Pocahontas*) at Kenova. He'd take dinner orders leaving Williamson and hand them off to the operator at Kermit, 19 miles out. The Kermit operator would phone the dinner orders to the operator at Kenova Tower, who in turn would place the orders at a nearby all-night restaurant for delivery to the depot.

We assistant road foremen of engines had to ride as many of these mail trains as we could, so I wound up covering Second 26 (the eastbound Powhatan Arrow) and the aforementioned Second 3 between Portsmouth and Williamson. This got me acquainted with a remarkable young engineer named Jimmy Marcum.

Marcum wasn't much older than I, but he'd gone firing on the Tadpole right out of high school and had established himself as one of the finest young runners on the district; indeed, he was among the best out there, of any age. He was popular with his fellow enginemen—he later was elected local chairman of the Tadpoles Brotherhood of Locomotive Engineers lodge—and equally so with the division's officialdom. Jimmy loved running a train;

he had been promoted on steam, and no one enjoyed running an A-class 2-6-6-4 more than he did.

Jimmy had bid in the mail trains for the holiday season in 1962 and had landed on the same turns I was covering. On Second 3 on December 8, as we were loading and unloading at Ironton, Ohio, Jimmy said, "Come on over here and sit down. You're not going to learn how to do this any younger."

Keeping in my mind Boss Tabor's orders and my enthusiasm, I still managed to fake reluctance. "But Jim, this is a passenger train."

"Sit down here. I won't let you get into trouble, and besides, I don't want to work for an assistant road foreman who doesn't know how to run a train."

So I sat down in Jimmy's seat. When Shirley Thompson gave the highball on the communication signal, Jimmy showed me how to get the slack out smoothly, and then said, "Get right after them. There's nothing between you and home but a 27-mile racetrack."

If I hadn't been hooked on that stuff before, I was then. Passenger Geep 511 and her companion were still new and lively. Jimmy had me start notching down on them somewhere in the low 70's, so we could cruise at 75 and never even have to touch the brake until Portsmouth. True to his word, he stood right there by the control stand and told me everything to expect and do.

The next night, Jimmy put me in the seat of the 501 leaving Williamson, so I could get a taste of the crooked country. Entering 2,626-foot Tunnel 1 at the legal 45 mph, I remembered having been told that I'd gain speed in the tunnel. I reduced the throttle a notch. "What did you do that for?" Jimmy asked. I related what I'd been told. He said, "Leave it where it was. You'll come out the other end at 46 miles an hour."

Sure enough, we came out the other end at 46, just like Jimmy said we would. I made up my mind right there that Jimmy was a guy I would get with at every opportunity. He not only knew his business, but could and would tell it to a rank amateur such as myself in terms I could understand. Many other engineers proved to be just as helpful, and I was able to see, and learn from, many highly skilled railroaders working at the top of their craft.

For example, let's watch Tadpole engineer Harry Spriggs get a coal train out of Williamson. In the interval between passenger trains, let's say they've made up

Harry's train on the main line; he's tied his two GP30's on, and the head end is about at the west end of the passenger station. The rear end is about 240 car-lengths—maybe 10,000 feet or so—to our east, and the grade is virtually level. The air has been pumped up; Harry has made the brake test and has been given the highball from the caboose.

Now, just because the carmen have said the brakes are released on the rear end doesn't necessarily mean that every brake in the train has released—this was before the days of the quick-releasing ABD car brakes, remember. And while the carmen would have walked the brake application, a pull-by inspection sufficed for the release. So, extreme care had to be taken in trying to start 'em. Two GP30's couldn't develop tractive effort anywhere near the strength of a car coupler, but when the head end got moving, the momentum of the two engines in throttle notch 1 or 2 and, say, the first 50 cars at 3 or 4 mph, would easily overstress a coupler knuckle if the rear end had some brakes hanging up and wasn't ready to come along. This train would have probably 250 feet of slack, the equivalent of six or seven hopper-car-lengths. So Harry Spriggs will very carefully "shake 'em loose."

Harry puts the reverser in forward, toots a highball, and opens the throttle to the first notch. He eases the engine brake off and lets the Geeps move forward, waiting to feel the resistance tighten up. As the resistance pulls his westward motion to a stall, he adds a throttle notch—at the most, two—and notes very carefully where the engines come to a stop.

"Well, that's as far as we can go this way. Let's see how far we can go that way," Harry says.

The stubby red lever goes into reverse, and Spriggs backs up against the train, very gently, and adds throttle as the resistance tightens up. He notes that the rearward stall occurs a car-length or so east of where the engines were located when he tied them on the train. Then he goes forward as before, noting that resistance does not tighten up until he's a couple of car-lengths west of the original westward stall. Now he knows that his next see-saw ought to get the caboose in motion.

If the caboose moves on the reverse, eastward shove—the conductor would notify him on the radio—Harry would shut the throttle off and let the train stop, knowing, then, that all the brakes were released and he can get them going for Portsmouth. If the caboose moves on the westward pull of the see-saw, he would add throttle with the intent of getting the train up to, say, 7 mph while pulling past the rear brakeman, who would be inspecting the train from about the east end of the passenger station. Once the rear man gets on the caboose and highballs Spriggs on the radio, Spriggs will wedge the sander lever open with a key and advance the throttle as high as the engine will hold the rail.

Eventually the throttle is in Run 8, the ammeters are at a steady 900, and forward movement slowly advances up to what will be a top speed of about 25 or 26 mph. (Those two GP30's will never get going fast enough to make the transition into parallel, which occurs at about 27 mph.) The speed will drop back to about 12 or 13 over the Ohio River crossing at Kenova, but the throttle will not come out of Run 8 until Ironton, where it will be reduced to Run 5 to minimize the possibility of a traction-motor flashover on the Detroit, Toledo & Ironton diamond. Except for this brief respite, the two GP30's will put out 900 amps until the shutdown just east of Sciotoville, where Spriggs will apply the dynamic brake so the train can head into the running tracks at Star Yard, at the extreme east end of the receiving tracks at Portsmouth's coal hump yard.

Once past the "shake-'em-loose" at Williamson, it became a ho-hum, run-and-whistle performance, watching the picket fences go by like telegraph poles, as they say, and listening to the turbo-charged 16-567's sing. Conveyor-belt

railroading, yes, but it was tremendously efficient and immensely profitable. Occasionally bad rail conditions would result in a two-unit train stalling at Kenova, necessitating the Kenova Yard engine giving it a boost over the bridge, but on the whole the operation was most dependable.

Coal business on the Cincinnati district amounted to about one train per day, varying from 30 or so cars to 140. The westward ruling grade on the Peavine was 7 miles of 1.4 percent from Lawshe up to Mount Zion. This included a series of reverse curves near the bottom known as "Sally's Backbone." Sally must've been a chiropractors dream to have a spine as crooked as those curves. Power for coal trains was still assigned with a built-in requirement to double this hill, a practice dating from the days of 4-8-0's.

Quincy Goff seemed a little paranoid about the train-handling problems we had been experiencing with the Peavine coal trains. When a break-in-two occurred, Boss Tabor would be less-than-gentle about calling it to Goff's attention. I'd been around about a month—my riding experience to Cincinnati mostly on the pre-Christmas mail trains and a couple of trips on the Sardinia turnaround local freight—when I was told to ride a coal train to Cincinnati with a young ex-tra-board engineer. If I was expected to keep him out of trouble, it was going to be a case of the blind leading the blind.

We had two GP9's and 32—thats right,

just 32—loads of coal. The young runner had done a good job of doubling the hill and slicking 'em through Sardinia, and I'd done a good job of observing him and keeping my unknowing trap shut except for calling signals. But somehow he cracked the whip with 'em at White Oak, 3 miles west of Sardinia, and broke the rear 12 cars off the train. It wasn't just a knuckle, it was a drawbar, an all-new break. Even though I had no idea what went wrong, I underwent some rough handling of my own when I got back to the office, and I wasn't even allowed to plead ignorance.

But over the months, tutelage by fellow ARFE Ray Morgan and engineers such as Forrest Nichols, Ray Scott, George Irvin, Ray Fultz, and Jesse Feagins got me to the point that I could get over the Peavine to Clare with any length of coal train. I couldn't do it in their fine style, or make their time, but I could get it there intact. It remains one of the most interesting (read: fun) jobs of train-handling I've ever seen, with a couple of situations requiring going uphill at about 45 mph with the dynamic brake full on, to keep the slack bunched for a drop-off beyond.

Otis Mullins had told me that first day that wind had a great effect on trains out in the open, but you couldn't fool me; I knew better. On the bright afternoon of January 8, 1964, I found myself invited to operate an empty hopper train from Columbus to Portsmouth. Detouring and duties on the Tadpole and Peavine had kept me from doing much running on the Valley, a circumstance shortly to be corrected. My gracious hosts were engineer Bob Schuler, one of the best anywhere, and his protege, fireman Wayne Phipps. Our engines were GP9 652 and RS11 314; we got our 177 empties right out of Joyce Avenue Yard. We were going straight south, there was a gale blowing out of the west, and I found that empty hoppers were just like sails. Our raging 3,550 hp was able to get that train up to almost 30 mph on the level. When we turned over the top of the hill at Kingston, facing 9 miles of descending 0.3 percent with the 35 mph speed limit over the B&O at the bottom, I started reducing the throttle.

After Schuler and Phipps enjoyed a few moments of laughter at the naivete of the new boy, Schuler said, "Leave them wide open."

Otis Mullins was right. I pulled that train down that hill just as hard as I could pull it and went across the B&O diamonds at 33 mph. Assistant Trainmaster Hank

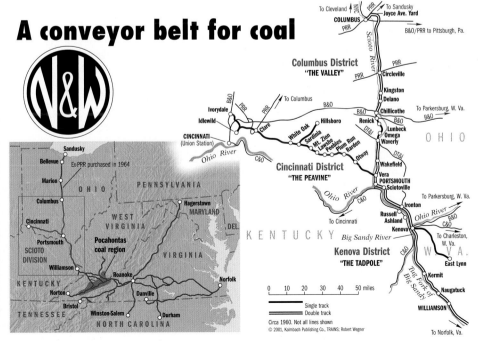

A conveyor belt for coal

Kinzel was at Renick Tower with the radar gun trained on me getting his speed checks in early that month waving and grinning as we went past. I'm afraid my reply wasn't as gracious. Our speed didn't approach 40 until we got into the single-track along the Scioto River between Lunbeck and Omega, where we were sheltered by the hills that provide the only topographical excitement between Portsmouth and Columbus.

On October 16, 1964, N&W merged with the Nickel Plate Road and leased the Wabash, although it had no direct connection with either. This was solved by N&W's simultaneous purchase of Pennsylvania's Columbus-Sandusky line, which crossed the NKP at its hub of Bellevue, Ohio. The Sandusky line was not in the best of shape and required much rehabilitation. N&W made it the Sandusky District of the Scioto Division, and took enough operating people from the old PRR to run it satisfactorily. We Scioto Division supervisors were given familiarization trips over it before merger date, and we rode everything that turned a wheel on the Sandusky for a month after the merger. It paid off. The crews were familiarized with N&W rules and methods, and the transition went off without a hitch. The only drawback was that we Portsmouth people had to live in a motel in Columbus for that month.

It was a pleasure watching the good hoggers run anywhere, but especially on that crooked, up-and-down Peavine. Riding with an old-timer like Bob Clark on the westbound *Powhatan Arrow* was a revelation. Bob could handle throttle and brake through those curves and humps and dips while telling you tales of the bygone days, and never miss blowing for a road crossing, calling a signal, or passing a station on the minute. And on December 10, 1964, Bob Clark gave me one of those moments you'd love to live forever.

That evening I got on the *Arrow's* power, Geeps 501 and 506, at Portsmouth, heading for Cincinnati to return on the first eastbound mail train of the season, the advance section of No. 4, the *Pocahontas*. "You take em," Bob had said, so I sat down in his seat and put my foot on the dead-man pedal.

Where for Bob Clark it was second nature, for me it was hard labor, even though I knew the road well enough—handling throttle and brake on that old narrow-gauge railroad, watching the speed carefully so as to not exceed the limits, and, almost as bad, to not be too slow and thus lose time, plus trying not to spill anyone's coffee back in the train. I fought my way through Otway and Rarden and enjoyed a brief respite letting the 501 and 506 have their heads up the comparatively straight hill into Plum Run, then worked at it again dropping down the hill out of Peebles to Lawshe.

Passing Lawshe, Bob Clark turned on the reading light on the fireman's side and looked at his watch.

"You're right on time," he said, turning the light off. Feeling no reply was necessary, I got ready to lay into those Geeps for the 1.4 percent climb up Sally's Backbone, when Bob dryly added the kicker: "Your boss, Quincy Goff, has usually gotten 10 minutes late by here."

Like I said, you'd love to live the moment forever. All that labor, plus that necessary to finish the job to get from Lawshe to Clare, wasn't wasted, and I got up out of the seat passing Clare Yard and gave it back to Bob, still right on time, feeling pretty good. He and his fellow engineers had taught me well.

While I was at Portsmouth, N&W leased 10 diesels from the Duluth, Missabe & Iron Range, six big Alco RSD15 "Alligators," Nos. 50-55 (purists insist that the DM&IR units weren't true "Alligators," having high noses), and four SD9's, 136, 140, 141, and 146. They were all immaculate when they came to us; you could have eaten dinner off their cab floors.

Since I'd never worked in Virginian Railway territory, these were the first six-motor diesels I had gotten a chance to run. Their dependability regardless of rail conditions was impressive; the only problem was that the Alcos had a tendency to kick the engine overspeed trip and die when making transition at about 19 mph. Their ability to dig in and lug may have influenced N&W's next motive-power purchase, a group of SD35's in the 1500 series. I quickly became a fan of these units, too. I had seen the first two of them, 1500 and 1506, going east, dead in train 94 to be put in service at Roanoke and get their first 1,000 miles in.

As I got into the routine of life as an ARFE on the Scioto Division, I developed an answer if Boss Tabor or anyone else asked me what I was coming back on. I would tell him No. 77 or No. 85, the westbound hotshots due out of Williamson before midnight, because it made a nice turn to leave Portsmouth on 78 about 4:30 p.m. or 84 about an hour later, and get off in Williamson about 7 or 7:30. I'd go over into town for a good, leisurely dinner, then hop on one of the westbounds back home. This fulfilled the riding requirement—ARFEs were expected to ride hotshots, too—and relieved me from getting to the office bright and early the next morning.

On July 8, 1965, about a week after I'd seen the 1500 and 1506 go east on 94, I'd gone to Williamson on 78, had dinner, and showed up at the yard office looking for a ride home. I was surprised to see the 1500 and 1506 marked up for 85 that night, with engineer John Johnson, so I jumped at the chance to run them on their first revenue trip on the division.

Number 85 had 139 cars that night after a small amount of switching at Williamson yard, and after the brake test and the highball, the two SD's lifted them right out of town. But, my oh my, how the flanges squealed and sang and protested as those new six-wheel trucks fought the curves! I caught the same two engines a couple of weeks later on an empty hopper train and they'd gotten broken in—they didn't protest a bit.

The SD35's proved to be slightly slower than comparable GP's, but earned respect because they didn't slip. Rain or snow, whatever the conditions, the 1500's would keep coming. They ran a 267-car test train, say 28,000 tons or so, up the Valley with three of them, and I watched engineer Gail Taylor walk 'em over the hill at Kingston at 11 mph with nary a slip.

Three years of this was all they'd let me enjoy. The merger had changed things forever on the N&W, and adventures on the former Wabash and Nickel Plate beckoned. Otis Mullins called me into his office in late November 1965, and told me the news: I was being plucked from my comfortable ARFE job and sent to Decatur, Ill., the heart of the former Wabash. But that's another story.

To wash, or not to wash—a UP gas-turbine

By Les Clark
Hostler

1962

From *Classic Trains* magazine,
Summer 2010

The Union Pacific operated some of its big gas-turbine locomotives on its South Central District between Los Angeles and Salt Lake City for a few months in 1962. At the time, I was a locomotive fireman and spent most of my workdays assigned to an afternoon hostling job at UP's Salt Lake City shop complex.

Until then, the turbines had worked mostly on the main line between Ogden, Utah, and Council Bluffs, Iowa, so when a turbine showed up at the Salt Lake shop, it was usually for major repair work. But for those few months in '62, when they became regulars at Salt Lake, things changed.

Except for the fact that they required No. 6 residual fuel oil (the so-called Bunker C), which was available only in a different area of the shop complex, the turbines were cared for at the regular service pits along with their diesel brethren. Bunker C was the same tar-like stuff that oil-burning steam locomotives had used, and the Bunker C stand pipe that had fueled steam engines at the shops still stood, so we fueled the turbines there.

Turning the turbines around also required special handling. The turbines, with their tenders, were too long for the shop turntable, so they were turned at the Grant Tower wye 2 miles south of the shop. This required the escort of a switchman-herder and, for a hostler and his helper, was usually good for at least an hour and a half of minimum labor and patient waiting. This interlude did offer the opportunity to snoop and gain experience with a turbine's operating characteristics, however.

At Salt Lake shop, standard servicing procedure for a hostler and his helper was for us to board the locomotives at the receiving track where the incoming road crews had parked them. As a hostler, I would then spot the locomotives at the sanding columns and slowly feed them through so my helper could add sand as needed. We'd then position the locomotives at the entrance to the run-through wash racks. As the photo below shows, these racks had high-pressure chemical and rinse-water pipes that arched around the locomotive. First a high-pressure wash solution was sprayed on the units, then a rinse, as we slowly advanced the locomotives through. When the wash and rinse were completed, we would move the units ahead to a spot on the inspection pits, where they would be fueled (the turbines each had a small auxiliary diesel engine, which used normal diesel fuel). All units were given water, cleaned, inspected, and had their air filters changed if necessary. If any running repairs were needed, those were then performed.

At the time, UP management was emphatic that, unless the temperature was

At the very wash rack where during summer 1962 turbines were washed (or maybe not), GP9's get the clean-up treatment. UNION PACIFIC RAILROAD MUSEUM.

141

Looking not unlike the servicing area at nearby Salt Lake, UP's shop tracks at Ogden in 1963 host 10,000-hp turbine 25 and year-old GP30's. Bruce R. Meyer.

below freezing, all units were to be washed. Woe to the supervisor who didn't ensure this rule was practiced. Thus did life on "the pit" become a routine pattern: Units came in, were washed and serviced, and units went out.

Then the turbines arrived.

One summer evening shortly after sunset, one of the 8,500-hp turbines arrived from Los Angeles. These were really fascinating and impressive machines. I quickly boarded this one so as to gain experience with it, not to mention that a break in the normal routine was always welcome. The turbine had been shut down by the incoming crew, making the locomotive much more tolerable to be around. With the turbine running, the loud, jet-like noise was annoying, to say the least.

Typical of gas turbines, they consumed about one-third as much fuel per hour at idle as under full load, making them real gas hogs. For this reason, the turbines were designed so they could remain shut down until just before leaving a terminal, and also upon arrival at the destination terminal, again could be shut down. The auxiliary diesel, a 1,000-hp Cooper-Bessemer engine in the front (A) unit of the 8,500-hp versions, was capable of moving the locomotive to and from the train and operating the air compressor to supply the necessary air-brake needs.

In practice, this didn't work out well on the earlier 4,500-hp units, because their auxiliary, a smaller 275-hp Cummins truck engine, lacked adequate power—it simply was too small to perform all the requirements at the same time: hostling, running the compressor, generating electrical power, and cranking the turbine. Even by itself, the cranking takes a whole lot of power. The 8,500-hp units, however, could be hostled to and from the train in a lively fashion. But I digress.

Back to our big turbine and the wash rack. After sanding the units, I positioned them at the entrance to the wash rack. My helper was busily arranging the wash pipes to provide a good bath, but just as we were about to start, the shop superintendent— an excitable person—came running out of the office, waving his arms and shouting

for us to stop. He yelled up to me that the turbine had to be running while the unit was being washed. I said, "OK, I'll start it up," and did so.

Now, this was not an arduous task on my part, as it involved pushing a button and watching a white light. It was, however, a complex operation involving 21 automatically controlled steps. The auxiliary diesel engine generator powered one of the four turbine main generators. This generator then began to rotate the turbine shaft. When the turbine shaft attained a certain rotational speed, diesel fuel was introduced by spraying it into the turbine burner chambers, where it was electrically ignited.

These igniters were a lot like oversized spark plugs. When the turbine had been running smoothly for a certain period on diesel fuel, the automatic transfer to Bunker C fuel began. Bunker C is of the consistency of tar until it is heated. The heating was supplied by a number of electric heaters placed in the sides of the tender fuel compartment and powered by the auxiliary engine. (On the smaller turbine locomotives, the heat was supplied from a steam generator at the rear of the unit.)

When a complete fuel transfer had been attained and certain automatic tests satisfied, then, and only then, was the turbine ready—as indicated by the white light going out and a needle on the notching guide indicator on the dashboard panel moving into the green zone. This meant that the locomotive was ready for full-load operation. The complete program was automatic and consumed about 11 minutes.

At this point, we were ready to wash the units . . . or so we thought. Just as we were about to turn on the water, out of the office came the shop "super" in a repeat performance. He yelled up at me to say that he'd consulted headquarters in Omaha and had been instructed not to wash a unit with the turbine running, and to shut it down first.

I said, "OK," and pushed the button again. The white light came on, indicating that the automatic, 11-minute shutdown sequence had begun. This was important, for if the turbine was shut down while operating on Bunker C, it would leave

such a mess in the burners that to make a restart without internal cleaning was very difficult. That was not a popular event with shop crews!

During the normal shutdown routine, the fuel transfer from Bunker C to diesel was made with the turbine operating long enough to ensure a complete purge of the fuel lines. After this, it was simply a case of waiting for the massive turbine rotor to coast to a stop. When the turbine stopped, the white light went out, indicating that a full shutdown had occurred. We were now ready to wash.

But wait!

Yep, you guessed it! Out of the office came our nervous leader again, to tell me not to wash the units at all and to instead place them on the service pit. So after an interesting hour of fun, it was now back to shuffling mundane diesel units for the rest of my shift. To my knowledge, none of the turbines received a run-through bath during their brief assignment at Salt Lake.

This was a fascinating time, and I hated to see the turbines transferred elsewhere. They were impressive, and perhaps one of the best train-handlers ever. The shop crews were not so enthusiastic about them, but the operating people liked them. Yes, the turbines were complex and noticeably different in many ways, with exclusive service needs, but this could be said of almost any new unit when introduced. And yes, the "Big Blows" were unpleasant to be near when the turbine was running. For a person to perform work on a running turbine bordered on severe torture.

Considering that they all were really experimental locomotives, the gas-turbine-electrics turned in a reasonable record of reliability. Over-the-road failures that required rescue were reduced by their being equipped with multiple-unit capabilities, so with diesel units in the consist, if a turbine failed, the diesels could keep the train moving.

I do feel that had Bunker C oil remained at the 3-cents-per-gallon level that had encouraged the turbine program in the first place, today we might be seeing their generational offspring.

Also, we probably would have figured out how—and when—to wash them.

From the Rockies to the Berkshires

By H.F. Cavanaugh
Mechanical Engineer

1963

From *Trains* magazine,
June 1976

The winter of 1962-1963 was severe in the eastern United States. Heavy snowfalls in early December were followed by temperatures colder than normal, and the weather created havoc on the New York Central—for which I was employed as an assistant mechanical engineer.

The NYC's fleet of diesel-electric locomotives was particularly affected. An unusually high number of locomotives were failing out on the road. The diesel engine would shut down, and as the dead unit was pulled along, wind-blown snow would collect in the traction motors and blow into the carbody, ending up in the main generator and electrical cabinet. When the locomotive was placed inside a shop for repairs, the snow would melt inside the electrical apparatus, resulting in grounded generators and traction motors.

In Colorado, the Denver & Rio Grande Western had been operating for about a year its three diesel-hydraulic locomotives built by Krauss-Maffei in Munich, Germany. The Rio Grande had decided to modify the KM's pneumatic throttle arrangement to an electric system to enable the units to operate in multiple with American-made diesel-electrics. Because of the size of D&RGW trains and the road's tonnage ratings, the three hydraulics had operated together. When the first unit, No. 4001, was shopped for the M.U. conversion, the others—Nos. 4002 and 4003—became surplus.

It was at this point that the New York Central, plagued with its locomotive electrical problems, decided to test a locomotive that did not require electric motors for traction and approached D&RGW to borrow for a short period the two surplus diesel-hydraulic units.

Arrangements were completed, and on February 8, 1963, Nos. 4002 and 4003 departed Denver on Chicago, Burlington & Quincy symbol freight No. 66 for Chicago for delivery to the NYC. Accompanying the diesel-hydraulics was the D&RGW's dynamometer car with three Krauss-Maffei technicians and two Rio Grande road foremen of engines who would instruct NYC engine crews in the operation of the locomotives.

When I was offered the chance to ride the diesel-hydraulic units in service on the NYC as a diesel inspector, I quickly accepted the assignment. Four of us from the headquarters office were to ride the units in turn, keeping a record of fuel used and noting any unusual occurrences in the operation of the locomotives. We, along with several other NYC mechanical department people and road foremen of engines, were to be in Chicago by Saturday, February 9, 1963, to inspect the units and become familiar with their operation. Numbers 4002 and 4003 arrived in Chicago that evening and were given a joint inspection by CB&Q and NYC mechanical personnel at the Burlington's engine terminal in Cicero, Ill.

Several factors impressed us the first time we were able to look over the units. The configuration of the cab in relation to the carbody was reminiscent of a Vista-Dome passenger car. Looking forward from the KM cab was like looking over the nose of an F7, but the hydraulic's cab seemed to have more glass area on the sides; and the sloping windows in the back of the cab roof (which provided exhaust-stack visibility) created the illusion of being in a bubble on top of the locomotive.

The cab was very quiet. We reasoned that this was due to the walls and ceiling, which appeared to be about twice as thick as those on an F7. The KM's cab also seemed more roomy.

Back in the engine room, the two Maybach 16-cylinder V-type engines seemed too small and compact to be capable of producing 2,000 hp each compared with the 2,000-hp diesel engines used in NYC's EMD GP20 or Alco RS32 (DL721) units. We were informed, however, that the Maybach engine operated at 1,585 rpm at full throttle, more than 50 percent faster than the Alco or EMD diesels. The hydraulic lines for propulsion and for driving the cooling fans gave the KM locomotives a maze of plumbing.

In the engine room we were shown the location of gauges for fuel-oil pressure and lube-oil pressure in each engine as well as the gauge indicating transmission-oil temperature. A tachometer for each engine indicated revolutions per minute. These gauge readings were to be recorded periodically by us NYC diesel inspectors.

The D&RGW dynamometer car was a converted World War II troop sleeper (basically a box car with windows). The car had its own diesel generator set for electric power; in addition to the instruments and test equipment, the car was equipped with facilities so that the crew could live aboard. The Krauss-Maffei technicians and Rio Grande personnel traveling with the locomotives lived on the car while they were on the NYC.

Following the inspection, the units and dynamometer car were towed to the NYC engine terminal at Englewood in Chicago to be dispatched in service from there. Since my first riding assignment would be from Buffalo east, I took the sleeping car on No. 90 out of Chicago that night.

On Sunday, February 10, the KM's were dispatched from Chicago to Elkhart, Ind., on freight CB-12; No. 4002 was in the lead. The train had 154 cars and covered the 100 miles in 6.5 hours, including three stops en route to pick up or set out cars. No problems were encountered.

After a layover of about 6 hours, the engines were sent eastward on Advance NY-4 bound for DeWitt Yard in Syracuse,

Two of Rio Grande's Krauss-Maffei diesel-hydraulics spent almost three weeks testing on the NYC in early 1963. Here crews on New York Central Advance BF-3 change at Bellefontaine, Ohio, on February 24, 1963. Si Herring.

N.Y. The 112-car train proceeded without incident from Elkhart to Cleveland, but there at approximately 12:50 a.m. the lead unit struck a 1960 Ford that had gone down onto No. 2 track off 63rd Street. The front end of the 4002 was damaged enough to require the units and the dynamometer car to be cut off the train and placed in the Collinwood diesel terminal in Cleveland for repairs.

The repairs were made on Monday morning, February 11, and that afternoon the units were coupled to Advance BF-NY-2. The KM's took 128 cars to Buffalo with no unusual occurrences en route.

At Frontier Yard in Buffalo, where I boarded, the train designation was changed to Advance CB-4 and the consist was changed somewhat. We departed Frontier at 10:10 p.m. with 85 loads, 20 empties, 5,924 tons. The engines handled the train satisfactorily into Batavia, where we stopped to pick up 19 loads, giving us 7,374 tons. Although this was to prove to be the heaviest tonnage handled by the KM's during their three weeks on the Central, the hydraulics had no trouble with the train since the grade eastward

from Batavia toward Rochester was descending. Stops were made at Rochester and at Lyons to set off cars and at Waynesport to ice some refrigerator cars. We arrived at DeWitt about 5:30 a.m. on Tuesday.

One characteristic of the KM's became evident to the engine crew on this portion of the trip: It was not possible to switch as fast with the diesel-hydraulics as with diesel-electric units. When reversing direction, each of the four transmissions in the locomotive consist had to shift fully into mesh for the reverse movement before power could be applied. If the unit was not at a complete standstill, no reversing action could take place; and if any gear teeth in one or more transmissions butted with other teeth, power could not be applied beyond one notch on the throttle stand (one notch turned the gears involved sufficiently to allow for engagement). A Rio Grande road foreman and an NYC road foreman were in the cab at all times to point out to the engine crews the intricacies of operating the locomotives. NYC men expressed the opinion that the two units handled a train as well as four GP9 units would.

The New York Central System was not all "Water Level," and the big test for the diesel-hydraulics was to be conducted later in the day on February 11 on the Boston & Albany Division. This line, extending from the Hudson River valley to Boston, crossed several high ridges of the Berkshire Hills in Massachusetts and had ascending grades of about 1.5 percent eastbound. A 5,000-ton train normally was assigned five Alco 1,600-hp units or four Alco 2,000-hp units. The diesel-hydraulics, rated at 4,000 hp each, were expected to take such a train across the Berkshires alone. Because the three axles in each truck of the KM's were coupled together with cardan shafts, NYC expected the units to experience less wheel slippage than diesel-electrics, which had individually motor-driven axles.

From DeWitt, the KM's took freight BA-2 down the Mohawk Division toward Selkirk Yard near Albany. They began the run at 1:35 p.m. with 85 loads, no empties, 4,973 tons. The temperature was around 30 degrees and light snow was falling. Except for a stop at Utica to check the train for dragging equipment, the trip was uneventful. Arrival at Selkirk was at 6:43

Rio Grande KM diesel-hydraulics pause during testing next to New York Central F units at Syracuse, N.Y., in February 1963. H.F. CAVANAUGH.

p.m. Although there is no record of it, we later suspected that at Selkirk additional cars were added to the rear of the train, boosting the total tonnage to well over 5,000 tons.

At 7:25, BA-2 left Selkirk and started uphill toward Pittsfield, Mass. The temperature had dropped to 10 degrees and snow was blowing. Operation of the train was normal from Selkirk up to Chatham, N.Y.; train speed varied from 25 to 30 mph. At Englishman's Curve east of Chatham, a series of wheel slips occurred and train speed dropped to 11 mph. After we passed Canaan, N.Y., however, speed increased and we maintained 15 to 20 mph on the grade.

East of Richmond, Mass., the eastward grade changed and became slightly descending through Pittsfield to North Adams Junction. From there, the track climbed steeply to the summit at Hinsdale on a ruling grade of 1.5 percent.

At North Adams Junction, BA-2 stopped to drop the swing brakeman (required at that time by New York State's full-crew law), and at 10 p.m. we were under way. The train reached a speed of 12 mph before the entire length of the consist was on the grade, but then violent slipping took place and brought us to a stall. The dispatcher was contacted, and he gave us permission to back the train to Pittsfield. Again we headed eastward, this time reaching 42 mph before starting up the grade. As our speed dropped below 12

mph, the locomotives again began to slip, and we came to a standstill about 2 miles from North Adams Junction.

An Alco RS1 based as switcher at North Adams Junction was called and was coupled to the rear of our train; but even with all locomotives working to capacity, the train could not be started. The decision was made to double the hill, so 25 cars were cut off the head end and taken to the top and set out at Hinsdale. The two hydraulics went back for the remainder of the train; and with the Alco shoving, they took the consist up to Hinsdale, where the train was reassembled.

On the descending grade from Washington to Chester, a single 10-pound brake-pipe reduction was made to set the air brakes on the cars, and the speed of the train was controlled by the hydrodynamic brake on the locomotives. This was the only time the hydrodynamic brake was used while the KM's were on the Central, and the brake was very effective in maintaining the 25 mph speed limit down the hill. At West Springfield, the train consist was reduced. We departed for Boston with 60 cars and had no more problems.

The return movement of the test units began on train LS-3 out of Boston at 7:09 p.m. on February 13. At West Springfield, cars were added, resulting in a consist of 40 loads, 61 empties, 3,606 tons. A single 1,500-hp Alco road-switcher also was

added behind the caboose, and the helper's engineer was advised to operate his unit in the No. 2 throttle position so as to take care of the weight of his locomotive only and not to help in the movement of the train. Just west of Chester, where the grade became more severe, our speed dropped in 2 miles from 30 to 12 mph. The locomotives experienced a violent slip, and train speed dropped to 9.5 mph before the slip was corrected. Speed continued to decrease and more slipping occurred, so the helper engine was contacted on the radio to assist. With all locomotives working to capacity, our speed gradually increased and we topped the mountain at about 15 mph.

The Alco helper was dropped at North Adams Junction and the train continued westward without further incident. The locomotives stayed on LS-3 all the way to Cleveland, and the only significant incident en route was a broken pipe in the hydro-static fan drive system for radiator cooling. This required the No. 2 engine in No. 4003 to be isolated and allowed only to idle; but even on three engines, the units made good time over the road with the train.

The locomotives laid over for about 24 hours at Collinwood, where the broken pipe was repaired, then were dispatched eastward on ML-12, leaving Collinwood at 10 p.m. on February 15. Again I boarded the locomotives at Buffalo to cover the trip to Selkirk.

Train ML-12, at that time fairly new in the NYC book of freight-train schedules, was designed to handle multi-level cars of new automobiles. Business had not yet developed to the extent that the train was solid auto racks, so cars of Flexi-Van containers were included in the consist. Although maximum speed on regular freight trains was 60 mph, ML-12 was allowed the 70 mph maximum accorded the Flexi-Van/piggyback Super-Van trains.

After we passed Batavia and started down the grade toward Rochester, our train reached a maximum speed of 71 mph. The Krauss-Maffei technicians and the NYC chief road foreman of engines riding in the dynamometer car behind the units were experiencing an extremely rough ride and radioed the head end to reduce speed. Thereafter the KM's were restricted to a maximum of 60 mph on NYC.

At Selkirk, the hydraulics were put on train BA-6 for another try at the Berkshires on the B&A Division. They left Selkirk at 6:08 p.m. on February 16 with 55 loads, 22 empties, 3,767 tons—a lighter train than on the first attempt. Twelve loads were dropped at North Adams Junction, and the train went over the hill with 3,076 tons. Two or three wheel slips occurred, but on the grade the speed did not drop below 18 mph. At West Springfield, the locomotives were turned back to Selkirk on train BD-3 with 14 loads, 86 empties, 3,185 tons. The lowest speed on the westbound ascending grade was 13 mph, and only one wheel slip was experienced.

To give personnel at New York headquarters a chance to examine these special locomotives, the KM units were dispatched down the West Shore on February 18 on train VW-6 to Wee-hawken, N.J. (excessive clearances of the units precluded sending them down the Hudson Division to New York City because they would not clear the third rail south of Croton-Harmon).

The hydraulics stayed a day in Weehawken, then were sent north on February 20 on train WD-1 with 93 loads, 32 empties, 6,320 tons. As the train approached Selkirk, the Krauss-Maffei technicians discovered that several fuel-injection lines were leaking on both engines of No. 4003. Leaking lines on one simply were tightened, but one line had to be renewed. At DeWitt, a bracket supporting a sanding pipe on 4003 was found to be broken, so the pipe was removed and was replaced with one from 4002 until the units could be shopped.

At DeWitt the units were put on train NC-1 destined for Elkhart and they proceeded to Collinwood without incident. We left Collinwood Yard at 4:16 p.m. on February 21 with 87 loads, 24 empties, 4,434 tons. Snow was falling, the temperature was 10 degrees, and we faced a headwind of 10 to 15 mph—it really felt cold. Nearing Elyria, O., the main air-reservoir safety valves on 4003 were observed to be blowing, and the main-res-ervoir air-pressure gauges showed a pressure of 150 to 160 psi (normal is 130 to 140). Within another minute, the high pressure air crossover pipe between the two air compressors on the unit had burst. The train was stopped, and a spare pipe carried in the dynamometer car was installed as a replacement.

We started again, but in several minutes the crossover pipe again burst. Evidently the extreme cold weather had caused moisture in the air to freeze in an aftercooler located outside the carbody on the end of the unit, and so the compres-sors could not pump air to the main reservoirs on that unit. However, the main reservoirs were getting air through the main-reservoir equalizing line from No. 4002, so there was sufficient air to operate the brakes. The crossover pipe connection was blanked off at the No. 2 compressor, and the locomotives continued on with three of the four compressors in the two units operating.

The air compressors on both units were belt-driven from the engines. Because of the extreme cold and its related problems, the air compressors were being overworked and the belts started slipping. As the train reached Airline Yard in Toledo, the belts on two of the air compressors broke. With one compressor on 4003 down because of the burst crossover pipe and the belts on two of the remaining compressors broken—and with no spares on board—the locomotives had to be cut off the train.

The units and the dynamometer car were turned on the wye at Airline and then were taken downtown and parked at the passenger station in Toledo until arrange-ments could be made to get them back to Collinwood diesel terminal. The decision was made to double-head the KM's with a diesel-electric unit ahead to supply air for operation of the brakes on the train; the one good compressor on 4002 supplied air for the two diesel-hydraulics only. GP9 No. 5915 was coupled to the front of the D&RGW units, and the three locomotives went back to Collinwood on train CDB-4. Upon arrival at Collinwood on the evening of February 22, the KM's were put into the diesel terminal for repairs and periodic maintenance.

Since the units still were covered under the manufacturer's warranty, a weekly inspection of the gearboxes and universal joints in the drive train for lubrication was required. A semi-monthly inspection on the whole locomotive also was required. A monthly inspection included changing the 116 gallons of lube oil in each diesel engine. These maintenance requirements were extensive compared with those for the average diesel-electric locomotive, which could run 30 days between any scheduled maintenance.

The hydraulic locomotives came out of Collinwood diesel terminal on February 24 and were dispatched down the old Big Four to Avon Yard west of Indianapolis on Advance BF-3. The trip was without incident until the train stopped outside Avon at Indianapolis. While the train was waiting to get into the yard, a broken elliptic spring was discovered on the No, 2 truck of the 4002, This necessitated shopping the units, so they were sent over to nearby Beech Grove, Ind., where the broken spring was repaired. On February 26, the units went back to Collinwood on Advance BF-4 without incident.

On February 27, the KM units started west to Chicago to go back to the D&RGW. They were dispatched from Collinwood to Elkhart on LS-7 with a 3,500-ton train. The weather was "warming up" into the mid-20's, and the trip was made without difficulty. The next day, the hydraulics went on to Englewood Yard in Chicago on LS-1. They were fueled at Englewood and then were sent over to the CB&Q with the LS-1 connection for that road.

In 19 days on New York Central tracks, the diesel-hydraulic locomotives operated a total of 4,116 miles. In handling fast freight tonnage trains between Chicago and Selkirk, their performance compared with that obtained from four EMD GP9 diesel-electrics. However, the NYC felt that because of the lack of sufficient weight on their drivers, the KM units in heavy-grade operation could not handle the tonnage that four 1,500-hp conventional units were regularly handling. When the speed of the KM's train had dropped to 12 mph on a grade with the units under full throttle, excessive slipping had occurred. Wheel slips also had been noted occasionally during high-speed operation.

The railroad found too that the maintenance required by the KM's was excessive. The NYC realized that the units still were under warranty, but the road nevertheless was concerned about the weekly and semimonthly inspections required for greasing and lubrication and the change of engine oil on a monthly basis—all in addition to the usual monthly inspection. During quarterly inspections, the cardan shafts were to be disassembled, relubricated, inspected, and reassembled; this was an extensive job.

For those of us involved in the testing of these unusual units on the New York Central, the experience was one never to be forgotten.

In 1964, diesel-hydraulics once more were tested on the NYC when Alco was preparing to deliver its three DH643 units (dubbed "Alco-haulics") to the Southern Pacific. However, this was strictly Alco's test and NYC's mechanical department was not involved. Earlier in 1964, Rio Grande had sold its three diesel-hydraulics to Southern Pacific, but by the end of 1968 these units and all of SP's own German-built hydrau-lics had been retired. The Alco hydraulics were written off by SP in late 1973, ending an interesting experimental period in modern American railroading.

The Peru 173: A close encounter on the Wabash

By Ed King
Road Foreman of Engines

1966

From *Trains* magazine,
Jannuary 1976

In 1966 British driver Graham Hill won the Indianapolis 500. I didn't run at Indy, but I was in the Peru 173 a number of times that year, and always finished.

In October 1964 the Wabash Railroad became part of the Norfolk & Western, and in December 1965 I became the first N&W operating supervisor to go to a similar position on the former Wabash, moving from assistant road foreman of engines on the Scioto Division at Portsmouth, Ohio [see page 134] to road foreman of engines at Decatur, Ill.—the heart of the Wabash.

The old Wabash had a reputation for fast running, and there were several racetrack districts over which it could—and did—really wheel 'em. The freight speed limit on most Wabash districts was 60 mph, but before the merger that limit was, often as not, honored in the breach. After the merger, speeding proclivities were toned down considerably; the 60-mph limits remained, but the official attitude toward violating underwent a considerable revision.

When I arrived at Decatur, I found that one of my responsibilities would be the Second and Ninth Districts, 173.1 miles of well-maintained, cross-drainage prairie railroading between Decatur and Peru, Ind.—"the Peru 173." The first 22 miles of this was double track to just beyond the Chicago line (the old Sixth and Seventh Districts) junction at Bement; except for double-track stretches between Tilton and Danville, Ill., and through Lafayette, Ind., the rest was single track with CTC signaling.

The usual routine for eastbound time-freight crews out of Decatur was to grab the first three units off the ready track at the enginehouse, go to the east end of the yard, and tie on to anywhere from 60 to 80 cars of merchandise or perishables or auto parts or whatever was going your way, make a brake test, and then "get out and walk about with 'em."

I had been on the Division almost a

year, then, when I showed up at Decatur Yard on a drab November 1, 1966, to ride hotshot KSB6 (Kansas City-St. Louis-Buffalo) to Peru. We were marked up for units 3515, 1315, and 3523, a U25B-GP35-U25B combo that should be equal to the task of "walking about" with the 71 cars lined up for the hotshot.

The 3515 was a lady with a past. Originally the 13th in Wabash's group of 15 U25B's numbered 500-514, she was wrecked in a collision at Hannibal, Mo., literally on the eve of the merger. Rebuilt by GE, she became the only N&W U25B with a split windshield (vs. one-piece glass) and the first to be repainted in N&W black (known in some quarters as "Roanoke's Rainbow"). She was then sent to the Scioto Division to see how we liked her down there. We didn't. I had run her on the Kenova District in West Virginia,

and the combination of GE's huge, unwieldy 16-notch throttle and no dynamic braking was too much even for those who were raised on Alco RS11's. So they sent her back to Decatur, where our paths crossed again.

KSB6's engineer that day was E.F. Sprinkle; the fireman, R.D. Taylor. Eddie Sprinkle was an old pro, a good engineer who could keep his mind on business and still regale you with some good tales whose interest and entertainment value was not diminished by the fact that some of them might have been somewhat true.

We made the air test and pulled out, and when the conductor and rear brakeman got on the caboose, Eddie went right to the whip. The three 2,500-hp units weren't picking the train up as they should have, though, and a quick check told us why. The third unit wasn't loading, and a further check determined that the m.u. jumper cable between the rear units was defective and we'd already found out that we weren't lucky enough to have a spare.

It happened that the second unit, GP35

A General Electric U25B leads EMD, Alco, and Fairbanks-Morse units on Norfolk & Western train KB6 near Hull, Ill., in October 1964, just weeks after N&W leased the Wabash. J. DAVID INGLES.

1315, was pointed east, so we decided to stop and move our good cable from between the first two units to the last two and set up the controls on the second unit so I could "double-head" Eddie over to Tilton yard, about 70 miles, where we could get a replacement cable.

This we did; it took only a couple of minutes for us to change the cables and for me to set up the 1315 to run the rear two units. I gave Sprinkle the high sign as Taylor went up to the lead unit. Eddie and I both went to the whip, and with all of the units doing business we were soon up at the 60-mph cruising speed.

I throttled back so Sprinkle could regulate the speed without any trouble and settled in to enjoy the ride. There was a certain perverse satisfaction in watching Eddie bounce and bob and weave as the U-boat hit the switches and road crossings while I enjoyed the better ride of the GP35.

Until we passed Sadorus, Ill., just west of the Illinois Central diamonds at Tolono.

We were minding our own business— and the N&W's—making time with the time freight, "walking the dog" across eastern Illinois at a flat 60 mph, when a farmer decided that he wanted to use his tractor to pull his double-bottom disc harrow across his private crossing from his south field to his north field.

It was chilly, so the farmer had the ear flaps down on his cap. The tractor was making a lot of racket anyhow. Eddie Sprinkle was heavy on the horn, but the farmer didn't hear, and I could see that this one might not be so good. The farmer was

still coming, so I shut off my throttle just before Eddie put the brakes in emergency. At the last instant the farmer looked up and tried to reverse, but you don't back up with a double-bottom disc harrow very easily and he didn't make it very far.

But he made it far enough. The brakes hardly had time to take hold—we were still running 60 when the handrail of the 3515 caught the counterweight in front of the radiator of the tractor and kicked it 90 degrees to the right, parallel with our path—and then I was past it. But I couldn't believe my last glimpse: The tractor was still upright and the farmer was still in the seat!

As we were stopping, we radioed the news to the conductor and finally came to a halt. It always takes an eternity to stop after you've hit something.

Sprinkle got everything reset after the emergency brake application and we backed the train up to the crossing, where we found the conductor taking the pertinent information from the farmer, who was apparently uninjured. It looked as though the tractor had suffered a minimum of damage, too, an amazing turn of events. He had, indeed, made it far enough.

And he was still sitting on that tractor! In fact, his hands were still locked onto the steering wheel, right where they had been when he looked up and saw the Pearly Gates personified by a large black GE locomotive bearing down on him. But he was calmly talking to the conductor and refusing medical or any other form of

attention. With a visible effort he got his fingers pried loose from the steering wheel and climbed down, a little shaky but okay.

After taking care of the formalities, we were off again, reporting everything by radio to Tilton for relay to the dispatcher in Decatur. In addition to the jumper cable, we now needed the attention of a shop man at Tilton since the 3515's front handrail was broken loose at the bottom and bent along the side at a rakish angle.

We finally got out of Tilton with a temporarily repaired handrail and a replacement jumper cable, which eliminated the necessity for doubleheading. The tractor episode, even though not fatal, had naturally dampened spirits on the head end tremendously. If we had broadsided that tractor and it had bunched up and rolled under the 3515 at 60 mph—well, that's not something you want to dwell on.

But you couldn't keep Eddie Sprinkle's spirits down very long. As we headed eastward, we began to realize just how much luck had been with all of us, including one Illinois farmer who would, no doubt, not fail to stop, look, and listen before he used his little private crossing again.

And as we got into the last lap of this somewhat tarnished version of the Peru 173, edition 11-1-66, we naturally began to speculate on what the farmer must be thinking and the two questions he must be asking himself: 1.) Why am I not taking harp lessons and being measured for a pair of golden wings? And 2.) Will my wife ever be able to get this underwear clean?

Battling blizzards on the Big G

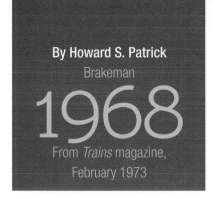

By Howard S. Patrick
Brakeman

1968

From *Trains* magazine, February 1973

Outside the temperature was 10 degrees below zero, and 40 mph winds whipped up the snow and buffeted our locomotives. Powdery white stuff driven by the blizzard sifted in around the window cracks. Conductor Ekberg on the hind end was bellowing over the radio, trying to raise the yard office at Willmar, Minn.

We had stalled in a drift on the main line, and if we didn't get moving soon we would be drifted in solid. Our hogger, Karl Schmidt, looked out again at the billowing snow, got up with a grunt, and slowly put on his parka.

As a fledgling brakeman on the Great Northern's Willmar Division, I was amazed at our situation. Turbocharged power and CTC were supposed to handle all but the worst a Minnesota winter had to offer. Yet here we were stuck fast in a storm that hadn't even excited the forecasters. It was rapidly becoming evident to me that all the excitement, hard work, and long hours on the rails had not gone out with the exit of steam power.

Of course our situation was due to more than whimsies of the elements. A broken steam pipe on No. 31 running ahead of us had thrown restrictive blocks in our faces; and only minutes before we lumbered into the drifted cut west of Atwater, alarm bells had heralded the shutdown of our second unit. The long drift and reduced power had been enough to bring us to a shuddering halt.

Karl was sweating it—he didn't want to be responsible for sealing up the main line. We had to get the Geep running to extricate ourselves; and besides, the alternative of draining the dead locomotive in a blizzard was not a particularly inviting prospect. So bundled against a wind chill close to minus-70 degrees, we crept down the gangway to see if we couldn't resuscitate our irksome GP7. Meanwhile, the wind-driven snow was filling in around the flanges.

The path leading to that icy night on the prairies had been a circuitous one for me. I had always wanted to work in train service, but lack of 20/20 vision had kept me ballast-bound as I boomed about the Midwest working a variety of jobs on the Illinois Central, the Milwaukee, and the Great Northern. In December 1968 my chance finally had come, however. The GN was hard up for brakemen and in apparent desperation had deleted the "un" from its "20/20 uncorrected" visual requirements. Before long I had switch key, lantern, and rulebook in hand and was ready to begin my student trips.

Normally a new man would spend about a week making these runs, since a total of four round trips were required: eastward to Minneapolis and westward to Breckenridge in both mainline service and on the local turns. For me, however, the process was accelerated. On my first run to Breckenridge I was tipped off by the regular brakey that another new man had made his first student trip west the day before. If I wanted to establish my seniority date before his, I would have to get my behind in motion.

So the marathon began. After dropping off 81 at Breckenridge, I caught No. 88 east and rode it all the way to Minneapolis, where I bedded down for a couple of hours in the roundhouse before hauling out of town on 97, the West Coaster hotshot. Number 97's hogger throttled down at Litchfield, east of Willmar, and there I hit the ballast and climbed on the East End local. The next day I finished up the student trips on the West End local and with a barest minimum of brakeman's skills got the trainmaster's O.K. to mark up.

In 1968, the Burlington Northern merger still was tied up in the courts, so the Willmar Division remained the principal route through Minnesota for the GN's through freight and passenger service. Traffic was heavy that winter, with four regular westbound freights scheduled out of Minneapolis along with assorted drags and "Minot Boxes." Movement often was denser eastbound owing to sugar beet extras and shorter trains coming in from the severe cold of the northern plains. Centralized Traffic Control reigned on the main line from Wayzata (13 miles west of Minneapolis) all the way to Breckenridge, rendering all movements except first class "extras" and simultaneously easing the mainline trainmen's work load.

Since new brakemen normally were restricted to mainline through freights until they really knew the ropes and were capable of working the locals, I looked forward to a fairly easy winter job, highballing down the main and enjoying warm diesel cabs and relatively short working hours.

Such was not always to be the case.

Barely 12 hours after my name went on the board, I received my first call—a message that soon became all too familiar and came all too frequently for the remainder of the winter.

"Patrick? You're called for an Extra East at 6:45 a.m." If I had listened between the lines I might also have heard the crew caller saying, "Congratulations, Patrick. You are now married to the telephone."

My first run was an easy one. It was the potash unit train—a new operation set up to handle movements of fertilizer constituent from southern Saskatchewan to central Illinois. Extra 312A East had 111 cars totaling 13,218 tons with 6 covered wagons on the point. We rolled nonstop to Union Yard with the hogger applying a delicate hand to the air since such heavy roller-bearing tonnage was a new experience for most of the crews. My sole duties that trip consisted of cutting off the power and throwing a few switches as we took the units back to the house.

That night we returned on 99, the catchall train which handles mostly empties and serves to move excess power west if needed. Number 99 normally picks up at Union and Lyndale yards and makes a straight shot for Willmar; but as luck would have it, on my first night run we had a message from the dispatcher to pick up a load at Delano where it had been set out by 97 the previous morning "account broken drawbar."

Such a pickup is an elementary task for the seasoned brakeman; but I, with the most basic skills barely in hand, was nervous. I cut off the engines all right, threw the mainline switch, and backed the units down the spur. In my excitement I wasted moves and must have climbed on that car six times checking the hand brakes and angle cocks. The hogger later declared, laughing, "Patrick, watching your lantern hop around back there I thought you were rebuilding the entire car."

Back on the main, I got the switch and the electric lock secured and backed 'em up to make the joint. I'd saved the air on the train line, so we started to pull right away. Then suddenly the air went with a ker-wham! At once the hogger and his fireman howled and the rear men yelled over the radio. We'd backed onto our train so gently that the pin hadn't dropped and I, of course, had neglected to check. Thus

the first of many lessons was well learned.

Within a week after I went to work the weather turned bad and it stayed that way with little respite into March. Old heads often said afterward that the winter was the worst since 1936. First the clouds dumped liberal quantities of snow. Then the skies would clear, the winds would come up, and the temperature would plummet. Branch lines to the west and the southwest were hit the hardest, and often trains and even dozer crews were drifted in for days. Men were taken from their regular jobs for snow service just when severe cold spells necessitated shorter trains and thus more crews.

Luckily we newer men were kept on the main line where operations weren't so complex, but even we amateurs got our guts full of blizzard railroading on the prairies. Soon the chain-gang crews were virtually demolished. Many crews were "setups," and more than once trains were held for lack of rested men. There was much pressure to "aggregate"—to work a train, for example, from Breckenridge to Minneapolis, right through the division point at Willmar. Several occasions even saw yard clerks hastily deputized as brakemen and sent packing in a caboose.

But I am getting ahead of myself. Before the winter storms and slow orders tempered action on the main line, I got a taste of high-speed running which reminded me that all drama has not left railroading even in the duller days of dieseldom.

One night I was called for First 88—a hot fruit manifest from the West Coast. We had 5,345 tons and big power (including two brand-new GE U33C's) in the 9,400-hp lashup. Our engineer was Henry Olafson, a friendly, portly fellow, but all business. Henry got a roll on 'em once we were over the hill, and soon we were running at the 65 maximum. East of Kandiyohi we passed Milepost 90 and Henry, muttering something about Milepost 30, pulled out his watch. The fireboy noticed my perplexity and informed me that Hank was a "grand-stander"—a speed demon who liked to show how fast he could roll the high cars. His favorite pastime on the East End was to see how often he could average 60 mph between the aforementioned mileposts. This he proceeded to do. No meets were in the offing, so our chances were good.

We slammed into the Grove City curve at a good 70. From there it was down-grade, one slight cant in the tracks, and

Number 48 prepares to leave Breckenridge, Minn., on a cold, snowy February day in 1969. With the lead two Geeps working and the trailing F unit off line, it will take author Patrick and crew six hours to get 6,500 tons of spuds the 112 miles to Willmar this day. HOWARD S. PATRICK.

The eastbound *Western Star* kicks up snow as it rolls past author Patrick's waiting freight train at the west end of the Tintah, Minn., siding on February 14, 1969. HOWARD S. PATRICK.

then 10 miles of tangent through Litchfield. Hank really had 'em wound up. The speed recorder showed 80 as we crashed through town. Needless to say, we kept our appointment at M.P. 30 with minutes to spare. Such was my first acquaintance with one of many distinctive personalities on Rocky's Road and also my initiation into real high-speed freight running in the old redball tradition.

As the weather grew worse, the work got tougher and time off between runs became shorter. By late December we almost always were getting called on our rest at Willmar, although sometimes we would sit as long as 16 hours or more at Breckenridge when trains from the west would fall down because of bad weather. Considering the operating problems, it was remarkable that we did as little deadheading as we did. By the time the new year turned I already had had a good taste of struggling with snow-clogged switch points in wind chills up to minus 65, but the first really hairy experience came on the night of January 8, and led to the snowbound situation mentioned earlier.

That night had begun badly when we demolished an automobile at the Montrose grade crossing. (The driver jumped in time.) At Howard Lake I had burned up most of my energy digging us in and out of the hole for the westbound *Empire Builder* and eastbound 438. Now we were fighting to keep our westbound drag from getting snowed in. Karl had taken a couple of cracks at the drift, but our big SD45 couldn't break us loose by herself. So we crept back to work on the Geep. Batteries were low and she cranked like an ancient Chevy, but after a couple of turns the V-16 roared to life. Karl scurried back up front and I stayed in the second unit to keep her running.

We took another rap at 'em and managed to back out of the deepening snow. We backed all the way through town and up the other side of the sag. Then, after a pause, we gunned our way westward, throttle in the last notch, building momentum. This time we busted through, and after ramming some more sizable drifts we finally reached the east end of Willmar Yard. Here all the leads were plugged. After abortive attempts to dig our way in, we finally got the O.K. to pull down the westbound main behind No. 31, and there we tied up.

Although I considered that run to have been a rough one, I kept my comments to myself, noting that the rest of the crew, aside from discussing some of the more harrowing moments, had not considered the night's events to be particularly unique. I trudged home wondering just what a really tough assignment entailed. Within two weeks I got my answer. The January 8 episode had been a mere training mission.

On the evening of the 23rd I went to bed early knowing that I was first out and that we had another raging blizzard on our hands. At 8 p.m. the radio had reported a temperature of minus-15 degrees with winds gusting to 45 mph. All roads were blocked and bus service had been halted. The phone rang shortly after midnight. I debated not answering, but out of sheer pride or stupidity I took the call: 438 at 1:45 a.m.

Clarence Olsen was our hoghead that night. He was a rather stubborn and opinionated fellow, but a master at his trade and a good man to be with in such conditions. Rumor had it that 438's train was a solid consist of sugar beets. Dead freight on a night like this? We looked at each other in disbelief, but a call to the yard office soon confirmed that such indeed was the case. Over on track 5 sat 5,000 tons of frozen beets in 65 barely serviceable gons and hoppers. Tonight, in this howling storm, the imperial powers in their warm and distant headquarters had decreed that this ponderous mass should be moved. Four GP9's were the assigned power, but two of these engines were off line going into Minneapolis for repairs and a third unit had one traction motor cut out.

A brief check of equipment on the engines revealed that all was not operating with perfection. Air horns and bells were frozen, and a long session with the torch was required to free the mechanisms from the day's icy grasp. The cab heaters were lukewarm at best and the defrosters were virtually ineffectual. When we finally were ready for the road, Clarence had to rock the power back and forth just to break us loose.

Now the real battle began. Frozen ties and rails groaned and squealed as we inched down the house track toward the south main. The dummy signal governing access to the high iron turned the swirling snow a misty blood red as we approached. The signal failed to change to green so we radioed the control operator. We were not surprised to learn that conditions had rendered the dual-control switches inoperative. So, with switch broom and lantern in hand, I descended into the storm and waddled up to the turnout.

After a brief struggle I managed to hand-throw the roundhouse switch, and Clarence trundled the units out on the south main. But now I couldn't get the points lined back again. The wind seemed to be gusting at well over 50 mph, and several times my 140 pounds nearly were upended as I wrestled with the hand-throw lever and battled with broom and shovel to keep the drifting snow from filling the switch mechanism. I finally abandoned my efforts, and after getting clearance from the operator we ran our engines down to the east end of the yard to see if we could get in on the lead.

But here matters were worse. Drifted snow was packed solid into the switches and piled high over the rails. Two sectionmen and the rear brakey joined us, but four men could do little more than one and soon we retreated to the relative warmth of the unheated rear unit to chart our next move against the blizzard.

Back over the south main we went, heading this time for the crossover near the depot. That recalcitrant roundhouse switch took another 30 minutes of our time, but with all of us grunting and heaving we finally got the points over and we rolled down another half-mile to the crossover. More sectionmen and Conductor Seidlitz joined the battle, and with the help of brooms, shovels, spike mauls, and brute force we managed to shunt our ice-covered behemoths from the south main to the north main.

By the time we reached track 5 and started to pump air, more than 4 hours had elapsed since we had gone to work. I figured that it also would take an unduly long period to charge the train line, since severe cold hardens the rubber gaskets in the air-hose couplings, thereby increasing leakage. In the interim we retired to the cab, where we found Clarence huddled like a mummy on the right-hand seat box. He was draped with an old blanket and wrapped with rags to keep out the drafts. One hour later the caboose gauge showed only 54 pounds. Seidlitz walked the train but couldn't find any leaks, so he joined us in the cab and together we cursed the unfeeling soul who had called us out on such a night.

At 7 a.m. we abandoned our units and headed uptown for breakfast. Word soon came that the yardmaster prudently had decided to let the beets ferment. We switched crews with No. 82, the eastbound hotshot which had just pulled in, and soon were preparing to leave town. More trouble was in store, however. Nothing had come down the hill from the east

since 99 had arrived a little after midnight, and now the cuts were thoroughly drifted in again. Clarence made a run at the hill with our two SD45's and 5,000 tons, but we stalled twice and the second time barely managed to back out. More delays ensued until we finally got the west lead morning switch job hooked to our tail, and with its help we plowed snow all the way to the top. After 8 hours in the yards we finally were under way.

The trip was slow and frustrating. We had block trouble east of Delano and met countless delays in the terminals where yards were plugged with snow and cars. Everything moved at a snail's pace and we cussed the switch tenders, the yardmasters, and the railroad in general. By the time we tied up it was getting dark and we were close to our 16 hours. This time everyone agreed we all had earned our pay.

Although battling the elements perhaps was the most challenging aspect of the job, a more subtle task lay in working smoothly with your hogger. A green man who frequently got his signals crossed could bring out the worst in an engineman. I was fortunate to encounter very few of the testy, cantankerous types, and usually when I received a chewing out I deserved it.

Hogheads, as we all know, are a distinctive breed and the GN's Willmar Division offered a good cross-section. Aside from those eagle-eye types you could consider as average, several distinct groups were recognizable. One of the grandstanders already has been mentioned, but there was another fellow I called "The Mad Frenchman" who merits comment. This man had a special talent for flogging overloaded diesels over the road. One evening we left Willmar with 3,600 tons and only one U25B. The "Frenchman" had her overloading a good portion of the way to the Twin Cities to the accompaniment of exploding ground relays and a cab filled with essence of ozone, overheating traction motors, and other ominous odors. We even lost the turbocharger approaching Minneapolis, but the Frenchman still delivered the goods with a flair.

Another group of engineers were called "mile hogs." These were the fellows who inched their trains along through the yards trying to make as many extra timecard miles as possible. Then there were the cussers. Many hoggers, such as Clarence Nelson, had their own special idioms that made it easy to identify them over the radio. Off the air, the terms often were interlaced with that particularly virulent form of profanity for which a certain segment of railroaders are noted—colorful and melodious but too earthy for inclusion here.

Other enginemen displayed a rich variety of habits and idiosyncrasies. One fireman perched on his seat like a rooster—a habit he claimed resulted from almost freezing his feet one night in a heatless diesel. Another fellow lugged a veritable jug of Gelusil tablets—nursing his ulcer with pills and milk as he nursed his train through the slow orders and blizzards. Earl (Playboy) Coleman was a source of wonder to many of us. Although he was well past 60, he lived it up dancing and carrying on with his girlfriend at the distant terminal (his wife had long ago thrown him out of the house). The nervous heads were easy to spot. These were the ones who had been in bad wrecks over the years and still were jumpy.

The "professionals" I found fascinating. One I nicknamed "The Otter" because of his quick, cunning, and alert nature. This chap was a wizard at improvisation in making recalcitrant equipment function, and at scrounging assorted pieces of gear to render his work easier and more efficient. Generally he went straight by the rulebook, but when he chose to fudge a bit, he did it with professional finesse. Another one of his tribe—Cletus Whitman—not only was a pro but was extremely orderly and methodical.

Imagine for a moment that you are head man on a drag east with Cletus as your hogger. On the ready track, Cletus, who tends to be on the corpulent side and likes his comfort, initiates the standard Cletonian operating procedure: After making an inspection of the running gear, he cleans the cab thoroughly—a task not to be entrusted to the lowly brakey—and carefully positions and adjusts the seatbox. Next the dead-man's control is subtly disconnected, since the pesky alarm buzzer—in Whitman's view—does nothing more than insult one's dignity and

assault the esthetic senses. Placing himself in regal pomposity at the throttle, he makes all the standard tests, but does so with such thoroughness and detail that you get the impression he is preparing to launch a fully loaded 747 into flight instead of dragging dead freight up the hill.

Once on the train and pumping air, Cletus assumes a more commodious semisupine position on the seatbox, feet up on the cab heater. He has tied a rag to the whistle cord on the SD9 so he won't have to stretch at the grade crossings. Now all is in readiness, and with plenty of air on the hind end you wait for the red dwarf signal on the lead to flick to green. Soon you're grinding out of the yards and up Willmar Hill at a steady 7 mph—warm, comfortable, and relaxed, lulled by the drumming chant of V-16's in the last notch. Behind your units, 4,300 tons drag through snowy turnouts and journals start to warm up under the masterly hand of the hogger.

Engineers received a larger meals and lodging allowance, so in Minneapolis they usually laid over in downtown hotels. We impoverished trainmen bedded down at a congenial flop house known as the Shifting Sands where a bed could be had for $1.50. Since some of the rooms were dormitory style, if you were a light sleeper you took some time getting used to the bustle of crews constantly arriving and departing. Most of us adjusted to this 24-hour traffic, but there was one problem few of us could handle. This was the snoring of Harold Livermore—one of our extra conductors. When this fire-breathing demon seized a rack in your room you could kiss your dreams good-bye. The Draconian noises and tremors emitted from Livermore's lips were of sufficient volume and force to awaken all creatures in past and present worlds. Death rattles, wheezes, grunts, pants, and sighs came forth in a steady barrage. All too frequent were the nights I lay staring at his prostrate form, toes curled out from under the sheets, jowls quivering and vibrating to an

orchestration of assorted bleats and bellows from his bronchial tubes. We even have documented observations of instances in which the sheet draped over Harold's mouth actually fluttered in the breeze while he pumped air for all he was worth.

Eventually I drew jobs on the snow dozers and runs on a couple of the locals, but even during the 16-hour trips there always was time to catch your breath and to observe some of the intrinsic beauty so peculiar to winter railroading on the prairies:

• A green block diffused by blowing snow beckons as No. 97 rounds the curve at Howard Lake, pushing tonnage to the limit.

• Ice-bound ties creak and crunch in protest as 99 works her way up the snow-covered lead and you trot ahead to bend the iron.

• Warm and cozy in the cab of a big new SD45, the crew is quietly excited as you buck 10-foot drifts at 55 mph east of Breckenridge.

• You stand in deep snow at West Tintah watching Second 88's headlight bore through the silent blackness as you wait to look 'em over.

I suppose the old heads seldom consciously appreciated such aspects of railroading as I, a newcomer, did that terrible winter. Yet in spite of their grumbling and complaining, obviously most of the crews not only loved their jobs but thrived on the added challenges. What is the essence of this work that makes it not only attractive but addictive even when the elements rage? Perhaps it is the sense of peace and humility you experience when plodding between endless strings of freight cars on a silent snowy night. More likely it is riding the point on a hot West Coast manifest, exulting as you crash through a small prairie town, with air horns bellowing and reverberating off the grain elevators, shattering the rural tranquility.

Life seldom was dull on Rocky's Road.

Of dispatcher Rosey, a blizzard, and a dark signal

By Dan Sabin
Operator

1969

From *Classic Trains* magazine,
Spring 2006

I was raised in a railroad family in Manly, Iowa, literally at the Rock Island depot, and spent most of my first 17 years riding trains of the RI, the Chicago Great Western, and the Minneapolis & St. Louis.

I started my working career at age 15 as a Rock Island student telegrapher at Manly, and worked as a section laborer during the winter of my junior year of high school and as an operator through most of my senior year. At age 18, I would become the youngest train dispatcher in the U.S. I dispatched the main line through Manly many times and enjoyed having tours of duty with my dad and brother Dave, who were engineers on back-to-back south-bound freights out of Inver Grove, Minn., RI's Twin Cities area yard. My brother Mark would be a conductor on Chicago & North Western train 19, a former M&StL operation, between Manly and Albert Lea, Minn. During 1969-70, I worked at 29 locations on the Rock Island, and I was one of the road's first dispatchers to have worked every trick and chief dispatcher's office on the system.

It was not uncommon during my junior and senior years at Manly High School for the railroad to call the principal to request that I come to work in an emergency staffing situation. Manly, with fewer than 2,000 people, was a railroad town, and it helped that the principal, Hartwick Roslien, had many relatives on the Rock Island and that my mentor, C.J. Stoffer, the Manly station agent, was also president of the school board.

On occasion, Mark and I would get a call to recruit a dozen of our friends and get down to the yard to sweep switches. One time, we were hired to grab enough helpers to shovel out the turntable pit at the old roundhouse. Another time, Stoffer hired Mark and me to transfer an entire carload of 100-pound bags of potatoes from a bad-ordered PFE reefer, inside the diesel shop, to another car. Jobs like that introduced me to the concept of inside work.

One morning in December 1969, Mr. Roslien called me out of a boring English class to tell me the depot had just called him. The chief dispatcher needed me to work the second-trick operator's job down at Iowa Falls, south of Manly on the Des Moines-Minneapolis main line. Since the job transferred on at 2 p.m. and it was snowing pretty hard, he suggested that I get home right away to pack a lunch and head out. I "always listened to my principal," so I soon was in my '62 Ford, heading south on Highway 65 for Iowa Falls, 52 miles away.

After a long drive busting through drifts, I turned into the snow-packed driveway behind the grain elevator that led to the Rock Island depot on Iowa Falls' east side. The first-trick operator was Russ Menning, who worked a five-day swing with four days at Iowa Falls and one third trick at Manly. Russ was an easygoing, soft-spoken guy and always good to work with. There was not much going on, so Russ took right off. As he was pulling away, he swung his car around on the platform and honked. I went out through the waiting room and opened the door, feeling the icy blast of the snow as I stuck my head out to see what he wanted.

Russ rolled down the window on his Mercury and called out, "I almost forgot to tell you, the light on the order board is burned out. The maintainer knows about it, but he's at Bradford with the section gang changing out a broken rail. With this weather, I don't think he'll get to it today, but we should be okay. The dispatcher knows about it, and there's nothin' much goin' on here." With that, he drove off.

Iowa Falls is about halfway between Manly and Des Moines, so it was convenient to have an operator on duty for handling trains during the night. After about 5 p.m., Iowa Falls, whose code was "AO," was the only intermediate open station between Mason City ("DF," the joint Chicago Great Western-Rock Island office) and Short Line Junction ("WX," the tower in Des Moines where RI's north-south and east-west main lines crossed). On the first trick, agents were on duty at Nevada, McCallsburg, and Hampton besides the first-trick operator at Iowa Falls, so advancing trains or changing meets during the day was pretty easy.

I grabbed a mug of the thick black ooze that passed for coffee and, placing the one-sided headset on, plugged in the dispatcher's phone. I listened for a while to Glen Watts (G.L.W.), the West Iowa Dispatcher in the offices at Des Moines, talking with the operator at Council Bluffs about cattle for Menlo on No. 60 tonight. The train would take the three cars into West Des Moines and have the west local spot them in the morning. No. 59 was OS'ed (reported) by Atlantic, out toward Council Bluffs, and the agent, Charlie Anderson, asked if he could clear No. 82, which was at Hillis for 59. Following the clearance of No. 82, the agent at Melcher OS'ed an extra south by, and Allerton, south on the Kansas City line, reported there was a set of bunk cars to move to Carlisle on No. 66. G.L.W. had a deep, gruff voice, and barked and grumbled a lot on the "d.s." phone, sometimes demonstrating impatience with the operators along the line.

There was a loud buzz on the dispatcher's phone, so I called "Beanie" (George Bean, the lineman) on the radio to see if he could check it out. He said he was coming by Purina (the siding adjacent to the feed mill about 2 miles south of the depot) and would be in there in about five minutes. He figured there was a "line wrap" somewhere because of the wind and could work with the relay office in Des Moines, using the circuit board in the office to patch around it.

There were no train orders on the

hooks for the main line, but I made additional copies of the slow orders for the Estherville branch (Subdivision 12-A) and for the Vinton line (Subdivision 19). Stu Erickson, the appointed agent, dropped by with some company mail and a fistful of wires for me to punch out on the teletype. He told me that the outbound Estherville job, No. 53, would have to wait for a unit off a Vinton line train (also numbered 53, but on the Illinois Division), and a unit off of 218, coming in off of the Dows branch. Everything was late and heavy, mostly owing to the snow, and outbound 54 wouldn't be made up for Cedar Rapids until after midnight. We were supposed to have an Iowa Falls turn behind 68 tonight, and he'd probably have another Geep to go back to Cedar Rapids during the night. Northbound 66 had been gone for some time, and I heard the CGW (actually, by this time, the C&NW) operator at Mason City OS him by Clear Lake Junction, on the south side of town where RI and the old CGW parted ways.

By this time, the 3 p.m. transfer of dispatchers had taken place on the West Iowa, and I could hear the old-head dispatcher, Harold "Rosey" Rosenberg (H.M.R.), talking to the operator at Short Line Junction. Until I became a student dispatcher in 1970, I thought Rosey was a

mean s.o.b. He didn't have much time for young operators and had chewed me out a few times over little stuff. He spoke with a nasal voice and was typically very sarcastic on the dispatcher's phone. I was eager to please him, though, primarily because I really wanted to be a dispatcher and needed all the good recommendations I could get from the trick guys, so I always listened pretty carefully, even when he was chewing my butt for some nit-picky thing.

About 3:15, the phone rang. It was the first-trick East Iowa dispatcher, Chuck Lamb (C.C.L.). He was always very patient and a good, calm kind of guy with an easy Kansas drawl. "Say, young man, what are you doing at AO?" he asked. We had a quick chat about the second-trick man having the flu, and he said he needed to make his transfer, but the Illinois Division Chief Dispatcher, Pat Mankins, asked him to find out where the Vinton-to-Iowa Falls job (No. 53) was. The superintendent in Silvis wanted a report of snow conditions on the Vinton branch. I called the train on the radio and passed along to C.C.L. that 53 was bucking some pretty heavy drifts between Wellsburg and Cleves but thought he would be into Iowa Falls Yard about 4:50 p.m.

"By the way," I said, "the hoghead says to tell you and the roundhouse foreman

that they've been bucking 8- and 10-foot drifts since they left Grundy [Center] and the 1353 [a GP18] has been kicking a ground relay ever since." I told C.C.L. that Erickson said they were pulling a Cedar Rapids unit off 53 to go to Estherville tonight and I heard the trainmaster on the radio say that 53 would need another unit with a pilot plow. The crew might not be able to be called back on their rest if we didn't have the power lined up. I also told him to tell his relief, Tony Knight (W.A.K.), that I needed to repeat some slow orders whenever he could listen. He to me to "call Tony back about 7 and he'll listen to them then." We hung up.

By this time, Rosey Rosenberg, the West Iowa dispatcher, was pretty busy, fixing up No. 43 at West Des Moines and taking down yard reports from agents along the line before they went home. I heard the agent at Stuart talking with him about the cattle on No. 60, and the agent at Earlham wanted to fix up the "Rock Roller," who was already at Winear and ready to come out on the main line to head for Short Line Yard. "He should be able to make West Des Moines for 43 if he can leave Winear ahead of 60." Rosey grumbled something and gave him his orders.

Meanwhile, up at Iowa Falls, outside the bay window I saw nothing but white. This was the life, I thought. I couldn't get enough.

About 5:15, I heard Jim Porter, the swing operator at Manly, give Rosey the call on No 67: two units, with engine 127 (an F7A) on the point and a B unit. He was extremely light this night, with only 14 loads and 5 empties for 1,115 tons with caboose 17177. He was called with a full five-man crew, including a fireman. I knew the crew well—they were a good, solid bunch of guys. Most of them had just lost their plush turns in July when the line's last passenger train, the Minneapolis-Kansas City *Plainsman,* had been discontinued. The fireman, Dick Armstrong, was a tall, thin guy who was an old-car nut and was always telling me he wanted to buy my '62 Ford Galaxie. He'd been a fireman on the passenger trains between Manly and Des Moines for many years.

Porter continued, "On duty at 7 p.m., has no work at Manly except to change crummies." (The Rock Island had pool cabooses by this time over most of the system, but not between Manly and Inver Grove, so every train changed cabooses at Manly.)

Author Dan Sabin works the operator's desk at Manly, Iowa, in July 1969, five months before his adventure at Iowa Falls. DAN SABIN COLLECTION.

Porter told Rosey the weather at Manly was heavy snow, strong northwest wind, and 17 degrees. He gave Rosey an OS on No. 66 arriving, and the delay report, and asked him what it looked like on No. 68 out of Short Line Junction. Rosey grumbled and rang WX and asked the tower operator to get on the intercom to find out from Virgil Rupe, the yardmaster, how much time they needed tonight to work No. 68 at Goody Brick & Tile, a spur south of Short Line Junction. The WX op said he would call him back "on the Bell" (city telephone) when he knew.

Rosey was not too patient and told WX to "copy five," meaning a train order with five copies. He then rang DF, the CGW operator at Mason City, and told him to copy five. Without giving the operators much time to get the order forms into their typewriters, Rosey started:

"Order number 248 to WX to C&E number 68, DF to C&E number 67, period. Number 67 engine 127 has right over number 68 engine 360 Clear Lake Junction to Short Line Junction. HMR." I listened as the operators repeated the orders and Rosey instructed DF to copy another order telling No. 67 that No. 66 with engine 263 had arrived Clear Lake Junction.

Every number, direction, and location had to be spelled out by both the dispatcher and each copying operator, a requirement of the *Uniform Code of Operating Rules*. It all sounded like a foreign language to an outsider, but I knew the language well—I'd been practicing since I was 8 years old and could spell most of the stations so fast I sounded like an auctioneer. Spelling Marshalltown, Minerva Junction, Mason City Yard, West Des Moines, Booneville, and Mitchellville were favorites. I always practiced copying every order I could, even when they were not meant for my station. I thought I was pretty good.

It sounded like I wouldn't be copying any mainline orders tonight, and I regretted not being busier. This was pretty cool, though. Here I was, just turned 17, making $3.20 an hour, out of school with permission, working as an operator during a snowstorm. It wouldn't be long and I would be out of school forever and could achieve my goal since childhood of becoming a train dispatcher for the Rock Island. Even so, I wished this night was busier, for with 67 going all the way to Short Line to meet 68, there wouldn't be anything interesting happening tonight. Boy, was I mistaken!

As the evening wore on, I listened to the action on the West Iowa dispatcher's phone. The weather west of Des Moines over to Council Bluffs was starting to get worse, and the snow kept piling up on the north end. We'd had about 2 feet of snow on the ground when it started today, and it had been snowing hard since before noon. We must have had 8 to 10 inches of new snow, and the wind was pretty strong. South of the depot, it was drifting heavily, but we were sheltered behind the big grain elevators just northwest of the low, cinder-block building.

North of Iowa Falls, wind-driven snow was always bad, with a long stretch of straight track from Hampton all the way to Flint, near Clear Lake Junction, and nothing but corn stubble in the open fields to stop it. I had grown up hearing stories of the bad drifts between Hampton and the open areas around Chapin. If I was really lucky, I thought, I'd get snowed in and have to miss school the next day. Better yet, maybe I'd be needed to stay on and be useful to the dispatcher through a good blizzard. I could stay all week if I had to. Ah, the dreams of a 17-year-old.

Tom Sawyer, the Illinois Central operator at Mills Tower just down the street east of the two depots where the lines crossed, called me on the Bell phone and we exchanged train information. He was a great old guy, having been closed out of the agency at Webster City after two decades and now working second trick at Mills. His old-head operator stories were something I always looked forward to hearing. He wanted to "go to beans" and wondered when No. 53 would be showing up off the Vinton branch.

The trains were getting later over the entire division, and 67 dropped back at Manly, finally leaving there at 8:15 p.m. after taking a pretty bad delay up at Gordon, Minn. They took a beating on the CTC territory for C&NW No. 1, whose crew was on short time after a broken train line, and then took the siding at Northwood for No. 66. I remembered that my dad was the engineer on 66 north of Manly tonight. By the time they were ready to leave Manly, Rosey was getting more information on 68, and it looked like something would have to be done to set up a meet north of Short Line Junction.

Rosey told Mason City to clear No. 67 with what he had and he would catch him at Iowa Falls to get No. 68 out of Short Line for him. My heart started pounding a little, knowing that I would be copying a meet order and handing it up to the men in the F unit on No. 67 on the curve here

at AO, with a fast engineer at the controls.

"Let me know when he clears Clear Lake Junction, DF."

"Okay, Rosey," said the former Great Western operator.

Then it was quiet for a while.

A few weeks earlier, I had worked at AO for several days, and on the first night, I had an order for No 67. When the train hit the block at Bradford, I told Rosey, and he barked, "Dammit! I don't get paid this big money to know when they get by Bradford!" So the next night I didn't say a word until 67 pulled to a stop at my order board, when I told Rosey that 67 arrived at 8:15 p.m. I was afraid to tell Rosey when the indicator light showed 67 was by Bradford, and now he was sitting here waiting for his orders and had not been cleared. Knowing that he had caused the delay to an important train, Rosey went berserk. "You're supposed to tell me when they get by Bradford! Don't you have a lick of sense? Do you think I have nothing better to do than sit here

Rock Island's *Twin Star Rocket,* bound for Minneapolis, leaves the depot (right) at Manly, Iowa, the author's hometown. Looking north into the yard, SW900 No. 904 is switching cars on this January 1965 day. DAN SABIN.

and guess what time 67 will go by Bradford? Clear him up, dammit! Tell the conductor to find a car number in his train and show an air-hose problem on the delay report."

Tonight, I wasn't going to let that happen.

It was now going on 8:45 and I hadn't heard Mason City OS No. 67 by Clear Lake Junction yet. With bad weather all over the Des Moines Division, I could tell that Rosey was on edge and not in a great mood. Finally, about 9:05, the DF operator came on and told Rosey 67 had just gone across the Iowa Terminal, the electric short line at Clear Lake Junction, having taken a delay at North Yard by the C&NW switch crew. He also said the conductor threw off a message that there were no working radios on either the head end or the caboose.

Rosey seemed upset and yelled, "AO!"

"AO," I answered.

"Copy five south," he barked.

I popped the switch to red on the train-order signal for southbound trains. "SD South. Did anyone tell you the train-order signal is out?"

"Yeah, I see it on the train sheet. WX copy five. We have a rule in the book that says the absence of a signal means the most restrictive, remember?"

Did Rosey know that it was a block-signal-type train-order signal instead of the traditional semaphore? When was the last time, I wondered, Rosey had even been to Iowa Falls, or even ridden a train?

I had a lump in my throat. "Well, you know, normally the office closes at 10 . . . will he be here by then? He won't be looking for a light in the order board after 10."

"Hell, no—he won't be there before 10. And you'll stay there until I let you go." Rosey was losing it, and I wasn't about to

get in an argument with a train dispatcher, especially Rosenberg.

"WX, where the hell are you? Copy five!"

"WX is ready," replied the op at Short Line Junction.

Rosey was quieter now. "Order number 279. T-w-o s-e-v-e-n n-i-n-e." He continued with the order as the operator at Short Line Junction and I typed it out on our typewriters.

"AO to C&E number 67, s-i-x s-e-v-e-n, WX to C&E number 68, s-i-x e-i-g-h-t, period. Number 68, s-i-x e-i-g-h-t, engine 360, t-h-r-double-e s-i-x n-a-u-g-h-t meet number 67, s-i-x s-e-v-e-n, engine 127, o-n-e t-w-o s-e-v-e-n, at Cambridge, c-a-m-b-r-i-d-g-e, number 68, s-i-x e-i-g-h-t, engine 360, t-h-r-double-e s-i-x n-a-u-g-h-t, hold main track at Cambridge, c-a-m-b-r-i-d-g-e. HMR, AO."

I was nervous now, but I still repeated

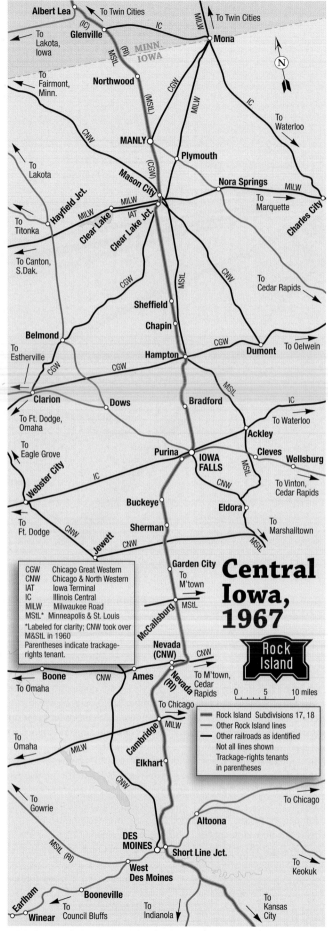

CGW   Chicago Great Western
CNW   Chicago & North Western
IAT   Iowa Terminal
IC   Illinois Central
MILW   Milwaukee Road
MStL*   Minneapolis & St. Louis
*Labeled for clarity; CNW took over
M&StL in 1960
Parentheses indicate trackage-
rights tenant.

Central Iowa, 1967

Rock Island

0   5   10 miles

Rock Island Subdivisions 17, 18
Other Rock Island lines
Other railroads as identified
Not all lines shown
Trackage-rights tenants
in parentheses

© 2006, Kalmbach Publishing Co., CLASSIC TRAINS, Jay W. Smith

the order flawlessly. This was my passion, and I did it well. I issued this same order at school a million times as I was ignoring a teacher, pretending I was a train dispatcher quietly issuing orders to a long subdivision of pretend operators. Rosey couldn't stump me now. He gave me the time complete, and I signed the order with what I thought was an old-timer's flourishing signature. WX finished with his repeat of the order and cleared 68 with just the meet at Cambridge with 67. Normally, 68 was superior by direction and did not have to be told to hold the main track. In this case, however, an earlier order had given 67 right over 68, so on this night, 67 was superior by right and did not have to clear the track for any train unless specifically told otherwise.

Number 68 got out of Des Moines in good shape, and I could hear static on the radio that I thought was 67, but I couldn't be sure.

Finally, I saw the indicator light come on, telling me a southbound train was by Bradford. I didn't want to screw up tonight. I cleared my throat and stepped on the foot pedal as I spoke into the ancient operator's mike, "AO, No. 67 is in the block, by Bradford." No answer.

It was well past my normal time to get off duty when I heard the Illinois Central's eastbound passenger train, No. 12, the *Hawkeye,* whistle through Rocksylvania Avenue and rumble over the diamond at Mills Tower. He must have hit some bad weather between Sioux City and Iowa Falls, because it sounded like his horns were nearly frozen. The snow was really blowing now, but it looked like it had stopped falling. A pretty good drift was just south of the depot, probably about 4 feet high. I heard Rosey bark at me, "AO, clear 67. What the hell, you want to stop him again?"

I was relieved he would finally realize that 67 was probably close. "Iowa Falls clear No. 67 on one order, number 279."

Rosey was ready to make his transfer to the third-trick man and anxious to get out of the chair. "Okay at 10:40 p.m., HMR." All Des Moines Division trick dispatcher desks transferred at 11 p.m., while Illinois Division trick desks transferred at 11:30 p.m. and assistant chiefs at 11:59.

I pulled the carbons out of the clearance pad and stapled the clearance to the onion-skin order. Grabbing a long-handled, Y-shaped order fork, I slipped two complete sets of the orders into the string and pulled it tight for the head end, then repeated the same action for the caboose on a shorter-handled order hoop. Pulling on my parka, I slipped two fusees into my coat pocket, something I always did, even though most operators didn't bother. I grabbed the electric lantern and the hoops and headed through the door to the waiting room.

I immediately heard the engineer blowing the horn for the crossing just north of the IC diamond. The glare of the F7's headlight was on one of the old buildings to the northeast of me, and I felt the blast of cold from the strong wind. The blowing snow stung my face as I walked the short distance to the main track and lined myself perpendicular to it, facing the oncoming beast. The orders tied in the strings were flapping in the wind like a child's pinwheel. I had to keep an eye on them to ensure they didn't literally twist the string off the order hoop.

I could hear the units throttle off to idle, then the bang of the lead trucks hitting the IC diamond. Immediately after the units throttled up again, I saw the headlight coming around the curve. As Stoffer had taught me, I quickly measured my distance from the rail by holding the longer train-order hoop against my hip, dropped it down level to the rail, then lifted it up for the delivery to the head end. I held the long hoop and my lantern in the same hand so the light would shine directly on the yellow flimsies, giving the crew a better chance at catching the string as the engine passed me. AO was a scary place to hand up to a fast train, with a sweeping curve in front of the depot, giving the appearance that the train was headed right for you as you stood close to the tracks. The superelevation of the curve also leaned the unit to the opposite side, into the curve, raising the cab window a few more inches on the depot side.

My adrenaline was pumping, and the F unit seemed to be coming too fast to pick up orders. Don Brink was always fast. With such a short train and 3,000 horsepower, he was blasting at me like a scalded dog. I used my left hand to wave a modest highball with the lantern, but didn't get a whistle reply. As the train came closer, the rails creaked and the wind howled. I held the hoop up, arms stretched to get the order up close to the engineer's window, and was blinded by the oncoming headlight. The snow was blowing in my eyes, and my glasses were fogging over. I could hear the roar of the EMD 567's on the two covered wagons coming at me, and a chill went up my spine. The pilot smacked the snowdrift in front of the

depot, spreading a huge cloud of heavy snow in every direction. I held my breath.

Within just a few feet of my body, the snow-covered nose of the F unit blasted past me, and I looked up for the familiar face of the engineer, whose son was in my older brother's class. Don Brink was a small, slender man, but he was a fearless engineer and was well known for being a fast runner.

Then I panicked. No one was at the window on the lead unit! The window was shut tight, and no one was visible in the cab from my close and low vantage point.

A cold chill ran up my spine as I swung around and grabbed for a fusee in my pocket. With the lantern in my right hand, I swung a wild stop sign to a blind engine, then cracked open the fusee. The engine had plowed through another snowdrift about two car-lengths south of the depot, and the obedient freight cars that followed steered themselves through the curve and kept the snow swirling like an ugly white tornado. The whole scene seemed like it was playing out in slow motion, and the heavy, wet snow between the rails muffled the wheels as they sort of hissed by.

Just then, I remembered that the train was short, and grabbed the other order hoop. I whirled around and tossed the lighted fusee down on the snow-covered platform. About five car-lengths northeast of me, I saw a light, telling me the bay window of the ice-covered caboose was swinging closer, around the curve in a massive cloud of powdered snow. This bad dream would end when the rear-end crew grabbed their orders, saw my stop signals, and pulled the air into emergency to communicate their orders to the head end. I held the shorter train-order hoop up and held my breath.

To my absolute horror, no one was at the caboose's bay window, and the sliding glass window was closed up tight!

I slapped the order hoop against the side of the caboose as it flashed by. The hoop hit the curved grab iron on the rear of the caboose and went flying as I swung around and reached down to the platform, looking for the still-lighted red fusee in the snow. I waved another frantic stop sign.

There was no response.

I quickly processed what was happening. The train-order signal was at stop, but the light was burned out. It was nearly an hour after the normal time for an operator to be here, and the crew possessed an order with "right over the world" to Short Line Junction. No. 68 had left there some time ago and was heading

north, planning to hold the main track at a siding in the middle of the frozen Iowa cornfields, to meet a train that had no working radio and had just missed their orders to take the siding at Cambridge. I was way too young to have caused a snowy, deadly cornfield meet.

I watched with terror and disbelief as the dim red marker on the roof of the caboose receded into the snowy night. With all my strength, and fruitlessly screaming at the top of my lungs, I passed another series of frantic stop signs, hoping someone would be looking back from the caboose.

In my mind, there was going to be a head-on collision of 67 and 68 somewhere south of Cambridge, with 68 running northward at full track speed, minding his own business, expecting to have 67 waiting patiently in the clear for him at Cambridge. The line had automatic block signals, but still, a head-on happened at the siding at Enterprise a few years back, despite the signals. In this weather, with poor visibility, the situation seemed hopeless. I sprinted into the depot and made a frantic call on the radio. There was no answer—not even static.

I grabbed the stem of the ancient black telephone mike on the dispatcher's phone and pulled the accordion-style holder back. My spine was wobbling like a bowl of Jell-O, and I started hyperventilating.

Slapping down the pedal with my boot, I yelled, "AO! AO! 67 missed the orders! Both ends missed the orders. Where's 68? He doesn't have the meet order!" I was screaming at the top of my lungs, I was so scared.

Rosey was still in the chair, obviously making a transfer to the third-trick man. When he answered me, he knew something serious was coming down. He yelled back, "Dammit, kid, call the agent at McCallsburg. Get him down there to stop 67."

I grabbed the clipboard with the phone listing, hung on a nail by the bay window, and picked up the receiver. I still had my gloves on and with my hands shaking so bad, I couldn't find the number. McCallsburg was only 25 or so miles south of Iowa Falls, and Iowans go to bed early. How could the agent get up, get dressed, and get to the depot in time to stop this train? Most of the roads are probably closed anyway. Could he get there at all?

I lost all sense of time. No. 67 was probably already blasting through Buckeye, so no one was going to be able to stop him before Cambridge. He would be blasting through McCallsburg before the agent had his pants on. Nevada was the next station—maybe there was time to get Glen French to the depot.

I was sweating profusely under my heavy parka in the hot office and nearly in tears. Just as I was running my gloves down the wet callsheet to find the agent's home number, I looked up and through the station's bay window. I thought I saw a faint red light coming toward me through the blowing snow from the south. I looked again. It *was* a red light. No. 67 was backing up, and I could see the Southern Pacific-style marker light on the caboose roof and the lights inside through the window. Two lit lanterns were on the rear platform. I stomped on the foot pedal and yelled into the mike on the dispatcher's phone, "They're coming back! Dispatcher, they're coming back! They got stopped and I can get the order to them!"

Without waiting for a response from Rosey, or whoever was now in the chair, I ran out the office door and around the ticket window to the waiting room. As I opened the outside door to the platform, I saw the conductor and the rear brakeman on the caboose's rear platform. The skipper swung down and spit a big mouthful of chaw when his five-buckle overshoes hit the snow piled high on the platform. The brakeman, hanging onto the back railing

on the caboose to protect the crossings as the boxcars creaked by, waved a finger at me.

I was so glad to see the conductor step closer to me under the platform light that I couldn't speak. He walked up to me and asked what was going on. Why was I here? My eyes were salty from tears, and my glasses were completely fogged over as I told him I had a meet with him and 68 at Cambridge. He stopped in his tracks.

The two F units were now garbling back and soon were in sight through the snow. The 127 stopped with its snow-covered nose in front of the depot, and the head brakeman and fireman slid down the ladder.

The fireman was the first one to reach me. He had on a light summer jacket and a heavy hat on with earflaps, looking like Barney Fife on a hunting trip. He looked at the conductor as I was telling him about the meet order and broke out in a nervous laugh. He said that as they had gone by the depot, the engineer had reached behind the control stand to grab a sandwich and a Thermos from his grip. Armstrong had been looking over the train on the left-hand curve but looked up and forward when they hit the snow drift at the south corner of the depot and watched the blast of snow fly up and out, hitting the hood of my old Ford.

Why, he thought, would the Sabin kid's car be here at Iowa Falls, especially at this time of night? There's no one on duty this late here. He had run over to the engineer's side of the cab and looked back through the cab-door window and saw my frantic fusee stop signs in the blowing snow. By the time they got stopped, they were already over the Iowa River bridge, around the next curve, and nearly to the north switch at Purina, over a mile away.

No one said a word after that. I found the order hoops, now buried in the snow, gave them their orders, and they got back on the engine. Brink, still at the window, just waved. With two short blasts of the horn, they pulled slowly away; the conductor jumped on the caboose as it went by. I watched the light dim into the winter night. The snow crunched under my boots as I made my way back into the operator's office. My whole body was still shaking, and I could feel I was dripping wet. I pulled on the old accordion mike, put the headset on, and, making sure I wasn't interrupting anything on the dispatcher's phone, said quietly, "OS, AO."

The third-trick man responded, "Dispatcher."

"Number 67 arrived AO at 10:48 p.m., departed 11:06 p.m."

The dispatcher said, "Okay, AO, good night. You can go on home now."

Rookie brakeman on the Camp 20 Graveyard Extra

By J.W. Schultz
Brakeman
1972
From *Classic Trains* magazine,
Summer 2009

On a tranquil Sunday evening in May 1972, the transportation equivalent of the infrequent complete blocking of one celestial body by another was about to occur when a phone call summoned me for work on a 10:30 p.m. extra switch engine at Camp 20, Milwaukee Road's yard in La Crosse, Wis. (The name recalled the railroad construction camp reputedly located on the spot occupied by the yard office.)

Ordering an extra switch engine was, in my limited experience, unheard of, and this night would be most memorable.

Alfie, our engineer, held down a regular Amtrak assignment and had been on passenger trains for years. That is to say, he hadn't worked in the yard in years, but had answered the railroad's plea for his services in its hour of need. Regular third-trick yardmaster Charlie Chase was on his day off, so our foreman, "Poodles," would multi-task, as is said now, in the capacity of "footboard yardmaster." I had concluded that Poodles was all-business, and I sensed he wasn't overjoyed to be working with either a rusty yard engineer or a relatively inexperienced 18-year-old helper (me). Rounding out our crew was the other helper, Lester, who despite having enough seniority to catch foreman vacancies on weekends, was more comfortable in the role of follower.

At 10:30 sharp, Alfie and I were driven over to the roundhouse to bring our switch engine back to Camp 20. For power, we were provided with a "donkey," one of the several little 600-hp Electro-Motive SW1's kept at La Crosse to work in multiple across the "Smokey Mountain" line to Austin, Minn., which was beset with light rail and frail bridges. Inadequate to the task awaiting us, the SW1 was sort of like being given a fly-swatter for a job requiring a ball-peen hammer. Returning to the yard involved entering the eastbound main at Copeland Avenue, running west the quarter-mile to West Wye Switch (where the two main tracks became one) and onto the Black River drawbridge, then reversing direction and running east on the westbound main (Track 1) back toward the passenger depot and the running track leading us into Camp 20.

The signal placement on the drawbridge was unique in that the east- and westbound signals faced one another, with just enough room in between to fit one unit. So the typical drill was to pull just west of the eastbound signal but without knocking down the westbound signal, then if necessary, send the junior crewman outside to watch for a favorable eastward signal.

Unlike with the Alco road-switchers sometimes assigned to the yard (and the Baldwin S12's usually assigned), the visibility afforded by the SW1 didn't require me to leave the cab to view the eastward signal. Nevertheless, I was again reminded of my predecessor, the previous new-hire switchman who—when asked to step outside and check the signal—scrambled down the north-side steps of the engine and, lantern flailing, kept right on going into the dark, chilly waters below. (He survived the ordeal unscathed, but resigned soon thereafter—I suspect from the burden of relentless kidding.) "Now don't forget, John, there's no walkway on the north side of the Black River draw!"

Switching at Camp 20 was conducted on the west end of the yard, kicking cars eastward. With about a dozen tracks, the yard was anchored on its west end by the yard office and on its east end by Grand Crossing, the interlocking where Milwaukee Road, Chicago & North Western, and Burlington Northern all

crossed. Milwaukee's two main tracks ran along the yard's south perimeter.

Poodles and Lester were waiting for us in front of Camp 20, switchlists in hand, when we arrived with the engine, and we went right to work. Not far into the evening's festivities (and our first switchlist), a gondola—heaped with scrap in flagrant disregard of AAR loading rules, its contents lapping out and beyond the car's top chord not unlike the foam on a freshly drawn glass of La Crosse's home brew, Heilemann's Old Style Lager—was set adrift by Poodles at the top (west end) of the north lead. The car was destined to one of the higher-numbered tracks toward the back of the yard (9 or 10), so I would mount the car as it passed the yard office and ride it into the track and tie a handbrake. (Initially, it would be the first and only car in an otherwise clear track.)

Climbing aboard, I swung around to the car's trailing end to prepare to tie the brake. Just as I rolled out of view, I tried to give the brake wheel a turn, only to discover that, apparently in the loading process, it had been bent backwards and thus would not revolve around the gear housing. (So much for a proper inbound mechanical inspection, and for our crew testing the handbrake before the car was kicked. Remember, I was relatively inexperienced.) A quick rearward glance confirmed that Poodles and Lester were out of sight.

With lurid visions of my errant scrap-laden chariot escaping the east end of the yard to explore the westbound main track beyond Grand Crossing (I chose not to dwell on the implications of BN interference at the diamond—but stay tuned), I unloaded and proceeded to discover just how fast I could run by lantern light.

It had been some time since local management had sponsored a yard clean-up, and a good thing too, for there was no shortage of discarded brakeshoes, air hoses, pieces of oak blocking from flatcar loads, wire, fragments of old ties, and an occasional tie-down chain lying

A "Maud," as Milwaukee railroaders at La Crosse called their Alco RSC2's, spends some quiet time in the roundhouse in 1971, eight months before a night of rescue. J.W. Schultz.

around on the ground. (In the interests of self-preservation and that of our fellow switchmen, all of us waged an ongoing effort to clear the toepaths of potential stumbling hazards.) By now I had sprinted perhaps three-quarters of the way toward Grand Crossing and, through judicious and repeated placement of the aforementioned yard flotsam on the north rail, had sufficiently retarded the gondola's progress that I sensed victory was within my grasp.

Then, from over my shoulder came a muffled shout. Like Mighty Mouse come to save the day and animatedly waddling from side to side, the SW1 had joined the chase. Perhaps Alfie had momentarily lapsed back into the routine of his real job, piloting the platinum-mist E9's of Amtrak's *North Coast Hiawatha* across Wisconsin. Decorating the donkey's front end were our newest heroes, Poodles and Lester, both yelling and gesturing for me to stand clear. In a blur of orange and black, Alfie was crowding the most liberal interpretation of "restricted speed." The report of couplers mating and the squeal of engine brakes was anti-climactic, and my esteem for SW1's suddenly rose to an all-time high.

The night was just beginning.

In contrast to the 25-degrees-below-zero third trick that had marked my debut as a switchman six months earlier, it was an utterly splendid spring night. A gentle breeze, sufficient to rustle the young leaves of the trees behind the yard office, was interrupted only by the eruptions of the SW1 as it attempted to kick cars. Aural counterpoint was provided by the corresponding run-in and run-out staccato of coupler slack, the stealthy creep of cars rolling down the leads before disappearing into the shadows, and momentarily, the sounds of coupler impacting coupler, reminiscent of distant artillery. Bound for Portage, Wis., and Milwaukee, three GP40's slipped past with 262, the Tacoma—Chicago *Thunderhawk,* its consist perfumed with fresh-cut lumber.

Along about 2 a.m., our donkey had hold of perhaps 15 cars, mostly loads, when a "kick" signal went unanswered. Our little engine could not. Perhaps 20 or 25 minutes passed before the mechanical department representatives responded to Poodles' summons for first-aid from the roundhouse. Their diagnosis: The patient could not be revived for now, so Alfie and I were chauffeured back to the roundhouse to secure another unit and then repeat the out-and-back Black River draw process.

To replace the fallen EMD, we were directed to a "Maud" (either 594 or 596, as I recall), the local mechanical forces' designation of an Alco RSC2. Actually, the term was applied to all Alcos at La Crosse, including the bigger RSD5's and the four RSC2's rebuilt at Schenectady in 1965 that came back with notched, lowered short hoods; new numbers (576–579); and a new classification (RSC2M). All were used on the 35-mile, light-iron branch down to Viroqua, Wis., from Sparta, 25 miles east of Camp 20. Now we'd have an engine that could kick cars with something that approached alacrity for the remainder of our shift. Alfie seated himself at the controls on the south side of the cab, as its "front," the long hood, was facing east. Out on the Black River draw, I checked the eastward signal from the south side and kept dry. Back at Camp 20, we completed switching the cut, set over the lifeless SW1, and went about our work.

The rest of the night's switching was uneventful—no other cars attempted to escape the yard. Maud took us down to the depot for a repast at the Track Shack, a dumpy all-night beanery on Copeland Avenue, where, over breakfast, we watched 99, the westbound overnight Chicago–St. Paul piggyback hotshot, noisily launch out of town.

Fortified, we returned to Camp 20 to embark on our final task, and one of comparative high adventure. For our grand finale, we'd deliver and pull the North Western interchange at Grand Crossing, an event that probably hadn't occurred after nightfall since the demise of steam.

Grand Crossing was appropriately named, as three railroads intersected there at grade. Milwaukee's east-west, double-track Chicago–St. Paul main crossed the north-south single track of Burlington Northern's ex-CB&Q Chicago–St. Paul main. C&NW's La Crosse city spur wandered in from Medary (a tower 2 miles east of Grand Crossing, where C&NW's line from Wyeville, Wis., to Winona, Minn., crossed our double track) and crossed first the BN and then the MILW on a northeast-to-southwest diagonal on its way downtown. The tower, a Milwaukee Road affair, sat just east of the BN between the C&NW and Milwaukee (today it is displayed in Copeland Park north of downtown La Crosse).

To effect the C&NW interchange, we got against the east end of the delivery and received permission, lineup, and signal from the leverman-operator at Grand Crossing. Exiting the east end of the yard

onto Main 1, we crossed the North Western and the BN, crossed over from Main 1 to 2, and stopped. After Grand Crossing relined the plant and gave us the signal, we shoved west back over the BN and entered the C&NW interchange track off Main 2. Poodles, perhaps weary of the events of the past six-odd hours, chose to spend this interlude in the company of Grand Crossing's "op," and had commissioned his second-in-command, Lester, to carry out the exchange of cars. I would "follow the engine," where I could pass lantern signals from Lester to Alfie. Lester would "work the field."

A word is in order about the "leaving signal" protecting our eastward main track from the C&NW interchange. It was a low or "dwarf" signal, mounted just above the ground, whose signal head was a disc perhaps 30 inches in diameter with a yellow background and a black line that, not unlike a semaphore blade, would indicate "proceed" (diagonal) or "stop" (horizontal) when the disc rotated in accordance with the movement of the proper lever in the tower. The disc was also equipped with white and red lenses, illuminated by a common light bulb, to indicate "restricting" (proceed) or "stop" in conjunction with the alignment of the black stripe.

This signal and a derail device were independently manipulated by separate levers in the tower, interlocked so the signal to proceed could not be given until the derail had been placed in non-derailing position. For a movement from the interchange eastward onto the main track, the signal also served as the home or absolute signal for the BN crossing, just east of the interchange track switch. Hence, a BN train could not receive a signal to proceed through the interlocking plant when the Milwaukee signal to leave the interchange indicated proceed.

Perhaps owing to not having had the benefit of any student trips at the onset of my switching career, or to the lack of any sort of genuine rules exam by that date, or being unfamiliar with the C&NW interchange, and certainly being preoccupied with passing lantern signals, I took no notice of the dwarf signal. (Actually, none of us had expected this Sunday night graveyard extra, and we were all beginning to show the effects of being short-rested.)

Meanwhile, our engineer continued to respond to my lantern signals to back up and pull ahead, the latter of which took him past the derail (immediately next to the signal) and onto our main track. Lester, in the depths of the interchange

Two GP40's and an FP45 lead a Milwaukee freight across C&NW's city line at Grand Crossing in La Crosse, Wis., in 1973. A close look will reveal—just to the left of the locomotive's nose—the disk of the "economized" dwarf signal. J.W. SCHULTZ.

track, was in no position to see the signal. Of course, the Milwaukee did not supply us with radios in those days.

Unknown to us in the midst of our labors, Burlington Northern's CX office at its North La Crosse yard (visible from the north window of the tower) notified Grand Crossing of the imminent departure of a southbound freight. Thus, in between one of our backups and pull-aheads, with our engine tucked safety behind the signal and derail, the tower op took away our lineup. The derail now was in position, and the signal displayed "stop." This established the lineup for the BN train.

As Alfie responded to yet another "pull ahead" command and eased toward the main, I became aware of an undercurrent of sound not normally associated with an Alco 244 prime mover. I looked east and south and saw nothing on either the Milwaukee or the BN. Our passing cut, though, afforded a momentary northward glimpse between two 40-foot boxcars, which revealed an approaching headlight and the strident chorus of Cooper-Bessemer chortles in GE's and EMD turbo-

charger whine—the aforementioned BN train! Meanwhile, our RSC2M had cleared the location of the derail unimpeded and was pulling slowly but steadily toward the BN diamond and what I envisioned would be a collision of apocalyptic proportions. And, oh yes—the dwarf signal was dark.

To this day, I remain convinced that my right arm is longer than my left as a result of the frantic washout signal I hoped my engineer would see before it was too late. In the application of *Consolidated Code of Operating Rules,* 1967 edition, Hand, Flag, and Lantern Signals 8(a) ("Manner of Using: Swung horizontally at right angle to the track; Indication: Stop"), my abandon was total.

Lester couldn't see what was about to transpire, but from my frenzied lantern-flailing, he correctly deduced that an immediate stop was desirable and promptly began swinging his lantern too. Unaware and looking eastward down the Alco's long hood, Alfie motored right up to the edge of the abyss, then at the last moment looked back just as Lester and I were about to achieve simultaneous liftoff. Alfie reacted immediately, and Maud ground to an abrupt halt the instant the

BN U33C emerged from behind our RSC2M's silhouette, green and gleaming in the Alco's headlight beam, the engineer's cab window filled with the faces of its three-man head-end crew. (I still wonder why they never placed their train in emergency, much less sounded the horn in warning.) We had stopped short of fouling the BN, but at what I adjudged to be less than half a car-length.

Even before the BN train's waycar had rattled over the diamonds, Lester and I stood at the derail, surveying the carnage. Instead of the derail lifting our engine off the rail and setting it down on the ties as intended, it had succumbed to old Maud; the Alco had literally yanked the device's heavy casting off the headblock ties by the spikes, broken it into five or six jagged pieces, and "kept right on truckin.' "

Moreover, our examination of the signal target revealed that the light bulb was missing! But no matter. My relief at our having avoided a collision was quickly replaced with a sense of foreboding. It had been a close shave, and in its aftermath I was beginning to suspect that my railroad career was over, that the prudent course of action might be to fling my lantern into the adjacent marsh and walk home. In the instant the BN train cleared the diamonds, we saw Poodles heading toward our engine with purposeful stride. But when we all converged on the ground beneath the cab, our foreman and engineer (who had dismounted from the Alco) were in the midst of a mirthful exchange. In effect, their attitude was one of, "Gee, that sure was a close one, ha-ha!" Whatever Lester and I were thinking at that moment we kept to ourselves.

After everyone had a good look at the signal and the remains of the derail, we concluded our business with the C&NW and made our out-and-back move past the tower and over the diamonds, shoving back into our yard. Back at Camp 20, Poodles' parting words were that we would all do well to keep the events of the past hour or so to ourselves. (Poodles also happened to be the United Transportation Union local chairman.) Later that morning before falling asleep, I concluded

that the arrival of a certified envelope from the trainmaster, containing a notice of formal investigation, was a foregone conclusion.

About three days later, though, having received no such piece of mail, I ventured up to Grand Crossing to visit the regular second-trick leverman-operator, Larry Lauffenberg. Had he heard about our contretemps in the predawn hours of Monday morning? Why, yes, he replied, grinning. Then he told me the rest of the story.

Knowing that the forces at Camp 20 made it their practice to exchange cars with C&NW during daylight hours, it seems the signal maintainer sensed an opportunity to economize. In a moment of sincere if misguided thrift, he removed the light bulb from the signal at the interchange, ostensibly to save money. In the light of day, the absent light wasn't noticeable. And unless it was after

nightfall and you were on the C&NW interchange seeking entrance to Milwaukee's eastbound main track, its absence was of no consequence and couldn't be observed from the main track. Quietly, both the section foreman and the signal maintainer had been summoned. Go ahead, said Larry. Go on down and see for yourself.

Behold! There, at the scene of the crime, a shiny new derail coated in black enamel guarded the entrance to the eastbound main, thick blue spikes firmly anchoring it to two equally new headblock ties, their creosote still damp and fragrant. All other evidence of Monday morning's events (the remains of the old derail, the old headblock ties, and even the old spikes) had been removed.

And there in the gathering dusk, a light bulb shone brightly from behind the signal target's red lens.

The Viroqua Patrol, with "Maud" Alco RSD5 in charge, crosses the Burlington Northern diamond at Grand Crossing on October 9, 1971, bound for Sparta and Viroqua. J.W. SCHULTZ.

Of Rule 93, Form S-C, and bow-and-arrow country

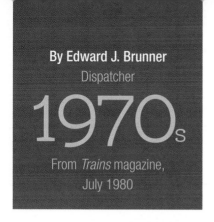

By Edward J. Brunner
Dispatcher

1970s

From *Trains* magazine, July 1980

I once startled a friend by insisting that, given the choice between a cab ride on the Rock Island from Chicago to Silvis, Ill., or a chance to spend eight hours with a Rock dispatcher in Des Moines, I'd unhesitatingly choose Des Moines.

After the first half hour or so, a cab ride starts to pall (especially if you're standing up). The rails are gliding below in a hypnotic effect; the conversation is down to an occasional nod or grunt (as everyone's throat, sore from straining over the throb of the engines, refuses to open); and the jarring constant "hunt" of the engine is creating a longing for the pliancy of rubber-on-pavement. Even the autos and gasoline trucks darting across the right-of-way start to seem tame.

My favorite cab-riding story concerned the night No. 5, the *Quad Cities Rocket,* was to have a visitor on the head end, a friend of the trustee. The dispatcher was dictating a message to the operator at Blue Island, advising the crew of their visitor, and the message ended: "Please show Mr. ___ every consideration."

"What does that mean?" the operator asked.

The dispatcher thought for a minute, then said, "I guess it means let him blow the whistle."

A dispatcher's office, on the other hand, is never dull. While the crew on No. 5 is innocently gliding along, whistling for crossings and setting the air, the dispatcher alone knows that 6 miles ahead, a drag freight is trying to outrun No. 5 to the crossover at Milepost 148. The drag freight can cross over to the other main and clear No. 5 *if* 02X, a perishable train, gets east of the crossover in time. No. 5 moves through the night, an isle of calm and serenity, oblivious to the drama unfolding around it. From the cab of No. 5, all is serene—green signals at every curve. From the office in Des Moines, though, a scenario involving three trains is working its way to its own resolution. And, no sooner will this be resolved than the center

of attention will shift to 02X, which unbeknownst to it, has an Ottawa Turn ahead of it, with work on both tracks at Morris. Then there is the threat of 201, just leaving Joliet, which soon will overtake the Ottawa Turn . . .

Only the dispatcher must participate in all of this, as he holds the volatile intricacy of the whole changing system in his mind. And the drama that actually unfolds—02X clearing at 148 in time to line over the drag freight and clear the signal for 5—is nothing compared with the possibilities he must entertain, thinking through all the options available. Next to this, a cab ride is a stroll in the park.

I'm not sure that the Rock Island dispatchers' offices in Des Moines were typical of dispatchers' offices in general. My suspicion is that typical dispatchers' offices don't exist. Each railroad maintains its own distinctive offices, with the offices reflecting the overall condition of the railroad in a concentrated form.

When I was applying for work on the Santa Fe, I received a fifty-cent tour of the dispatchers' offices in Fort Madison, Ia. A solemn hush pervaded the two rooms, both dominated by a wall of Centralized Traffic Control (CTC) machinery. One man handled from Kansas City to Fort Madison; the other from Fort Madison to Chicago. A third board could be cut in during rush times to oversee from Joliet east. The lighting was muted, the atmosphere redolent of a graduate school library. In one corner stood a tall, lean cabinet like a modern grandfather's clock with reels of tape unwinding behind glass. Everything on the dispatcher's phone was automatically recorded. "You'd be surprised how easy that makes an

investigation," said the chief clerk who was showing me around.

One didn't talk to the dispatchers. If one had a question, the signal maintainer stood by, ready to answer—just as he was ready for action if anything acted up on the CTC. When I called later, hoping to talk to the chief dispatcher, he'd already gone home at 4 p.m.—just like a guy with a normal job! (In Des Moines, the chief always had arrived by 6 a.m., and he counted himself lucky if he was out at 6 p.m.) But after all, what else would one expect of the Santa Fe? Looking across the rows of neat desks in the clerks' office, I saw people chatting and consulting each other over coffee. (And, having worked for the Rock Island, my instinctive response was: "I'll bet they could cut one-third of these people and still do the job"—but then, I always was a company man.)

In the only other dispatcher's office I had visited, the Milwaukee Road's in Ottumwa, Ia., the atmosphere was just the opposite. The dispatcher sat in a tidy back room of a small depot. The office was the size of a generous broom closet, and he was packed in with a CTC board, an enormous train sheet, a train-order log, and a typewriter. When the agent went home at 4, the dispatcher became his own operator, copying orders directly on his typewriter as he dictated them, then writing them in the log when the other end repeated. People wandered in and out; the superintendent chatted with the crew hauler; someone brought in a load of sandwiches; an engineer showed off a trinket he'd picked up for his grandchild.

Business was talked all the time, but as an undercurrent, as part of the gossip. Was 2011 still acting up? When was someone going to look at the switch at Rubio? Why did Clinton hold our trains for the North Western? There was an air of breezy professionalism, suitable for the necessary ad hoc quality of that part of the railroad. One exclamation—"Okay you guys, hold it down, I'm putting out some orders"—and the door was quietly closed.

The Rock Island offices in Des Moines fell somewhere in between these two. As in Ottumwa, the Rock offices were in a depot, but an enormous one, a relic of the days of *Rockets* and *The Californian* and the *Rocky Mountain Limited.* A substantial waiting room, its allure much faded, still was intact inside. The dispatchers, however, occupied only the northwest corner of the second floor, away from the tracks, as at Fort Madison. The offices were isolated from the outside world—the windows covered by wallboard. The rooms had been modern once, in the 1950's to judge from the design, but nothing had been added since. The walls were scored with the marks of lounging feet, the floors mottled with scars of crushed cigarettes, the ceilings stained where pipes had leaked.

Each office was unlike any other (a quality that carried over to the train sheets, each arranged in its own way). Office No. 1,

the "Missouri side," was all CTC. Territory covered: Missouri Division Junction (Davenport, Ia.) to Armourdale Yard (Kansas City); and Manly, Ia., to the Twin Cities. The dispatcher sat in a pit created by walling him on four sides with the black, silver, and olive boards (the colors dated them, revealing their post-World War II origin).

Office No. 2, the "bow-and-arrow country" was all train orders; during second and third tricks (3 p.m.-7 a.m.), the work was done in office No. 4. Territory: Manly-Des Moines-Allerton, Ia., and the branchline network in northwestern Iowa.

The next two rooms consisted of desks only, surrounded by sheets, charts, train lists, and filing cabinets. The two assistant chiefs sat here, at the center of activity. Next door, in the third office, a small CTC machine had been joined to a larger one. This dispatcher worked the "Illinois side,"

handling movements through the throat of the system from Missouri Division Junction to Chicago, plus Illinois branches. Most of his railroad was invisible—his CTC ended at Atkinson, Ill., 25 miles east of Silvis. The main line was all double track and east of Atkinson was handled with block signals and train orders; Bureau and Joliet each had their own local CTC.

In office No. 4 stood a modern CTC machine—silent, with none of the clicking, coding relays that simmered in the other rooms. Since this office was sometimes consolidated with No. 2, there were two of everything—two train sheets, two microphones, two train-order logs, two sets of buttons to ring in operators. On first trick, office No. 4 handled only "east Iowa"; Missouri Division Junction to Des Moines on the east-west main; Manly to Burlington on the north-south line; and Vinton to Iowa Falls. Newton-Des Moines was CTC,

Rolling through Marengo, Ia., in May 1979 was 43's Extra. This Davenport-Des Moines section of the main was one of the Rock Island's busiest, but this portion was train-order territory. The condition of the depot reflected the Rock's financial straits. R.B. OLSON.

the remainder train orders; the operator at West Liberty (the crossing of the two mains) controlled his own interlocker plus the passing siding at Iowa City.

Across the hall, apart from the others (which were in a row connected by an open hallway), stood office No. 5, the "Colorado side." From Des Moines to Denver, this was entirely train-order territory. Two clocks on the wall indicated the time change that occurred, for railroad purposes, at Goodland, Kans. A mammoth train sheet, pasted together out of four separate sheets, was draped across a desk which could never accommodate it—one end of the sheet always drooped across the floor. No lights were here, no bright colors, no clicking relays, just the gray of the desk, the silver of the microphone, and the white of the train sheet.

But these were the offices as they never appeared—vacant and quiet. There was always a buzz of activity. The assistant chief was roaming about, searching for up-to-date information. Other dispatchers wandered past, tracking down trains that would be leaving another's territory and coming onto their own, or trying to run down the chief, who "was here a minute ago." There was an endless babble of background talk, as the conversation from one office filtered into another (some stations broadcast loud and clear, while others were barely audible). Underneath this babble was the mutter of radio transmissions—since three of the offices handled trains in and out of Des Moines, dispatchers had to keep one ear open to the radio. And somewhere, always, a telephone was ringing.

Dispatchers were talking, or talking and writing, or trying to listen, or leafing through the pile of various-sized papers that were the record of previous messages, or reaching up to line a switch and code a

signal, or staring at a blinking light on the board, or hastily calculating on a piece of scratch paper, or recopying slow orders. One or two sat smoking, sipping coffee, gazing off into space with a glazed look, waiting for the chief to return their train sheets, or thinking what next to do, or simply, thankfully, resting.

Why, you may ask, would that man be so tired? Why is he rubbing his eyes and kneading his brow? Why is he turning back to his desk with a slump in his shoulders? What about the excitement of three trains clearing a track for each other, right in a row? Where is all the drama of railroading, that drama of which the crew on No. 5 remained so blissfully ignorant?

A large part of a dispatcher's life is detail work. Is the train-order log up to date? Is every OS ("on sheet," a report of a train passing a certain point) in? Is the delay on 56 written down? Has 43 got a message to pick up? What time will 62 leave Manly (better walk down the hall and find out if it's called in)?

"Dispatcher, I've got a slow order to repeat." (Hold on just a second.) "OS, Iowa Falls, on 53, and a call on 54 and a 411; 411 has work at Dows." (Better find out if Estherville has anyone figured against 54, if there's anyone at Estherville—he may be out checking the yard).

"Dispatcher, dispatcher, this is the brakeman on 56 at Brooklyn. 43 is doubling the hill at Homestead." (Marengo's gone home; maybe Iowa City can talk to 43.) "How long are we gonna be at Brooklyn? Can we go to Marengo? I've got something to write an order on." (Won't be any good unless 43 comes to the phone). "This is train 82, dispatcher, the conductor speaking. Look, we got a message to pick up at Argon, but one engine is dead and we've already got 6,300 tons. Now I'll pick up if you really want me to but I can't guarantee . . ."

It's not enough, though, to point out the stress of the job; most railroad jobs are stressful at one time or another. The dispatcher, however, remains the medium for everyone's problems. To provide a true insight into dispatching, it is necessary to cross that dark divide that separates dispatchers from operators and engineers and conductors. It is necessary to examine that most cumbersome, that most outmoded, that most traditional aspect of railroad operations—the train order. The crew need only know how to follow it, and the operator need only know how to type it, but the dispatcher must know everything about it.

One of the difficulties of learning train orders (at least when I was on the Rock Island) was that there was no set method of instruction. The apprentice system was in effect. The student sat alongside a dispatcher for the first day or two, watching him work. When conditions permitted, it was proper to ask questions. After a while, the student was invited to "sit down," though he at first performed only bookkeeping functions—taking the call on a crew, writing a delay report, getting an OS, perhaps updating a slow order. If a train order was required, the dispatcher usually dictated it to the student as the student dictated it to the operators. By the end of a week, the student was in the chair the full eight hours and the absences of the dispatcher became more frequent and less noticeable.

There were a few dispatchers whom I avoided like the plague, for they simply sat you down on your first day, then vanished—the "sink or swim" method of pedagogy. One man, who later went to another railroad, was apparently a master at literally hiding from his students. The helpless student, stuck on some fine point of the rules, would wander the halls in vain, searching for his mentor who was,

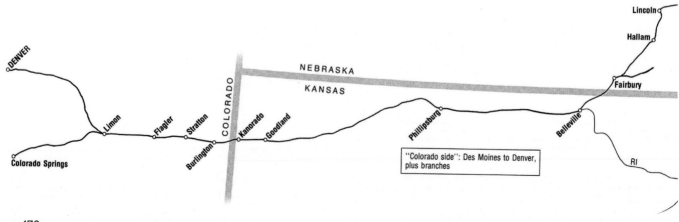

"Colorado side": Des Moines to Denver, plus branches

someone confided to me, holed up in the furnace room on the first floor, reading *Playboy*.

The end result of the method I went through is that one learned train orders in a haphazard, catch-as-catch-can manner. I wasn't really able to think clearly about them until I'd worked as a student for a month and happened, one morning, to work with a dispatcher on a light day. "Two kinds of orders can get you in trouble faster than anything else," said B.S.F., "the flagging order and the right-over order." (Dispatchers are universally known on a railroad by their three initials, which they append to every order. To protect these employees, fictitious sets of initials for each person are used.)

I could see how a flagging order might cause problems. This type of order, introduced to me by B.D.K. as a "foot-ease" order, is designed to relieve a conductor from protecting the rear of his train with a flag when the train is stopped. Quite simply, it restricts all trains from passing a set location before a specific time, and it was used frequently on the "bow-and-arrow country," the portion of the Rock Island in northwestern Iowa that was a spiderweb of branch lines to grain terminals.

The bow-and-arrow country deserves a lengthy aside, if only to serve as an example of how the Rock Island could be flexible. Except for on the main stem between Iowa Falls and Estherville, most lines were restricted to 25 mph or less. A train crew simply could not make a round trip—especially if its objective was to gather up a unit grain train—within its 12 hours. A train could be out on the line three or four days. One member of the crew, therefore, would follow the train in his auto, and at the end of 12 hours, the working crew would tie up at a convenient point and ride home in style.

Just where a train would be on any given day was known only to the crew until the next morning, when the dispatcher's telephone would ring (there was no wire left in this area; all work was handled by telephone), and an agent somewhere would ask for orders for a train at, say, Hayfield Junction en route to Round Lake. As may be imagined, train lineups for this territory were arranged with room for trains that might surpris-

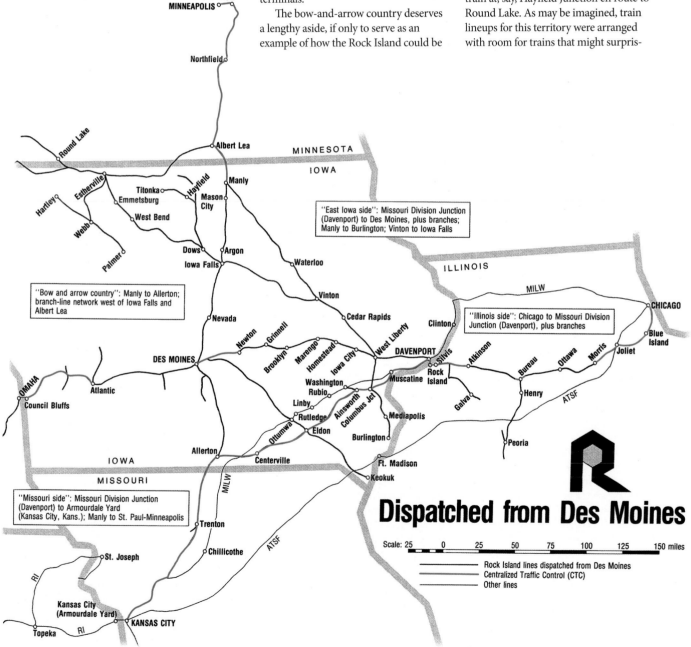

"East Iowa side": Missouri Division Junction (Davenport) to Des Moines, plus branches; Manly to Burlington; Vinton to Iowa Falls

"Bow and arrow country": Manly to Allerton; branch-line network west of Iowa Falls and Albert Lea

"Illinois side": Chicago to Missouri Division Junction (Davenport), plus branches

"Missouri side": Missouri Division Junction (Davenport) to Armourdale Yard (Kansas City, Kans.); Manly to St. Paul-Minneapolis

Dispatched from Des Moines

Scale: 25   0   25   50   75   100   125   150 miles

Rock Island lines dispatched from Des Moines
Centralized Traffic Control (CTC)
Other lines

ingly appear: "EXTRA EAST LEAVE EMMETSBURG NOT BEFORE 1001 AM."

The objective in dispatching is to move trains without yielding control of any line. Yet in the bow-and-arrow country, where everything was under train order, a train could appear at any moment anywhere—Dows or Emmetsburg, for example—and ask for orders. If the main line was owned by another train, not due to arrive anywhere for another four hours, there was no way to change orders without complications. I once made the rash confession to an assistant chief that I was finally beginning to understand the way things worked in the bow-and-arrow country. "Oh my," said C.B.K., "now I know it's time for you to take a day off!"

B.D.K. seemed expert at adopting the flag order (Form Y in our *Book of Rules*) to a variety of conditions. One time I'd worked third trick with F.W.A., and I thought we'd done a careful job, but when we turned the transfer over to B.D.K., he spotted a mistake right away. "How's it look?" asked F.W.A., ready to bounce out the door.

"Well, not too bad," said B.D.K., "except you've got 'em lapped up here."

"Lapped up" are the ultimate words of censure. They derive from the phrase "lapse of authority" which is the result of a dispatcher having two trains in operation, one of which knows nothing of the other. To "lap 'em up" is, classically, to set the stage for a collision, and while I'd heard the phrase bandied about as a nervous joke ("Don't bother me now, I'm on orders and I'd rather not lap 'em up"), I never thought I would participate in a real-life situation.

Our mistake was simple, once it was explained. We had two westbound trains running on the main stem from Iowa Falls to Estherville. The first, Extra 4300 West, had left about 4 a.m., and since it had no work, we had not felt it necessary to give the train a flag order. The second train, Extra 4314 West, called about two hours later, had cars to peddle and had received appropriate protection. Our Form Y order read: "WESTWARD EXTRA TRAINS EXCEPT EXTRA 4314 WEST WAIT AT IOWA FALLS YARD UNTIL 1201 PM."

"How have we got 'em lapped up?" F.W.A. asked belligerently. "I don't see it."

"This second guy's got a flag order, right? He's not expecting any trains behind him—no one can follow out of Iowa Falls till noon," said B.D.K. "So he's boogyin' on down the track, doin' his work. Meanwhile, this first train gets hungry, or maybe

he's got a bad order to set out. Whichever, he decides to get in the hole at West Bend. First train's in the hole; second one goes around him. No problem, right?"

"Nothing wrong with that."

"All right, second train is now first. But it's not got a care in the world—it's got a flag order. It stops to do work at Emmetsburg; the conductor stays inside where it's warm. Meanwhile, the first train, which is now second, finishes up the flapjacks at West Bend, takes off, and bingo—there's your lap."

He was right, of course. The second train, if it somehow became first, would be excused from protecting its rear end, expecting nothing westward behind it. But there was the chance that the first train could turn out to be behind it. It was a lapse of authority. No matter that F.W.A. had brushed it off ("Aw, nothing can happen—that track's all twenty-five mile an hour anyway"), the principle had been violated. And if it could happen here, under circumstances which were benignant, it could be allowed to happen elsewhere, on fast track.

F.W.A. shrugged it off, but I was new enough to be shaken, so I hung around to find out how we should've done it.

"Very simple," said B.D.K. "You don't need to get hold of your first train. All you need to do is to let your second train know there is a first train. Here's the way you do it: 'WESTWARD EXTRA TRAINS EXCEPT TWO EXTRAS 4300 AND 4314 WAIT AT IOWA FALLS YARD UNTIL 1201 PM. EXTRA 4300 WEST HAS LEFT IOWA FALLS YARD.'

"The trick is to include that final sentence, which informs train two that train one is out ahead. Now, train one never has to know about this order, which is okay; if train one stops, it'll send out a flag as a matter of course. Everyone is adequately covered; if train two passes train one, train two will know there is a live train behind it not simply some dead train tied up on a siding waiting for a new crew."

If a simple order, the Form Y, can tie up the railroad, imagine the problems created by a complicated order, the Form S-C, which is often combined with another form, S-E, the time order. Form S-C ("S" for single track), the "right-over" order, is frequently used, especially on main lines, unlike the Form Y, which usually is restricted to branch lines and locals.

Any train must have some knowledge of traffic opposing it, even if that knowledge is that there is no traffic. On the Rock Island main line between Iowa

City and Newton, for example, trains operated under train orders on single track with sidings. A westbound leaving Iowa City (or an eastbound leaving Newton) usually would have one of three kinds of train orders.

Example: 59's train, Extra 199 West, rolls past West Liberty, and the engineer scoops up his orders. Aside from the Form X orders (slow orders indicating reduced speed zones not listed in the timetable), he may have a straight Form G order: "ENG 199 RUN EXTRA IOWA CITY TO NEWTON." Along with authorizing his train as an extra (and all trains on the Rock Island dispatched from Des Moines in 1978 were extra with the exception of the two *Rockets* until their demise), the order informs him that he has no opposing trains to counter: 59 owns the track to Newton.

Suppose, however, that 56 has been called at Des Moines. If that is the case, the engineer would likely receive, in addition to the Form G running order, a Form A order, a straight meet with 56, operating as Extra 4308 East: "EXTRA 199 WEST MEET EXTRA 4308 EAST AT GRINNELL. EXTRA 199 WEST HOLD MAIN TRACK AT GRINNELL." Result: 199 knows there is an opposing train, Extra 4308 East, but no problem—both will meet at Grinnell and neither must pass that location until the other has arrived.

The meet order is blatant. On the "Colorado side," between Council Bluffs, Ia., and Limon, Colo. (Limon to Denver was on Union Pacific track), where trains were enormous, meet orders were almost always used. A straight meet was a necessity because each subdivision had only one place that could accommodate two trains. The subdivisions were relatively short, and the dispatcher could afford to salt away a train for an hour or two without jeopardizing the crews' ability to complete their run in 12 hours.

What happened, though, when trains operated over a long subdivision—for example, the 182 miles on the "east Iowa side" between Silvis and Des Moines? This subdivision handled the hottest train on the Rock Island—57, the General Motors auto-parts train. That called for the subtlety and finesse of the right-over order, coupled with the time order.

The right-over order has evolved considerably since its initial usage. When timetables were supreme, all eastbound (or northbound) trains were superior to westbound (or southbound) trains. At its most elemental, this simply determined which train held the main at a meeting

Author Brunner looks over his extensive train sheet as he dispatches the "East Iowa Side" in Office 4 of the Rock Island's Des Moines dispatching center in the 1970s. R.B. OLSON.

point. The Milwaukee Road timetable I used as an operator at Culver Tower in Muscatine, Ia., showed No. 75 leaving Culver at 10:40 a.m. and meeting No. 64 at Linby at 12:10 p.m. Likewise, the timetable showed No. 64 leaving Ottumwa at 11:35 a.m. and meeting No. 75 at Linby at 12:10 p.m. The timetable also stated: "Eastward trains are superior to westward trains of the same class." Both 64 and 75 were second-class trains, so upon arriving at Linby, 64 stayed on the main and 75 headed into the siding. What could be simpler?

If life were only that simple! Example: 64, it turns out, is hours late today and has no hope of making Linby even close to his scheduled time. Will 75 simply sit, waiting for 64? Technically, yes. But the dispatcher can nullify this delay by issuing an order to 75 that, in effect, alters the timetable: "NO 75 HAS RIGHT OVER NO 64 FROM LINBY TO RUTLEDGE" (Rutledge is an interlocking at the edge of Ottumwa). The order must also be addressed to 64 at Ottumwa. Number 64, of course, cannot leave until 75 arrives, because its superiority has been temporarily borrowed and bestowed upon 75. It is contrary to the timetable, but that is precisely what a train order is: a

momentary deviation from the strict (and ideal) realm of the timetable, a modification necessitated by exceptional events.

Variations on this order are endless, since the dispatcher can assign right as he pleases. The timetable imposes, but the dispatcher disposes; or, what the timetable giveth, the dispatcher taketh away. He can move 75 against 64 for part of the way, if 64 is only delayed for a short spell. But be must never forget that eastward trains rule the road as a matter of convention. If 75 is hours late, 64 needs nothing, because 64 is top dog; 75 stays out of 64's way. A student dispatcher can raise quite a chuckle from his operators by issuing 64 right over 75. Since 64 already has right over 75, operators find this highly entertaining, at least the first time (response is disappointing the third or fourth try).

Right-over orders are invaluable when one wants to assign floating meets that can change depending on circumstance. With 57, Murphy's Law ("If anything can go wrong, it will") attained a certain refinement. The railroad corollary of Murphy's Law is: If a hotshot westbound is running, then a hotshot eastbound also will be called. Example: How does one move 57 against 56 without taking the

cowardly option of holding 56 at Newton until 57 arrives, or running 56 to a siding and salting it away for an hour?

The solution is to create a temporary schedule for 57's train, a schedule it can well live within, but which also will give 56 an opportunity to move against it. First requirement is to give 57's train (say, Extra 4337 West) right over 56's train (Extra 4326 East), because 57 is hotter—57 doesn't see an approach signal, let alone handle a siding switch. (The first time I, as an operator, stopped 57, to call attention to sticking brakes, I received in rapid succession a call from the chief dispatcher, a call from the power bureau at Kansas City, a call from the assistant superintendent, a call from the area trainmaster, and a call from a man in Chicago who never did identify himself [the prerogative of being a high official].)

The next step is to calculate the approximate time that 57's train will arrive at the three sidings where 56 can meet it. The calculations result in an order that might read: EXTRA 4337 WEST HAS RIGHT OVER EXTRA 4326 EAST FROM IOWA CITY TO NEWTON AND WAIT AT
   MARENGO UNTIL 615 PM
   BROOKLYN 640 PM

Rock Island engineer Phil Reynolds, at the controls of a new GE U25B, rolls a westbound freight between Davenport and West Liberty, Iowa, in 1963. Author Brunner says he finds a visit to a dispatcher's desk much more interesting and preferable to a cab ride. ED WOJTAS.

GRINNELL 701 PM

FOR EXTRA 4326 EAST

Hence 57's train has been given its own unique schedule. The use of the word "wait" in the order is euphemistic: 57 cannot realistically run to fulfill its unique schedule. The schedule is actually for the benefit of 56, which now knows approximately where 57 will be. More specifically, 56 knows precisely where 57 will not be: 57 will not pass Marengo before 6:15 p.m. Therefore, 56 has until five minutes before that time to be in the clear at Marengo. If 56 cannot run that well, it may be able to make Brooklyn by 6:40 and wait there for 57. Just where 56 ultimately goes for 57 depends on how well it can accommodate itself to 57's "schedule."

There is a further twist in this order. As it states, Extra 4337 West is to wait for Extra 4326 East. Once 57 has met 56, the time restrictions in the order no longer are binding; it can outrun its schedule, if it dares, because, as the order specifies, it was to "wait" at the locations for a specific train. Once the train is behind it, the order has been fulfilled.

Understanding the *Book of Rules* would be simple if the rules were applied in a strict, legalistic fashion. Any one rule by itself is (relatively speaking) clear, concise, and to the point. But in its application, a rule can become charged with nuances, implications, and innuendoes.

My favorite example of this centers on Rock Island's Rule 93. Every railroad has a variation on Rule 93. In its simplest form, it states that within yard limits, the main track may be used by trains or engines that can move in either direction. Most railroads add a few extra clauses: regular trains must be cleared, but not extras; any train moving within yard limits must proceed "prepared to stop short of train, obstruction, or switch not properly lined."

To begin with, Rule 93 was the center of a small controversy because the *Uniform Code of Operating Rules* had a form T order which could establish "temporary" yard limits. Every day but Sunday, the "temporary" yard limits went into effect at Lincoln, Neb., and Waterloo, Ia., and woe to the third-trick dispatcher who neglected to issue this order: "801 AM UNTIL 401 PM (DATE) RULE 93 IN EFFECT BETWEEN MP (SUCH-AND-SUCH) AND MP (SO-AND-SO)." The reason was that switch engines at both locations had industry switching for several miles along the main. Without the rule, the switch crews would need to work under track and time limits or with a flagman. Just why the rule was only placed temporarily in effect at these two locations was a puzzle, but the real rub of contention, I believe, was that no dispatcher liked the idea of a snake-wagon (switcher) out on "his" main line, especially since both locations were in train-order territory. If a meet turned sour, was it because the snakes delayed a mainline train for an hour while they happily switched?

Rule 93 worked wonderfully well under one set of circumstances, though. Various branch lines throughout the Rock Island system saw only one train a day. Why not decree these to be yards? A train running from Iowa Falls to Titonka would require orders only to Dows; after Dows, the train would operate exclusively on subdivisions 12B and 12C, both of which were annotated in the timetable: "Trains and engines will operate per Rule 93." The whole branch was a yard, and any train on it would need to move at "Restricted Speed," watching out for open switches, obstructions, and other trains (which didn't exist except in principle).

One afternoon I walked over to the Missouri side to visit with K.F.N., an opponent of the Form T order. "Ever see an order like this?" he asked me abruptly, holding up the train-order log. I had to squint to read his writing, notoriously casual, but it appeared to state: "RULE 93 IS SUSPENDED FROM AINSWORTH TO WASHINGTON . . ."

"It's an anti-Form T order," I said. "Is this the beginning of a new campaign?"

"Horsefeathers," he said (or some such

phrase). The explanation was odd, indeed. On this day, the branch from Ainsworth to Washington would see not only the usual one train a day but also a second train, a Rock detour over the Burlington Northern from Washington to Mediapolis. Two trains would occupy the branch, thus the rule had to be suspended and the dispatcher had to revert to the regular routine of train orders. But the purpose of Rule 93, ostensibly or at the very least originally, was to permit a number of trains to move in the same area of designated limits, each watching out for the others.

I summed up my lesson. "The only time Rule 93, which covers two or more trains, is legal, is when there are not two or more trains?"

"You're finally catching on, kid," K.F.N., said (he called almost everyone "kid"). "I have hopes for you yet."

I shook my head in wonderment and bewilderment.

Much to my surprise, I realized one day that a few dispatchers had their own distinctive ways of composing train orders. Not everyone slavishly imitated the examples given in the Book of Rules. Most dispatchers believed the formulae therein were sacrosanct, but a few deliberately roamed as far as possible from established models.

One of the finest train-order dispatchers, S.K.S., had the unusual tendency of combining a slew of train-order forms in one order. The *Book of Rules* sanctioned this, up to a point; a footnote advised which forms were allowed to combine with others. Very few dispatchers combined more than two forms in one order—except S.K.S. It was characteristic of him to jam all his information into one staggering order. Here is an extreme instance:

ENG 211 RUN EXTRA GOODLAND TO LIMON WITH RIGHT OVER TWO EXTRAS 298 AND 4324 EAST AND MEET EXTRA 298 EAST AT KANORADO INSTEAD OF BURLINGTON WAIT AT

    BURLINGTON UNTIL 115 AM

    STRATTON 145 AM

    FLAGLER 225 AM

    FOR EXTRA 4324 EAST

In one order, Forms A, S-C, S-E, G, and P.

I think he positively relished deviating from the obvious examples in the rule book. One morning, three eastbound trains were called out of Fairbury: 56's train, Extra 4317 East; a Lincoln Turn (346), Extra 4314 East, which would turn

at Lincoln and become a westbound; and 58's train, Extra 4315 East. The problem: the Lincoln Turn had to receive all its orders at Fairbury, including orders permitting it to return as a westbound (yes, the agent could've been called out to copy an order, but that would've been the easy way out). His solution was an order unlike the way anyone else I know would've done it:

ENG 4314 RUN EXTRA FAIRBURY TO LINCOLN AND ARRIVAL EXTRA 4317 EAST RETURN TO FAIRBURY WITH RIGHT OVER EASTWARD TRAINS AND MEET EXTRA 4315 EAST AT HALLAM

Quite simply, he combined the return trip running order with a meet: 4314 can only return to Fairbury after the arrival at Lincoln of Extra 4317 East, and en route, 4314 meets 4315 at Hallam. The conventional way would've been to issue a meet with 4314 and 4317 at Lincoln, but S.K.S. always opted to be as brief as possible.

This order resolved a messy situation so compactly—and was so dazzling to me, who would've issued a half dozen orders—that I immediately began to rifle through my notebook, looking for a spare corner to write it all down. S.K.S. heard me turning pages hurriedly and said over his shoulder, "If you're lookin' for an example in the rule book, I wouldn't bother. There isn't any."

At an opposite extreme from S.K.S. was C.M.T. While S.K.S. reduced his orders to the bare minimum, compressing them so not one nonessential word appeared, C.M.T. created orders that attained, in my mind, a certain degree of elegance. They were unusual for their subtlety and sophisticated knowledge of the rules. At the time, he was working on the Illinois side, where little opportunity existed for writing orders, except on one subdivision—the line between Bureau and Peoria. This not only was single-track, train-order territory, it also was the last part of the system having a scheduled train. The *Peoria Rocket,* Nos. 11 and 12, had the honor of holding the final regular run on the Rock Island. The *Quad Cities Rocket,* Nos. 5 and 6, also had a timetable schedule, but since the train did not operate in unsignaled train-order territory, the designation was meaningless.

The *Peoria Rocket* was a thorn in management's side. For several years, applications for abandonment of the train had been postponed or denied, often at the last moment. About 1977, the word went out—freight trains on the Peoria branch were not to be delayed by the

passenger train. The crews on 11 and 12 rankled under their revised status and came to believe the dispatcher's motives were all malignant. C.M.T. strived to live within the edict of management while at the same time working to give the passenger trains every break. It wasn't always possible, though, and when push came to shove, No. 11 came out on the bottom. But 11's crew still had plenty of fight left in them.

One night, 11 arrived at Bureau a few minutes early, a frequent occurrence owing to improved mainline track condition not reflected in a revised schedule. At Bureau, the crew saw the following order: "ENG 202 RUN EXTRA PEORIA TO BUREAU WITH RIGHT OVER NO 11 PEORIA TO BUREAU." The crew decided that, because No. 11 was a scheduled train and Extra 202 East was no more than an extra, No. 11 could run down the line to Henry and clear Extra 202 East there.

This was nonsense—the order plainly stated the extra was running with right over No. 11, period. (Possibly the crew was confusing this order with another kind of order, an order that would read: "ENG 202 RUN EXTRA PEORIA TO BUREAU, NO 11 HAS ENG 652." Under that order, Extra 202 East could move against No. 11's scheduled times in the timetable. The engine number of the regular train must be mentioned so Extra 202 East will know when it has passed No. 11.) Fortunately, the crew decided to inquire whether their interpretation was correct.

C.M.T. went up in smoke. "The order reads, 'with right over,' not 'has right over'; 'has right over' is the wording for a Form S-C order to an intermediate point on a subdivision, while 'with right over' confers superiority for the entire subdivision." I can't believe the crew understood this technical explanation, but they could surely guess from the dispatcher's tone of voice that they had strayed from the fold.

It was unfortunate that C.M.T. worked under these strained conditions, for the crews on 11 and 12 were so sensitive to any unusual order that they misinterpreted his motives. A classic example occurred one evening. Peoria had called a freight train east for 6 p.m. Normally, this would have meant that the freight might arrive at Bureau about 9:30, knocking a half-hour hole in 11's schedule. But the engineer on this job was exceptional—with a bit of luck, it was possible he could make Bureau by 9. Number 11 was due out of Bureau at 9:02. Still, intangibles were involved. Would the freight depart Peoria soon? Would it develop trouble on the way?

C.M.T. knew the freight could make Henry, but he thought that, with the engineer pressing it, there was a good chance the freight could get to Bureau. How to keep open this possibility of running from Henry to Bureau? There was no operator on duty at Henry, and if the crew stopped to copy an order by radio, they would lose just enough time to render the order useless.

The problem was solved in this particularly elegant manner: "ENG 213 RUN EXTRA PEORIA TO BUREAU, HAS RIGHT OVER NO 11 PEORIA TO HENRY, NO 11 HAS ENG 655." With right over No. 11 to Henry, 213 owns the line up to there; beyond Henry, 213 can run against 11's schedule, if time permits. As things worked out. Extra 213 East ran in superb fashion, clearing Bureau by 8:55 p.m. There even was time to annul the orders that would have informed No. 11 of the move, which left one and all blissfully unaware of the tight squeeze.

Not all crews appreciated these subtle orders, especially one nicknamed "the stinger" which was usually reserved for branch-line operations. A stinger is a sentence added to a running order that annuls the order after a certain time. Typical situation: Engine 238 will be working on the line between Albert Lea and Estherville for at least three days. Instead of allowing its running order, authorizing it to move as an extra without any opposition, to remain in effect for a long three days, the dispatcher issued it a running order with a stinger: "ENG 238 RUN EXTRA ESTHERVILLE TO ALBERT LEA, THIS ORDER IS ANNULLED AT 330 PM." (The time in the order is 12 hours later than the call time of the crew, the hour when the crew is dead under the Hours of Service law.)

The stinger accomplished a number of things. At 3:30 p.m., the order was dead, and the dispatcher could consider it fulfilled. Furthermore, the crew had to have its train off the main and in the clear by 3:30 p.m., for quite simply, their authority to exist ceased at that time. After 3:30, the dispatcher could assume he had his main line back. And the next morning, when the crew resumed its work, they would have to call in for new orders, thus advising the dispatcher of their location, and in addition, giving him the opportunity (in the unlikely event he had an additional train to run opposing them) to issue a meet, if necessary.

On main lines, a stinger on an order was a rarity because, of course, crews were supposed to complete their runs well within their 12 hours. They weren't always able to, though, for a host of reasons, and nothing annihilates the operation of a railroad more thoroughly than a train tying up on the main, dead under hours of service. Most railroad slang is obsolete, if indeed it ever existed (K.F.N, was fond of asking, "I've never heard a sectionman called a 'gandy dancer'—have you? We call them 'sectionmen,' goddamit!"). The exception involved train crews who have run out of time; it is no accident that the most contemptuous terms are reserved for such occasions. A crew is "hog-lawed" (one of the rare times when "hogger" is resuscitated from the past) or "goes to the dogs" a result of the crew dogging along, or dogging it. A relay crew for the stranded one is called "a dogcatch crew."

C.M.T. introduced the stinger to the main line, and when be did it he was experimenting. By automatically attaching a stinger to the running order of mainline trains, he created a situation where a train crew couldn't simply lie down on the main when their 12 hours expired. They had to be in the clear, off the main, before their authority to exist evaporated—no more tying up the main and pressuring the dispatcher to call a dogcatch crew quickly.

This policy, exclusively maintained by C.M.T, came to a bitter end one day. A westbound had a bad trip—getting no farther than the siding at Iowa City, where it tied up. The dogcatch crew, arriving to take the train on to Des Moines, received the characteristic running order with its uncharacteristic stinger. Since the crew had been called for 5:30 p.m., the stinger annulled the running order at 5:30 a.m. But the engineer balked. "I have a running order," he explained, "dated August 14 which states that 'this order is annulled at 5:30 a.m.' It is now 7:18 p.m., and therefore my running order has already been annulled." Efforts to convince the engineer that the 5:30 a.m. figure applied to August 15 were made to no avail. The engineer demanded a new order; C.M.T. maintained the order was adequate as it stood. An intermediary finally suggested that the superintendent would decide—later.

Much to everyone's amazement, the higher authority sided with the crew. The order was ambiguous, he maintained, and besides that, what was the point? No one attempted to question the judgment or

explain how a stinger could keep the main line free.

It would be perverse to conclude that the situation in Des Moines was the very condition under which dispatchers thrive. Certainly with the Rock Island financial situation, there was an alarming amount of attrition, with the Burlington Northern a special beneficiary. "Someone could make a lot of money," one dispatcher said, "running a shuttle bus between Des Moines and Alliance." The Rock's financial condition aside, the dispatchers who chose to remain became, of necessity, exceptionally skilled individuals. My guess is that the Milwaukee dispatchers at Ottumwa could discern the attractions of a job in which the unexpected is a daily occurrence. And with all due respect to the Santa Fe men at Fort Madison, I submit that the anxiety of having your every word taped is nothing compared with the anxiety you feel hearing that the eastbound is down to one unit and doubling the hill in front of the hottest westbound on the road.

As it happened, I decided that the dispatcher's life, at least at Des Moines, wasn't what I wanted for myself. Yet the decision was difficult to make. I still look back on the job with nostalgia and affection.

Two remarks stay with me, hauntingly; they seem to sum up, as nothing else can, the whole of my experience. The first was made one morning by K.F.N., after he had sat down in the middle of a particularly messy situation on the Missouri side. "I make more decisions in one hour," he said, "than the president of Monkey Ward makes in a year."

The other was made by a young dispatcher who arrived a few months before I did. He already had the reputation for excellence—a scrupulous and thorough worker. We had just spent an unbroken four hours together on the Iowa side, overseeing 57, expediting 56, untangling a derailment tying up subdivision 12, prodding the West Liberty local, and wrestling with the usual tangle of trains in the bow-and-arrow country. It was 7 p.m. and the system was, at last, in fairly good shape; now, time for supper. I handed him his lunch box, but he ignored it. He was lost in thought, surveying the train sheets, shaking his head and saying, to no one in particular, "It's impossible to do a good job; it just can't be done."

Alcos over Lineville: Big Centuries on SCL

By Ed King
Road Foreman of Engines

1970s

From *Trains* magazine,
September 1983

"Ed, the Frisco's screaming about all the South cars they've got for us at East Thomas. I've got an extra called out of there at 10 a.m., and they want you to ride him. I've already got the power over there on the train." A.K. Conner, then Seaboard Coast Line Chief Dispatcher at Manchester, Ga., was on the phone early one summer morning.

"OK, A.K.," I replied. "What power is it?"

"The 2204 and the 2207."

Omigod. "How much train we got?"

"Oh, about 5,800 tons."

In the early 1970's, I was Road Foreman of Engines for the SCL in Birmingham, Ala. Although I had some responsibility for operations on the former Seaboard Air Line to Atlanta, my primary concern was the Birmingham Terminal and the former Atlantic Coast Line district to Manchester, Ga., thence to Waycross, Ga., and Jacksonville.

Trains on this former Atlanta, Birmingham & Coast line originated and terminated at Louisville & Nashville's Boyles Yard in Birmingham and used the L&N's main line from there to Parkwood, Ala., 16 miles. From Parkwood to Manchester, 180 miles, the line passed through some of the prettiest and most remote country in the Southeast. On this district, there were several long 1 percent compensated grades; about 6 miles north of Lineville the track passed the highest elevation on the old ACL—1,119 feet above sea level. The site was marked by a concrete monument which still bore a Champion McDowell Davis-purple sign commemorating the fact.

The Lineville Subdivision, as this district was known, was well maintained by Atlanta Division engineering forces under Division Engineer A.C. Low; except for restrictions on curves and by town ordinances, the freight speed limit was 55 mph. Locomotive maintenance standards, however, were not up to the same level.

Run-through trains were just becoming popular at that time, made possible by some changes in the labor agreements with the operating crafts. The SCL had initiated two run-throughs with the Frisco at Birmingham: one through Atlanta to Richmond, Va., and the other through Manchester to Jacksonville, Fla. As a result, our crews were familiar with Frisco's East Thomas Yard and the terminal trackage between there and the L&N main.

Back to the 2204 and 2207 and A.K.'s 5,800 tons. The units were Alco Century 628's, rated for 2,950 tons apiece on the Lineville Sub when they were new—and they were far from new. Among other things, they had the reputation for heavy use of cooling water. I hoped that there were hoses available at places like Pelham, Talladega, Lineville, Roanoke, and La Grange. With that much tonnage and the 628's reputation, I could envision stopping for water more often than a steam locomotive. It had been done.

I called my wife and told her I was going to Manchester instead of riding the Coosa Pines local, and to "pack me a b-i-i-i-g lunch. It's gonna be a long day."

Home to change clothes, pick up the b-i-i-i-g lunch, back to the office, hitch a ride to East Thomas with Trainmaster Ed Lambert . . . and there they were, sitting at the east end of the yard as Conner had promised. Our two jewels, the 2204 and 2207, oily black flanks dull in the bright summer morning sun, little curls of blue smoke from crankcase exhausters.

"Thanks, Ed. You sure you don't want to go with us?"

"No way, buddy." Engineer Spencer Tracy (no kidding) and the rest of the crew showed up at about the same time—a couple of minutes this side of calling time.

Spencer and I looked over our two hogs—the 2-10-2's of dieseldom—and climbed up into the 2204's cab.

"All the traction motors are cut in," he said. "Lube oil is OK, and cooling water's right up to the line."

"Good. It'll need to be."

"Do you want to run, Ed?"

"Yeah, I'll take it for a while and then you can have it."

The brake test was OK; the head brakeman lined the yard lead and we pulled out, heading east toward the L&N wye just south of Boyles Yard. Slow running through a congested part of town, the old 16-cylinder 251's cha-cha-ing easily through their turbos.

We made a short stop at the wye to get permission to enter the L&N main, then pulled out slowly so the rear man could close the gate behind us.

Running speed through town was around 12 to 15 mph; we loafed easily across Southern's Alabama Great Southern main at 14th Street at the specified 10 mph.

Red Mountain rears its ugly head about a train length south of the AGS crossing. Since, with most trains, the engines are heading into the hill before the caboose clears the 10-mph restriction, there is not any room to make a run for it. About 3 miles long, the grade is in the neighborhood of .7 percent and is a good indicator of what a southbound SCL train can expect on the 1-percenters on its own railroad. The old-timers said, "If you can get over Red Mountain doing 14 mph, you'll make it over our hills." Under their breath they undoubtedly added, "If your power holds together and it doesn't start to rain."

Our rear-end crew radioed that our caboose was over the AGS; I started notching out on the throttle, listening carefully as the 251's picked up their pace. As the turbo pressure built up, the whistling, sighing cry came in that would let you know, without benefit of load meter, that those Alcos were doing their thing. Those old hogs accelerated that 5,800 tons on Red Mountain—the lead unit passed the summit at the requisite 14 mph.

As the speed built up going down the other side, the amperage went back to zero at transition speed—18 mph. I waited for the "hunting season" (the popping of relays in the electrical cabinet) and the buildup of amperage in the second step of transition. And waited. And waited.

"We got a problem, Spence," I said.

"What's the matter?"

"This one's not making transition."

The speed slowly increased as the 2207, going it alone for now, pushed the 2204 and pulled the train down the south side of the mountain. Finally, at about 32 mph, hunting season opened again and the 2204 got back in business. The Century 628 had two steps of transition, series-parallel and parallel, both of which employed shunting with progressive resistances in the traction motor field circuit. These resistances were controlled by a shunting indexing motor which operated in steps to connect the different resistance circuits. Evidently, the 2204's shunting indexing motor was out of adjustment, a not-uncommon problem but one that I couldn't fix. I carried fuses and hairpins and other replacement parts for EMD's, but nothing for Alcos.

This was going to be an especially annoying problem on an up-and-down railroad like the Lineville Sub. After topping one hill, we would be handicapped in making a good run for the next one since we couldn't accelerate very well between 18 and 32 mph.

I said, "I don't know of anything we can do to fix this one. She's loading above 32 mph."

Tracy said, "Just keep after 'em. We'll make it OK."

In spite of the problem, we did fairly well. After getting onto the SCL at Parkwood, I power-braked the train down the hill to the Cahaba River bridge (no use even trying the dynamic brake) and really laid into those 628's through Pelham, trying to get a swing for Simmsville Hill.

Speed loss going into a hill was rather rapid; there was no loading between 18

and 32 mph, either accelerating or decelerating.

We got over Simmsville about 11 mph; fortunately, the downside of that one was long enough to let us get over 32, so we held the speed up pretty well through Chelsea, Westover, and Coosa Pines. Renfroe Hill was the next bad one, though; sharp curves, including a 30 mph'er at the top, made it a little tougher than Simmsville.

As we approached the top of Renfroe, grinding along at about 10, I said, "Spence, come over here and watch them while I go look at the water."

I went back, opened the little door at the top of the hood of the 2207, and—wonder of wonders—it was right up to the top of the glass. Amazed, I went to check the 2204. Same thing—right up to the top.

Tracy moved aside as I went in the cab door.

"Something's wrong with them, Spence. Neither one of them has used a drop."

"Think we better radio for help?"

I laughed.

I sat down just in time to see the white light go on at the defect detector house, and to hear the recorded "SCL Railroad, Shocco, Alabama" start its repeated monotone over the radio. We slowly accelerated down the hill toward Shocco siding; as our caboose passed the detector, we received one last blessing from the recorder: "SCL Railroad, Shocco, Alabama—no defect."

I was reminded of a story told me when I first went to work on the SCL. The first talking detector had made its appearance on a certain division, and an old hogger, hearing it say "no defect," picked up his radio and said, "Thank you." Another engineer, waiting on a train in a nearby siding, picked up his radio and said, right on cue, "You're welcome." The first engineer, on arrival at the terminal, went on at great length to all who would listen about the social graces built into the new machines.

The big hill for a southbound train on this district is from Talladega, about Milepost 910, up to Milepost 888. The maximum grade is 1 percent; there are short stretches of easier grade but the bulk of it is a dead pull, with Talladega's 25-mph city ordinance to keep you from getting any kind of a run for it. (Of course, getting a 55 mph run for a 22-mile hill wouldn't help that much, but it would make you feel better about it.) With our handicap of only having one unit between 18 and 32 mph, it

was going to be a matter of lugging 'em over the top. We'd soon find out whether those two old Schenectady mules had any starch left in 'em.

The 2204 and 2207 did get the train up fast enough to make it necessary to power brake for the Talladega restriction; we chug-chugged lawfully through town at 25. The 2204 persisted in her policy of not loading when I got them out in Run 8, but the speed dropped rather rapidly as we got into the hill, and as we got back to 18 mph, the welcome cannonade of the hunting season and the stirring of the ammeter told us that she had decided to help out.

The speed varied between 12 and 15 mph as we whined up through Carara; we had ample opportunity to admire the wild country between there and Weathers.

Just south of the Weathers defect detector (Milepost 898) there is a particularly sharp S curve—right-left—that is rough on a long train. We had already gotten down to 10 mph as the 2204 swung into it. She started to slip a bit in spite of being on sand; the ammeter edged into the red between the buzzes of the wheel-slip alarm as the speed further lessened … 9, 8, finally stabilizing at 7 mph as the big Alco straightened out and leaned into the left-hander. I entertained thoughts of doubling to Lineville, but the 251's, shouting to the world through their turbos, let me know they weren't ready to quit yet. I kept after them; the rail was a little bit better in the left-hander and the slipping abated somewhat. We actually gained a mile—we came out of that curve at 8 mph.

After we got out of the sharp curves, we gradually got back up to about 11. Approaching the summit at Milepost 888, Tracy went back to check the water.

"Both of them OK, Ed. Right up to the mark."

"!"

Only 100 miles to go.

The long dip north of Lineville enabled us to get the 2204 working in the higher transition; we went blasting over the little hump at Lineville station at about 40 mph, answering with a wave the highball given by the agent-operator.

Between Lineville and Cragford, southbound, is a 9-mile, 1-percenter like falling down a crooked well. The curves get sharper the farther down the hill you get; 50 mph near the top, then 40, then 35 at Cragford as you come out along Muddy Prong Creek and join the beautiful Tallapoosa River valley. Two air applications and judicious use of the throttle did the trick.

Seaboard Coast Line Century 628 No. 2201—sister of transition-troubled 2204 and 2207—leads a mixed lashup of locomotives at Colliers Yard near Petersburg, Va., waiting for a cut of cars. The six-axle Alco was built in 1963 for the Atlantic Coast Line. WALTER GAY.

Back in Run 8 again after passing Cragford, I stood up.

"Come on over here and go to work, Tracy. I've enjoyed all of this that I can stand."

I sat down on the left side and relaxed as Tracy handled the train beautifully down the river. Through Wadley, the sharp curve to the left and the truss bridge across the Tallapoosa (pulpwood trimmers, some called them; there were always a few sticks of pulpwood at the entering end of truss bridges from shifted loads)—over the little hump into Abanda (named for the original railroad, the Atlanta, Birmingham and Atlantic) and through Blake we charged, 251's shouting.

After lugging up the short grade through Roanoke, it was rip-rap (or hogback, if you prefer) country all the way to Manchester. Except for the 25 mph ordinance through La Grange, which made for a hard pull up the little hill to South La Grange, Tracy was able to hold their feet to the fire all the way, and the 2204 and 2207 rewarded us by staying over 32 mph the whole distance.

I checked the water again going into Manchester; again both were still right up to the top.

Tracy was on duty less than 11 hours for the trip. I still had some of my b-i-i-i-g lunch left over for my trip back.

And, when asked my opinion of Alcos, my answers since that trip have been less vehement. A little bit.

R.I.P., DY— Culver Tower on the Rock Island

By Edward J. Brunner
Tower Operator

1970s
From *Trains* magazine,
April 1986

Culver Tower was unique just because it wasn't special. It was an example of one of those countless small, average, ordinary towers that railroads built wherever two lines crossed each other at grade, or wherever an important junction occurred.

That major towers remained standing into the 1970's was not surprising, for those brick-and-mortar buildings with their motorized switch machines, their flip toggles on Centralized Traffic Control (CTC) panels, and their hotbox and dragging-equipment detectors housed therein were placed at the hottest spots on the railroad. What was rare was that one of those typical, common-as-pennies towers should endure so long, one with clapboard siding and a shingled roof and an interlocking of ancient armstrong levers with throw rods descending to the tracks and spreading out to switches and signals.

A sister tower to Culver, protecting the crossing of the Rock Island's direct Chicago-Kansas City route with the main line of the Chicago, Burlington & Quincy at Fairfield, Ia., had fallen years ago. There was a rumor that somewhere in Texas, an identical tower still existed from which replacement parts could be taken, but no spares ever arrived in the years I worked there. The other Rock Island towers I knew—WN at West Davenport, Ia., WX at Short Line Junction in Des Moines, and MC at Joliet, Ill.—were either CTC or push-pull pneumatic action, and most hot spots and junctions (W at West Liberty, Ia., and AU at Bureau, Ill.) were covered by depots with a CTC board inside.

But Culver Tower in Muscatine, Ia.—DY on the dispatcher's train sheet to distinguish it from Muscatine proper—was the real thing, the antique that still worked, a bit of medieval technology lasting from the turn of the century, when the railroads were beginning to emerge from the Dark Ages of operating by timetable and train order only.

Armstrong levers—they were called "strong-arm levers" by most—should have been a simple technology. And in essence they were ingenious: the towerman threw a lever that, in turn, moved a rod only a few feet away; that rod, when moved, tugged on another rod which in turn tugged on another, all connected in a Z-shaped fashion which eventually ended in a rod attached to switch points. Each rod was only moving the rod attached to it, but that rod shifted another down the way. The kinetic energy expended by the towerman, throwing his one lever about 3 feet, was multiplied, as it were, and sustained throughout the system. The backbreaking chore of heaving switch points over, difficult enough even when standing by the points themselves, was made into an easy task . . . usually.

One of the difficulties was that each switch lever had its own quirks, quirks so subtle that they were impossible to describe to anyone else. A new man coming into the tower had trouble heaving a lever, while veterans could line up the same switch with ease. Strength wasn't necessary. I saw a 200-pound section foreman, who was used to pushing track cars on and off the rails, wrestle with a lever that a 135-pound operator, who was used to punching a typewriter keyboard, handled in a second.

Each lever had to have a certain "English" applied to it: One lever threw with a twist toward the end of its arc; another needed a strong heave at first, then went smoothly. The operator didn't think of a lever as "Number 22." He thought of it as "the crossover from the main to west siding," and he knew what it felt like to line up that movement and applied his body weight accordingly.

Everywhere I worked on the railroad there were certain initiation ceremonies unique to each place, tests designed to show how the new man reacted under pressure or to circumstances that suddenly turned disastrous . . . tests to separate the men from the boys, the operators from the clerks. At DY, the levers alone were the test—if you could line up a series of switching moves without complaining, you were on the way to going to work.

But the experienced operators spoke of the special test they sometimes offered to those they didn't want in the tower. The test hinged on the fact that some levers were incredibly easy to throw. Some of the levers simply yanked on a rod that unlocked the switches, others simply closed a relay that changed a signal lens. To a new man, those levers were indistinguishable from the switch levers, and he would be invited, in his preliminary tour of the interlocking plant, to throw a series of switch levers, all of them lining up various turnouts and crossovers. After he was panting with exhaustion, the operator would graciously tell him to stand aside and, while delivering a brief lecture on how a few months at Culver would enable him to throw the levers easily, he would reach over and with a flip of his wrist toss a signal lever. The new man usually decided to stick with rates and demurrage claims.

Partly because of the levers, extra-board men dreaded working Culver and would go to great lengths to avoid it. Since this meant more overtime for the regulars, no one went out of his way to set them straight. In fact, Culver had a reputation for being terrifyingly complex. In a sense, this was earned. DY was in the crux of the junction where Kansas City-bound Milwaukee Road trains left their Rock Island trackage rights from the Davenport area to strike out on their own main line, and the DY op worked with two dispatchers, one in Des Moines on the RI, the other in Ottumwa on the Milwaukee. And the op had two radios, one for each railroad, plus an annoying intercom

This view of Culver Tower in 1950 shows the Milwaukee main line (foreground right) and passing siding, with the double-track Rock Island main visible behind the tower. ROBERT LAWLER.

directly connected to the Rock Island's Muscatine Yard. West of DY, the Milwaukee was a dark, train-order-only railroad, still running on timetable rules, which required train orders to be copied "without erasure or interlineation."

DY had no real warning lights to inform the op that a train had showed up. Westbound freights on the double track rang a bell, but by the time this happened the train was already looking at an approach signal and needed a clear indication right away. Eastbound freights were on separate tracks; Rock Island trains could be seen when their headlights rounded the curve at the foot of Letts Hill and entered a long, 4-mile tangent, but Milwaukee freights were out of sight until they were literally at the doorstep of the tower.

To stay on top of things, the operator had to keep his own running schedule of who was where and when they might arrive, which meant not only catching the departure times of trains from their terminals but also knowing which crews ran hot and which ran cold. Some Milwaukee crews tripped through the dew from Ottumwa to Culver in a little over 2 hours, while others were lost in the weeds for nearly 3 hours. Radio was a help,

except that all the crews had a habit of using nicknames for locations. If the extra-board man asked RI 23 for its location, he might find out it was "by the fish farm" (the Fairport state fish hatchery) or "by the bluffs" (I located Wyoming Bluffs once on an old map from the 1920's).

All this necessary inside knowledge made extra-board men shudder when vacations at Culver rolled around and the regular operators weren't able to show all the ropes to a new man. A regular op quickly identified the levers by their function—e.g., lever 25 was the crossover from the westbound to the eastbound used by Milwaukee Road trains, and when the lever was in its back position, the crossover was lined for Milwaukee traffic. A regular op could glance at the levers and tell in a second which way the plant was lined.

Extra-board men were told to follow the chart on the wall—a dim, fly-specked, dusty map peppered with numbers so small they could hardly be seen. It purported to show "Instructions for Tower Manipulation," and it did, in painstakingly intricate fashion. To follow it, one had to locate the oncoming train at a point designated by a number on the map, then

find another point on the map, designated by another number, where one wanted that train to end up. Then one had to search out references on a diagram to those two numbers. Once the numbers had been located—"Move 19 to 4," or whatever—the chart then listed a new series of numbers: the numbers on the levers that needed to be thrown, in strict sequence, in order to line and signal the route from spot 19 to spot 4. This may seem reasonable enough, printed here in black on white and read in the comfort of wherever you read this, but it was a different story in the Real World.

Aside from appearing on a yellowing map 8 feet in the air (and swimming just outside the cone of light from a single bulb), the schematic depended on all the levers in the plant being placed in a forward position after each move. The engineers who drew the diagram assumed that after each movement, the operator restored the plant to a neutral position. If the extra-board man forgot that, he was on the edge of being lost. Instead of going from one move to another as a regular op would, the student had to throw all the levers forward before he could begin his manipulation. This took time, and it meant work. Furthermore, DY was either very busy or very quiet, and when two or three trains were lobbying for a signal at the same time, it took a remarkably calm personality to follow the wall diagram patiently.

And of course, if you lined up switches for a westbound move, then cleared a signal for an eastbound, you had to "run time." The plant was locked up for 4 minutes, with no lever able to be thrown at all, while the manual timer clicked away the seconds. By that time, the commotion would have increased to riot proportions.

DY was around as long as it was because, at certain times, it was genuinely busy. According to the station agent, Muscatine was second only to Chicago in the revenue it generated for the Rock Island. The city of 23,467 (1980 census) was blessed by numerous industries that required rail service; in the 1970's, three switch engines worked round the clock weekdays, servicing the upper, lower, and middle yards. Blessed, but also cursed by tracks wedged between the Mississippi River on one side and the town on the other, leaving no room for expansion. The middle yard, then, held only a few hundred cars, and when it overflowed, the yardmaster simply built the next eastbound pickup on the only space left . . . the eastbound main. (The dispatcher went through the roof, and eastbound trains detoured around the pickup by running wrong-main up the westbound to the next crossover.)

The upper yard was not really a yard at all but a maze of spurs that were actually the remnants of an engine servicing facility and branch lines to Nichols and Wilton Junction (see the map on page 185). The lower yard, on "the island," as it was called, where there was room to expand, had expanded, but wildly some of its spur tracks were miles in length, and they wandered off to quarries and cement plants. Switch engines could disappear for hours in that mysterious realm.

Prosperous but crowded—that was Muscatine. But the headache was that, at the same time, it was also the junction for the two rival railroads' main lines. East of Culver, the Kansas City-Chicago routes of the Rock Island and Milwaukee shared double track for 26.4 miles to West Davenport. The railroads diverged at Culver, though they generally paralleled for the whole distance to Kansas City, crossing each other at Seymour, Ia., and sharing more trackage for the last 39 miles from Polo, Mo., to K.C. This was the result of a grand scheme by that latecomer to the

Armstrong levers—so named because they took some arm strength to move—were used to throw turnouts and change signal indications. Especially in older installations, each lever had its own personality and required various amounts of finesse to operate. Union Switch & Signal.

Midwest, the Milwaukee Road, undertaken at the turn of the century as a kind of warmup to its truly grand scheme to reach Puget Sound. In 1887 the Milwaukee had completed a so-so line to Kansas City, dropping south from its Chicago-to-Omaha line at Cedar Rapids and wandering through some river valleys to arrive at Ottumwa, from where it headed toward Kansas City. At least two drawbacks made this route unattractive by 1902: it was fragile, built along the beds of creeks that turned into swollen streams in the spring; and it was circuitous, built to tap the center of the state where river traffic could never reach. A forward-looking road like the Milwaukee by then recognized the need to accommodate the long haul between major points, which required straight lines—read "air lines"—between big cities.

The solution also resolved the perennial problem of flooding between Cedar Rapids and Ottumwa. By arranging trackage rights on the Rock Island and the Davenport, Rock Island & Northwestern (the "DRI Line," jointly owned by the Milwaukee and the CB&Q), the Milwaukee could run from Clinton, Ia., to Muscatine; and by boldly laying a bee line across Iowa from Muscatine to Ottumwa, the Milwaukee had its Kansas City Cutoff completed by 1904. Major freight traffic, as well as the *Southwest Limited,* funneled through Muscatine thereafter, and although the origin of DY is lost in the mists of time, it must have been built to handle this trade, as its expenses were shared by both roads.

Muscatine, then, was precisely like the elephant viewed by the three blind men in the parable; depending on what each touched—trunk, hide, or tail—it was a snake, rhinoceros, or mouse.

To the Rock Island yardmaster, Muscatine was a series of wayward yard tracks that just happened to have a main line linking them together; mainline trains were always interrupting his switching maneuvers, and some of those trains didn't even belong to his road.

To the Rock Island dispatcher in Des Moines, Muscatine was the Kansas City main line with some yards that happened to be adjacent; it was also the point where double track ended and CTC began, and it was a convenient and necessary waiting point for westward trains to hold till the single track ahead of them was clear of eastward trains.

To the Milwaukee dispatcher in Ottumwa, who didn't have much CTC on his mostly dark, single-track railroad (there was a patch of CTC in Missouri) and who was struggling to hold together his train-order-only railroad with no operators between him and Culver (except the agent at Washington, who went home at 4 p.m.), Muscatine was where his westbounds had to wait for eastbounds with rights over them; to him, the double track was a long passing siding, with the next meeting point a long way off.

Each railroad had its own killer hill to climb to get out of the Mississippi basin, and neither dispatcher could be sure that his westbound would get to Letts (Rock Island) or Cranston (Milwaukee) without doubling the hill. The yardmaster, of course, had no sympathy for mainline trains that spent more time backing up than going forward.

Finally, the authority of all three men was just about equal. The yardmaster was promoted to a higher status than usual just because his yard generated so much revenue—the apocryphal "hot switch engine" was a daily fact of life in Muscatine if it was switching a cut promised for a.m. delivery in Chicago. And the Milwaukee dispatcher had as much clout as his Rock Island counterpart, even though ordinarily trains of a foreign road get short shrift on tracks of a home road. Outside Kansas City, you see, the Milwaukee controlled the tracks and Rock Island was the foreigner, and if Milwaukee 65 was sitting at Muscatine blocked by an RI switcher working the main, the Rock Island DS might find that his 01 would be following a Milwaukee local with work at every station between Polo and Birmingham on the way to Kansas City.

The Culver operator was the one who had to live with the fact that the elephant was not a snake, not a rhinoceros, and not a mouse, but a composite—a dreadfully complex composite—of all the conflicting qualities no one else wanted to see. He was at the center of the controversies, the mediator who worked equally with all those who were opponents of each other, with the aim of keeping everyone happy, perhaps even shielding them from the horrible truth that the elephant was an elephant.

The best operators at DY were those who, aside from working with antiquated equipment and charting the progress of invisible trains and knowing which crews were reliable and which were not, combined the attributes of international arms negotiator, country lawyer, and stand-up comedian. No one could be all three at once, but second-trick operator Kenny Shumate came close, largely because he had the skill and intelligence to make difficult decisions while at the same time presenting things so as to make them seem less complex than they were. His advice: never let on that you're excited.

"You're in the driver's seat—not one of these trains moves till you say so." And though you may be running around like a lunatic, writing with one hand and answering the phone with the other, two cigarettes burning in the ashtray and a third in your mouth, the intercom chattering away as though you dropped everything the moment the yardmaster

spoke, and two trains wondering out loud on each radio if they'll ever get a signal—don't ever show it.

Easy for Kenny to say. He'd worked up and down the system, starting on the Wabash as a telegrapher. He seemed to know everyone on the railroad, and he had a distinctive voice—a slow Missouri drawl, instantly identifiable, which made him seem half-asleep and half-intoxicated, and had the effect of calming (or at least slowing) everyone at once. (Certainly the introduction of train radio and dispatching by phone must have been as traumatic for railroaders as the shift from silent to sound movies was for film stars: Those with a distinctive voice, who could speak wittily, with a flair for language, found the change exhilarating, like a new tool to work with, while those who were tongue-tied or naturally terse found verbal communication to be a drain on their authority. It was always a pleasure to work with Jerry Marsengill, a dispatcher who would answer a switchman's request to enter the main track by saying, "Come home! All is forgiven!" instead of "Rule 350, examine the switches.")

Kenny had his own unique phrase to cover any contingency. To a dispatcher rushing him to copy an order: "Now hold on just a minute. I've already got both shoes off and I just ran out of toes to count with." To a trainmaster who'd worked out a horrifyingly elaborate pickup for a train and was wondering what the logjam was: "These ain't no tiddlywinks we're playing with" and "You can't play leapfrog with these engines."

It would be going too far to say that events took on a kind of mythic dimension when Kenny was in the middle of them, but he had an ability to remind others, in a way at once off-hand and humorous, that there were advantages to their positions, whatever they thought of it at the moment. It was as though he intuitively sensed the way individuals saw themselves. To hard-pressed dispatchers who always felt they were overworked and under-appreciated for the many split-second, long-range decisions they had to make, Kenny would begin a lengthy report on a train's tonnage changes with, "While you're resting, here's some totals." To train crews, who usually knew they had a good job, what with arbitraries and adventurous times away from home, Kenny would not simply give the "okay" sign as they rumbled by the tower; he would rub thumb and forefinger together and shout, "Easy money! Hello, easy money!" To trainmasters, who thought operators had

an easy time of it with long rests between trains, Kenny would anticipate their telephone call and, instead of answering with "Culver Tower, Rock Island Lines, Kenny speaking," he'd respond: "Maisie's Boarding House—Maisie's not here and the girls are all busy. What can I do for you?"

If anyone accused Kenny of being capricious, he would say, "Just tryin' to break up the monotony a little bit." If he had been inept, if his repertoire had been designed to smooth over errors, he would have been in hot water, but he was the sharpest operator on the railroad. Train crews, yardmasters, trainmasters, and clerks universally addressed the operator as "Culver," as though Culver was the name of whoever was working: "Culver, can I get a signal?" and "We're comin' down the hill, Culver." But when Kenny's distinctive voice was heard, it was, "Okay, Kenny" and "We'll notch 'er down, Kenny." It was easy to get the orchestra to play in tune when it followed the concertmaster.

Kenny was the master of the second trick at DY, the shift when it seemed all the trains on the two railroads decided to funnel themselves through the tight neck of Culver. Come 4 p.m., just as the parade was under way, usually led by the first of two or three sections of Rock Island 02, the SP perishable train, the phone started ringing off the hook as the agents reported their yards for the day—information needed for the RI east and west locals and the Milwaukee stone train (years ago, it turned at a quarry, and the name stuck). The agents were eager to go home, but so was the crew on Milwaukee 64, which always had work up the line at Nahant Yard near West Davenport and which, if it went ahead of 02A and 02B and 02C, might delay the parade.

Rock Island 01 (02's westbound counterpart) was by "West Dav Tower" and rolling down the river, not to be delayed except that ahead of it rattled Milwaukee 65. Milwaukee 65 couldn't go anywhere till Milwaukee 64 was clear of dark territory and on double track; 01 couldn't go anywhere till 65 was out of its way; but if 64 ran out on double track, the 02's would be following it up the river, and suffering their own delays. Second trick once again would have hit the jackpot: six trains all converging at once, all threatening to end up eyeball-to-eyeball.

Kenny, handling everything with his own brand of graceful aplomb, would recognize 64 as the center of the problem, in danger first of delaying 65 and therefore

An exercise in towerman's logic

Compared to many towers, DY was in the bush leagues: the plant consisted of three crossovers, a turnout, and a siding switch; in addition, the operator could run reverse traffic on the westbound main to the hand-thrown crossover on the edge of town. By contrast, Rock Island's AU interlocking in the depot at Bureau, Ill., controlled six crossovers, two turnouts, and a siding switch. But at times, DY had to run as many trains as AU, with nowhere near its facilities to handle them.

In the absence of the proper tools, ingenuity took over. A typical example facing DY, involving three trains watched carefully by three immediate supervisors: the Milwaukee "Stone Train," a local, is a caboose hop arriving to turn at Muscatine and to pick up 12 cars off the Middle Yard; the yardmaster is monitoring it with an eagle eye. Rock Island 20 is an eastbound junk train with 45 cars just showing up at the west end where CTC ends; 20 has a cut of 38 cars to pick up which will clear the eastbound main, and the RI DS is eager to see that happen. Milwaukee 64 is a heavy train, just starting down the hill toward the tower; the Milwaukee DS hopes it won't be stopped and can run through town as fast as possible. The trains should leave town in this order, all heading east: Milwaukee 64, the Stone Train, Rock Island 20.

Some do's and don'ts: RI 20 can't bring the bulk of its train uptown because that would block grade crossings, and the Stone Train can run around its caboose by dropping it on the fly into the spur switch off the Milwaukee siding. Milwaukee crews can throw hand switches for Milwaukee trains but not for Rock Island trains. On the map, all three trains are an equal distance from Culver.

We'll assume that all three engineers are asking for signals at the same time. Tell RI 20 to cut the engines off from his train and head toward DY; he'll be picking up 38 cars off the eastbound. Tell Milwaukee 64 to take it easy down the hill; he will go through town right away, but running wrong-main to the Old High Bridge. Tell the Stone Train to keep on coming, and line the siding switch for him.

As soon as the Stone Train has entered the siding, run 20's engines up the depot crossover, where they will hand-throw themselves over to the eastbound main; by the time 20 lines back the crossover, Milwaukee 64 should be coming around the corner and expecting a signal to run wrong-main up the westbound.

Ten minutes later the scene should look like this: Milwaukee 64 is halfway through the High Bridge crossovers, dragging his train east. RI 20 has coupled onto his pickup and is shoving it west

01; second of delaying itself as it waited for three 02's. Moving 64 off the Milwaukee and onto double track, Kenny would run it up the eastbound only as far as the old High Bridge crossovers, a set of hand-thrown turnouts. ("If you just sit a spell," he'd tell the crew, "I might be able to build me an Oh-Two Sandwich.")

As 02A's headlight grew larger and larger on that tangent track off Letts Hill, Milwaukee 65 kept plodding down the westbound, through the Milwaukee turnout and onto the dark territory vacated by 64. As soon as 65's caboose cleared—"Easy money, easy money!"—02A would run wrong-main up the westbound, around 64, to the High Bridge crossovers which 64's crew had obligingly lined up for it ("Don't bother buttoning up those switches, 02A—got some moguls from the Milwaukee on the ground taking care of them").

As 02A crossed to the eastbound, 01 showed on the warning light, but the route was lined. 02B and 02C were still coming on that single-track CTC west of Culver, so it was the west siding for 01 as their headlights grew larger and larger. However, 64 was pulling with a "Much obliged" from Kenny for handling the crossovers—a favor negotiated because of the crew's eagerness to run ahead of 02B and 02C. But 02B and 02C never saw as much as an approach signal from 64's train—they wouldn't see any signals at all until they reached West Dav Tower, because Kenny had been, in his words, "wheeling and dealing" with the DS.

As soon as 01 cleared, he read back an order to the DS (already delivered and posted at West Davenport Tower), giving 02B and 02C rights over all trains on the westbound track between Culver and West Dav. With no westbounds due past West Dav for an hour or so, the last two sections of 02 had the track to themselves; they'd

pass 64 as it stopped to work Nahant. The delays? Train 01 showed an obligatory 5 minutes at Culver to "head through West siding" and 02C showed 5 minutes at Culver to "follow 02B." Not bad for running six trains in three directions in 40 minutes.

"I guess there's just no rest for the wicked," Kenny would say, usually to the Milwaukee dispatcher when he rang up to fix another eastbound out of Ottumwa. But the action was not nonstop. Though second trick sat down to a hornet's nest at 3 p.m., by 9 o'clock or so most of the dust would have settled. At that time, it would seem as though a remarkable peace and quiet had settled over the tower, though the place was never truly quiet at all: the radio still picked up conversations from West Liberty, 25 miles away on the Des Moines Division; the teletype continued to spill out messages and consists; and the through the Rock Island crossover, back against his train. The Stone Train has his caboose where it belongs and is coming back to the siding signal.

This solution is working because, at this point, you still have some flexibility. If 20 is shoving back slowly, run the Stone Train wrong-main. If 20 is going to clear the eastbound in another minute, plan to run the Stone Train up your brand-new eastbound main. If 64 is running poorly, have the Stone Train promise to line the switches back after it leaves the High Bridge crossovers, thus saving 64's crew start-and-stop time. Whichever way, by the time 20 has coupled up and pumped its air, the Stone Train should be coupled onto its short train and ready to follow 64 up the river.—E.J.B.

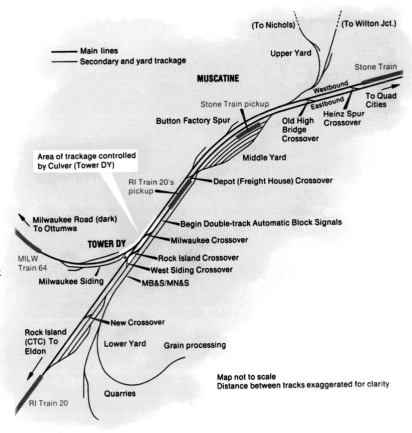

dispatchers kept asking for call times and totals and tonnage changes. But the operator only had to overhear all this, knowing that it did not directly concern him. It was pleasant, at such times, to hear the DS clear a train leaving West Wye Tower in Kansas City or to listen to totals on 81's train out of Minneapolis. You felt in touch with a far-flung system, a small point in an enormous network of tracks and trains.

And this time was pleasant for another reason: without the pressure of trains to run, the equipment in the tower no longer seemed like the necessary tools one used, rapidly, unthinkingly, to solve the problems of the moment. In the quiet, the tower began to appear as the extraordinary relic that it was. You sat at a desk surrounded by train orders typed on the same flimsy paper in use 50 years ago. The dispatcher's phone pivoted out on an accordion extension. And the levers, paint

worn away at the tops, were as firm and substantial and upright as when they had been installed long ago by gas or kerosene lamp. There even seemed to be an underlying smell of coal smoke in the corners.

At such moments it was hard to believe that time would ever run out for DY—the calendar on the wall said 1976, but it could have been 1922, or 1946, or 1904. What finally closed Culver? Hoping to qualify for track rehabilitation money under the 4R Act, the Rock Island persuaded the Milwaukee to shift its Kansas City traffic to its rails. The agreement was a fiasco for both parties: Milwaukee, which made money operating 150-car trains, found that the sidings on the Rock Island's line were too small; the Rock Island, under the cloud of bankruptcy, somehow never qualified for the Federal loan. After a few months of bad experimenting, the railroads returned to their own tracks, but

in the meantime, DY had been unnecessary for both and was taken out of service in November 1977.

The dispatchers were calling the Muscatine yard clerk, who in turn advised Milwaukee trains when to hand-throw themselves onto the Rock Island main and soon, of course, there was no Rock Island main, for there was no Rock Island. The old Milwaukee turnout into dark territory was lined exclusively for Milwaukee traffic.

And even that was not permanent, for in 1980 the Milwaukee purchased the Rock Island main as far as Ainsworth and an RI branch from there into Washington and abandoned its dark territory, further erasing all signs that there ever had been a Culver Tower.

Swapping power to keep cars moving

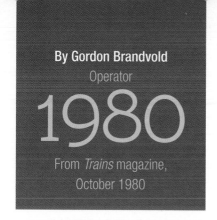

By Gordon Brandvold
Operator

1980
From *Trains* magazine,
October 1980

It seems that, more often than not, one hears what is wrong with railroading. The complaints range from inadequate freight-car availability to taxpayer-supported "featherbedding" to excessive terminal delays. The list goes on and on.

I, for one, am tired of hearing these gripes. It is time to talk positively and to believe that conditions can get better. It is time not only to implement improved methods of operation but also to know that there are people who are trying to do the job and to do it well. In line with this, allow me to cite one occasion when a railroader attempted to expedite the movement of freight.

The setting was Devils Lake, N. Dak., on the 9th Subdivision of Burlington Northern's Dakota Division, in the Twin Cities Region. This railroad was the original westward mainline extension of the St. Paul, Minneapolis & Manitoba, later the Great Northern. Devils Lake—86.1 miles west of PA Tower in Grand Forks and 113.5 miles east of Gavin Yard near Minot—is the terminal for all operations on this segment. Traffic on the Ninth Sub is relatively light, the only regular trains being through freight trains 127 and 128, local freights, and Amtrak 7 and 8, the *Empire Builder*. Other movements include reroutings; unit potash, bentonite, and grain trains; and work and inspection extras. (The majority of BN's northern transcontinental traffic moves between Fargo and Minot on the Surrey Cutoff, completed in 1911; this runs 40 or so miles to the south of Devils Lake.)

All trains receive orders and/or change crews (enginemen only on passenger trains), and/or pick up or set out at Devils Lake, and four regularly scheduled branchline locals call it home. In addition, Soo Line's Drake-to-Fordville branch interchanges here with BN, most traffic from the Soo being coal loads destined for the University of North Dakota at Grand Forks. Train 127 operates between Superior, Wis., and Minot; 128 travels the

reverse route. Usually there will be more than one section of each of these trains on line at one time, owing to length of route. Both do a lot of way-freight switching. Usual motive-power policy is for the engines to go through to either Grand Forks or Minot, as long as a connection is available or the power does not consist of locally assigned units.

On Wednesday, February 6, 1980, train 127 (designated 01-127GK-06) had arrived in Devils Lake at 3:20 p.m. (1520 railroad time), operating as Extra 1942 West with units 1942/733/834, a 5,000-hp GP9/F7B/F9A set. The crew tied up for 8 hours to await train 128. The power was scheduled to turn back east, with the caboose going through to Minot.

Train 128 out of Minot (01-128-06) had 28 loads, 17 empties, 3,305 tons for east of Devils Lake. Running as Extra 1351 East, it had units 1351/6912/6620, a 7,950-hp GP7M/SD40-2/F45 set. These locomotives also were scheduled to turn, returning to Gavin.

As the evening progressed, 128 picked up 6 loads of grain en route—typical of the line, which sees tonnage grow eastward, most of it grain bound for either Duluth-Superior or Minneapolis-St, Paul. At Devils Lake, another 41 loads and 2 empties awaited 128, so out of the terminal, the train would have 75 loads, 19 empties, 8,266 tons. To the east, 5 loads and 3 empties were to be picked up, so into Grand Forks, 128 would have 80 loads, 22 empties, and approximately 9,000 tons.

The problem of matching power and tonnage was apparent; the question was how to solve it. Should only some of the Devils Lake cars be taken? Should no

pickups be made? Would 5,000 horsepower handle the full tonnage on the slight ascending grade out of the yard and eastward? Could 128's power be used?

There were more points to consider. Geep 1351 was a locally assigned unit and was needed back in Minot. Booster 733 was due in Grand Forks for a test the next day, and cab unit 834 had to be there for the same reason in three days. Also, 6620 was due in Havre, Mont., in three days for a test. The time necessary to break apart and reassemble units at Devils Lake was a factor, as was the undesirability of using big units for en route switching. Finally, the dispatchers at Minneapolis and Minot had to be updated concerning the cars already at Devils Lake.

The operator at Devils Lake briefed the Minneapolis dispatcher, qualifying his analysis by stating he was not trying to do the dispatcher's job. The op suggested perhaps 128 could borrow the 6912 and the 6620 in order to move all the tonnage.

After the Minneapolis trick dispatcher consulted with the Minot chief dispatcher and with diesel control in St. Paul, the Minneapolis man agreed: 128 would have units 6912/6620/733 (8,100 hp), while 127 would have 1942/834/1351 (4,850 hp). The latter was adequate for the 3,449 tons with which 127 would depart. The new assignments had the stipulation that 6620 must go back on the next 127 while 1942 and 834 must leave Gavin on the next 128. These assignments were met the following day.

Train 128 arrived at Devils Lake at 10:45 p.m., and made its setout; the crew then made up the new power lashup for 127. The westbound departed at 1:30 a.m. (February 7), just 10 minutes after 128's crew reported back to work. The eastbound crew put their diesel lashup together, grabbed the Devils Lake cars, and tied onto their train. They departed at 3:30.

This was an example of how tonnage can be moved. The power swap put the

Four Burlington Northern SD45s lead a westbound freight through the shadows of grain elevators at Des Lacs, N. Dak., in November 1973. JOHN M. ROBINSON, JR.

revenue-producing loads and the needed empties miles—perhaps even days—closer to their destinations. Loaded rolling stock does no one any good sitting in a yard awaiting the next train. The movement of cars is what helps determine the amount of black ink on a company's ledger and what ultimately gives many people a paycheck. In keeping the cars moving, all people concerned derive benefit.

This does not happen all the time, of course, for many factors affect car movement, but any railroad employee worthy of the name owes it to the company and to himself or herself to see that the goods are moved as expeditiously as possible.

Yes, I was the second-trick operator at Devils Lake on February 6, 1980. I do not tell this tale for any self-glorification, for I have found on the BN that most employees whom I have met feel the way I do

about service. If railroading is to survive as private enterprise, we all must do our part. If we do not, the alternative is either government control or drastically reduced rail transport, with many areas losing all service. All you "rails"—professional or fan—out there, remember the examples set by the likes of Conrail and the Rock Island. Then remember those of us who are trying to move the tonnage. A lot of us care. I know that I do.

Braking toward Bethlehem: Iron ore on Conrail

By Jonathan W. Reck
Engineer

1980s
-'90s

From *Trains* magazine,
January 2004

No train gave a young engineer on Conrail's east end as much anxiety as the Bethlehem iron-ore trains. I joined Conrail in 1988 and was promoted to engineer in 1990, and I can tell you, manning those heavy trains left the throttle and brake levers wet with perspiration. The combination of heavy loads, old ore jennies, temperamental air brakes, and a roller-coaster profile made every trip a challenge. Ride with me on the head end and you'll see what I mean.

The ore came in by ship at Conrail's Greenwich Point Pier in South Philadelphia, and Conrail hauled it 110 miles to Bethlehem Steel in that company's namesake Pennsylvania town. Generally, one ore boat would yield between eight and 12 trains. If iron production at the blast furnaces was high and stockpiles at Bethlehem low, two or three trains would run each day; otherwise, one train would run every other day. When the ore ran heavy, Conrail's Saucon Yard in Bethlehem was filled to capacity with inbound loads and outbound empties, and the Philly pools would turn on their rest every eight to 10 hours.

Each ore train, symboled ZBB, ran about 100 cars and grossed between 10,000 and 11,000 tons. At first, they ran with a mixture of former Pennsylvania Railroad ore cars (called "jennies") and standard coal hoppers. Later, Bethlehem Steel realized they were losing a lot of ore pellets through the hoppers' pocket doors, which after years of abuse no longer closed tightly, so the trains were assigned ore jennies only.

Most of the jennies had the same friction-bearing axles they were built with in the 1950s. Only a few had been rebuilt with roller bearings. When the cars were turned upside down to empty their load of ore in Bethlehem Steel's rotary dumper, the lubricating oil in the journal boxes spilled out, coating the wheels in oil. The empties left an oily film on the rails as they ran back to Philadelphia. If you were the unfortunate engineer following an empty ore train—especially on wet rail—you hoped you didn't have a heavy, underpowered train.

Empty ore cars were assembled into trains at Saucon Yard in Bethlehem. Depending on the time frame for reloading, empty trains, symboled XGW, ranged from 80 to more than 200 cars. The longest train I ran had 204 cars. The difficulties were with the loads, however.

It was one thing to run the Bethlehem ore train with an experienced training engineer guiding your brake and throttle moves every foot of the way. It was another once you were promoted and on your own.

One major problem was with the air brakes on the jennies: They only worked well when the jennies were loaded. In that case, you could apply almost any amount of brakes, make a release, and be fairly assured that none of the brakes would stick in the applied position. But when the jennies were empty, you needed to make a full-service reduction and bring the train to a complete stop. If you didn't, you had stuck brakes and an unhappy conductor walking the train to release them manually. Most of the time, however, your locomotives' dynamic brakes were sufficient to control the train and you didn't have to touch the air.

If you could go back to 1990, this is what your trip was like: Leaving Philadelphia, your locomotives have their work cut out for them climbing out of the Delaware River Basin with a trainload of ore. After snaking south of town, your tracks join the "High Line" at CP (Control Point)-Field, and your train climbs over Philadelphia, across the river from Center City. As you pass the Post Office, you can look back and see the rear end crossing the former Schuylkill River swing bridge at CP-Gray. A little farther along, you pass Amtrak's 30th Street Station and begin your descent to Zoo Tower.

Speed through Zoo interlocking is restricted to 10 mph, as the line drops down a steep connection to reach the former Reading at Belmont. You make certain to keep the train under control. If you've drawn a set of locomotives with good dynamic brakes, you can usually hold your speed, but if the dynamics suddenly drop out, you'd better grab some air, or your speed will jump to 17 or 20 mph in no time.

Once on Conrail's Harrisburg Line— the former Reading main—the tracks are mostly river-grade and double, except for the single-track tunnels at CP-Rock and CP-Phoenix. Approaching the city of Reading at CP-Titus, the railroad splits. If you go straight, you'll go through downtown Reading; if you turn left, you'll travel over the "Belt Line" around downtown. Nearing Titus, your best bet is do what most engineers do and hold your speed to about 17 mph, keeping your locomotives under power while the train winds through the tight curves around Neversink Mountain. If the dispatcher has you lined for the Belt Line, you'll need to switch to dynamic brakes as soon as your locomotives clear the Titus interlocking, anticipating a slight dip in the tracks beyond the junction's curves that could have your train pushing the 30 mph speed limit in no time.

At CP-Belt, the line through downtown Reading rejoins the Belt Line, and the Blandon low-grade leaves the main line to begin a 3.2-mile climb to CP-Blandon. The low-grade line, built to bypass a 1.1 percent climb up Temple Hill, has a 0.6 percent maximum grade.

The low-grade is your moment of truth: If you can make this, you'll probably be able to make the climb up Saucon Hill in Bethlehem at the end of your run. But if your speed on the low-grade drops below 18 mph, you'll need to notify the dispatcher that Saucon Hill looks iffy. One of three things might happen: The Saucon drill (switch engine) might meet you and assist your train; an extra unit might be added at Allentown Yard; or you'll hear those dreaded words, "Do the best you can."

At CP-Belt, you enter Conrail's Reading Line, the former Reading Company East Penn Branch to Allentown. You've now made the equivalent of a U-turn and your nominally westward train from Philadelphia is now headed timetable east to Bethlehem.

The Reading built the East Penn Branch inexpensively, following the lay of the land and without much cut-and-fill work, resulting in a roller-coaster railroad. It's easy here to have all the slack run in or out—and you'll sure know when the rear-end comes in!

Each engineer has his own technique on the East Penn. Mine is using power-braking—setting the train brakes while keeping the locomotives under power. That keeps the train stretched out with little slack action. I was schooled in the art of power-braking while training on piggyback trains with former Erie Lackawanna engineer Steve Bonscher. When I joined the Philly pools, former EL engineers Al Watson and Joe Sullivan broke me in. I don't know what it was with those EL men, but they were masters of power braking. Yet, using power braking on ore trains seemed to dumbfound some people: Bonscher, for one. He later became a road foreman, and in a conversation about train handling, I told him of my style of running ore trains. His response was first amazement and then disbelief: "You what? Jesus, Jesus, Jesus!"

On another trip, heading downgrade on the East Penn with the brakes set, a voice over the radio warned us we had a number of cars with smoking brakes and we'd better stop and inspect the train for stuck brakes. I explained I was power braking. That brought silence—I guess whoever it was thought I was just plain nuts.

In Allentown, at CP-Burn, the Reading Line becomes the ex-Lehigh Valley main line east to CP-Bethlehem. There, the Bethlehem Secondary branches off for Saucon Yard, which includes the dreaded stretch of 0.9 percent grade known as Saucon Hill, a distance of about three-quarters of a mile. Speed on the Secondary is limited to 10 mph, so there is no way you can get a run for the hill. Worse, low joints in the stick (jointed) rail hurt traction.

The best you can hope for is to maintain 10 mph upgrade for as long as possible. At the crest of the grade under the Lynn Street bridge, the speed will probably be down to 3 mph, the sanders will be full on, the units will be slipping and lurching regardless, and the ammeter will be pushing into the red zone. You'll be on pins and needles hoping your train doesn't rip in two or stall. If it stalls, probably a few of South Bethlehem's road crossings will be blocked. If the drill is unable to help you, you'll have to take your train uphill in two pieces. Later, the trainmaster at Allentown will receive a greeting from the Bethlehem police asking the railroad for a contribution to the city's general funds.

After coaxing your train up Saucon Hill, you'll be thinking the worst is past, but it's not. The track drops steeply down the other side into Saucon Yard. If you forget about this and get moving on the downgrade, go to full dynamic brakes and make a full service application on the air brakes, then wait for the train to stop. The yardmaster always has the route lined into the yard just in case. Still, I've witnessed some pretty wild entrances!

You'll probably have enough time left of your 12 hours to deliver the ore to Bethlehem Steel, which requires spotting the train at the "ore tip," a set of stub-end finger tracks next to the dumper. This requires cutting the train in two and backing each cut into the tip. This got harder when Conrail prohibited employees from getting off moving trains. Now, you'll have to stop twice; first to drop off the conductor and second to make the cut. This is a little tricky, since the train is on a downslope and as soon as the brakes began to release, it will quickly gain speed, making it difficult to stop at the right spot

to make the cut.

I discussed this once with veteran yard engineer Gordon Fegley. He suggested two tricks: First, as soon as the train starts to move, apply the brakes immediately; the second trick is to put on more air as the train is stopping and stretch it. This will put slack into the train, aiding you in getting it started when you start shoving each half back uphill toward the ore tip.

Now the train is stretched out on the downgrade. As soon as your brakes begin to release, wind the throttle out and shove hard to get the train moving backward. Don't worry about banging it around. As one engineer says, "That's ore you're shoving, not crystal."

You'll know if you're on the correct track—just look for the ore pellets covering the ties. Watch that all the hand-thrown switches you'll encounter in the yard are properly lined, and look out for switch engines and men from the Philadelphia, Bethlehem & New England, the switching road owned by Bethlehem Steel.

The tracks up to the tip run parallel to the Secondary. That means another encounter with Saucon Hill as you back toward the crest under Lynn Street. The farther up the hill you progress, the more cars will have crested the hill, and instead of pushing, now you're being pulled down into the tip. Once again, you'll have to set some air in order to control the speed using the throttle.

The ore tip consists of nine finger tracks. Conrail crews use tracks 4 through 9. The tracks are not very long, so every foot counts. Nearing the bumper, apply yet more air so the trailing car will stop just three to four feet— you hope!—from the bumper. Five hand brakes are applied on each cut of cars. Depending on how full the tip is, you'll repeat the process for the second half of the train, or pull the balance into one of the yard tracks. A PB&NE crew will take over from here, pulling cars from the tip and shoving them through the rotary dumper. Your work, however, is done. If an empty train is planned, the power might stay at Saucon or head over to the hump yard at Allentown, about five miles away.

You can't make this run anymore, because steel production ceased at Bethlehem on November 18, 1995. Conrail subsequently removed Saucon Yard and tore down the yard office, which also housed Lehigh Tower. The tracks under Lynn Street were reconfigured to directly enter the PB&NE's Iron Hill Yard, severing the Saucon running track and Bethlehem Secondary. Interchange with the PB&NE is now done along the ex-Lehigh Valley main line (now part of Norfolk Southern) at the north end of Bethlehem Steel's property, on five tracks called the "River" tracks.

Despite the grueling runs, I do have some fond memories. On one trip with a loaded train, we had four GP38's and a GP35. The GP35 broke down right out of Philadelphia. Climbing the low-grade out of Reading on a crisp fall morning, the four GP38's were wide open, shooting white exhaust 30 feet straight into the sky. It formed a cloud over the train that perfectly followed the line's curves. The sun was just coming over the horizon and the scene was brilliant in the morning sun.

Another time, a train I passed at Phoenixville Tunnel reported we had smoke coming from a car midway in the train. Upon inspection, the conductor found we had a "sneaker"—the handbrake was slightly applied. I notified the dispatcher of the car's number and location, stating it had a sneaker.

There was a brief pause. Then, "What kind, Reebok or Nike?"

A Conrail ZBB ore train exits Black Rock Tunnel at Phoenixville, Pa., on March 9, 1984. ROBERT PALMER.

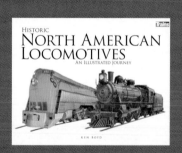
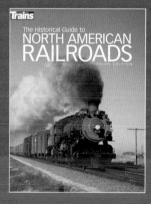
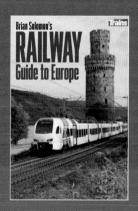

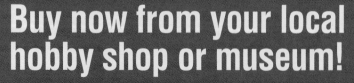